Data Communications & Teleprocessing Systems
Second Edition

Trevor Housley

Prentice-Hall, Inc.,
Englewood Cliffs, New Jersey 07632

Library of Congress Cataloging-in-Publication Data

Housley, Trevor (date)
  Data communications and teleprocessing systems.

  Includes index.
  1. Computer networks. 2. Data transmission systems.
I. Title.
TK5105.5.H68 1987   384.3   86-16847
ISBN 0-13-197393-2

Editorial/production supervision
  and interior design: Sophie Papanikolaou
Cover design: Ben Santora
Manufacturing buyer: Gordon Osbourne

©1987, 1979 by Prentice-Hall, Inc.
A division of Simon & Schuster
Englewood Cliffs, NJ 07632

Printed in the United States of America
10 9 8 7 6 5 4 3 2 1

ISBN 0-13-197393-2   025

Prentice-Hall International (UK) Limited, *London*
Prentice-Hall of Australia Pty. Limited, *Sydney*
Prentice-Hall Canada Inc., *Toronto*
Prentice-Hall Hispanoamericana, S.A., *Mexico*
Prentice-Hall of India Private Limited, *New Delhi*
Prentice-Hall of Japan, Inc., *Tokyo*
Prentice-Hall of Southeast Asia Pte. Ltd., *Singapore*
Editora Prentice-Hall do Brasil, Ltda., *Rio de Janeiro*

To
JOCELYN, LARA, and KRISTIE

Contents

Preface to the Second Edition

Data communications is still the fastest-growing aspect of computing. I said that in the preface to the first edition and it is just as true today. The subject has always been made artificially complex, and modern developments tend to complicate the issue even more. Satellite communications, local area networks, optical fibers, digital networks, the integrated services digital network, and the open system interconnection are examples of the rapid growth in the communications industry.

Although things seem to be changing at a dramatic rate, in reality it is not so hard to follow. After all, the basic principles of communications never change. If you have a good knowledge of the fundamentals, you will see that most of the change in the industry is really only on the surface and that underneath the same old things are happening. For example, today we use a microchip to do what would have required a cubic foot of electronics a few years ago. The way the thing works, however, is basically unchanged.

Regardless of where you live, there are still universal principles that lie at the heart of all data communications. This book deals with these principles and addresses them in simple terms and in a logical sequence so that you will be able to locate easily the essential information you need to know to have a good understanding of data communications.

The book is based on a successful series of training courses that I have been running for several years and that have proven to be of great use to beginners and experts alike. Although we start out assuming no knowledge of data communications, experienced members of the field will find that the book consolidates information they have learned piecemeal during their careers.

Numerous worked examples take you through the basics of network design. If you follow these examples and build models on your personal computer, you will be able to experience the satisfaction that is related to network design.

acknowledgment

I would like to thank all of the people who have attended my training courses over the years and have provided me with feedback and encouragement.

Trevor Housley

Index to Examples

This example illustrates the approach to calculating the throughput efficiency of a simple point-to-point link using a half-duplex protocol. The aim of this example is to illustrate the effect of network delays such as propagation delay and modem delay on the throughput of a link.

Loop delay is one of the most important concepts in network design. This example shows how loop delay can be calculated and illustrates its use in finding how long it takes to transmit a block of data through a simple point-to-point satellite communication line.

This example extends Example 11-1 to working out the throughput of the communication line, and shows how the throughput of the line can be improved by increasing the speed of transmission.

This example takes the parameters from Example 14-1 and shows the effect on
system throughput of modifying the protocol to use a more modern protocol, such
as HDLC. This gives a dramatic increase in system performance.

This is a real-life example illustrating how the throughput of a link can be calculated even when all the parameters may not be known. Under these circumstances an educated guess may be made which gives reasonably accurate results
of system performance. This example compares the theoretical results of the
analysis with practical results obtained when the system was up and running.

This example illustrates how to calculate the length of time it takes to poll a
terminal and receive a no-traffic response. This example then goes on to calculate
the poll cycle time, which is the time it takes to poll all the terminals on the
network. From this we can then calculate the polling delay, which is an important
component of the response time in an on-line inquiry system.

This example illustrates the effects on polling cycle time and polling delay if the
polling is slowed down below the maximum speed at which polling could normally
proceed.

This extensive example illustrates how to calculate the performance of a half-
duplex multipoint line with four drops. The example first works out the polling
delay and then goes on to find the line utilization at a given traffic volume. This
involves the analysis of half-duplex multipoint protocols in some detail.

This is a more detailed analysis than that of Example 16-1. Using a typical half-
duplex basic mode bi-sync style protocol, running multithread, we calculate the
line utilization and response time for transactions in an on-line inquiry system.

This involves building a detailed model of the system and incorporates queuing theory to work out response times.

example 16-3: calculation of delays caused by queuing   272

This example shows how to use queuing theory as explained in Chapter 28 to work out the average time delays caused by interference between messages from different terminals for the communication line in Example 16-2.

example 16-4: half-duplex point-to-point line
with printers and a cluster of visual display terminals   273

This detailed example illustrates how to calculate the throughput of a system and shows the dramatic effect that seemingly small time delays can have on system performance. It also illustrates how easy it is for system implementers to inadvertently make mistakes which can cause the network performance to be less than adequate.

example 20-1: HDLC network no. 1—point-to-point line
with printers and terminals   311

This is similar to Example 16-4 except that we are running with full-duplex protocols. This example illustrates two things. First, it is generally much easier to calculate the throughput of a full-duplex system than the equivalent half-duplex; and second, the throughput of the full-duplex system is far superior to that of the half-duplex. It also illustrates that the throughput of the full-duplex system is to a large extent independent of the time delays encountered through the network.

example 20-2: HDLC network no. 2—with remote
concentrators, remote job entry, and on-line inquiry
terminals   312

This extensive example illustrates how to calculate the performance of a network involving front-end processors, remote concentrators, remote job entry terminals, and on-line inquiry terminals. It calculates the throughput of the system from the point of view of RJE terminals and calculates the response time for on-line inquiry terminals going through the concentrators. This example illustrates the analysis of HDLC networks and also incorporates the effects of higher-level protocols as used for flow control.

example 25-1: calculation of the utilization for a simple system   385

This example shows a generalized approach to the calculation of utilization which can be used in any type of system.

example 25-2: investigation of the behavior of a simple on-line inquiry system   393

This example illustrates, in qualitative terms, the behavior of a simple on-line inquiry system as the load on the system is increased. It illustrates how bottlenecks occur within the system, which will have a limiting effect on the system throughput and cause response time to be extended. These bottlenecks can be removed in a number of ways, and this example illustrates several techniques that can be used to improve system performance.

example 28-1: queuing example no. 1   440

This example illustrates how we can analyze the performance of a simple single-server queue as we apply a load to it. It goes on to examine the behavior of the system as more servers are provided and the queue thus becomes a multiserver queue.

example 28-2: queuing example no. 2   445

This example demonstrates the use of multiserver queuing to work out average queuing size and queuing time for a typical small system.

example 28-3: queuing example no. 3   445

We are not always given problems in a straightforward way. We are often faced with one that cannot be solved directly, where an educated guess needs to be made. This example illustrates such a problem.

example 28-4: queuing example no. 4—simple system   447

This example describes a simple on-line inquiry system which is a quantified version of the simple on-line inquiry system used in Example 25-2. It shows how to work out average queue sizes, queuing times, and waiting times for users of an on-line inquiry service.

This example illustrates a multipoint environment with single-thread operation and shows how you can work out the behavior of the system under different loading conditions. It also illustrates the impact of having queues within queues and shows how results can be misleading. Although the results look good on the surface, in practice the behavior of the system could be disastrous.

This example modifies the system of the previous example, turns into a multi-thread environment which changes the queuing behavior of the system quite dramatically. This illustrates the basic approach that would be used to analyze the performance of such a system.

The communications rules of the previous example are changed from half-duplex to full-duplex. Once again, this modifies the model for analysis. This example illustrates the general approach that would be used in analysing this system.

1
Introduction to On-Line Systems

This chapter is intended to help to bring all readers of this book to a common level from which we can attack the main material, which starts in Chapter 2.

From the outside looking in, the world of data communications seems to be very complex. This has been brought about by three major items. First, in the field of data communications there is very little standardization; second, there is a lot of strange terminology; and (3) there is a lot of conflicting terminology. Figure 1-1 illustrates some of the strange terminology. As far as conflicting terminology is concerned, with one or two exceptions, the acronyms on the right-hand side of Fig. 1-1 refer to fundamentally the same thing.

These things tend to confuse the subject and make it difficult for beginners; in fact, they can even cause trouble for specialists. However, underneath this seeming complexity, the subject really is quite straightforward, and it is the intention of this book to present the topic in its simplicity.

As we all know, the fields of computers and communications are merging. Practically all new computers have communication capability, while nearly all new communications equipment includes one or more computers. The rapid growth in the industry, of course, is due to technological advances, which now make it relatively inexpensive to do things that we always wanted to do.

It is interesting to realize that the basic principles of operation of modern data communication systems have changed very little over the last century. Tech-

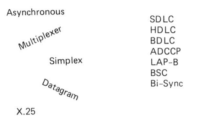

Asynchronous

Multiplexer

Simplex

Datagram

X.25

Duplex

SDLC
HDLC
BDLC
ADCCP
LAP–B
BSC
Bi–Sync

Figure 1-1 Strange and conflicting terminology.

nological advances allow us to do things faster and more economically. The presence of a computer in a communications system enhances the range of user facilities available. Let us first look at some of the applications that people are using for on-line systems.

applications for on-line systems

On-line inquiry systems

Probably the most common application today is the on-line inquiry system. Such a system is illustrated in Fig. 1-2, where we have a configuration of equipment with a host computer that has a file of some sort attached to it, and the operator has a terminal connected into the host via a communication line.

Typically, the terminal operator wishes to access the file to extract a record from it and examine the contents of the record. Alternatively, the operator may wish to add a record or perhaps modify an existing record. Regardless of the detail of the application we can normally break a single transaction into three or four component parts, as shown in Fig. 1-3.

Let us assume that the terminal is buffered. This means that the terminal has a memory buffer inside it, so that as the characters are entered on the keyboard they do not go down the communication line; rather, they are stored in the terminal and displayed on the screen. When the terminal operator hits the transmit button, the contents of the screen are transmitted down the line into the computer.

The block diagram shown in Fig. 1-3 illustrates the major component parts of an on-line inquiry transaction. The first component is data entry, where the terminal operator enters the transaction into the terminal. When the operator is ready, he or she hits the transmit button, which causes the contents of the terminal

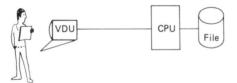

Figure 1-2 On-line inquiry system.

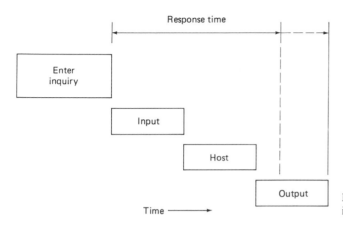

Figure 1-3 Block diagram of on-line inquiry system.

to be transmitted down the communication line to the computer. The box labeled "input" contains everything that is necessary to get the message from the terminal into the computer. The computer then processes the message, looks up the file, extracts the record, and prepares a response. This is illustrated in the box labeled "host." Then the computer transmits the output message back to the terminal, where it is viewed on the screen by the terminal operator. The box labeled "output" contains everything that is necessary to get the message from the computer out to the terminal screen.

Although a transaction looks simple in block diagram terms, in reality it is more complicated because the system designer must determine precisely what happens in each of the boxes shown in Fig. 1-3. The designer is normally designing to meet a particular performance specification, which usually contains a response time and a throughput specification.

Response time is a measure of the speed of operation of the system and is defined, in the case of a buffered terminal, as the time from when the terminal operator hits the transmit button until the first character of the response appears on the screen. This time is illustrated on Fig. 1-3. Response time normally finishes somewhere in the output box. It could finish at the beginning of the output box in the case of a terminal that displays the characters on the screen as they come off the communication line. Alternatively, some terminals wait until they get the complete message before they flash the message up on the screen. In this case the response time would terminate at the end of the output box. In any case, the system designer needs to be able to work out precisely what happens inside the input box, the host box, and the output box to determine how long each component of response time is going to be so that he or she can add the components together to work out the response time.

Throughput is a measure of the load on a system and we need to know if the system can carry the load we intend imposing on it. Suppose that the terminal operator is entering a certain volume of transactions per hour. If we know how long the line is going to be occupied for the input sequence, and how long the line is going to be occupied for the output sequence, we can work out how long the communication line will be occupied for one message. From that we could work out the time the line will be occupied over a complete hour for the given number of transactions per hour. In this way we can determine the line loading and if the system can carry the load we are going to impose on it. In later sections of the book we deal in detail with the contents of the blocks labeled "input" and "output."

Data entry and data distribution

A very rapidly growing application area for on-line systems is what I am calling *data entry and data distribution*. This is illustrated in Fig. 1-4. The intelligent terminal, and now the personal computer, allows a lot of processing to be done at the user site. Either of these machines can support disks or floppy disks. We can use the intelligence in the terminal to edit data as they are entered; then we can store the data on the disks or floppy disks. Editing the data as they are entered is the best place to do the data editing because we can catch a high proportion of data entry errors then and there, on the spot, while the operator still has the source document in front of him. Corrections can be made immediately. Of course, it is not possible to catch all data entry errors at the point of entry, but we can catch a high proportion of them and end up with a relatively clean file on the disk.

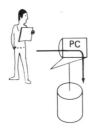

(a) Data entry using personal computer

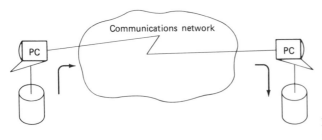

(b) File transfer with personal computers

Figure 1-4 (a) Data entry using personal computer; (b) file transfer with personal computers.

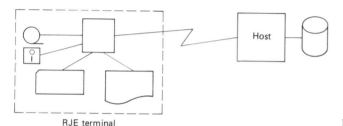

RJE terminal

Figure 1-5 Remote job entry.

Later, as shown in Fig. 1-4(b), the operator can establish a communication link through the telephone network or packet switch or any other communication network and transmit the contents of the floppy disk from her terminal to another terminal at a remote site, or perhaps into a mainframe computer.

Remote job entry

Remote job entry, a very well established application, is illustrated in Fig. 1-5. Typically, we have a host computer with all its peripheral units at one location. At a remote site we have a collection of input/output devices connected to a control unit, which in turn is connected to the host via a communication line. Users submit their jobs to the remote job entry terminal and the data are transferred down the line to the host. The host executes the job and transmits the results back to the remote job entry terminal for printout. Thus users at the remote site think they have the power of the host computer right there in their own offices, but in reality it is miles away at a central site.

Message switching

Probably the oldest application for data communications in the world is message switching. This is best illustrated by means of an example, as shown in Fig. 1-6. Here we have five branch offices of a company, we need to have communication between them, and we want hard copy for administrative purposes.

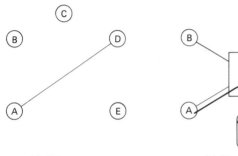

(a) Telex network

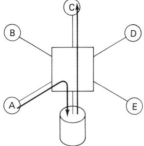

(b) Message switching

Figure 1-6 (a) Telex network; (b) message switching.

A simple way of providing such a facility is to give each branch office a Telex set so that we can establish temporary point-to-point connections through the Telex network and exchange messages between the cooperating terminals. In Fig. 1-6(a) terminal A is talking to terminal D. If terminal E wishes to send a message to D, it cannot because D is busy; terminal E has to keep trying until D becomes available. The Telex network, although providing great flexibility, has limited traffic-carrying capability, and in a situation like this the system tends to fall apart as the traffic increases. This is because as the traffic increases, everybody is busy while everyone else is trying to call them.

We can solve this problem by putting a computer into the system, as shown in Fig. 1-6(b). Here the terminals interface directly into the computer, which has mass storage, and message flow takes place along the lines shown in the diagram. A message from A to C coming into the computer is first stored on the disk and then forwarded to C. We call this a *store-and-forward message-switching system*; that is, the message is stored before it is forwarded. When we handle messages in this manner, we can do a number of good things. First, if terminal E wishes to send a message to C while the other message is being transmitted, he can do so because the message will be stored on disk and placed in a queue, and will be forwarded when C becomes available. Indeed, C could be broken down or switched off; the other terminals can still send messages. They will be placed in a queue and held until C becomes available.

The presence of the computer allows us to do many other good things, such as communicating between terminals that would otherwise be incompatible. In the case of the Telex network, where we have effectively a physical hardwired connection between the two terminals, the terminals need to be exactly compatible with each other. They need to operate at the same transmission speed, using the same character set, using the same message formats, and so on. In the message-switching system the computer can carry out conversions. It can perform speed conversion, code conversion, format conversion, and protocol conversion to enable us to communicate between a low-speed teleprinter and a high-speed intelligent terminal.

Many other facilities can be provided by a message-switching system, but to go into this is beyond the scope of this book. We should also point out, however, that the more modern Telex systems do indeed have store-and-forward capability built in, so that a lot of problems related to Telex are disappearing.

Packet switching

A derivation of message switching, which is of more interest to computer communication users, is packet switching. Although we describe packet switching in detail later in the book, a broad overview is provided here.

In Fig. 1-7(a) we have a network that consists of three switching computers interconnected with high-speed communication lines. This part of the network forms the common network which is shared between a number of users. Users

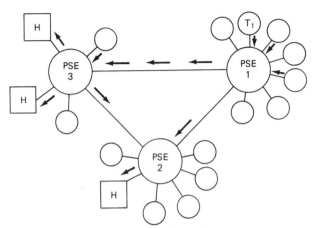

PSE: Packet switching exchange

(a) Packet switch

PH: Packet header, includes address information
PT: Packet trailer, includes error detection codes

(b) Packet structure

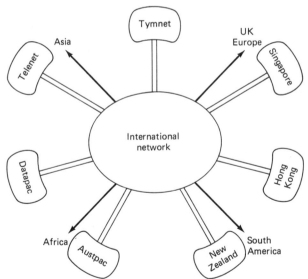

(c) Interconnected packet switching networks

Figure 1-7 (a) Packet switching; (b) packet structure; (c) interconnected packet-switching networks.

connect their host computers and their terminals into the nearest packet-switching exchange and the network switches data from the terminals to the computers in the form of packets.

A packet consists of a collection of bits of user information, typically up to 1024 bits, wrapped up in an envelope that has an address in the front and an error-detecting mechanism at the back, as shown in Fig. 1-7(b). The packets are shown in the diagram as arrows and the packet coming from terminal T1 into the first switching center is examined by that switching center, which determines from the address that the packet should be routed down to the second switching center. The second switching center looks at the address and routes the packet to the host. Basically, a packet-switching network provides a facility whereby any terminal or computer connected into the network can communicate with any other terminal or computer in the network.

In this regard it is rather like the public telephone network. The telephone network allows any telephone to communicate with any other. In fact, you can get on the telephone right now and call the President of the United States. The network allows you to do this. Whether or not the President wishes to speak to you depends on your relationship with him.

It is a similar situation with packet-switching networks. The network will allow anyone to communicate with anyone else; however, whether or not the call is consummated depends on the relationship between the calling and the called parties.

Packet-switching networks in various countries are being interconnected [Fig. 1-7(c)] via the international telecommunications networks, and before long, we will end up with a worldwide interconnection of packet-switching networks, rather like our present worldwide interconnection of telephone networks. When this happens, in theory, any terminal or computer connected into any packet-switching network in the world should be able to communicate with any other terminal or computer provided that it is connected into this common packet-switching cooperative network.

Value-added services

Sitting on the back of the packet switch or perhaps on other networks, we are going to come across value-added services. A value-added service is a service whereby a common carrier or perhaps an entrepreneur takes a basic telecommunications service, adds intelligence to it, and in the process provides a new telecommunications service that has more value to the end user than the basic service had. A good example of a value-added service is the packet switch. The common carrier takes its own basic wires, adds intelligence in the form of switching computers, and thereby produces a new network which has more value to the end user than do the basic wires.

Sitting on the back of these services we are likely to see a number of other value-added services, such as electronic mail, Teletex, electronic message services, and so on. Let us examine these briefly.

Electronic mail

The term *electronic mail* means different things to different people. To me it means a transmission of textual information via electronic means. In reality this communications application has been in existence for years in the form of Telex and facsimile, both of which have been transmitting text information via electronic means.

The thing that is making electronic mail more of a popular buzzword nowadays is the thought of communicating word processors. Most organizations now have word processors and many of them are setting up communication links between them so that they can transmit information and get better-quality output, and thus bypass the postal system or certain courier services.

This is fine if we are communicating between word processors of the same brand. However, word processors of different brands generally cannot communicate because they use different communication protocols, perhaps different character sets, and different control functions.

In the early 1980s, a standard was developed by the International Telecommunications Standards–setting body, CCITT. The acronym CCITT, translated from the French, means Consultative Committee for International Telephones and Telegraphs. It consists of representatives of most of the common carriers in the world, and it operates under the auspices of the United Nations. CCITT develops standards for telephony, telegraphy, and data communications. It is because of the work of CCITT that the various telephone networks around the world interface with each other; you can get on the telephone and dial Afghanistan and it works.

CCITT also developed standards for communicating word processors and the standard is called Teletex. The Teletex standards are an international standard for communicating word processors that define the character sets, the control functions, the communication rules—in fact, it defines everything that is necessary to enable us to get an exact copy of a page of information from the memory of one word processor to the memory of another. As word processor suppliers implement the Teletex protocols into their products, we will approach a point where we can have easy communication between different brands of word processors.

The common carriers around the world are implementing Teletex networks, some of which are based on packet switches and some of which are based on circuit-switching networks, which will provide, in effect, a super-duper Telex service. Teletex operates much faster than Telex. It operates at least 2400 bits per second (bps), which enables us to transmit an A4-size page of data in 5 to 10 seconds, whereas to do the equivalent with Telex would take several minutes.

Also, the quality of output for Teletex is limited only by the quality of the printer attached to the word processor. This means that it can be absolute letter quality, whereas the print quality of Telex messages is quite poor.

Teletex is not intended to replace Telex but rather, to complement it. There will, in fact, be interfaces between the two networks via a gateway machine that is called a *conversion facility*. This will allow Telex users to communicate with Teletex users, and vice versa. Teletex should provide competition to courier services and to some postal services in that it will enable instantaneous high-quality communications.

Electronic message services

Electronic message services are commonly called *mailbox services* and can be provided on your own in-house computer or by a public service, perhaps through a packet-switching network. The aim of an electronic message service is to minimize the effects of a game known as "telephone tag." Telephone tag is what happens when person A tries to call person B—there is usually about a 72% chance of person B not being available. A therefore leaves a message for B to return the call. When B does finally return the call, guess what—there is a 72% probability that A will not be available. This goes on and on until finally they do speak to each other.

With an electronic message service, A and B would have access to terminals perhaps on their own desks, which would be connected into a mailbox computer. User A would log into B's mailbox and put the message in the mailbox. When B comes back to work, he or she would interrogate the mailbox, find A's question, and probably respond to it on the spot; the answer will automatically be put into A's mailbox. Later, A will come back and interrogate his or her mailbox and thus we have communicated between the two people, but we have done so on a non-real-time basis. A high proportion of interpersonal communications can take place in this way, in that it is not necessary for the people to be physically there at the same time to achieve meaningful communication.

Mailbox services can be provided in a number of ways. For example, most computer suppliers can provide software that will sit on the back of their existing network which will provide these facilities. Local area networks for personal computers usually have a simple mailbox service which enables the different users on the local area network to communicate with each other. Public mailbox services are offered by many common carriers around the world and many are accessible from international destinations, which is extremely useful for the executive on the move. Finally, the electronic Private Branch Exchange (PBX) or the digital PBX in many cases offers a mailbox facility as well.

The latter, the PBX mailbox facility, is particularly useful in view of the trend in telephone instruments. The latest telephone instruments contain both personal computer and telephone, connected into the PBX via a single port. The communication technique employed is such that it is possible to be talking and using the terminal simultaneously, so that we can be communicating by voice with a person and at the same time can use the personal computer as a freestanding personal computer. Alternatively, we can communicate via the PBX to a database on our own computer, or perhaps access the packet-switching network, and thus get access to any computer connected onto the packet switch. These executive workstations or computer telephones are proving to be a tremendous asset to executives today.

Scientific and industrial application

The realm of scientific and industrial applications belongs to the microcomputer. Practically all manufacturing processes can be either partially or fully computer controlled. Such things as controlling traffic lights and fire alarms, mixing dog food, rolling steel, rolling paper, and blowing plastic bags are all computer controlled.

differences between batch and on-line

Most users are experienced with batch-processing applications, and the trend seems to be more and more toward the use of on-line systems with data communications. Although on-line systems tend to be more complex than batch systems, particularly from the systems development point of view, there are a number of good reasons why we should want to go on-line. We may wish to eliminate intermediate processing between the users and the machine—that is, capture the transaction at its source. This is typically what is done in on-line order entry systems where people ring up to place orders. Their orders are captured by terminal operators and the order is fed directly into the computer. This eliminates all the intermediate data entry and verification steps that would otherwise have taken place. Hopefully, it also eliminates many of the errors that could have been associated with these intermediate steps.

Another reason to go on-line might be to reduce the time required to produce full reports and to reduce the amount of paper that is required by providing selective inquiries. Instead of printing out reams of paper every day for standardized reports that nobody ever reads, the trend seems to be toward giving executives and other users the capability of inquiring on a file so that they can extract the precise piece of information that they need and not get bogged down with extraneous information.

Another reason is to provide access to up-to-date information. In the area of inventory control it is said that the more perishable the product we are dealing with, the more accurate our knowledge has to be about the status of that product. For example, one of the most perishable products of all is an airline seat. If an airline seat takes off without a person sitting in it, that space can never be sold. That is perishable! The airline needs to know precisely how many seats are available at this instant, not how many were available 10 minutes ago or even an hour ago, but right now. This can be performed only by a real-time reservations system.

Another reason to go on-line is to provide a service that cannot be adequately provided by any other means. For example, in police departments the police have all their files on the computer: criminal names, the names of people who have warrants out against them, driver's licenses, vehicle registrations, firearms licenses, and so on. This becomes a marvelous operational tool for the police, and a police officer in the field can find out all about a person in a few minutes through the computer system rather than taking several weeks, as would be required using the old style of manual file.

Given that there are a number of good reasons to go on-line, we should now look at some of the differences between batch and on-line processing. There are, in fact, major differences in areas such as performance, reliability, and recovery, just to name a few.

Performance

In the case of a well-established batch operation, performance is typically measured in terms of turnaround. Assuming that the user gets the correct answer to his or her question, the user usually judges the system based on the time it takes to get the answer to the question, and this turnaround is typically measured in hours or days. When we go on-line, the turnaround is typically measured in seconds, and this clearly introduces problems in the areas of reliability and system capacity.

While there are many performance criteria for a system—reliability, availability, cost, and so on—the two major performance criteria, assuming that the system is reasonably reliable and works reasonably well, are response time and throughput. Response time is a measure of the speed of operation of the system; throughput is a measure of the load the system can handle. These two performance criteria are related and the relationship between them is nonlinear, as shown in Fig. 1-8. This diagram shows that as the throughput on the system increases, the response time increases slowly until it gets to a certain point where it streaks up past the top of the page.

This curve shape is caused by queuing in the system. In later chapters we examine queuing theory in more detail. In general, as the load on a system increases, the transactions compete for the available system resources. As this competition increases, we get queues of transactions lining up to get onto the available system resources, such as communication lines, disk input/output channels, and so on. Where queuing occurs, we have nonlinear behavior, as shown in the diagram.

The system designer must be able to work out approximately where on that curve the particular on-line system is operating. For example, we may have a response-time specification that states: "The response time must be less than 3 seconds at a load of 10,000 transactions per hour."

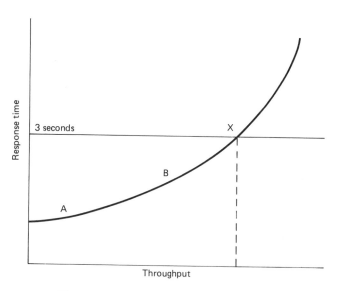

Figure 1-8 On-line system performance curve.

In Fig. 1-8 we have indicated where 3 seconds is. As long as 10,000 trans-actions per hour is anywhere to the left of point *X*, we are in business. Let us say that 10,000 transactions per hour is at point *B* on the curve. We are meeting the response-time specification and all looks well. However, things are not as good as they seem because we do not have very much room to move. If the load increases slightly, the response time will go through the roof. On the other hand, if 10,000 transactions per hour had been at point *A* on the curve, we could double the load or perhaps even treble the load before getting into trouble.

You can see, therefore, that it is important to know approximately where we are on the curve. Later we spend a lot of time working out where we are on this performance curve.

Reliability

Reliability is extremely important in both batch and on-line systems. How-ever, in the case of batch systems, where we have a typical 24-hour turnaround on jobs, there is plenty of time for the computer to break down for 5 to 6 hours. The users will not necessarily know the difference because they still get their reports on time.

In an on-line system we have terminals in the user departments. If the com-puter breaks down for 5 or 6 minutes, everybody knows about it. This means that the reliability requirements of an on-line system are going to be much more strin-gent than those of a batch-processing system. It may be necessary to duplicate parts of the equipment so that if we have an equipment failure they still continue to provide service.

User interface

In the case of a batch-processing system, the user typically goes down to the data processing (DP) department with the job to be processed and gives it to a DP person. The DP person feeds the job through the computer and speaks a cryptic language to the computer which has little room for error. The DP person then gets the output from the computer and gives it to the user. If the user has a problem, he or she can resolve the problem by talking to the DP person in his or her own natural language.

When we go on-line, the user interfaces directly with the computer and does not wish to use the same specialized, cryptic language to talk to the computer that DP people typically use. The user wants the machine to communicate in a meaningful way regardless of what sort of rubbish the user may input into the machine. This means that the human–machine dialogue needs a lot of work.

Nowadays the buzzword is that the human–machine dialogue must be *user friendly*. Whatever we call it, a great deal of work needs to go into these dialogues to make sure that they cater properly to the user.

Recovery

Recovery involves what you do when the system breaks down, and when you finally fix it, how you get back to where you would have been had the computer not broken down. In the case of a batch job, if the computer breaks down halfway through a job, typically, when we fix the computer we resubmit the job or perhaps restart from a checkpoint. In the case of an on-line system, we do not want to resubmit all the transactions; we need to be able to pick up the threads from where we were when the system went down. This means that the system needs to be set up such that when it fails it captures its own environment, so that when we repair the system we need only reenter the transactions that were in the process of being processed when the failure occurred.

This means specialized software, which, luckily, tends to come with computers nowadays. In the early days we had to write this software ourselves and it was very complicated. Even though the software does come with the computer, we still need to check it out very thoroughly: first, to ensure that the software does what the supplier says it will do, and second, to ensure that it is indeed suitable for our application.

management problems

One of the largest problems in the development of on-line communication-based systems is not in the technical area but in the management area. This is because the design and implementation of on-line systems differs greatly from the design and implementation of batch-processing systems. In a well-established batch-processing installation, the data processing department and the user department can generally join forces, specify an application, and design and implement it without calling upon the resources of the mainframe supplier.

As soon as we consider the implementation of an on-line system, we start to involve outside organizations, such as the following, in our design and development efforts:

- *Terminal supplier.* There are hundreds of terminal models on the market, and it is quite possible that we will consider using a terminal that is not supplied by our mainframe supplier. This is because we can probably find a terminal that is better, more versatile, cheaper, or more readily available than the products offered by our mainframe supplier.
- *Mainframe supplier.* The mainframe supplier is likely to be involved for several reasons. For example, if we are using terminals from an outside organization, we need to make sure that the terminal is indeed compatible with the hardware and software supplied by the mainframer. This immediately introduces problems, because the mainframer and the terminal supplier may not necessarily like each other. Also, we will be using communications hardware and software, and if it is our first experience with on-line systems, it is likely that we will not be familiar with these products and therefore will need assistance from the mainframer.
- *Data communications equipment suppliers.* Modems, network terminating units, multiplexers, modem sharing units, protocol converters, concentrators, and other pieces of data communications equipment may be used in your network. There may be several suppliers involved in providing these components.
- *Consultant.* If we are just moving into on-line systems, we may call on the services of an outside consultant to assist in the design and development effort.
- *Software house.* For similar reasons to those for employing consultants, we may employ a software house. In the design and implementation phase of an on-line system, we often need personnel of higher caliber than those needed to keep the system running once it has been cut over to operational use. Experienced on-line design-and-implementation personnel are very expensive, so we may choose to hire over the short term from a software house or consulting organization rather than add to in-house staff. The problem with employing such people is that the average organization does not have a sufficient variety of work to keep these people interested once the project is completed, and they are likely to leave and look for work elsewhere.
- *Communication carriers.* If you intend to install terminals outside your own premises, it is likely that you will need to obtain communications facilities from your communication common carrier(s). The number of carriers you will need to deal with depends on the country you are in and whether or not you are contemplating international communication.

- *Power, air conditioning, etc.* Because we are going on-line, the reliability and recovery requirements for the system are going to be much more stringent than those of the batch system. A batch-processing system can be out of action for several hours, and nobody apart from the electronic data processing (EDP) department would be aware of it. In the case of an on-line system, however, when the system stops everybody involved knows about it, including all the users. We often go to great lengths to duplicate items of hardware so that we can allow an item to fail without putting the entire system off the air. If we are going to go to these lengths, we need to consider whether we should have alternative sources of air conditioning and power.

Each of the organizations listed above may have its own ax to grind, and it will not always row the boat in the same direction. The data processing manager therefore has a management problem involving the coordination of the activities of the outside organizations. In many cases, he or she does not have experience in handling this type of problem and, in fact, may not realize that there is a problem until it is too late. There have been many instances in which the project time scales have elapsed, budgets have been exceeded, and no real work has been accomplished, because of poor coordination on the part of the project manager.

There are established procedures for handling projects of this type and for coordinating the activities of the various parties involved. If from the beginning the data processing manager or project manager recognizes the possibility of problems, he or she can minimize their rate of occurrence.

2
Basic Communications Theory

Communications plays a very important part in our lives because we are almost always involved in some form of communication. Figure 2-1 illustrates some of the following everyday examples of communication:

- A face-to-face conversation
- Reading a book
- Sending or receiving a letter
- A telephone conversation
- Watching a film or television
- Looking at paintings in an art gallery
- Attending a lecture

There are thousands of other examples of communications, and *data communications* is one specific area of the entire field of communication.

From the examples given, we can see that each communications system has its own characteristics but that there are a number of properties that are common to all communication systems. The principal common attribute is that the aim of communication is to transfer information from one point to another. In data communications systems, we generally call this information *data* or a *message*.

As indicated in Fig. 2-2, the message may take a number of forms. It may

Figure 2-1 There are many examples of communication in our lives.

be composed of factual information as in a well-prepared lecture, or it may be composed of emotional information, as in a painting or in the arrangement of a piece of music. The message, however, is all-important, and all the processes of communication have been developed because there is a message to send.

Figure 2-2 A message may take a number of forms.

Figure 2-3 Basic communications system.

To send a message from one point to another, three system components must be present. We need a *source*, which generates a message and places it on a *transmission medium*, which carries the message to the third element, which is the *receiver*. These elements are the *minimum* requirements for *any* communication process, and if one of them is absent, communication cannot take place. A common communication system is illustrated in Fig. 2-3, and a more formalized arrangement of the three basic components is shown in Fig. 2-4.

These fundamental elements can be present in many different forms depending on the particular communication system, and we can analyze some everyday examples to determine the source, medium, and receiver in each case:

- In a conversation taking place in the kitchen, the source may be Mrs. Jones; the medium is the air, which carries the sound waves from her voice; and her son, John, is the receiver of the message.
- In a telephone conversation, the source might be Mary in London; the medium is the telephone network connecting her to New York; and the receiver is Sally in New York.
- When I give a lecture, I send a message through the air to a number of individual receivers, who are the members of the audience.

Having established the components of a communications system, we now examine some factors that are relevant to its *performance*.

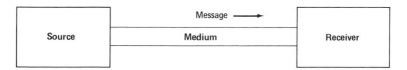

Figure 2-4 For communication to take place, three elements must be present.

- *For communications to be effective, the message must be understood.* Figure 2-5 shows that the receiver must be able to correctly interpret the message. If while talking to a friend, you use a word that he or she does not know, you have not communicated meaningfully. If you pick up a Japanese version of this book, you would probably not understand it. No matter how well presented the material, if you cannot read Japanese, the message is meaningless to you. Similarly, if a computer is expecting information to come along a data line at a particular speed and in a particular code, and the information comes at a different speed or in a different code, effective communication has not taken place.

- *The overall characteristics of a communications system are defined and limited by the individual characteristics of the source, medium, and receiver.* The type of information to be conveyed often dictates the type of source, medium, and receiver that will be used in a communications system. A color film of a horse race can convey visual and sound information about the race; we can see whether the sky is blue or overcast; we can see what colors the jockeys are wearing; we can see who wins the race; but we cannot smell the training paddocks, due to a limitation in the particular communication system involved.

In Australia, computers are used to handle betting on horse races. By looking at the data coming in on the communication lines, the computer can

Figure 2-5 The receiver must understand the message for effective communications to take place.

Figure 2-6 Noise.

tell how much money is being bet on which horse so that it can compute the odds and work out how much money to pay the winner. But due to a limitation in the communications system, the computer cannot sense the feeling of anticipation in the queue of bettors in front of each betting window.

Later in the book you will see how a single component in a communications system can limit the performance of the entire system.

- *In a communications system, interference can occur during the transmission process*, and the message may be corrupted. Any such undesired disturbance in the system is called *noise*. A low-flying jet plane is a source of noise that interferes with a conversation; a person in front of a movie projector, as in Fig. 2-6, is noise interfering with the visual message being projected; and static on a telephone line is noise that interferes with the conversation.

signal-to-noise ratio

Communications engineers like to talk about the *signal-to-noise ratio* (S/N). They say that all communications channels have a background of noise and that the larger the signal in relation to the noise, the easier it is to detect the signal. Also, the larger the signal, the more information that can be carried by that channel.

In satellite communication systems, for example, the size of the earth station basically determines the communication capability of a link. All other things being equal, the noise picked up by and generated in an earth station is about the same regardless of the size of the antenna. However, a big earth station intercepts more signal energy than is intercepted by a small earth station. Therefore,

$$\text{large earth station} \rightarrow \text{large } S/N$$

$$\text{small earth station} \rightarrow \text{small } S/N$$

Common carriers use large earth stations because they need to provide a service to a large number of users. Corporate communications networks use small earth stations because they are much cheaper. As a consequence, however, the communications capability of a small earth station is limited by the small S/N ratio.

data communications

Knowing the basics of general communications allows us more easily to investigate the specific area that is of interest to us: *data communications*. Data communications involves a combination of message source, medium, and receiver in various kinds of communication networks. The term *communication network* often causes something like the arrangement of Fig. 2-7 to spring to mind. Here we have a computer with an in-house teleprinter and visual display terminal (VDT) and a number of remote terminals connected by communication lines.

For data communication to take place, it is not necessary to use telephone lines or special-purpose data lines. In fact, most organizations indulge in data communications right now. If you want to send information from one point to another, there are various media available to perform this task. You can use the mail for transmitting documents, cassettes, or floppy disks. You can use air express, you can transmit the data along a telephone line, or you can physically carry a box of cards from one point to another. In each case, the aim is the same— to get the information from one point to another and to get it there in one piece. The particular medium that you use is determined by examining a number of factors, such as the cost, the speed, the reliability, and the availability of the medium as well as the urgency of your own requirements. You should go through the exercise of evaluating the various media that are available for two reasons: (1) to determine which particular medium or combination of communications media is optimum for your purposes, and (2) to select a suitable backup in case the prime system fails. For example, if you rely on using air express to carry cassettes from one city to another, what do you do if there is an airline strike?

In this book we analyze data communications systems as though the medium in use were a telephone line or a special-purpose line from another kind of electronic communication network, such as a packet-switching network or a digital data network. The principles involved, however, apply to other communications media, and if we develop analytical techniques to analyze a communications system based on telephone or data lines, we can use the same or similar techniques to analyze systems using other communications media.

A data communications network usually involves a computer with one or more terminals connected by communications lines. These lines carry the messages between the computer and its associated terminals, or between terminals. Terminals can be any one of a number of devices, such as teleprinters and other keyboard devices, line printers, credit-card readers, visual display terminals, and

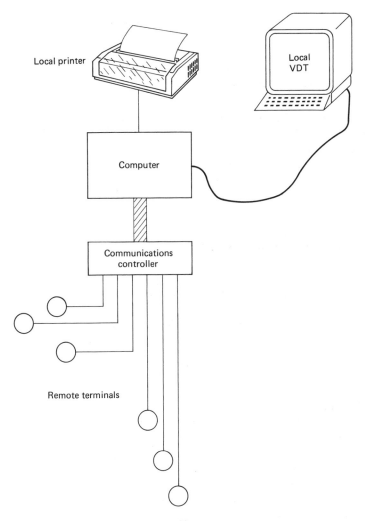

Figure 2-7 Simple network.

even computers. We shall learn more about data terminals later and see how the terminals and the computer can act as a message source or a message receiver, or in some cases as both a source and a receiver.

The communications lines are generally telephone lines, although they may come from special-purpose data networks such as digital data networks. Most communications lines come from the telephone network, and this will continue to be the case for a long time. In many countries, special networks, such as the Australian Digital Data Network, have been introduced. Also, the use of digital transmission techniques in telephone systems is increasing as carriers aim at the Integrated Services Digital Network (ISDN). Digital transmission lines provide far superior performance to telephone lines. We discuss the ISDN in more detail later in the book.

transmission definitions

The *communications line* is the medium that carries the messages in a data communications system. This line usually comes from the telephone network, so we often call it a *telephone line*. We send data along the line, so we often call it a *data line*. As you have seen, we often just call it a *line*. (Some people use the term *data link* to refer to the communication line, but this can be confusing; the term *data link* means different things to different people. As outlined in Chapter 12, a data link generally consists of more than just a line.)

One-way transmission

The line consists of one or more *channels*, where a channel is defined as a means of *one-way* transmission. A channel can carry information in either direction but in only one direction at a time. The direction of information flow is determined by the characteristics of the devices at each end of the channel.

A hose pipe is a good example of a communication channel. It can carry water in either direction, but the direction of flow depends on which end is connected to the water tap. Radio and television broadcasts are examples of one-way transmission. The signals travel from the broadcasting station to be picked up by the receiving sets in our homes. Our radio and television receivers cannot send information back to the transmitter because the receivers in our homes are not designed to transmit, nor is the broadcasting station designed to receive information. Cars traveling in a one-way street, as in Fig. 2-8, provide another example of one-way transmission. If a vehicle travels in the wrong direction along a one-way street, there is likely to be a collision. The same thing happens in data communications if we attempt to send information along a channel in both directions at once. The result is that the messages become garbled or unrecognizable.

A simple electrical example of a one-way communication system is shown in Fig. 2-9. Here we have a person in room A and another in room B. We give A a battery and a pushbutton switch, and we give B a light bulb. We connect the system together with two pieces of wire, which enables A to send information to B by pressing the pushbutton switch. This closes the circuit, allowing electric current to flow from the battery through the wire to light the lamp. When the switch is released, the current stops and the lamp goes out. By using some predetermined sequence of flashing the lamp on and off, A can communicate with B. However, there is no way that B can communicate with A because of the limitations in the equipment at each end of the line.

Figure 2-8 One-way system.

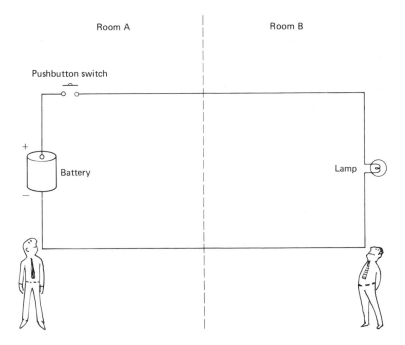

Figure 2-9 Simple one-way communication system.

This is a one-way communication system, and one thing we should observe is that two pieces of wire are used to connect the source and the receiver. This is a simple example of what is known as a *two-wire line*. The information is transmitted by varying the electrical signal on these two wires. As a general rule, two wires are required to produce a communication channel, although, as outlined in Chapter 7, there are some exceptions to this rule.

Either-way (half-duplex) transmission

By using suitable terminal equipment, we can alternate the direction of data flow along the channel. Let us upgrade the equipment at each end of the channel so that it is capable of *either* transmitting or receiving. We can initially send from A to B; however, at the end of the message, we can turn the system around so that B becomes a transmitter, A becomes a receiver, and we can send information back the other way. This way we have a two-way alternate data flow situation, which is correctly called an *either-way* transmission system but is more commonly referred to as a *half-duplex* system (abbreviated HDX).

Polite conversation is half-duplex. I talk to you, then you talk to me. Press-to-talk radio systems such as those used in police cars and taxis are half-duplex. When the taxi driver presses the button on his microphone, he can talk to his base but he cannot hear his base; when he releases the button, he can hear the base but he cannot talk to the base. Tennis is a half-duplex game. The one-lane bridge in Fig. 2-10 is a half-duplex system: It can carry information in either direction but in only one direction at a time, and the direction of data flow is determined by the boom gate at the end of the bridge.

Getting back to our simple electric communication system in Fig. 2-9, we can make that into a half-duplex system by giving each person more equipment. We will give A a lamp and B a battery and a pushbutton, and we will give each person another switch that we will call a *transmit/receive* switch. We will connect

Figure 2-10 Either-way (half-duplex) system.

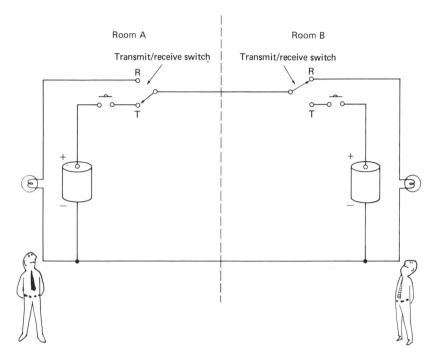

Figure 2-11 Simple either-way (half-duplex) communication system.

the arrangement as shown in Fig. 2-11. With A in transmit mode and B in receive mode, A can communicate with B by pressing the pushbutton and sending current through the loop to lamp B. At the end of the communication, both people can switch their *transmit/receive* switches to the opposite position, and then B can communicate with A by pressing his pushbutton and sending current through the loop and lighting lamp A.

There are two points that we should notice about this simple communication system. First, it uses only two wires to connect A and B. In Chapter 7 we look in detail at two-wire and four-wire communication systems, but for the time being, notice that in the simplest half-duplex communication systems we need only two wires to physically connect the source and the receiver.

The second point to notice is that the action of reversing the direction of data flow takes a finite amount of time. You can imagine how long it takes to recognize the end of a transmission and switch the *transmit/receive* switches over so that we are ready to transmit in the opposite direction. This *system turnaround* time is the combination of *reaction time*, which is the time it takes the operator to recognize the end of a transmission, and line *turnaround time*, which is the time it takes to physically flick the switches and get ready to transmit in the opposite direction. Most communication systems have a finite turnaround time, and we generally need to find out how long it is for the particular system under consideration. We examine this in more detail in Chapter 7.

Both-way (full-duplex) transmission

If we set up a communication line with two channels, we have the capability of sending information in both directions at the same time. Usually, one channel carries information in one direction, and the other channel carries information in the backward direction. If the terminal equipment at each end of the line is capable of transmitting and receiving data simultaneously, the entire system is capable of simultaneous two-way data flow. Such a system is correctly known as a *both-way* system, but more colloquially it is referred to as a *full-duplex* system (abbreviated FDX). As shown in Fig. 2-12, most roads are full-duplex.

The easiest way to turn our simple electrical system into a full-duplex system is to duplicate the arrangement shown in Fig. 2-9 to give us a system like that in Fig. 2-13. This system is capable of two-way simultaneous data flow, because B can press the pushbutton that sends current through the loop to lamp A while A is sending current through the other loop and lighting lamp B. You will notice that in this system we have a total of four wires connecting A and B. This is a simple example of what is known as a *four-wire line*. In Chapters 3 and 7 we explore the operation of communication lines in more detail, but for the time being, we will note that in the simplest case we need four wires to provide full-duplex capability.

Another point to note about this full-duplex arrangement is that although the communication channels and terminal equipment are arranged to give us full-duplex capability, we may not be able to use the system as a full-duplex system. This may be because of limitations imposed by operators A and B. An experienced operator can possibly interpret an incoming message and transmit an outgoing message at the same time, whereas most operators would only be able to do one or the other but not both. So in this case, we can see that the overall characteristics of the system are going to be limited by the characteristics of the operators.

By providing full-duplex capability, however, we do improve the efficiency of the system, in that we eliminate the line turnaround time that would have been required in the half-duplex arrangement shown in Fig. 2-11. We still have the

Figure 2-12 Both-way (full-duplex) system.

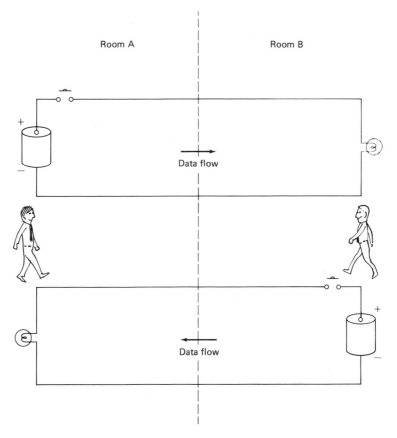

Figure 2-13 Simple both-way (full-duplex) communication system.

reaction time identified earlier, but the total turnaround time will be shorter. It is very common in data communications for half-duplex terminals to be connected by two channels. There are two reasons for the popularity of this organization: (1) in many telephone networks, the telephone lines come with two channels because that is the way they are used by the telephone system; and (2) by using this configuration, we can minimize system turnaround time.

The telephone network—full-duplex or half-duplex

People often ask whether the telephone network is full-duplex or half-duplex. The answer depends on the configuration of the network. The following explanation relates to the analog telephone network, which is basically a two-wire network.

If you refer to Fig. 2-14(a), you will see that your telephone is connected into the network by two pieces of wire which we call a *two-wire line*. The telephone

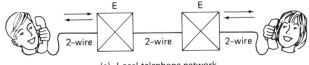

(a) Local telephone network

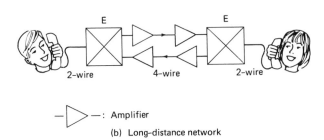

—▷—: Amplifier

(b) Long-distance network

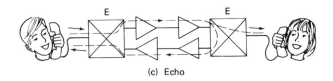

(c) Echo

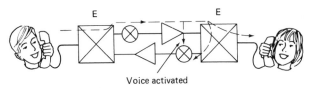

Voice activated

⊗: Echo suppressor

(d) Echo suppression

Figure 2-14 (a) Local telephone network; (b) long-distance network; (c) echo; (d) echo suppression.

is connected to the nearest telephone exchange (or central office) by this two-wire line. The central office contains all the switching equipment used to route the calls through the network.

If you make a call over a very short distance, say a few kilometers, you could probably trace a physical path through the network over two-wire lines. We all know from experience that both parties can talk at once on such a connection. This implies that the telephone network is capable of full-duplex operation, and indeed it is under these circumstances. It is unlikely that you could have a sensible conversation in full-duplex mode but at least the network is capable of it. We capitalize on this ability when using two-wire full-duplex modems over the dial-up telephone network.

Over a longer distance, say over a toll circuit, you would find that the carrier does not dedicate physical pairs of wire to each telephone conversation. Rather, it groups a number of conversations together on a bearer circuit which may be derived from coaxial cable, microwave, and so on. The bearers have amplifiers, or repeaters, at appropriate intervals to boost the signal to send it along the next piece of bearer. The amplifiers are purely one-way devices, and as we need the capability of two-way conversation, there will be a second bearer running in the opposite direction. This means that the long-haul part of the circuit is indeed a four-wire line, as shown in Fig. 2-14(b). During the conversation, the man's voice goes over one pair of wires and the woman's voice goes over the other pair of wires.

When the man speaks, his voice travels along the top pair of wires to the other end. Due to the way the telephone network is constructed, his voice not only gets to the destination but also bounces off the electronic equipment at the other end, as shown in Fig. 2-14(c), and comes back along the other pair of wires as an echo. The echo is amplified on the way back and eventually returns to the man about as loud as it was when it originally left him. Generally, the man does not hear the echo because the round-trip delays are so short that the echo comes back superimposed on his own voice. Basically, therefore, echoes do not cause a problem on most telephone calls within one country because the round-trip delays are very short.

Let us now make the line longer, perhaps an international circuit going through a satellite link. In this case the round-trip delay is something in excess of $\frac{1}{2}$ second, due to the time it takes the radio wave to get from the earth station up to the satellite and back again. In this case the man speaks and his voice arrives at the other end approximately $\frac{1}{4}$ second later. As before, his voice bounces off the equipment at the other end and comes back on the second pair of wires as an echo, and the echo returns to the man half a second or more after he spoke. The echo has been amplified on its return journey and therefore it returns just as loud as his voice was when it first left him. It is difficult, if not impossible, to carry on a sensible conversation when confronted with your own voice in the form of an echo.

The common carriers overcame this problem with the use of echo suppressors. An echo suppressor is effectively a switch placed in each communication channel as shown in Fig. 2-14(d). Echo suppressors are voice activated by signals on the other communication channel. When the man speaks, his voice goes along the top channel to the other end and activates the echo suppressor on the other pair of wires. The echo suppressor effectively opens the return circuit so that the echo of the man's voice is blocked at the echo suppressor. The echo suppressor remains activated for as long as the man keeps talking. While the echo suppressor is activated, if the woman should speak, her voice would also be blocked at the echo suppressor. When the man finally stops talking, the echo suppressor drops out; the woman can then speak, and in turn her voice activates the echo suppressor in the other channel, which once again blocks off the echo and also, as a by-product, stops the man's voice getting through if he should attempt to speak.

The operation of a system with echo suppressors is clearly half duplex. Those who use the telephone network for data transmission will find that modems, which are used to interface terminals and computers to the telephone network, generally transmit a special tone [at a frequency of 2100 hertz (Hz)] for about 1 second prior to transmitting their own carrier down the line. This special tone deactivates the echo suppressors so that the communication line can be used for full-duplex data transfers. In the case of operation with modems, echoes do not cause a problem because the echoes are electronically filtered out at the modem.

More modern devices that achieve the same purpose as echo suppressors are called *echo cancelers*. Such a device fits in the communication line at the same position as the echo suppressor; however, rather than opening the return circuit to physically block the echo, it performs some mathematics on the original signal and the echo. The echo canceler takes the echo and subtracts it from the original signal, which produces a balance of nothing to go back along the return channel to a speaker. This allows the recipient to speak, and his/her voice will go straight through the echo canceler because the person's voice is subtracted from, in effect, nothing, and therefore the voice goes straight through. Echo cancelers therefore allow full-duplex operation on the voice circuit.

Other terminology

Note that confusion can arise due to the use of different terminology. Most people use the term *simplex* transmission to mean *one-way* transmission, but some people use the term as though it means *half-duplex*. Similarly, some people use the term *duplex* on its own without a prefix. When they do this, they usually mean *full-duplex*, but some people use the term as though it means *half-duplex*. It is advisable to use the full terminology—that is, *one-way, full-duplex*, or *half-duplex*—and to clarify the definitions if you are talking to somebody who uses other terms.

transmission codes

In data communications systems, we usually wish to transmit a stream of characters, such as letters, numbers, or special symbols, from one point to another. (There is a trend toward the transmission of pure binary data streams, which is covered in Chapter 18.) The information usually originates in a form that a human being can understand, and we wish to reconstitute it at the other point either in a form that a human being can understand or in a form that a computer can handle.

The characters cannot be transmitted along a communication line the way we see them in print. Figure 2-15 shows how the characters must be encoded from the form that we understand into a form that the line can handle and that the receiving device can interpret. The receiver can then decode the received signals and put them into a form that we can understand or perhaps into a form that the computer can handle.

All data communication codes are based on the *binary* system. Binary means *two*, and in data communications, the term is used to describe any condition capable of existing in two different states. For example, the light switch in a room can exist in two states: on or off. The two states used in communications are called the *zero* state (0) and the *one* state (1). By using this binary system of 0 or 1, we can encode the message into a meaningful string of 1s and 0s that can be transmitted along a data line and decoded by a receiver. The string of 1s and 0s is meaningful because it is defined by a *code* that is known to both the source and the receiver.

A detailed discussion of the physical transmission of 1s and 0s on a line is beyond the scope of this book, but the basic concept is that the line presents a defined electrical state to signify a 0 and a different electrical state to signify a 1. For example, in the situation shown in Fig. 2-9, the presence of electric current in the loop can signify the 1 state, and the absence of electric current in the loop can signify the 0 state. These states are physically represented by the pushbutton at room A being either on or off and by the lamp in room B being either lit or unlit.

A code is limited by the number of *bits* it contains—the term *bit* being a contraction of the words *binary digit*. In data communications, the bit is the smallest unit of information in the system. We sometimes call the bit an *element* or a *level*, so the character-handling capability of the code is limited by the number of bits, elements, or levels that the code contains. For example, a one-bit code means that you can have two characters, so that we could encode the letter A and the letter B where the letter A was represented by the 0 state and the letter B was represented by the 1 state.

A two-element code would enable us to handle four characters. We could encode, for example, the letter A as the binary combination 00, B could be combination 01, C could be combination 10, and D could be combination 11. If we had a three-bit code, we could encode eight characters because there are eight

Figure 2-15 Transmission encoding and decoding.

possible combinations of the three bits. The general rule is that if we have an N-level code, we can encode 2^N characters. So in the case of our three-level code, we have $2^3 = 2 \times 2 \times 2 = 8$ combinations. Given this rule, we can invent any code that we wish. We could produce a 27-bit code and dream up all kinds of exciting possibilities for the 2^{27} available combinations. (If everyone did this, we would have chaos.)

However, just as the English alphabet has been standardized so that we can communicate with people all over the world, certain standardized data communication codes have been developed. Two of the more commonly used codes are *Baudot* code and *ASCII*, and we now examine these in detail.

Baudot code

Baudot code is named after a French postal engineer who worked on telegraphy around 1874. A New Zealander named Murray also worked in this field, and some people refer to this code as *Murray* code. In international communication circles, there is a body called the International Telegraph and Telephone Consultative Committee (CCITT). This body meets to produce standards for telephony and telegraphy, and they also produce data communications standards. (The CCITT standards are actually called "recommendations.") A standardized version of Baudot code is called CCITT Alphabet No. 2. Because CCITT is an international body, the code is often referred to as International Alphabet No. 2. This is the code that is used on the international Telex network, and it is therefore often called *Telex code*. The code is very widely used in private telegraph networks and among approximately 1,500,000 Telex sets that are interconnected through the international Telex network.

Baudot code is a five-bit code, which means that we can represent 32 characters. This is not enough to handle a full alphanumeric character set, so we extend the character-handling capability of Baudot code by designating two of the characters as code extension characters. Refer to Fig. 2-16 while you read the following description. This figure has three columns, the first containing the binary representation of the 32 Baudot code combinations; the second column is headed "letters characters," and the third is headed "figures characters."

The code extension characters are known as the *letter shift* character (LTRS or LS) and the *figure shift* character (FIGS or FS). The letter shift is binary 11111, and the figure shift is binary 11011. The figure shift is graphically presented by an upward arrow (↑) and the letter shift is graphically represented by a downward arrow (↓). These code extension characters tell the receiver which column of Fig. 2-16 to use when interpreting an incoming character stream.

If a figure shift appears in a character stream, the characters following it are interpreted as though they have the meaning in the "figures character" column of Fig. 2-16. If a letter shift occurs in a character stream, the characters following the letter shift are interpreted as though they have the meaning in the "letters characters" column in Fig. 2-16. The figure shift and letter shift characters operate

Binary	Letters Characters	Figures Characters
00000	Blank	Blank
00001	E	3
00010	≡	≡ Line feed
00011	A	—
00100	SP	SP Space
00101	S	'
00110	I	8
00111	U	7
01000	<	< Carriage return
01001	D	⌖ Who are you?
01010	R	4
01011	J	🔔 Bell
01100	N	,
01101	F	%
01110	C	:
01111	K	(
10000	T	5
10001	Z	+
10010	L	)
10011	W	2
10100	H	£
10101	Y	6
10110	P	0
10111	Q	1
11000	O	9
11001	B	?
11010	G	$
11011	↑	↑ Figure shift (FS)
11100	M	.
11101	X	/
11110	V	=
11111	↓	↓ Letter shift (LS)

Figure 2-16 Baudot code conversion chart.

in a similar manner to the "shift lock" key on a typewriter. When you press the "shift lock" key, all the characters you type come out in uppercase. When you release the "shift lock" key, all of the characters that you type come out in lowercase. As on the typewriter, it is not necessary to precede each character with a figure shift or a letter shift character.

For example, if we wish to transmit this character stream:

293 NORTH 14TH AVENUE

we would insert figure shift and letter shift combinations as follows:

(FS) 293 (LS) NORTH (FS) 14 (LS) TH AVENUE

or graphically we could represent this as

↑ 293 ↓ NORTH ↑ 14 ↓ TH AVENUE

By using the letter shift and figure shift combinations, we can almost double the number of characters that can be handled by the code. Certain character combinations, such as *carriage return* (CR), *line feed* (LF), and *space* (SP), have the same meaning in both figures mode and letters mode.

From the foregoing we can see that Baudot code is rather cumbersome to handle. Also, because all five bits are used for information, there is no inherent means of error detection. Given these restrictions, if you were to set out to design a new computer-based communications system, it is unlikely that you would pick Baudot code for use in the network. On the other hand, many organizations do have quite extensive Telex networks or telegraph networks that already use Baudot code; in this case, it often makes sense to use these preexisting networks for data transmission.

You may wonder why a five-bit code was initially developed rather than a six-bit code, which would have the capability of handling 64 characters. The reason is that when Baudot code was developed, transmission speeds were around 20 to 30 bps and the messages transmitted were in what we call *natural language*. This book is written in natural language and if you were to transmit a page using Baudot code, you would find that you do not need to shift between figures case and letters case very often. In transmitting natural text of this nature, we use an average of about 5.05 bits per character with Baudot code compared to six bits per character with a six-bit code. With very low transmission speeds and long messages, this means a considerable saving in transmission time.

ASCII code

ASCII (American Standard Code for Information Interchange) is an eight-level or eight-bit code that consists of seven information bits plus one bit for parity checking. ASCII is one of the most widely used data transmission codes. There are a number of standardized versions with different names, but basically they refer to the same code. CCITT has a version known as CCITT Alphabet No. 5 or, as it is sometimes called, International Alphabet No. 5. In international circles, there is an organization called the International Standards Organization (ISO) which has produced a standard called "ISO Seven-Bit Coded Character Set for Information-Processing Interchange." There are national options available within the code so that you can elect to use special characters that are peculiar to a given region. For example, in the United Kingdom, the pound sign (£) is required, whereas it would not normally be used in the United States.

Seven information levels give us 128 combinations, which allows us to encode a full upper- and lowercase alphanumeric character set with additional graphic and control characters. A common method of representing the character set is shown in Fig. 2-17. This chart lays the character set out in 8 columns and 16 rows. The columns are numbered 0 through 7, and the binary representation of the column number corresponds to the three most significant bits of the seven-bit pattern for the character. The rows are numbered 0 through 15, and the binary

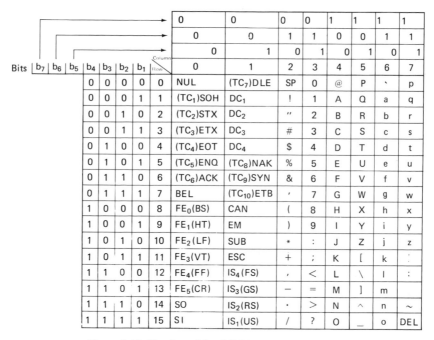

Bits b7 b6 b5	b4	b3	b2	b1	Col/Row	0	1	2	3	4	5	6	7
	0	0	0	0	0	NUL	(TC$_7$)DLE	SP	0	@	P	`	p
	0	0	0	1	1	(TC$_1$)SOH	DC$_1$	!	1	A	Q	a	q
	0	0	1	0	2	(TC$_2$)STX	DC$_2$	"	2	B	R	b	r
	0	0	1	1	3	(TC$_3$)ETX	DC$_3$	#	3	C	S	c	s
	0	1	0	0	4	(TC$_4$)EOT	DC$_4$	$	4	D	T	d	t
	0	1	0	1	5	(TC$_5$)ENQ	(TC$_8$)NAK	%	5	E	U	e	u
	0	1	1	0	6	(TC$_6$)ACK	(TC$_9$)SYN	&	6	F	V	f	v
	0	1	1	1	7	BEL	(TC$_{10}$)ETB	'	7	G	W	g	w
	1	0	0	0	8	FE$_0$(BS)	CAN	(	8	H	X	h	x
	1	0	0	1	9	FE$_1$(HT)	EM	)	9	I	Y	i	y
	1	0	1	0	10	FE$_2$(LF)	SUB	*	:	J	Z	j	z
	1	0	1	1	11	FE$_3$(VT)	ESC	+	;	K	[	k	
	1	1	0	0	12	FE$_4$(FF)	IS$_4$(FS)	,	<	L	\	l	
	1	1	0	1	13	FE$_5$(CR)	IS$_3$(GS)	−	=	M	]	m	
	1	1	1	0	14	SO	IS$_2$(RS)	.	>	N	^	n	~
	1	1	1	1	15	SI	IS$_1$(US)	/	?	O	_	o	DEL

Figure 2-17 Version of the CCITT No. 5 code chart.

representation of the row number corresponds to the four least significant bits of the character. When writing ASCII code combinations in binary, it is conventional to number the bits from one through seven and to place the least significant bit on the right.

There are two common methods of identifying any one character in the ASCII character chart. First, we can use the binary representation of the character to identify it; for example, the bit pattern 1001000 corresponds to the character H. Another method is to use column and row numbers to uniquely identify a particular character. For example, the representation 4/08 would represent the same character H as the character appearing in column 4, row 8. Similarly, 2/04 identifies $ as being the character in column 2, row 4. This is also the hexadecimal representation of the character.

In the following pages we examine some of the more important characteristics of the ASCII character set. We do not precisely define all the characters because this is done in documents produced by the various standards organizations. If you are interested in exploring this topic in detail, consult your national standards body for a copy of its version or one of the internationally recognized versions of the code.

Looking at Fig. 2-17, you can see that the two left columns, "column zero" and "column one," contain *control characters*. These characters are used to control the transmission of data, to control the format of data, to control the logical relationship of data, and to control physical functions in terminals. The remaining six columns contain the information characters we use to encode the messages we wish to transmit [with the exception of the DEL (Delete or Rubout) character in position 7/15, which is, in effect, a control character].

Some terminals use a 96-character subset of ASCII, which means that they do not handle the lowercase characters. In these cases, if we were to transmit a code combination corresponding to one of the lowercase characters, the terminal would interpret that character as though it had its uppercase meaning. Looking at Fig. 2-17, we see that each code combination corresponds to one and only one character, unlike most of the Baudot combinations.

Control Characters. There are 32 *control characters* included in the character set. Within these there are four generic classes of control characters and a number of individual characters. The four generic classifications of control characters are:

- *Transmission controls:* used to control the flow of data along the lines
- *Format effectors:* used to control the physical layout of information on the printed page or the screen of a visual display terminal
- *Device controls:* used primarily for controlling auxiliary devices at terminals
- *Information separators:* available for use to logically delimit elements of data

The transmission controls are perhaps the most important from our point of view, and we now review briefly the characteristics of the other control characters and then spend some time looking at the transmission controls.

Format effectors. There are six *format effectors*, designated FE_0 to FE_5, and they are found in column 0, rows 8 to 13. The first character, FE_0, corresponds to the *back space* (BS) character, and as on a typewriter, this causes the printing head on a printing terminal to move back one position, or in the case of a visual display terminal, it causes the cursor to move one position to the left. FE_1 is *horizontal tabulation* (HT), which causes the print head or cursor to advance to a predetermined position in the horizontal direction. FE_2 is *line feed* (LF), which causes the print head or cursor to advance to the same character position on the next line. FE_3 is *vertical tabulation* (VT), which causes the print head or the cursor to advance to the same character position a predetermined number of lines further on. VT usually operates within the same page, whereas FE_4, *form feed* (FF), causes the print head or cursor to advance to the same character position on a predetermined line of another form or page. FE_5 is *carriage return* (CR), which causes the print head or cursor to return to the first position on the same line.

In some terminals there is a control function that performs a *line feed* and a *carriage return* at the same time. When this happens, the function is commonly known as *new line* (NL) and is usually performed by FE_2.

From the description of the format effector characters, you can see that these characters are used to control the physical layout of information on the printed page or on the screen of a visual display terminal to make it easy for us to handle the data.

   Device controls. There are four *device control* characters, designated DC_1 to DC_4. These generally are used to control physical functions at a terminal. For example, DC_1 could cause a cassette recorder connected to a terminal to be switched on. DC_2 may switch off the cassette recorder. DC_3 may cause the contents of the screen of a visual display terminal to be printed on an auxiliary printer. DC_4 may cause the keyboard of a visual display terminal to be locked so that the operator cannot enter data. The implementation of the device control characters is generally determined by the terminal manufacturer.

   As outlined in a later section, the characters DC_1 and DC_3 are often used for flow control purposes when transmitting data to simple character-oriented asynchronous terminals. DC_1 is often called "XON" and DC_3 is often called "XOFF." These characters are used by the character-oriented terminal to temporarily halt the flow of data from the host computer to the terminal when a fault such as a paper jam occurs, or if the terminal is engaged in a time-consuming action that could prevent it from accepting any more data. This form of flow control is described in a later chapter.

   Information separators. There are four *information separators*, designated IS_1 to IS_4, and these are available for us to logically delimit information to make the records easy to handle by the computer. They are generally used in a hierarchical order, where IS_1 is used to delimit a *unit* of information, and hence it is called a *unit separator* (US). IS_2 is used to delimit a *record* of information, where a record consists of a number of units, and IS_2 is therefore called a *record separator* (RS). IS_3 is used to delimit a *group* of information, where a group consists of a number of records, and IS_3 is therefore called a *group separator* (GS). IS_4 is used to delimit a *file*, where a file consists of a number of groups of data, and IS_4 is therefore known as a *file separator* (FS).

   There is no requirement imposed upon you to use information separators in the manner described. You can, if you wish, define their specific meanings for each application. Many people, in fact, use combinations of format effectors and other characters to logically delimit data blocks.

   Transmission controls. The *transmission control* characters are used for two main purposes: They are used to frame a message into an easily recognized format or sequence that can be handled by the receiver, and they are also used to help to control the flow of data in a network.

   The transmission control characters are used for message framing purposes with character-oriented protocols such as binary synchronous communication. Different techniques are used with bit-oriented protocols such as SDLC or HDLC. These techniques are outlined in later chapters.

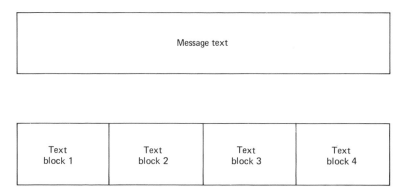

Figure 2-18 Message segmented into four blocks.

Message formats. The information content of a message is called the *text*. With long messages, many terminals segment the message into a number of text blocks, as shown in Fig. 2-18. These blocks are transmitted one at a time along the communication line, and depending on the system used, they may or may not be preceded by some kind of *header* information. The message header, if used, contains addressing and/or administrative information relating to the message text. For example, the header may identify the address of the receiving terminal, the address of the originating terminal, the identity of the person who is to receive the message, and the identity of the originator of the message. It may include priority information; it may include date and time information relating to when the message was sent; it may identify the communication line that carried the message; it may contain security information; and so on.

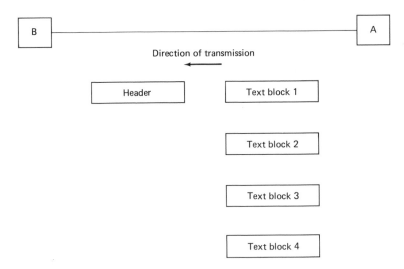

Figure 2-19 Segmented message.

The header is not usually relevant to the information content of the message; rather, it indicates how the message is to be handled on the way from the originator to the final recipient. The decision as to whether or not a header is to be used in a message is based partly upon the characteristics of the hardware and software used. Many systems require terminal addresses and such information to be included in a header at the beginning of every text block that is transmitted. On the other hand, your system design may require that you include information such as priorities, security, date/time stamping, etc.

A typical message sequence consisting of four text blocks may be transmitted in the format shown in Fig. 2-19. This shows the first text block being transmitted with a header that describes the message in some way. Subsequent blocks are sent without a header. In this case, the receiving terminal must be able to relate the subsequent text blocks to the preceding text blocks.

Figure 2-20 defines each of the transmission control characters. This figure gives the mnemonic code for each control character, the TC number, the column

TC_1	0/1	*SOH Start of heading*—a transmission control character used as the first character of a heading of an information message.
TC_2	0/2	*STX Start of text*—a transmission control character which precedes a text and which is used to terminate a heading.
TC_3	0/3	*ETX End of text*—a transmission control character which terminates a text.
TC_4	0/4	*EOT End of transmission*—a transmission control character used to indicate the conclusion of the transmission of one or more texts.
TC_5	0/5	*ENQ Enquiry*—a transmission control character used as a request for a response from a remote station—the response may include station identification and/or station status.
TC_6	0/6	*ACK Acknowledge*—a transmission control character transmitted by a receiver as an affirmative response to the sender.
TC_7	1/0	*DLE Data link escape*—a transmission control character which will change the meaning of a limited number of contiguously following characters. It is used exclusively to provide supplementary data transmission control functions. Only graphics and transmission control characters can be used in DLE sequences.
TC_8	1/5	*NAK Negative acknowledge*—a transmission control character transmitted by a receiver as a negative response to the sender.
TC_9	1/6	*SYN Synchronous idle*—a transmission control character used by a synchronous transmission system in the absence of any other character (idle condition) to provide a signal from which synchronism may be achieved or retained between terminal equipments.
TC_{10}	1/7	*ETB End of transmission block*—a transmission control character used to indicate the end of a transmission block of data where data is divided into such blocks for transmission purposes.

Figure 2-20 Transmission control characters.

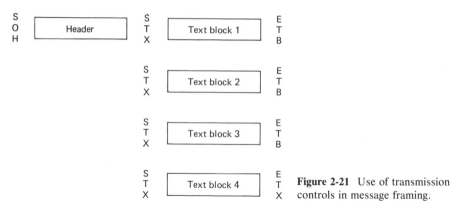

Figure 2-21 Use of transmission controls in message framing.

and row positions in the ASCII character set, and a brief description of the use of the character.

The following paragraphs outline how some of the transmission controls can be used to identify the component parts of a multisegment message. While reading these paragraphs, refer to Fig. 2-21.

The SOH (Start of Header) character is placed before the header of the message, and this tells the receiver that the information following the SOH is to be interpreted as header information. Similarly, the STX (Start of Text) is placed at the beginning of the text, and this tells the receiver that the information following STX is the text of the message. In this particular context, STX is also used to terminate the header. As we are sending a multisegment message, we will terminate the first block of data with ETB (End of Transmission Block). This tells the receiver that the message segment is complete, but it implies that there are more blocks to come in that particular message.

The next message block is preceded by STX, and it is terminated once again by ETB. Similarly, Text Block No. 3 is enveloped by STX and ETB. Finally, Text Block No. 4 is started with STX but is terminated by ETX (End of Text). ETX terminates the text of a message, and this means that the entire message has been transmitted. In some systems, a heading would be placed on each block of the message so that each transmitted segment would look like this:

```
S           S       E
O (HEADER)  T (TEXT) T
H           X       B
```

Not all terminals allow segmented blocks to be terminated by ETB. In many devices all message segments are terminated by ETX, and if we are sending a multisegment message, we would have to incorporate information within each text block to enable the receiver to link the correct text blocks together to form a complete message.

Note: In Baudot code, there are no special control characters that are equivalent to ASCII controls such as SOH and ETX. Message framing sequences must be built up from strings of characters. These sequences are picked so that they are unlikely to show up in natural text and therefore be misinterpreted. For example, it is usual to use the sequence ZCZC for Start of Message and NNNN for End of Message.

The remaining transmission control characters are used to control the flow of information in a network. The use of the characters in this way is described in detail in Chapters 14 and 15.

The parity bit. Bits 1 through 7 of each ASCII character contain the information we wish to transmit, and bit 8 is the *parity bit*. The purpose of the parity bit is to give us some error detection capability. We can have either *odd* parity or *even* parity. In the case of odd parity, the sense of bit 8 is determined so as to make the total number of 1s in the encoded character (including the parity bit) an *odd* number. Similarly, for even parity, the sense of the parity bit is determined so as to make the total number of 1s in the encoded character (including the parity bit) an *even* number.

If we were encoding the character found in position 3/07 of the ASCII chart, the seven information bits would be as follows: 0110111. In an *odd*-parity system, the parity bit would be 0, and for an *even*-parity system, the parity bit would be set to 1.

The way the parity system works is quite simple. The transmitting terminal appends a parity bit to each character and transmits the encoded character down the communication line starting with the least significant bit (bit 1). As the receiver receives the seven data bits, it computes its own parity bit. The receiver then compares the received parity bit with the computed parity bit, and if they match, it declares the character valid.

Figure 2-22(a) illustrates the sequence of events that occur if a transmission error takes place while a character is being sent. The receiver is expecting odd parity, and based on the first seven bits it receives, it computes a parity bit of 0 and receives a parity bit of 1. The receiver therefore knows that a transmission error occurred.

If two bits had been reversed, as shown in Fig. 2-22(b), the receiver would not have detected the error because the incoming character would have passed the character parity check. This shows that the simple character parity checking procedure is not foolproof because it can only detect changes in an odd number of bits.

If changes occur in an even number of bits, the parity check will be passed, and the receiver will assume that it has received a valid character. To detect multiple errors, more sophisticated techniques can be used, and we examine these in Chapter 10.

The parity bit is not always used, even though it may be present. In some cases we talk about "mark" parity, or "space" parity. In a *mark parity* system

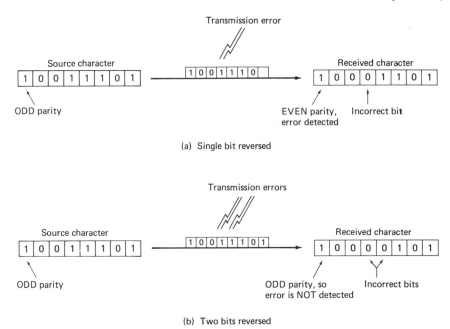

(a) Single bit reversed

(b) Two bits reversed

Figure 2-22 ASCII character parity checking.

the parity bit is always set to 1, and in a *space parity* system the parity bit is always set to 0. In other systems the parity bit is totally ignored, so it can be either a 1 or a 0; it is just not checked.

Other transmission codes

There are many other data transmission codes that are used from time to time—the more commonly used being BCD code and EBCDIC code.

BCD Code. BCD (Binary Coded Decimal) is a six-level code that is used as an internal code by some computers. Six information bits gives us $2^6 = 64$ possible code combinations. For data transmission purposes, the code is sometimes implemented as a seven-bit code containing six information bits and one parity bit.

EBCDIC Code. EBCDIC (Extended Binary Coded Decimal Interchange Code—pronounced "eBB-sID-iK") is an eight-level code in which all eight levels are used for information (unlike ASCII, which uses the eighth level as a parity bit), giving 256 possible combinations. The code is an extension of the BCD code. EBCDIC is used as an internal machine code in many computers; therefore, it is often used as a data transmission code with those computers.

transmission modes

So far, we have defined a communication line as consisting of one or more channels, and we have examined methods of encoding characters to enable them to be transmitted along these channels. We now examine two basic approaches to transmitting data along a communication line: *parallel transmission* and *serial transmission*.

Parallel transmission

In parallel transmission, all bits of an encoded character are transmitted simultaneously, which means that each code level has a unique channel dedicated to it. For ASCII characters, we will therefore need eight channels. Figure 2-23 shows how all the bits of a character leave the source simultaneously and how they also arrive at the receiver together. Note that the term *parallel transmission* refers to the fact that the bits of the character are transmitted in parallel, whereas the characters themselves are transmitted serially—that is, one after the other.

Parallel transmission is often used for on-site communications and for the transmission of data between the computer and its peripheral devices (such as printers, magnetic tape handlers, disk subsystems, etc.). With this kind of interface we can achieve very high data transfer rates. Over long distances, however, problems arise, due primarily to the cost of providing all these parallel channels.

Serial transmission

Serial transmission is by far the most commonly used method of communication. In serial transmission. the bits of the encoded character are transmitted

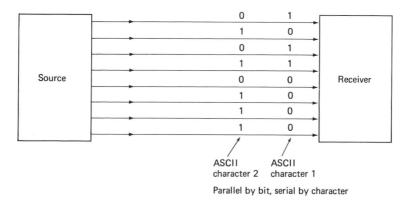

Parallel by bit, serial by character

Figure 2-23 Parallel transmission.

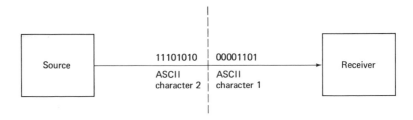

Serial by bit, serial by character

Figure 2-24 Serial transmission.

one after the other along one channel, as shown in Fig. 2-24. The receiver then
assembles the incoming bit stream into characters. Serial transmission presents
two synchronization problems related to the receiver first achieving *bit synchronization* and then achieving *character synchronization.*

Bit Synchronization. The receiver must be able to correctly interpret the bit
pattern generated by the source. This means that the receiver has to know when
to look at the line to take the bits off the line. We overcome this problem by
placing a clock at each end of the line, as shown in Fig. 2-25.

The source clock tells the source how often to put the bits onto the line,
and the receive clock tells the receiver how often to look at the line. If we wish
to transmit at 100 bps, we set the source clock to run at 100 bps, which tells the
source to put the bits on the line 100 times per second. At the receive end, we
would see a bit appearing at the input of the receiver every 1/100 of a second.
We set the receive clock to run at 100 bps, and that clock would tell the receiver
to sample the line 100 times a second. As long as the clocks are running at the
same speed, the receiver will collect all the bits as they come down the line. (If
we set the receive clock to 50 bps, it would only receive every other bit.)

The processes of "putting bits on the line" and "sampling the state of the
line" vary considerably from system to system. In the simple system illustrated
in Fig. 2-9, a 1 could be represented by the presence of electric current in the

Figure 2-25 Clocks help us achieve bit synchronization.

line (i.e., the lamp is on), and a 0 could be presented by the absence of current in the line (i.e., the lamp is off). If we wish to transmit a string of alternate 1s and 0s at a rate of 1 bps, the state of the line over a period of time could be depicted as in Fig. 2-26. The length of each bit is the same because we have a clock that tells us how long a bit should last.

A human receiver can see the lamp flashing on and off and can interpret the incoming bit stream. If the lamp and the human operator were replaced by an electronic terminal, we need to ensure that the terminal can correctly decipher the incoming information.

A terminal usually samples the state of the line for a very short time to see whether it is in the 1 or the 0 state. If it samples the line during the transition from a 1 to a 0, we would get an indeterminate result. The ideal place to sample a bit is in the center of the bit, and the receiver can do this by using one of the 1/0 or 0/1 transitions as a reference point. The receiver can trigger itself from one of these transitions, wait for one-half of a bit time, and then sample the line. Thereafter, as shown in Fig. 2-26(b), it samples the state of the line at intervals of one bit time, and provided that the transmitter and receiver clocks are running at the same speed, the bits will be sampled at the correct instant. If the transmit and receive clocks are not running at the same speed, the receiver will not correctly identify the incoming bit stream.

In practice, if we have independent clocks at each end of the line, they will probably be running at slightly different speeds. Although the speed difference will be small (probably less than 0.01%), they will ultimately get out of step unless they are resynchronized periodically. Later in this chapter, when we discuss asynchronous transmission systems, we will see how the receive clock is resynchronized at the beginning of every character.

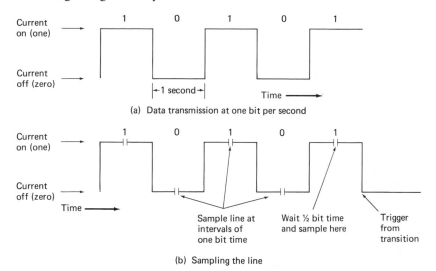

Figure 2-26 Bit timing in a simple system.

In other systems, timing signals are propagated through the network so that the receiver can derive a clock that is precisely in step with the transmit clock. This is examined in more detail in Chapter 7 under the heading "Timing Considerations."

Character Synchronization. When the receiver has achieved bit synchronization, it is faced with the problem of achieving character synchronization. This is the problem of determining which group of bits belongs to a character. In Fig. 2-24, two ASCII characters are being transmitted serially along the communication line. The two groups of eight bits belonging to the first and second characters have been labeled for you. The bit stream is not labeled in this manner when it appears at the receiving device, and the receiver is faced with the problem of determining which particular set of bits belongs to a character. This problem reduces to that of determining which bit is the first bit of a character. If the receiver knows (1) how many bits there are in a character, and (2) the speed at which the bits are coming down the line, it can count off the required number of bits and assemble the character once it has identified the first bit of a character.

There are two common approaches to determining which bit is the first bit of an incoming character. One approach utilizes a technique known as *synchronous transmission*, and the other approach utilizes a technique known as *asynchronous transmission*.

Synchronous Transmission. Synchronous transmission is used to transmit whole blocks of data at once. In synchronous transmission, the duration of each bit is the same, and in character transmission systems, the time interval between the end of the last bit of a character and the beginning of the first bit of the next character is either zero time or a whole multiple of the time required to transmit a complete character. There is a trend toward pure binary transmission systems, in which a message may consist of a number of bits that are not necessarily divided into fixed-length characters.

SDLC and HDLC are examples of protocols that will transport any bit patterns. These protocols do not depend on the use of any particular character set for their implementation, and as a result there are no characters such as SOH, STX, ETB, ETX, and so on, which are used for message framing. The beginning and ending of a frame are identified with a particular bit pattern known as a *flag*. The flag not only identifies the beginning and end of the frame, but it is also used to enable frame synchronization to be achieved. The technique for achieving frame synchronization is described in Chapter 18.

Figure 2-27 shows how the letters of the alphabet could be transmitted using synchronous transmission. With all the characters jammed together with zero time between them, the receiver only needs to identify the first bit of the first character, and then, knowing the character size and transmission speed, it can count off groups of bits and correctly assemble the incoming characters. In the case of ASCII data, each character has eight bits, and having identified the first bit of

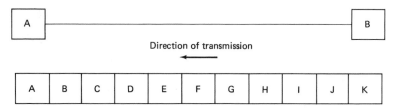

Figure 2-27 Synchronous transmission.

the first character, we could count off groups of eight bits and thus assemble an incoming message.

To correctly identify the first bit of the first character, we precede each block of data with a unique synchronizing pattern. This makes use of the SYN transmission control character (TC$_9$: character position 1/06 in the ASCII chart). The SYN character has a bit pattern of 00010110 (with odd parity), and the receiver is designed to continually sample the latest set of eight bits that it has received and to compare these bits with the unique SYN pattern ("Looking for Sync"). When the receiver has detected a SYN pattern, we may expect it to be in a position where it can count off groups of eight bits and thus assemble the incoming message character by character. This is not the case, however, because we could achieve "false synchronization" if the receiver were to lock onto a pattern that looked like a SYN character but was not a genuine SYN character. This situation can arise, as shown in Fig. 2-28(a), where eight bits taken from two contiguous characters could look like a SYN characters. This would be "false synchronization," and if the receiver were to start counting off groups of eight bits based on this false synchronization, it would incorrectly assemble characters.

To guard against false synchronization, we place two SYN characters in front of a data stream, as shown in Fig. 2-28(b). The receiver, having identified

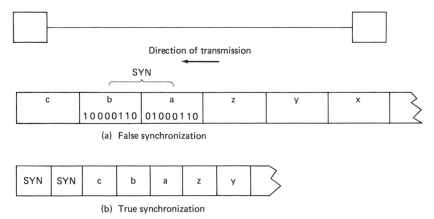

(a) False synchronization

(b) True synchronization

Figure 2-28 Two SYNs guard against false synchronization.

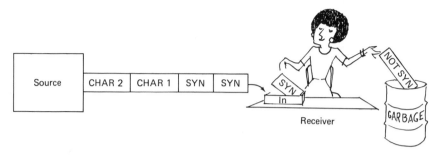

Figure 2-29 Synchronous transmission—receiver looking for sync.

the first SYN pattern, requires the next eight bits to be a SYN pattern. If the second character is indeed a SYN, the receiver declares itself synchronized, and it then starts counting groups of eight bits to assemble the message. If the second character is not a SYN character, the receiver declares false synchronization and throws itself back into the "Look for Sync" mode, where it looks at the line and once again compares the latest set of eight bits it received with the SYN pattern. Figures 2-29 and 2-30 illustrate the sequence of events. In most systems we put three or four SYN characters in front of the data block to make sure that the receiver achieves synchronization.

There are variations on the theme used for obtaining synchronization. In some cases, two different characters are used in the synchronizing pattern so that the receiver recognizes one unique character and then requires the next set of bits to be the other unique character. In pure binary transmission systems (where we do not necessarily have individual characters), the synchronizing pattern is called a *flag*. This is described in detail in Chapter 18. In all cases, the technique relies on the receiver being able to identify and verify the presence of a special bit pattern at the front of a data block.

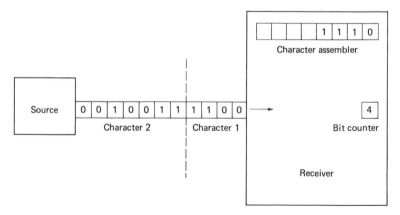

Figure 2-30 Synchronous transmission—receiver counts off bits for each character.

Buffered terminals. As we transmit many characters in a block in synchronous systems, we avoid situations in which an operator enters data and sends them straight out to line, because (1) operators usually cannot maintain synchronization between characters, and (2) the line speed is usually quite high—faster than the operator is able to type. So we need to make use of *buffered* terminals. Figure 2-31 shows how a buffered terminal contains a memory that will accumulate the characters as they are entered by the operator. This procedure allows the operator to enter characters at his own speed and when he is finished, to hit the transmit key and send the whole message down the line at once at the line speed. The hardware/software of the system puts the required number of SYN characters in front of the data stream and sends it down the line. At the other end of the line, we need another buffer to accept the data as they come in.

Synchronous transmission makes very good use of the data-carrying capacity of the communication line. While data are being transmitted, almost the entire data-handling capacity of the line is being used. Soon we will compare this with the efficiency of transmission utilizing the other technique of obtaining character synchronization.

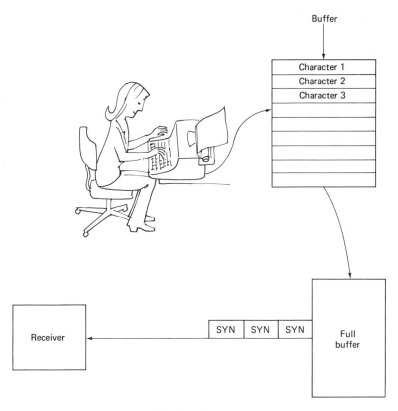

Figure 2-31 Use of buffers in synchronous transmission.

Asynchronous (Start/Stop) Transmission. Asynchronous transmission is used in systems in which characters are sent one at a time without necessarily having any fixed time relationship between one character and the next. This is the case with unbuffered terminals. An unbuffered terminal is one in which the characters are sent to line directly as they are entered on the keyboard. That is, there is no buffering of the characters from the keyboard for temporary storage in the terminal prior to transmission. In this case the receiver has to reestablish synchronization for every character. Alternatively, we may use a buffered terminal in which the characters are held temporarily in a memory device after they have been entered on the keyboard. When the operator is ready, he or she initiates the transmission of the block of data down the line. The characters are effectively all jammed up together with zero time between, as in the case of synchronous transmission. The receiver must still be able to recognize the first bit of each character, and we do this by preceding each character with a *start pulse*, which tells the receiver that it is starting to receive a character.

The receiver detects start pulses by monitoring the condition of the line, which, as we have seen, can be in either the 1 state or the 0 state. When the line is *idle*—that is, when no information is being transmitted—it is conventional to leave it in the electrical state corresponding to the 1 condition. (In some systems, this is known as the *mark* condition. The opposite state of the line, the 0 condition, is sometimes known as the *space* condition or perhaps as the *open line* condition.) In the idle state, the transmitter will therefore be sending a continual string of 1s.

When it wishes to send a character, the transmitter precedes the character with a 0, which acts as a *start bit* to tell the receiver that the bits following the start bit are information bits. In electrical terms, as shown in Fig. 2-32, the transmitter generates the start bit (or *start pulse*) by switching the state of the line from the *idle* (1) condition to the 0 condition for one bit time. The information bits are sent out following the start bit.

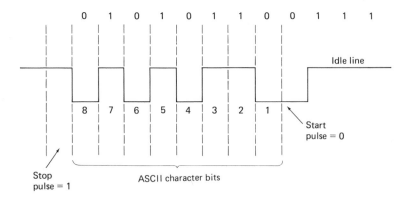

Figure 2-32 One character transmitted asynchronously.

The receiver detects the change of state from 1 to 0 and starts its clock. Half a bit length later, the clock tells the receiver to sample the line to see if it is still in the 0 state. If it is, the receiver accepts this 0 as a start bit; it then samples the state of the line at intervals of one bit length, and it assembles the incoming character. If on initially sampling the line, the receiver found it to be in the 1 state, it would regard the initial transition from 1 to 0 as part of a short noise impulse, and it would take no further action. (If the receiver acted purely on the 1/0 transition without verifying the existence of a start bit, a noise impulse could cause it to assemble a "garbage" character.)

The receive clock is thus resynchronized at the beginning of each character, and we can therefore tolerate slight variations in speed between the transmit and receive clocks. At the end of each character, a *stop* bit is transmitted to allow the receiver to stabilize itself before another character is transmitted. As shown in Fig. 2-32, a character is surrounded by *start* and *stop* bits. For this reason, asynchronous transmission is often called *start/stop* transmission.

The stop bit is the 1 condition, and its duration varies from system to system. For ASCII transmission, the stop bit is either one or two bit lengths. For Baudot systems, the stop bit is often 1.5 bit lengths, although in other cases it is 1.42 bit lengths. The purpose of the stop bit was originally to enable electromechanical terminals to act on a character once the information bits had been received. These terminals would receive the incoming data bits, and during the stop bit time, it would determine what to do with them (such as punching a hole in a paper tape or perhaps printing a character).

The length of the stop bit was determined to give the terminal enough time to act on the character and get back into a condition whereby it could receive the next character. Early ASCII terminals required two stop bits to enable this operation to take place. As electromechanical components became lighter and faster, the terminals were able to interpret and act on a character within one bit time; hence later ASCII terminals only use one stop bit.

Efficiency of Transmission. Figure 2-33 compares the efficiency of data transmission using synchronous or asynchronous transmission. In Fig. 2-33(a), which illustrates synchronous transmission, we can see that almost the entire capacity of the line is being used to carry information. Figure 2-33(b) illustrates the overhead of the start and stop pulses on each character and also includes the variable intercharacter gap. In the case of ASCII transmission, with eight bits being transmitted for each character plus an overhead of one start bit and, say, one stop bit, we need to transmit a total of 10 bits for every character. If we have zero time between characters, the maximum efficiency we can achieve is therefore 80%. This compares unfavorably with the efficiency of transmission in a synchronous system.

Let us quickly compare the transmission efficiency of synchronous and asynchronous systems for sending a block of 240 ASCII characters. In the case of

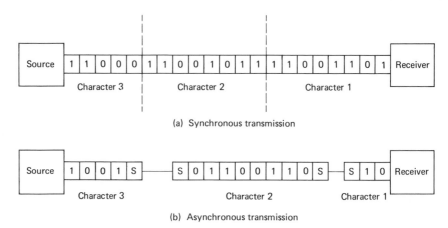

Figure 2-33 Comparison of synchronous and asynchronous transmission.

synchronous transmission, let us assume that we precede each block of data with three SYN characters. The information content of each data block is:

240 characters × 8 bits per character   = 1920 bits

3 SYN characters × 8 bits per character =   24 bits

Total number of bits transmitted   = 1944 bits

The ratio of information transferred to total number of bits transmitted is

$$\frac{1920 \text{ information bits}}{1944 \text{ bits transmitted}} \approx 99\% \text{ efficiency}$$

We have already seen that the maximum efficiency we can achieve with asynchronous transmission is 80%. In this case the efficiency of asynchronous transmission was 19% less than that of synchronous transmission (the actual reduction might be more depending on the time between characters). If the stop bits had been two bits long, the efficiency would have been reduced even more.

The efficiency figures mentioned above represent the efficiency with which we are using the line during the actual transmission process. The overall efficiency with which we use the line, however, is another story and is influenced by other factors, such as the protocols employed and the time delays encountered in the network. These factors are discussed in Chapters 12 to 20 when we look at line protocols and line utilization. Also, although synchronous transmission seems to be far more efficient than asynchronous transmission, it can be seen that for small blocks of data the efficiency of synchronous transmission drops off quite sharply due to the overhead caused by the SYN characters.

In general, synchronous transmission uses a communication channel more efficiently than asynchronous transmission. A channel capable of transmitting

4800 bps can handle 600 ASCII characters per second in synchronous mode. However, it could only carry 480 characters per second in asynchronous mode (assuming a single stop bit).

The advantage of asynchronous transmission is that inexpensive and unsophisticated equipment can be used for low-speed transmission; for example, an operator can type directly to line at whatever character rate he or she chooses because there is no inherent time limit between the characters. In many cases, there will be a system limitation on the maximum time allowed between characters. It generally has been cheaper to build simple asynchronous terminals than it has been to build more sophisticated, buffered, synchronous terminals. This price difference is decreasing, however, as technology progresses. With new techniques it will soon be possible to make a sophisticated buffered terminal for about the same cost as an unsophisticated unbuffered terminal. (Whether it will be sold for the same price is another question!)

The trend in the industry is toward synchronous transmission because it makes better use of the communication line. However, we will still need asynchronous transmission to maintain compatibility with the millions of asynchronous terminals that are in use at present.

Asynchronous transmission has, however, become more popular in recent years due to the development of simple statistical multiplexers. These devices, which are described in Chapter 4, also allow us to achieve extremely efficient use of the communication line. In addition to improving the efficiency of line utilization, the statistical multiplexers add error detection capability and can provide switching facilities for messages going to and from simple asynchronous terminals.

3
Communication Lines

A data communication network can be a very simple collection of terminals, lines, and computers, or it can be a complex system with hundreds of terminals and many computers connected across thousands of kilometers. However, even the most intricate communication network can be constructed using very few different component types. Due to the wide range of equipment that is available, specific brands of equipment are not discussed, but the basic principles of operation of each type of component are outlined to enable you to analyze your own situation in detail.

In this chapter the word *terminal* is used in its generic sense to mean anything from a basic teleprinter-style terminal to a computer. When necessary, we qualify the term to identify a particular style of terminal.

modems and network terminating units

One of the basic components of a data communication network is a modem. A modem is a device that enables us to transmit digital data over the telephone network. In earlier sections we said that lines from the telephone network are not ideally suited for data transmission. The telephone network was designed specifically to carry human voices and all the circuits in the network have been

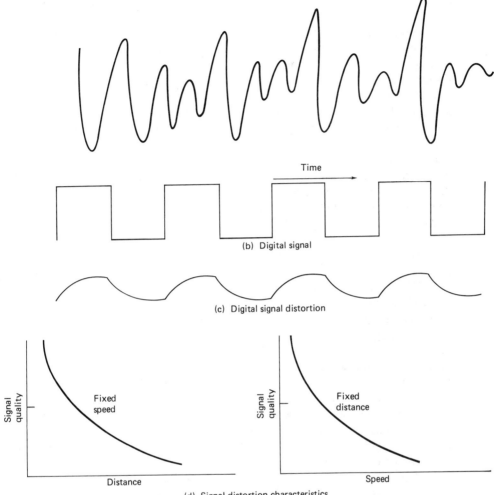

Time

(b) Digital signal

(c) Digital signal distortion

Signal quality

Fixed speed

Distance

Signal quality

Fixed distance

Speed

(d) Signal distortion characteristics

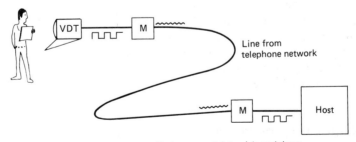

VDT

M

Line from telephone network

M

Host

Modem = modulator / demodulator

(e) Position of modems in network

Figure 3-1 Modems.

engineered around the characteristics of the human voice. The human voice is a relatively smoothly varying signal and if it were displayed on an electronic device such as an oscilloscope, you would see a smoothly varying signal such as that shown in Fig. 3-1(a). This is called an *analog signal* because the electrical signal is analogous to the vibrations of the human voice. The whole telephone network has been designed to carry such an analog signal and it does so beautifully.

A digital signal coming out of a terminal or a computer looks nothing like a voice. As shown in Fig. 3-1(b), the digital signal has only two states, the 1 condition and the 0 condition, and there are very sharp edges between the 1s and the 0s. It is called a digital signal because it is numeric; that is, it has two states, the 1 and the 0. If we send such a signal through the telephone network, the sharp edges become rounded off as shown in Fig. 3-1(c); we call this phenomenon *distortion*. The distortion gets worse with both speed and distance.

In Fig. 3-1(d) the graphs indicate the deterioration of signal quality with speed or with distance. These factors limit to a relatively short distance the distance that we can transmit a pure digital signal through the telephone network.

We normally wish to transmit over long distances, and this is where the modem comes in. As indicated in Fig. 3-1(e), the modem sits in the interface between the terminal and the telephone network, and between the host computer and the telephone network. The job of the modem is to take the sharp-edged digital signal from the terminal or the computer and turn it into a smoothly varying analog signal that will go nicely through the telephone network. At the other end, the receiving modem takes the incoming analog signal and reconstitutes the original digital signal.

This is the sole purpose of a modem—to perform the digital-to-analog conversion at one end and then to form the analog-to-digital conversion at the other end. Most modems are capable of full-duplex operation so that they can transmit and receive data simultaneously.

The word "modem" itself is contraction of the words "modulator/demodulator." *Modulation* is the process of putting the digital information onto the analog signal and *demodulation* is the process of extracting digital information from the analog signal.

Having identified the modem as an essential piece of communications equipment, you will find that most of the network diagrams in this book do not include modems. This is because modems tend to clutter up diagrams and make them too busy, and we normally just assume the presence of a modem at each point where there is a terminal. Where it is absolutely necessary for the purposes of clarity, we include the modems in the diagrams.

digital data networks

Referring back to the graphs in Fig. 3-1(d), it can be seen that at a particular transmission speed the signal quality drops off as a function of distance. In new

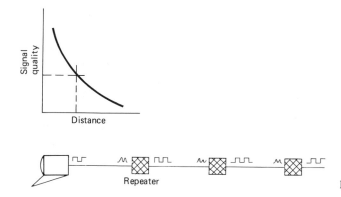

Figure 3-2 Digital transmission.

digital transmission networks, we capitalize on this characteristic as illustrated in Fig. 3-2.

In this diagram we have indicated the minimum acceptable signal quality where we can still tell the difference between the 1s and the 0s. If we catch the distorted digital signal before it gets to this minimum signal quality, we can feed the distorted signal into a piece of digital electronics and regenerate the signal, that is, turn it back into its original sharp-edged digital self for transmission on the next piece of wire. Once again, we catch the signal before it becomes too distorted and feed it through another repeater to regenerate the signal for transmission along the next piece of wire. As long as we have repeaters at suitable distances we can transmit pure digital information through the telephone network. The speed of transmission we can achieve depends on the distance between repeaters. To give you a feeling for this, if we are using conventional physical telephone wire pairs and the repeaters are approximately 1 mile apart, we can achieve a digital transmission rate of approximately 2 Mbps (2 million bps).

Common carriers around the world are implementing digital transmission

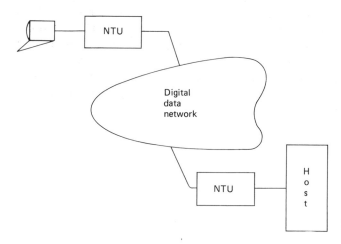

Figure 3-3 Network terminating units.

networks, which are described in more detail in Chapter 23. Even though the networks use pure digital transmission, an interface box similar in appearance to a modem is generally needed between the terminals and the digital network. This is because the form of the digital signal in the network is generally different from the form of the digital signal as it comes from a terminal or a computer. This interface box, usually called a *network terminating unit*, also sits in the interface between the terminal and the digital data network or between the host computer and the digital data network, as shown in Fig. 3-3. Once again, in the diagrams in this book, unless they happen to be essential for purposes of clarity, network terminating units are omitted because they tend to make the diagrams too busy.

types of data communication lines

Point-to-point line

The *point-to-point* line shown in Fig. 3-4 is a fundamental component of a communications network. A point-to-point line is a communication line that connects two terminals. The length of the line is unimportant; it can be 3 meters or 10,000 kilometers. The line can be one-way, half-duplex, or full-duplex, and it can operate synchronously or asynchronously.

Star networks

Perhaps the most common network configuration in the world is the *star network* shown in Fig. 3-5, in which each terminal has a point-to-point relationship with the central site. As long as the host has sufficient power to handle all of the terminals simultaneously, the star configuration provides excellent performance. Each terminal has unrestricted access to the host and the network component of response time is virtually instantaneous. The star network can become expensive, due to each terminal having a dedicated line. People are always on the lookout for methods of improving the utilization of expensive communication lines in order to reduce system cost. There is great scope for improving the utilization of lines in a star network—if the terminals have human operators indulging in on-line inquiry or similar applications, it is difficult for a person to generate enough traffic to use more than 10–15 percent of the line capacity. In reality, many such lines are running at much lighter loads than this.

Figure 3-4 Basic point-to-point network.

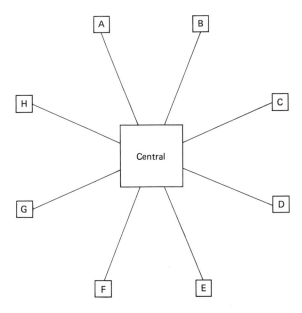

Figure 3-5 Star network—an expanded point-to-point network.

Multidrop (or multipoint) lines

Because communication lines are expensive, we go to great lengths to optimize the way we use them. There are several approaches to this, and Fig. 3-6 illustrates a common configuration utilizing *multidrop lines*. A *multidrop* (or *multipoint*) *line* is a line with two or more terminals connected to the one communication line. It is possible to use simple unbuffered terminals on a low-speed line in this configuration, but it is more common to use buffered terminals on a relatively high-speed line. This is because the buffered terminal (1) makes very efficient use of the capacity of the communication line while it is transmitting, and (2) does not use any line capacity while messages are being entered by the operator. This means that we can share the capacity of the line among a number of terminals.

Figure 3-6 indicates that two or more terminals should not transmit simultaneously because the data from the terminals would collide on the line and become garbled. To control the flow of data in such a network, a set of *line control procedures* are necessary, and these are covered in detail in Chapters 12 to 20.

Multidrop lines are particularly suitable for applications in which each terminal transmits intermittently and does not need to utilize the line constantly. We therefore make more efficient use of the lines in the network than if each terminal were connected to the central site by point-to-point lines, because most of the time the point-to-point lines would be idle and the cost would probably be prohibitive.

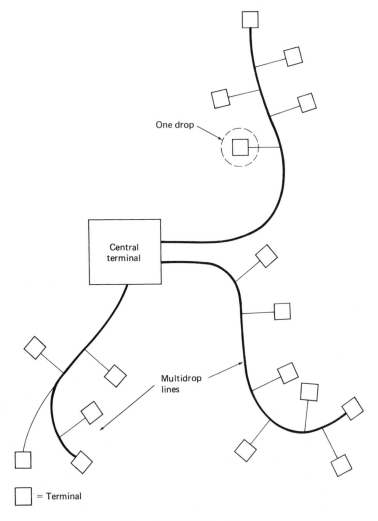

One drop

Central
terminal

Multidrop
lines

☐ = Terminal

Figure 3-6 Multidrop lines.

There is a limit to the number of terminals that can be connected to a multidrop line. This limit varies considerably from system to system and is determined by the following factors: (1) the inherent capacity of the hardware and software involved, (2) the amount of traffic generated by the terminals (i.e., the length of the messages and the rate at which messages are generated), (3) the speed of the line, and (4) any restrictions that may be imposed by the common carrier that supplies the communication line. (Many carriers will not permit more than some predetermined number of drops on the one line.) For example, an airline reservation system may have 50 or 60 terminals on one line, with each terminal handling an average of one transaction per minute. With a high-speed communication line, each terminal may utilize the line for half a second for each transaction. Obviously, such a line would be able to support many terminals. We examine the method of operation of multidrop lines in more detail in Chapter 7 under the heading "Modems" and also in Chapter 15.

Switched networks

In many applications, there may be terminals that only need to transmit data for a relatively short time each day. It would not be economical to install a private line for the terminal when the line is being used for such a small part of the time. In these cases we can make use of the various switched networks that are available. Switched networks enable us to establish, on demand, a point-to-point connection between two terminals and to maintain the connection for as long as we wish. As a general rule, charges are applied only for the duration of the call, although in some cases the charges relate to the volume of data that we transmit rather than to the length of time that it takes to transmit.

There are four basic types of switched networks:

- Telephone networks
- Telex/TWX networks
- Packet-switching networks
- Specialized digital networks

Although the details of operation for each type of network are different, as outlined and detailed in Chapters 22 to 24, the basic principle of operation in establishing a connection between terminals is similar to the process involved in making a telephone call. When using the telephone network, you pick up the telephone and dial a number. The telephone network automatically establishes the connection between your telephone and the receiving telephone, and, at the end of the conversation, you clear the call by hanging up the telephone. At this point you could, if you wish, establish another point-to-point connection with any other telephone in the network. Most countries have well-established telephone networks and most of these are interconnected via international networks, so that it is possible to establish a point-to-point connection between virtually any two telephones on the earth.

The public switched telephone network (PSTN), or *dial-up network* as it is sometimes called, is in regular use for data communications. The telephone network is a two-wire network, which means that it is easy to run half-duplex at speeds up to 9600 bps. It is also possible, using special modems, to achieve full-duplex operation at speeds up to 2400 bps in most countries and up to 9600 bps in others. The maximum transmission speed is related partially to the quality of the telephone network in a particular country and partially to the regulations imposed by the communication carrier in that country.

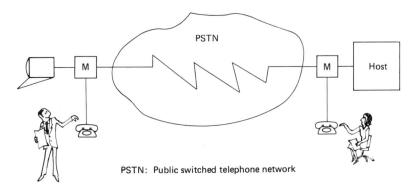

PSTN: Public switched telephone network

Figure 3-7 Temporary connection via dial-up network.

As illustrated in Fig. 3-7, terminals and computers can be connected into the telephone network using a combination of a modem and a switching device. Often the switching device is built into the modem, or alternatively, it may be a separate device, such as the switched network adapter (SNA) shown in Fig. 3-8. You will notice that the modem has a telephone connected to it, which means that either the telephone or the modem can be connected to the telephone lines. Calls can be set up manually or automatically and answered in the same way, depending on the configuration of the equipment.

In the simplest case, manual call origination and manual answering is used, whereby the terminal operator picks up the telephone, dials the call, and the telephone at the other end rings. The person at the other end answers the telephone and at an agreed point in time, they each activate the switch which disconnects the telephone and connects the modem at each end to the communication line. At this point we have a two-wire point-to-point line set up through the telephone network.

It is possible to use automatic answering modems which eliminate the need for the person to answer the telephone at the receiving end, and it is also possible to have automatic call origination, whereby the computer could dial up the remote

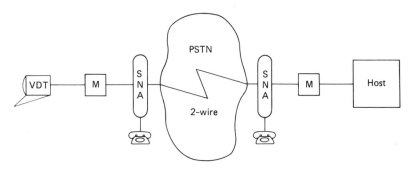

Figure 3-8 Switched network adapters for dial-up operation.

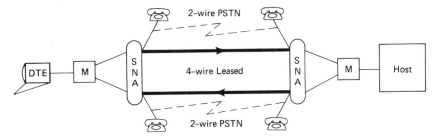

Figure 3-9 Dual-dial backup.

site but have the call automatically answered so that files could be transferred from the remote site to the central site, or vice versa, untouched by human hands. This is often desirable for use in after-hours situations because in many countries the long-distance telephone tariffs drop considerably in the evening. Autodial is often used with personal computers because manual dialing detracts from the functionality of the personal computer. One of the variations on the theme is the dual-dial backup arrangement shown in Fig. 3-9. Here two telephone calls can be made to provide a four-wire connection in the event of a failure in the four-wire leased line.

Packet-switching networks, on the other hand, operate on principles different from those employed by the telephone network. *Packet switching* can be defined as the routing of data in discrete quantities called packets, each of controlled format and with a maximum size. The technique differs fundamentally from the circuit switching employed in the telephone network, in that physical circuits are not switched and dedicated to the user for the duration of the call. Instead, the information to be transferred between the source and destination is transmitted in the form of packets over logical links called *virtual circuits*. A packet-switching network, as shown in Fig. 3-10, consists of a number of packet-switching exchanges, which are switching computers. The packet-switching ex-

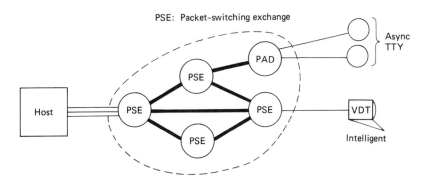

Figure 3-10 Packet-switching network.

changes are interconnected in a kind of mesh arrangement, and individual hosts and terminals are connected into the nearest packet-switching exchange. Packets are transmitted from the host to the packet-switching exchange and then routed through the network to the destination. This routing is based on addressing information contained in the packet. Packet switching is described in detail in Chapter 24.

4
Multiplexers, Statistical Multiplexers, Concentrators, and Front-End Processors

multiplexers and concentrators

Another method of increasing the effective utilization of expensive communication lines is to use *multiplexers* or *concentrators*. The dividing line between these components can be hazy, and the following paragraphs serve as clarification.

Multiplexers

A multiplexer is a transparent device that divides the capacity of a communication line between a number of terminals. It is transparent in that it does not do anything to the data on the way through; apart from being slightly delayed, the data that come out one end are the same as the data that went in the other. We now examine the two basic approaches to multiplexing: *time division multiplexing* and *frequency division multiplexing*.

Time Division Multiplexing (*TDM*). We describe the principles of time division multiplexing by means of an example. Suppose that an organization has a computer in one city and four branch offices in another city. If the organization wishes to install a 300-bps terminal in each of the four branch offices, these terminals could be connected to the computer via point-to-point lines, as shown in

Figure 4-1 Point-to-point configuration.

Fig. 4-1. This would give each terminal unrestricted access to the computer, but it could be expensive due to the high cost of the lines.

　　If the load on each terminal is relatively light, a multidrop line that links all the terminals to the computer could be the answer. Such a configuration is shown in Fig. 4-2. This is probably the most economical method of linking all the terminals to the computer, but it can be operationally feasible only if the traffic volumes are low enough that transmissions from one terminal do not interfere with the transmissions from other terminals.

　　Let us assume that each terminal is in use 60% of the time. In this case, the multidrop line approach would not work, and we must look for another solution. By using a *multiplexer*, we can take the four streams of low-speed data and merge them in such a way that we can transmit them down a high-speed channel. To transmit data from several terminals on one line, the data from the terminals must

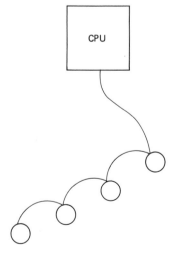

Figure 4-2 Multidrop configuration.

be interleaved or interwoven in some way. Figure 4-3 shows the four terminals connected to the computer via a high-speed communication line and multiplexers. This diagram shows the low-speed character streams from each terminal going into multiplexer B, which takes the characters from each line, interleaves them, and transmits them along the high-speed channel to multiplexer A, which then demultiplexes the interleaved character stream and reconstitutes the original low-speed data streams. This particular diagram shows characters being interleaved on the high-speed line, although in real life many multiplexers interleave bits rather than characters.

Commercially available multiplexers cater to a wide range of line speeds on the low-speed side, handle different codes, and can often intermix synchronous and asynchronous transmission. In these cases, the bit stream on the high-speed

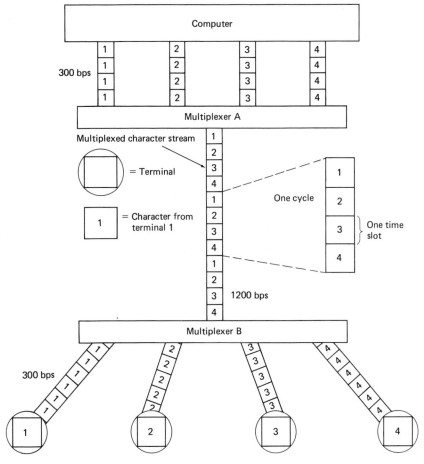

Figure 4-3 Time division multiplexing.

circuit can be quite complex, but this is not a problem because it is demultiplexed at the other end and reconstituted into the original data streams.

In this kind of configuration it can be seen that multiplexers are transparent to the network and that each terminal thinks it has a point-to-point relationship with the computer. The performance of the network would not be markedly different from that of a point-to-point network; there would be some time delay introduced by each multiplexer, but this would not be significant, and of course, the data are not modified on the way through the system. One thing that we should note is that there is a one-to-one relationship between time slots on the high-speed channel and time slots on the low-speed side, so that if a terminal is not transmitting, there is still a time slot assigned to it on the high-speed channel.

In some installations, the high-speed data stream is fed straight into the computer, and the bit stream is demultiplexed by the software in the computer. This saves some hardware in the form of line termination units on the computer, and of course, it saves the computer-end multiplexer, which saves some money. On the other hand, a software cost that involves two components would be incurred. First, there is the cost required initially to develop and implement the software demultiplexing, and then there would be continuing overhead in terms of memory space and computer time required to hold the program and to execute it. Considering hardware and software prices, it is usually not worthwhile to consider software demultiplexing except in the simplest cases, such as when all the terminals are identical and when there is a relatively simple bit stream on the high-speed channel.

As time goes on and electronic technology develops, front-end processors are becoming more and more powerful. In many cases it will then become possible to dispense with the multiplexer at the computer end of the connection and use software or firmware in the front-end processor to demultiplex the incoming data stream. Indeed, one of the facilities available with new digital data networks operates along these precise lines. This facility, known as the X.22 multiplexing facility, is available from some common carriers.

A typical multiplexer configuration is shown in Fig. 4-4. Here we have four terminals each running at 1200 bps; they multiplex together onto the single line running at 4800 bps. Due to the nature of time division multiplexing, typically the sum (aggregate) of the low-speed lines must be equal to or less than the speed of the composite link. In many cases, the sum of the low-speed lines cannot equal

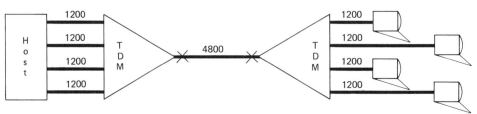

Figure 4-4 Typical multiplexer configuration.

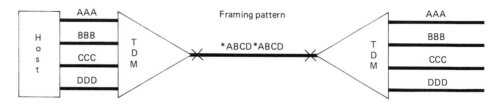

Figure 4-5 TDM framing overhead.

the composite because there is an overhead associated with the multiplexing process. As illustrated in Fig. 4-5, a framing pattern is usually needed to enable the two multiplexers to stay in step with one another.

In the example of Fig. 4-4 we may be able to have 4 × 1200 bps = 4800 bps because the 1200-bps terminals are asynchronous; that is, the individual characters have start and stop bits, while the 4800 bps is synchronous and thus does not have start and stop bits. In this case the multiplexers strip the start and stop bits from each of the incoming characters to forward the characters along the composite link using synchronous transmission, and then the receiving multiplexer adds the start/stop bits onto the characters at the other end for transmission on the outgoing low-speed ports into the host computer.

If the low-speed lines had been synchronous, it would not have been possible to have 4 × 1200 bps = 4800 bps, because of the overhead involved for the framing pattern. In this case as shown in Fig. 4-6, one of the lines would have

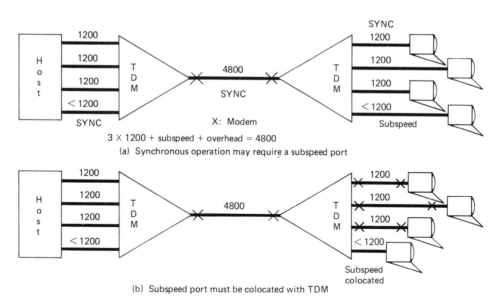

Figure 4-6 (a) Synchronous operation may require a subspeed port; (b) subspeed port must be colocated with TDM.

had to run at a lower speed, so that the sum of the low-speed lines and the overhead would then equal the composite link speed. In this case we say that the line running at less than the nominal speed is a *subspeed* port. It is important to note that the terminal connected to the subspeed port should be colocated with the multiplexer; that is, if the four terminals are at different locations in a distant city, the time division multiplexer would be colocated with one terminal and this terminal would be connected directly into the time division multiplexer in the subspeed port. The other terminals would be connected via modem tails as shown in Fig. 4-6.

For synchronous transmission, modems have a very tight tolerance on speed of transmission, and typically this tolerance is $\pm 0.01\%$. If the transmission speed is outside this tolerance, the system will not work. The subspeed port on the time division multiplexer is typically outside the tolerance, which is why we colocate the terminal with the subspeed port. From the point of view of the terminal operator, the difference in speed between the normal speed port and the subspeed port would usually be imperceptible.

Multistream Modems. There is an example of a multiplexer that does allow for synchronous lines to be handled by a composite link that is running at the same speed as the sum of the incoming lines. This particular case is a multistream modem, which is a modem that has a time division multiplexer built into it. For example, a 9600-bps modem may accept the following data streams and combine them onto the 9600-bps link:

$$1 \times 9600 \text{ bps} = 9600 \text{ bps}$$

$$2 \times 4800 \text{ bps} = 9600 \text{ bps}$$

$$4 \times 2400 \text{ bps} = 9600 \text{ bps}$$

$$2 \times 2400 + 1 \times 4800 \text{ bps} = 9600 \text{ bps}$$

$$1 \times 2400 + 1 \times 7200 \text{ bps} = 9600 \text{ bps}$$

With 9600-bps modems, the multiplexing function is typically integrated with the modulation process, which means that there is no multiplexing overhead. This situation arises because the modems themselves must be synchronized with each other in order that the modulation/demodulation process will work. Given that the modems are already synchronized at this level, there is no need for an additional level of synchronization to keep the multiplexers in step. In this case we can achieve perfect multiplexing, so that it is possible, for example, that 4×2400 bps can be combined together onto a single 9600-bps line. These modems allow us to achieve economies, as indicated in Fig. 4-7.

We can replace Fig. 4-7(a) with the configuration of equipment shown in Fig. 4-7(b). In this diagram we are assuming that all the terminals were colocated, that is, located within the same building. If the terminals had been located in different buildings, modem tails would have been required to connect the terminals into the 9600-bps multistream modem. Generally speaking, a configuration such

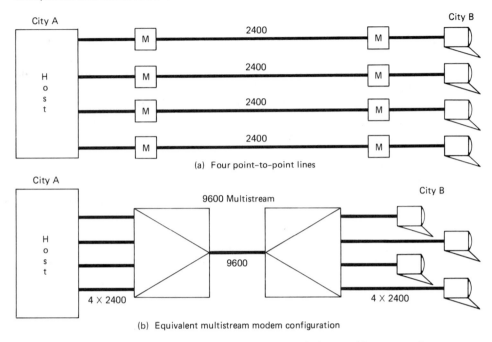

Figure 4-7 (a) Four point-to-point lines; (b) equivalent multistream modem configuration.

as that shown in Fig. 4-7(b) should be cheaper than the configuration shown in Fig. 4-7(a). Many variations on the theme are possible and the ingenious network designer can come up with quite intricate networks using combinations of multistream modems running at different speeds.

The reader should note that not all multistream modems allow us to achieve perfect multiplexing. The situation described above is a special case and there are, in fact, modems on the market which although they have multiplexers built in, have a multiplexing overhead involved as well.

Frequency Division Multiplexing (FDM). Frequency division multiplexing is often used to derive a number of low-speed data channels or telegraph channels from a voice-grade communication line. The voice-grade line (telephone line) is capable of carrying a particular range of frequencies, and in the case of frequency division multiplexing, each terminal entering the multiplexer is assigned a unique frequency range within the range that is available for use on that telephone channel. This is broadly similar to the way in which each radio broadcasting station is assigned its own particular frequency to transmit radio programs. The telephone line joining the multiplexers effectively carries a number of bands of varying frequencies, with each band carrying its own data stream.

Time division multiplexing is the most common form of multiplexing in computer networks. It is generally more efficient than *frequency division multiplexing* because it can make better use of the available capacity of the communications line. FDM requires "guard bands" between the frequency ranges that have been assigned to each terminal device, and this reduces the efficiency of the transmission because the guard bands utilize some of the capacity of the line. Broadband local area networks use frequency division multiplexing to divide the capacity of the coaxial cable into a number of independent communication channels.

Concentrators and front end processors

A *concentrator* or *communications processor* is a computer-based device that often has some form of mass storage attached. Functionally, the concentrator is similar to the multiplexer in that it combines the data from a number of terminals onto a high-speed line for transmission to a host computer. It is, however, a more sophisticated device, because it can alter the form of data streams prior to merging them onto a high-speed line. Figure 4-8 shows how a concentrator can interface a communication network to a computer. The concentrator itself is usually connected to the host computer by a high-speed synchronous line, and the terminal network is interfaced directly into the concentrator. In Fig. 4-8 a concentrator is interfacing a varied network ranging from low-speed asynchronous terminals through medium-speed synchronous and asynchronous lines to a higher-speed remote job entry station.

By handling the communication network, the concentrator can take some load from the host. Communications processing is not a computationally demanding task, in that it does not require high-powered instructions to handle the lines and the data. On the other hand, it is a time-consuming task, because each character needs to be checked many times to ensure that it is the right size, the right shape, in the right sequence, has no errors, and so on.

This is particularly true for low-speed asynchronous traffic, which tends to have very little error-detecting capability. The integrity of the data must be thoroughly checked by software. In the case of higher-speed traffic from buffered terminals, there is usually some error-detecting mechanism built in (as described in Chapter 10) that can be automatically checked by the communications hardware.

For performing this work, a fast cycle time is more critical than a high-powered instruction set, and it turns out that an inexpensive minicomputer can handle communications traffic just about as well as an expensive data processing computer. So by putting the communications handling outside the main computer in a concentrator, we can relieve the main computer of a lot of the load and make this capacity available for data processing purposes.

If equipped with mass storage or sufficient main memory, the concentrator can act as a *store and forward* device, in that it will assemble complete messages or blocks of messages from the network terminals, store them in its memory, and

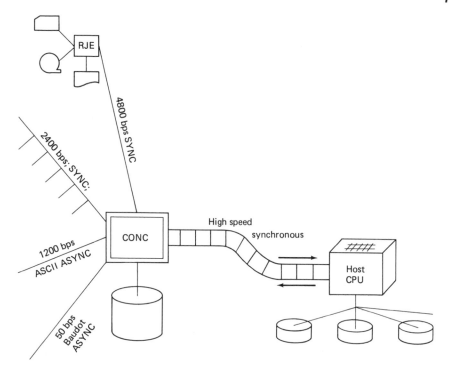

Figure 4-8 Concentrator-based network.

then forward them to the host. This is particularly useful in the case of low-speed asynchronous data coming from unbuffered terminals, because the concentrator can assemble a complete message and send this to the host at high speed in a standardized format.

This implies that the concentrator is performing code conversion, speed conversion, and format conversion. These functions are usually required if we wish to interface terminals that were not supplied by the manufacturer of the host computer.

Most mainframe manufacturers supply communications-handling software that enables networks to be put together fairly simply if the terminals come from the same manufacturer. These days there are so many terminals available from third parties that it often becomes attractive to buy third-party terminals and interface them to the host. Such "plug-compatible" terminals can be directly interfaced to the host as though they were supplied by the host manufacturer.

In the case of terminals that are incompatible with the host (due to differences in speed, code, format, line protocol, etc.), something has to be done to make them compatible. We could modify the host software and/or hardware to make it handle the different terminals. This poses problems because it is often difficult to get enough information to be able to efficiently change the host to make it compatible with the network. Also, if we do change the host, we are faced with the problem of keeping the changes updated every time the host supplier brings out a new version of software, or when hardware field changes are implemented.

By using a concentrator to perform code, speed, and format conversion, we can effectively make the network compatible with the host by presenting messages to the host in a standard form so that it thinks it is talking to its own terminals. (A special case of this kind of device is a *protocol converter* which allows foreign terminals to emulate the host's own terminals.) A concentrator, having intelligence, can make better use of the high-speed line by compressing the data before transmission. This involves removing redundant information such as trailing spaces, converting digital information into binary rather than translating it into ASCII characters, and so on. There are a number of other methods of compressing data so that fewer bits are required to carry a given amount of information. Some of these methods use *Huffman coding* techniques, whereby the data characters are translated into a variable-length code. In most systems, some data characters occur more frequently than others, so they are translated into short codewords. The less frequently occurring characters are translated into longer codewords. The result is that the average number of bits per character should be fewer than if the characters had been transmitted in their original form. The degree of compression that can be achieved depends heavily on the data and on the compression algorithm that is used, but in many cases a compression ratio of 50% or more can be achieved.

The concentrator can also improve the utilization of the line by statistically averaging the traffic from the network onto the high-speed line. The intelligence in the concentrator and the presence of storage can enable the concentrator to queue traffic for the communication line, which means that we do not need to have a one-to-one relationship between high-speed line time and terminal time. That means that if a particular terminal is not transmitting, we do not assign any high-speed line time to that terminal, and we use that time for some other terminal. The result of this is that we can support more terminals on the one high-speed line because the line only needs to be able to handle slightly more than the average amount of traffic generated by the network rather than the *total* amount of traffic that can be generated by the network. In other words, the concentrator statistically averages the traffic from the network onto the high speed line.

Depending on the application, the concentrator may be able to increase network reliability. In some cases the concentrator is used as a data collection center that collects data from a network and later forwards entire blocks of messages to the host. In this case, if the host computer or the high-speed line fails, the concentrator can still continue to assemble data without interfering with the operation of the network. When the host or the line comes up again, the blocks of data can be transmitted to the host. In the opposite direction, the host processor can transmit an entire file of data to the concentrator, which can keep it on mass storage. The concentrator can then deliver the messages to the terminals when they are ready for them. In this case, a terminal that is out of action for any reason does not need to hold up the production process in the host computer.

A special case of the concentrator is the *front-end processor*, which is the same kind of thing except that it is installed at the same location as the host. A front-end computer handles the communication network on behalf of the host and transmits complete messages to the host. As with the concentrator, the front-end processor may or may not have auxiliary mass storage. With auxiliary storage, such a machine could collect messages and data and hold them until the host is ready to process a batch of data. Similarly, it could receive a batch of output data from the host and distribute it to the terminals at their own speed and in their own time.

Most modern computer systems have front-end processors. Large mainframe computers tend to have minicomputer front ends; minicomputers have other minis or perhaps microcomputer front ends. Even microcomputers nowadays have other microcomputers as front-end computers. This is particularly prevalent in the case of personal computers, which have front-end processors in the form of add-on circuit cards that handle the communications on behalf of the processor in the personal computer (PC). This practice originated because in most cases, the processor in the personal computer was rather busy doing its normal job and the overhead involved in handling a communication protocol took up so much time that there was very little capacity left for doing data processing. An additional printed circuit card containing another processor was used to handle the communication line on behalf of the processor in the PC, which means that the basic processor was able to go about its normal business without being overloaded by communication-handling difficulties.

The link between the host processor and the concentrator or front end is usually a point-to-point line, whereas front-end processors and remote concentrators can be connected to the terminal devices that they control by either point-to-point or multipoint lines. Indeed, it is not uncommon to have concentrators connected to concentrators in a hierarchical fashion. The type of connection used depends on a number of factors such as the geographical layout of the system, the terminal types, the message rate for each terminal, the response-time requirements, and, of course, cost.

"Intelligent" multiplexers or statistical multiplexers

The concentrator and multiplexer as described so far represent two ends of a spectrum. Some concentrators do not have mass storage, which means that they have limited store and forward capabilities. On the other hand, some multiplexers have intelligence built into them so that they can perform statistical multiplexing by averaging the traffic from a low-speed network along a high-speed line. They can also perform automatic error detection and correction on the high-speed line, which is something that is not done in a simple multiplexer. In this case, we have

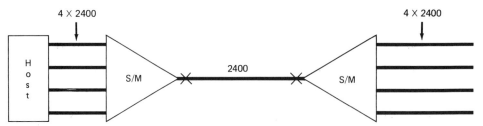

Figure 4-9 Simple asynchronous statmux.

a configuration similar to that shown in Fig. 4-4 except that the multiplexers do have some memory capability and intelligence to control the flow of data along the high-speed line. Such a device could also handle data compression so as to give a significant improvement in performance over a standard multiplexer. This type of machine does not relieve the host of any communications-handling load, because it still presents the host with a number of individual data streams just as in the case of a normal unintelligent multiplexer. This form of multiplexer can introduce significant time delays due to characters queuing for the high-speed line.

A typical statistical multiplexer configuration is shown in Fig. 4-9. The statistical multiplexer works by averaging the traffic from the low-speed lines onto the composite link. If the low-speed lines are not carrying data 100% of the time, the sum of the low-speed lines can greatly exceed the speed of the composite link. In the illustration, the composite link is, in effect, carrying data from four lines running at the same speed, which means that the average loading on each of the lines over an extended period must be less than 25% in order that the system will operate properly.

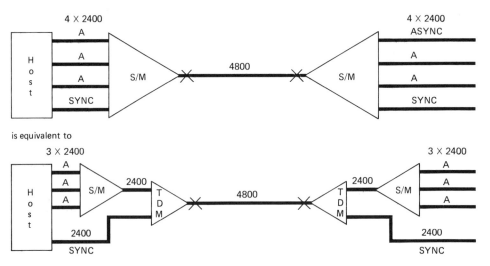

Figure 4-10 Simple asynchronous statmux with synchronous channel.

Due to the nature of asynchronous traffic, it is relatively easy to statistically multiplex asynchronous lines. Synchronous data are harder to statistically multiplex, partially because the idle time on a line may be relatively small (or even nonexistent), and partially because blocks of data need to retain their integrity as they go through the combination of statistical multiplexers. Generally, we find that the statistical multiplexers that handle synchronous traffic tend to be more expensive than those which handle only asynchronous. Some inexpensive models handle synchronous traffic by using time division multiplexing techniques to split the composite channel into two. This is illustrated in Fig. 4-10. In this case the synchronous traffic goes along a TDM channel, while the asynchronous traffic is statistically multiplexed on the remaining time division multiplex channel.

The configuration in Fig. 4-9 works fine as long as the terminals are relatively lightly loaded. Buffering is needed in the statistical multiplexers to handle a situation that arises when the sum of the incoming bit rates exceeds the composite bit rate. This can happen, of course, so data are temporarily stored in the buffer in the statistical multiplexer while the data are discharged down the composite link. The buffer size needs to be large enough to cater for the size of the peak that is likely to arise.

Statistical multiplexers can often be configured in interesting network configurations. An example is the ring configuration shown in Fig. 4-11. In this case

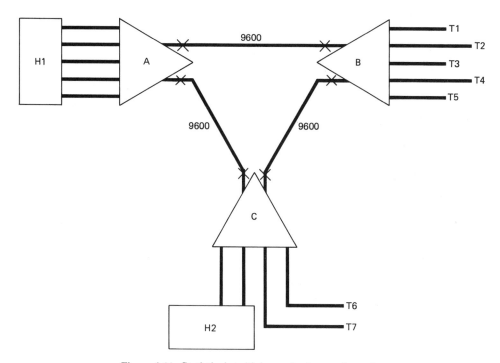

Figure 4-11 Statistical multiplexers in ring configuration.

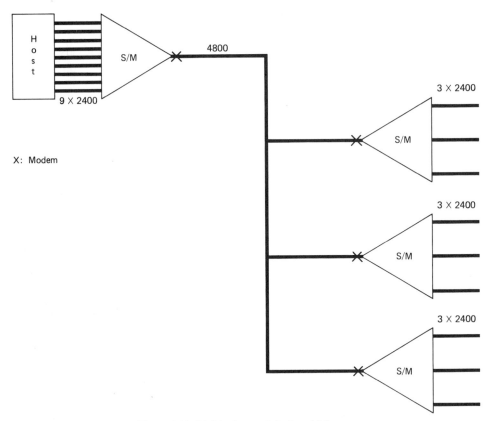

Figure 4-12 Multipoint statistical multiplexers.

we have two host computers and a number of terminals. Terminals 1 to 3, for example, could be connected through host 1, while terminals 4 and 5 could be connected through host 2. Terminals 6 and 7 may be connected to host 1, and at the same time host 1 and host 2 are connected together. There are many products on the market to enable this kind of configuration. In many cases this network can have some redundancy built in such that if we were to lose the 9600-bps link between multiplexers A and B, we could automatically download new configurations to all three multiplexers so that the traffic from terminals 1 to 3 is still routed to host 1, but in this case via multiplexer C.

Switching Multiplexers. In yet another configuration, statistical multiplexers A, B, and C in Fig. 4-11 may have dynamic switching capability, so that a terminal (e.g., terminal 1) can be connected on demand to either host 1 or host 2. This connection is typically established by the terminal operator indulging in a brief dialogue with the statistical multiplexer to ask that it be connected to a port on the appropriate host. The statistical multiplexer will not only switch the call but will statistically multiplex the traffic with the traffic going to or from other terminals on the same link.

Multipoint Configurations. It is also possible to use statistical multiplexers in multipoint arrangements, as shown in Figs. 4-12 and 4-13. In the case of Fig. 4-12, the data from the remote statistical multiplexers are combined over a single multipoint line which is operated under the control of the statistical multiplexer at the host computer site. Data from the remote terminals are first combined into frames within the remote statistical multiplexer, and then on command from the instation statistical multiplexer these frames are transmitted down to the instation statistical multiplexer. This statistical multiplexer then breaks the frame into its individual components and feeds the characters out to the appropriate host ports. Note that we have the same number of terminations on the host as we have presentations at the outstation statistical multiplexers.

In the configuration shown in Fig. 4-13, the composite link on statistical multiplexer C is itself statistically multiplexed with data from terminals connected

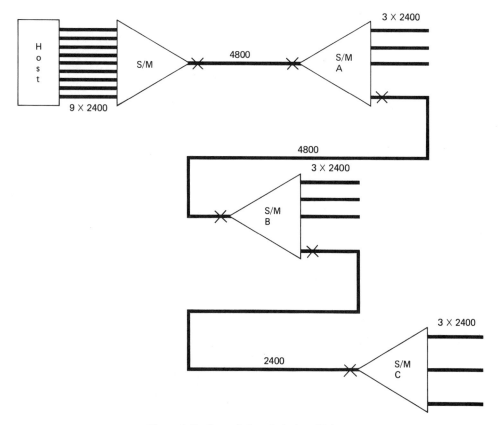

Figure 4-13 Cascaded statistical multiplexers.

to statistical multiplexer B. It, in turn, is statistically multiplexed with data from terminals connected to multiplexer A, and the composite link of statistical multiplexer A is fed into the statistical multiplexer at the instation, where the data streams are broken down into their individual component parts and the characters are presented to the host on individual channels representing the individual presentations at the remote statistical multiplexers.

As you can imagine, time delays could be rather long, particularly in the configuration shown in Fig. 4-12. On the other hand, if it is lightly loaded situation, the time penalty may be relatively small compared to the amount of money that is saved over the cost of an equivalent network made up out of three point-to-point statistical multiplexer configurations.

5
Network Configurations

types of network configurations

There are four basic network configurations that can be used: the *star* network, the *ring* network, the *mesh* network, and the *hierarchical* network.

The *star* network, shown in Fig. 3-5, is probably the most common form of network. In this network, each terminal is connected to the central site by a point-to-point line. Multipoint lines can also be used along with point-to-point lines in a star configuration. A star network is very dependent on the integrity of the central site, and if it is performing a critical function, such as airline reservations, it may be necessary to duplicate some or all of the equipment in order to maintain service in the event of an equipment failure.

A common approach to data processing is to decentralize the computer systems around a number of cities. In any one city, the local computer handles the local network, which usually would be a star configuration. The computers in the various cities may also be interconnected back to a master computer, as in Fig. 5-1, to form another star network. This type of system is, if you like, a distributed star in that the computer in each remote site has its own star network and then the remote computers themselves act as the distant terminals in yet another star network. In a star network of this nature, there is only one data path between any two terminals in the network. If terminals in two different cities wish

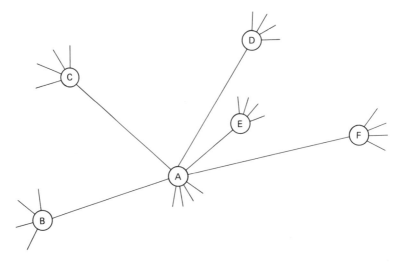

Figure 5-1 Star network.

to communicate with each other, the connection has to be established via the
central site. If the central site fails, this connection cannot be established.

The system can be improved somewhat by using the *ring* network approach.
Figure 5-2 illustrates a ring network, which, as the name implies, consists of a
number of computers connected together in a loop or ring. In this case, there are
two paths that can be established between any two computers in the network,
and if for some reason one of the paths fails, the other route can be used as a
backup.

If there is a need to handle large volumes of traffic from many terminals in
many cities, it may be advantageous to implement a *mesh* network, as shown in
Fig. 5-3. The decision as to whether to use star, ring, or mesh networks is based

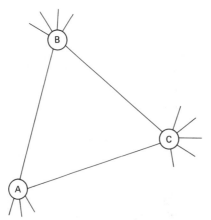

Figure 5-2 Network with ring
configuration.

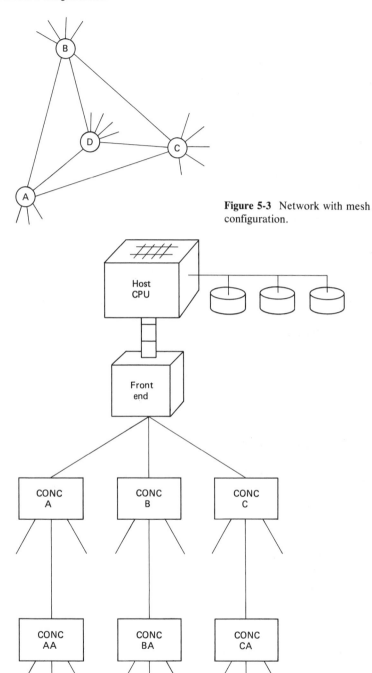

Figure 5-3 Network with mesh configuration.

Figure 5-4 Hierarchical network.

largely on the cost of the lines, the geography of the network, and the volume of data that has to be transmitted around the network. For example, in a country such as Australia, where there are few major cities and these are separated by thousands of kilometers, the most common network configuration is a star. In Europe and the United States, on the other hand, with many medium-size to large cities, mesh or ring networks are common.

A *hierarchical* network such as the one shown in Fig. 5-4 should be self-explanatory. Various levels of computers can be interconnected as shown in a similar manner to the way an organization chart in a corporation is developed.

By looking at the diagrams of star, ring, and mesh networks, it can be seen that network reliability and capability increases as the network becomes more complex. In the star network, if the central site fails, the network ceases to exist as a network. Of course, to guard against this type of failure, we can duplicate critical items in the central site.

In the ring configuration, the failure of one center on the ring puts out of action only the terminals directly connected to the failed center, because the remaining sites can communicate by using other parts of the ring. Similarly, the mesh network is more reliable, again due to the increased number of interconnections.

The star, ring, and mesh networks involve different lengths of communication lines, and they provide different degrees of reliability. In designing a network, trade-offs are usually made between reliability, efficiency, and costs, with the result that any one system may contain different types of networks, some based on the star configuration and some based on the ring or mesh.

private networks

In addition to traditional networks of leased lines and switched services from common carrier networks, there are several options for the installation of private switched networks. These options include:

- Multiplexer networks
- Satellite networks
- Private packet-switched networks
- Private microwave
- Laser and/or infrared links
- PABX networks

A brief description of each follows.

Multiplexer Networks. We have already had a brief look at multiplexer networks, which can be constructed using combinations of time division multiplexers and statistical multiplexers. These networks are often configured in a ring or mesh configuration, interconnecting multiple host locations with many terminals. If switching multiplexers are employed, terminals have the capability of being connected to one of a number of host computers through the multiplexer network. This is of great benefit to unbuffered asynchronous character-oriented terminals, which otherwise have to be connected to a particular port on a particular host via a point-to-point line. Great flexibility and reliability can be designed into such networks.

Satellite Communication Networks. These networks are also in widespread use in data communications, particularly for domestic communications, as a means of bypassing common carrier networks or for providing backup for common carrier networks in the event of failures in the carrier networks. Satellite communication systems have an inherently long time delay related to them, which can severely affect the performance of the network, depending on the kind of communication protocols used. As outlined in Chapters 12 to 20 the choice of protocols is critical for systems with long time delays. The newer protocols, such as SDLC and HDLC, allow us to achieve extremely efficient operation, even on networks with long time delays. This is discussed further in Chapters 17 to 20.

Private Packet-Switched Networks. These networks are also in widespread use both on the domestic scene and in international networks. Their beauty arises because of the capability of interconnecting numerous computer locations with many terminal locations. The ability to have dissimilar computers communicating with dissimilar terminals is also an advantage. Generally, the networks can handle not only data traffic for computers but other traffic as well, such as electronic mail and electronic message services.

Private Microwave Links. These links are often used to provide point-to-point communications line of sight between locations, typically within the metropolitan area of the city. In many instances the communication lines within the city are not capable of high-speed operation, and a private microwave link can be designed to carry speeds of 2 Mbps, 8 Mbps, or even more between two locations. These links can be used with a time division multiplexer or a statistical multiplexer at each end to combine transmissions from computer terminals, voice systems, PBXs, electronic mail, and other internal business telecommunication services.

Laser and/or Infared Links. Links of this type are also used for short-haul point-to-point communications. Both of these facilities use light as the transmission medium and therefore require a point-to-point configuration. They are susceptible to bad weather conditions, such as heavy snow, very heavy rain, or fog. Typically, they are used over relatively short distances, carrying data at speeds of perhaps 2 Mbps or thereabouts. It is also possible to transmit digitized voice over a laser or infrared link.

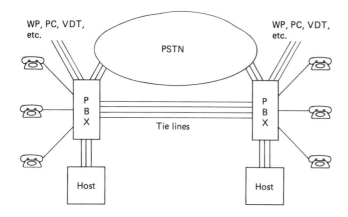

Figure 5-5 PBX voice/data network.

PBX Networks. The PBX (private branch exchange) is a very important component in data communication and office automation networks. Every organization needs a PBX for its telephone system, and the new digital PBXs, which are computer-controlled, are capable of interfacing computers and terminals and in the process, of providing a switching capability whereby any terminal connected to the PBX can be switched to any other terminal or computer that is connected into the PBX. As illustrated in Fig. 5-5, PBXs are often interconnected via tie lines, so that PBXs in different cities can be connected in the form of a network with overflow capability via the public switched telephone network. Generally speaking, the tie lines are designed to carry the peak voice traffic between the different cities. As the traffic fluctuates dramatically with time as shown in Fig. 5-6, for a high proportion of the time during the day the tie-line network is idle. With a computer-controlled PBX, the PBX is able to manage the use of these tie

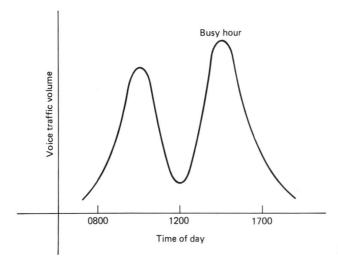

Figure 5-6 Tie-line traffic distribution.

lines so that when they are not being used for voice, they can be used for data transmission. This means that we can share an expensive resource among a number of different users.

Local Area Networks. We discuss local area networks in more detail in Chapter 8. Local area networks are short-haul high-speed networks capable of interconnecting computers and terminals in such a manner that any device on the network is capable of communicating with any other device.

conclusion

To summarize, then, as shown in Fig. 5-7, a typical computer system in modern times is likely to be interconnected to a wide range of different communication facilities, ranging from the conventional public switched telephone network and leased line services through digital services, packet switching, private networks

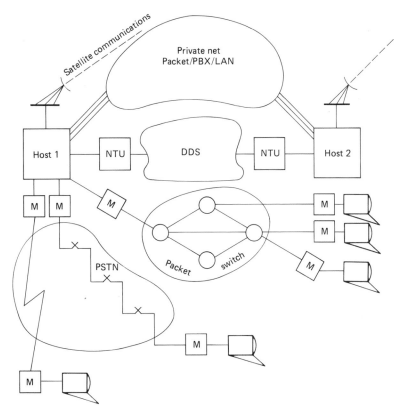

Figure 5-7 A modern computer network uses many forms of communication.

that may be packet, PBX or local area networks, or satellite communication networks.

Selecting which network is suitable for a particular communication is a very important task. Some transactions will be ideally suited for transmission through the packet switch, whereas high-volume file transfers are more suited to the local area network or a high-speed satellite communication link. One of the functional layers of the open system interconnection protocol hierarchy, layer 4, is responsible among other things for selecting the particular network to be used for a particular transaction. This is discussed in more detail in Chapter 13.

6
Terminals and Personal Computers

types of terminal equipment

The choice of a terminal for a particular application is an important aspect in the overall design procedure for a communication network. Several variables must be considered in order to select the correct terminal for the job. The terminal should be able to fulfill particular requirements for data transfer regarding quantity, quality, and speed of transmission. If necessary, it should be compatible with other components in the network, and it should be an acceptable device for human use if a human–machine interface is required. The cost of the terminal in relation to its performance is also, of course, an important factor in the selection process.

Terminals exist to handle practically any communication function that is needed, and, if a new requirement appears, a new type of terminal is fairly quickly designed to accommodate it. There are so many terminals available that we do not attempt to describe any particular style of terminal. Rather, we look at the common elements that are at the heart of all terminal equipment. First, we see how terminals *communicate*, and then we classify terminals *functionally* so that we can identify the differences between the main classes of terminals.

Terminal communication modes

From the communications point of view, terminals operate either in a *free-wheeling* mode or in a *controlled* mode. Freewheeling operation means that the transmission of data from a terminal is under the control of the terminal operator. This is to be contrasted with the controlled mode of operation, which means that the transmission of data from the terminal is controlled by the device at the other end of the line (usually a computer). This control involves the use of *line control procedures,* which are a set of rules defining the requirements for the transmission of data between terminals. (Line control procedures are covered in Chapters 12 to 20.) In systems with several terminals connected to one line, we must usually operate in a controlled mode; otherwise, we run the risk of having two or more terminals attempting to transmit simultaneously, with the result that the data become garbled.

Freewheeling Communication. Most unbuffered asynchronous terminals are freewheeling in that as the characters are entered into the keyboard of the terminal they are transmitted down the line. We should therefore use only one terminal

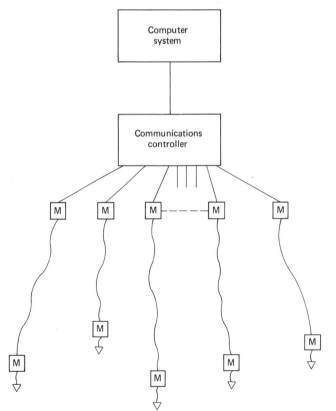

Figure 6-1 Network structure with freewheeling terminals.

per line in freewheeling mode unless the traffic is so light that it is unlikely that two terminals would transmit simultaneously.

As an example, let us consider a computer that has 20 terminals connected to it. If we have freewheeling input, we will require a point-to-point line for each terminal, as shown in Fig. 6-1. As the computer has no control over the input data, it must always be ready to accept data from each line. This means that it must have an input buffer assigned to each line, and the system must regularly monitor every line (either by hardware or by software, depending on the particular equipment in use) to see if data are coming in.

In a large system with many terminals and many lines, a large amount of system resources could be diverted to the communication functions. These resources include hardware facilities, such as the main memory required for input buffers, and the line interface hardware and modems required to terminate the lines. Not so apparent are the software resources that are required to handle abnormal conditions such as all the lines inputting data simultaneously. The simultaneous filling of many input buffers could require that a large number of fresh buffers be rapidly assigned to the lines in order not to lose any incoming data, and the contents of the buffers that have just been filled need to be processed or written to mass storage very quickly in order to release the buffer space for reuse. This can place an excessive load on the processor and/or mass storage subsystem during the period of heavy traffic.

A system with freewheeling input traffic must be designed to handle the peak load that may be imposed on it when a large volume of input data transmission occurs. If we were a plot a graph of the load on system versus time, we would find that most systems have a variable load, perhaps with quite severe peaks, as in Fig. 6-2.

For example, an airline may have a traffic peak at Easter and another at Christmas; a bank may have heavy traffic during the lunch hour and again just prior to closing, and so on. In most organizations, seasonal and/or daily variations can create large peaks. In commercial systems, it is generally unacceptable to

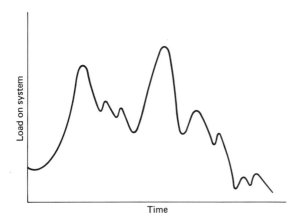

Figure 6-2 The load on a system varies with time.

lose input data, so in a system with large traffic peaks, we need to provide sufficient computer power to be able to handle the heaviest peak. This means that the system may be grossly underutilized during the remaining time.

Controlled Communications. We now examine the same situation using *controlled* terminals. Controlled terminals are usually buffered, which means that we can run them at high speed and therefore share the capacity of a line between a number of terminals. The way this is done depends largely on the geographic distribution of the terminals. For example, if 8 of our 20 terminals are in one building, they could be connected to one line through some sort of cluster controller or perhaps by a daisy-chain (concatenated) connection, depending on the type of terminal in use.

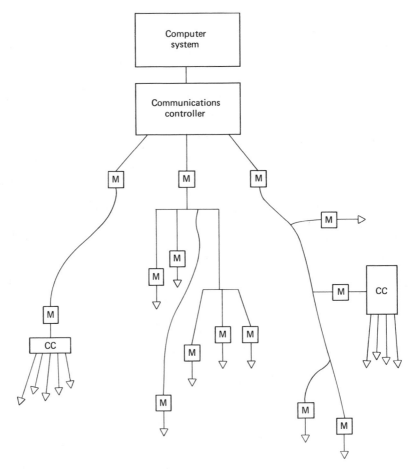

Figure 6-3 Network structure with controlled terminals.

Figure 6-3 shows a typical system connected with point-to-point and multipoint lines. The resources consumed at the central site in supporting this kind of network differ from those used in the freewheeling system. We have reduced the number of line interface units and modems required because many terminals are sharing each modem and interface unit. We have also reduced the number of input data buffers because we have buffers assigned on a line basis rather than on a terminal basis.

On the other hand, we have introduced software to handle the *line control procedures,* which control the flow of data along each line. This represents an overhead in terms of memory space and computer time. If the system becomes temporarily overloaded, it can reduce the load by not allowing the terminals to transmit. This can reduce the load-carrying requirement in the central site, because it can average out a traffic peak by temporarily storing the traffic at the terminals rather than in the computer as in a freewheeling system.

Generally, the terminals used in a controlled environment are more complex and consequently more expensive than their freewheeling counterparts. This is because each terminal must be capable of being addressed by the central site, and this requires extra hardware. This price differential is becoming smaller as time goes on due to the advances that are being made in the construction methods of terminals and computers.

classes of terminals

We now examine some of the terminal types that are found in today's data communication systems. As indicated earlier, there is an extremely wide range of terminals, and it is difficult to create a suitable general classification for terminal types. In order to reach such a classification, we use the terms *simple, sophisticated,* and *intelligent* to describe classes of terminals. The dividing line between them is very hazy, and indeed, a particular terminal may straddle two classifications depending on its configuration.

Terminals vary from simple electromechanical devices to computer-based machines. The main advantage of very simple terminals has been the fact that they are inexpensive. However, modern electronic techniques have substantially reduced the manufacturing costs of terminals. In the future, rather than giving us further large reductions in price for terminals, the suppliers will tend to give us more capability per unit cost. The trend in the industry is toward producing more-intelligent terminals, which enable us to do more processing at the point where the data are generated. Also, they enable us to make better use of expensive communications lines. On the other hand, simple terminals will still be manufactured for years to come if for no other reason than to maintain compatibility with the millions of simple terminals that are in use today.

The general characteristics of simple, sophisticated, and intelligent terminals are summarized in Table 6-1 and discussed in the following paragraphs.

TABLE 6-1 GENERAL CHARACTERISTICS OF SIMPLE, SOPHISTICATED, AND INTELLIGENT TERMINALS

Simple terminals

Inexpensive
Unbuffered for keyboard data entry
Freewheeling
Asynchronous
Low speed
Little or no error detecting capability
Little or no storage (paper tape)

Sophisticated terminals

More expensive
Buffered
Synchronous/asynchronous
High speed
High-level line control procedures
Automatic error detection and correction
Storage
Clustered operation
Multidrop operation
Security (e.g., badge reader)
Auxiliary devices (e.g., printers, cassettes)

Intelligent terminals

Same as for simple or sophisticated terminals plus:
   Computing capability
   On-line storage
   Data editing
   Data compression
   Local storage of "forms" and operator prompting
     messages

Simple terminals

We describe a *simple* terminal as being inexpensive (usually), having little data-handling capability (i.e., no editing or data-manipulation capability), having little or no data buffering, and generally operating at low line speed. The lack of data buffering means that the data are transmitted as they are entered, and hence the terminal uses asynchronous transmission. Also, this means that the line speed is constrained by the data-handling capability of the terminal.

These terminals are often referred to as *character-oriented terminals* because of the fact that characters are handled one at a time as they are entered on the keyboard. For example, a simple teleprinter as used on the Telex network will transmit a character to line as soon as the key on the keyboard is pressed.

Similarly, the speed at which an electromechanical terminal such as a teleprinter may operate is restricted by the time required to recognize a character and print it out by mechanical means.

Of course, many terminals are unbuffered from the point of view of transmitting data, but they are buffered from the point of view of receiving data. Many visual display terminals and printers have large buffers so that the received data can be stored and displayed or printed. In these situations, the terminals may, in fact, be run on a relatively fast communication line to maximize the speed at which the buffer can be refreshed with data from the host. This means that generally speaking, the communication lines are very lightly loaded, but this is a good example of the type of terminal that lends itself to statistical multiplexing. As each terminal contributes only very light loading to the composite link between the multiplexers, a number of terminals can be statistically multiplexed together on a single line.

In many instances, the fact that the terminal operates asynchronously and at low speed and therefore makes poor utilization of the communication line is not a problem. For example, on in-house lines, short communications lines, or local area dial-up lines, there are usually no great economic consequences if we dedicate a line to a simple terminal. In many countries, for the price of a local telephone call, a subscriber can utilize a telephone line all day, and, under those circumstances, there is little to be gained by optimizing the use of that line.

Simple terminals have little or no error-detecting capability. They often ignore errors such as in the case of terminals handling administrative messages. In other cases, they rely on the echo technique (see Chapter 10) or on character parity checking, which, as we have seen, is of limited use on its own.

Simple terminals generally have no inherent data storage capability, although many of these terminals are equipped with paper tape reader/punch units and are able to generate data and store it on a paper tape that can be transmitted later. This is effectively a form of off-line data storage.

Simple terminals generally operate in a freewheeling mode, but some terminals can be connected in such a way as to operate under controlled conditions. In other words, they become somewhat more sophisticated in their operation. A version of the teleprinter known as an *automatic send receive* (ASR) machine can transmit a message from a roll of paper tape upon a command from the master station. The terminal contains circuitry or, in electromechanical terminals, a device known as a *stunt box*, which can recognize an address function enabling the computer to poll the terminal and ask it if it has any traffic to send. If the terminal has traffic, it will proceed to send the information on the paper tape. Similarly, on the receive side of the terminal, circuitry can detect a terminal selection address (a receive-select code, or RSC), which determines which machine of many connected to a communication line will receive a message transmitted by the computer. In some instances, it is possible to address more than one terminal on the line at the same time.

Simple terminals therefore, although they are inexpensive, tend to consume central site resources as well as generally making inefficient use of communications lines. In many instances, the use of an inexpensive simple terminal could represent a false economy due to the hidden costs associated with these other resources. The advent of inexpensive statistical multiplexers has had a dramatic effect on the use of simple character-oriented terminals. They are in widespread use with statmux and switching multiplexer networks.

Sophisticated terminals

We define a *sophisticated* terminal as a device that generally has more logical functions than a simple terminal, often having additional bulk storage units such as cassette tape drives. Sophisticated terminals operate either synchronously or asynchronously at high line speeds and are generally buffered to enable efficient use of the line. The change from synchronous to asynchronous operation is often switch selectable or under software control. In other cases, an interface card in the terminal needs to be changed. These terminals usually have a high-level line control procedure to take care of automatic error detection and correction and to make efficient use of the communications line by enabling the line to be shared by a number of terminals. This enables flexible configurations to be designed using multidrop lines and clusters of terminals.

The increased logic capability of sophisticated terminals enables the use of communications control characters for cursor addressing in visual display terminals, for the control of auxiliary devices such as off-line printers, cassette drives, and so on, and for the establishment of protected format fields. This increased logic capability can also enable some manual editing functions to be incorporated, such as the shifting of all characters in a line to the left or right, the deleting of single characters or fields, and the performing of more advanced functions such as roll and scroll (i.e., when all data on a VDT move up or down one line at a time, similar to the way the credits on a movie move up the screen).

Sophisticated terminals can provide added security; for example, a key may be required to operate the terminal, or a badge reader may be incorporated that requires that an operator insert an identification card before using the terminal. This is important in many applications such as banking and allied fields.

Sophisticated terminals with auxiliary devices such as printers and cassette units can be used for off-line data capture. Data can be entered into the terminal and recorded on the cassette, and later be transmitted down the communication line to the computer.

Intelligent terminals

The outstanding characteristic of an intelligent terminal is that it has computing capability which is user programmable. In the past many intelligent terminals had cassette and paper tape storage capability, whereas nowadays most have on-line storage capability such as disks and floppy disks.

From a communication point of view, an intelligent terminal can behave like either a simple terminal or a sophisticated terminal, depending on how it is configured. Most intelligent terminals can communicate like a simple unbuffered character-oriented terminal, and with the aid of a suitable software package or add-on printed circuit card, many of them can also emulate one of the protocols employed by the more sophisticated terminals. Personal computers and small business computers are playing a prominent part in the terminal world by their capability to emulate either simple or sophisticated terminals.

In this book we use the term *intelligent terminal* to refer to devices that are user programmable. There is a difference between an intelligent terminal and one that uses built-in computer power to provide sophistication. Many sophisticated terminals are built this way, but the computers cannot be programmed by the user.

An important feature of an intelligent terminal is its data handling capability. These terminals are often used for remote data entry, and the intelligence allows the terminal to pick up many data entry errors. It can then draw the operator's attention to the error, which can be corrected on the spot. The data can then be transmitted to the host computer, where they can be fully edited. This will probably detect some errors that could not have been picked up at the terminal. These erroneous data can be transmitted back to the terminal for correction. The number of rejects should be small, because most errors would be picked up at the terminal.

This is to be contrasted with the unintelligent terminal approach, which would allow data to be entered onto cassettes without editing. In this case the data are transmitted to the host computer, which then performs the edit. Any rejected data are then transmitted back to the terminal for correction. This process obviously takes much longer than that using intelligent terminals.

In many cases, both with intelligent and unintelligent terminals, data entry is assisted by means of a *form* that is displayed on the screen. This form can be protected by the terminal so that the operator can neither destroy the form nor enter data on top of it. Data are entered by filling in the spaces on the form. In these instances, when the data are transmitted to the computer, only the significant information is transmitted (i.e., the form itself is not transmitted to the computer).

With unintelligent terminals, these forms are held on the mass storage associated with the host computer, and the host has to be interrupted every time a terminal operator wants a new form. This places an additional load on the host and also on the communication line. With an intelligent terminal, the forms can be held on the terminal's mass storage, and the operator can retrieve different forms locally without interrupting the host.

Similarly, the intelligent terminal can store messages and phrases that can be used to prompt the operator. This capability is useful for guiding new operators through the use of the terminals. These prompting messages can also be retrieved locally without interrupting the host computer.

A prime feature of the intelligent terminal is its capability of acting as a freestanding data processing system. Such systems are finding wider application today, because local data processing can be performed on local files and transactions that are of little or no interest to any other location, and communications can be established with other locations as the need arises (e.g., to transmit daily statistics to head office).

personal computer communications

Personal computers are now in widespread use as terminals for file transfer or for terminal emulation. Personal computers are used in three major classes of application: file transfer, terminal emulation, and resource sharing. Looking briefly at these, we can see the general characteristics of each application class.

File transfer

File transfer is used either between personal computers or between a personal computer and a host computer. For example, it is fairly common to use file transfers between personal computers over a data communication link because of the incompatability of disk formats used between different brands of personal computer. This means that disks created by one computer cannot be read by another. A communication link can be used to transfer files from one personal computer to another regardless of differences in design between the personal computers. Of course, a software package would be required to handle a communication protocol used on the link and also perhaps to perform any character translations that may be required to cater for differences between the computers or between the application programs being run on the computers.

Personal computer-to-host communications can arise for a number of reasons; for example, the disk storage capacity on a personal computer is usually limited by the size of the floppy disk or perhaps by the size of the hard disk attached to the personal computer. The bulk storage on the mainframe can be used as an extension of the storage attached to the personal computer, and this storage can be accessed via a data communication link. Of course, a software package is required at each end of the link to manage (1) the communications, and (2) the file retrieval and file storage mechanisms. Using the host storage to emulate the personal computer storage in this way, although it looks attractive, is relatively slow in that the data transfer rates experienced over communication links are very slow compared to the natural data transfer rate off a floppy disk or a hard disk attached to the personal computer. It is not unusual for users to have to wait many minutes for a file transfer over a communication link, whereas that file transfer may take place in a few seconds from a locally attached disk.

PC-to-host communications are also valuable for sending files to or from the host. For example, a personal computer may be used as a freestanding data processing machine during the day and may accumulate a transaction file relating to business activity during the day. At the end of the day a link may be established with the mainframe and the contents of the transaction file streamed down the line to the host, where they can later be amalgamated with results from other PCs. In the opposite direction, data transfer from the host to the personal computer is often required because the personal computer users, once they have experienced the capability that the PC can provide for them, may wish to have access to the main corporate database, which is held on the host. With suitable software packages at each end of a data link, information can be retrieved from the main databases on the host and transmitted down the line to local storage on the personal computer, where these data can be accessed.

Terminal emulation

Terminal emulation is another reason many users get involved with personal computer communications. Practically all personal computers can emulate a simple character-oriented terminal because most PCs have an asynchronous communication port and they also come with a software package which allows them to emulate a character-oriented terminal. There are many software packages that will also allow the personal computer to transfer files from the disk to another personal computer or host, as mentioned in the preceding paragraph.

Many personal computers are capable of emulating the more popular sophisticated terminals, which are the ones that have been put out by the mainframe computer manufacturers for many years. This terminal emulation is generally performed on an add-on printed circuit card which is plugged into a spare slot on the personal computer. The reason for the add-on card is that the communication protocols employed by the sophisticated terminals are relatively complicated and consume a lot of computer power when software is used to control the protocol. If the main processor in the PC were used to handle this communication link, it would leave relatively little processing power to handle the normal jobs and applications that are to be run on the personal computer.

The add-on printed circuit card contains another processor, which in effect makes this card into a front-end processor for the PC. The additional processor is responsible for handling the communication protocol and, to an extent, the "personality" of the terminal being emulated, leaving the processor in the PC free to perform application tasks for the user.

Resource sharing

Resource sharing is another reason why people get involved in personal computer communications. Nowadays, the PCs are relatively inexpensive; however, the peripheral devices, such as hard disks and letter-quality printers, tend to cost as much as, if not more than, the personal computer itself. As the number of PCs in an organization grows, the number of hard disks and letter-quality printers does not grow as fast, because on a per computer basis the activity on the hard disk and the letter-quality printer is relatively light. It is therefore feasible that these expensive resources could be shared between a number of personal computers. The techniques used for sharing these resources vary considerably, but most are based on the use of local area networks (LAN), which are described in more detail in Chapter 8.

One of the more useful developments in the area of personal computers is the integration of the PC with the telephone. This means that the resulting workstation can be used as a telephone, using the intelligence in the PC to keep track of phone numbers and perform automatic dialing. While the person is conversing on the phone, he or she can be using the computer as a freestanding data processing machine or can use it to access various databases. This PC/telephone workstation would typically be connected into the organization's PBX and then via the PBX would be linked into the public telephone network, data networks, packet-switching networks, and so on, so that the operator can access any database assessible to any computer connected into the networks while he or she is talking on the telephone. This is an extremely useful feature which will be exploited more and more in the future.

7
Modems and Interfaces

data communication networks

In most countries, the lines that we use for data communications are taken from the telephone network. This is because telephone networks are so extensive and the circuits from the network are available for use in data communications. The telephone network was designed to carry the human voice, and such a system is not the best medium for data transmission. In some countries, special networks have been established specifically for carrying data, and these will provide much better service than telephone networks. In the meantime, most of us must continue to use the telephone network for data transmission.

Baseband signaling

The digital data signals generated by terminals and computers have sharp transitions between the 1 state and the 0 state, so that a raw digital data stream looks like a series of square or rectangular pulses. Over short distances and/or at low transmission speeds, we can send these digital data signals straight down the line using a technique known as *baseband signaling*. Many terminal manufacturers supply a *current loop interface*, which allows us to use this type of signaling.

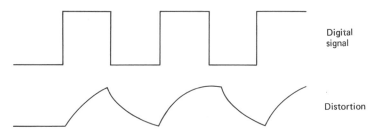

Figure 7-1 Square pulse distortion.

The current loop interface sends 1s and 0s by varying the direction of current flow through a loop of wire. The technique is not unlike that used in the simple battery/lamp/pushbutton arrangement described in Chapter 2 when we were discussing one-way, half-duplex, and full-duplex communications.

Current loop interfaces are usually used on in-house lines that do not go through the common carrier's network. In fact, many common carriers will not permit direct current interfaces to be used on their lines.

If these signals are fed into the telephone network, they tend to become distorted, as shown in Fig. 7-1, so that the square edges of the pulses become rounded. If the distortion becomes too severe, the signals cannot be correctly decoded by the receiving device. In general, this effect becomes more pronounced as the distance increases and as the transmission speed is increased. Also, in some parts of telephone networks, the digital signals just would not go through, owing to the nature of the components used in setting up a telephone network.

Modems

To use the telephone circuits for data transmission, we generally need to convert digital signals into a form that will go smoothly along the telephone line and at the other end convert that signal back into digital form for use in a computer or terminal.

One suitable signal for transmission along a telephone line is the sine wave shown in Fig. 7-2. Such a signal can be used as a *carrier* wave, which will carry the digital information along the communication line. A process shown as *modulation* places the digital information on the carrier wave at one end of the line, and at the other end of the line, a process known as *demodulation* takes the digital data from the carrier wave.

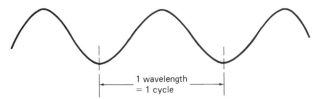

1 wavelength
= 1 cycle

Figure 7-2 Sine wave.

The process of modulating and demodulating the digital data is performed by a *modem* (the word "modem" is a contraction of the words modulator and demodulator). In some parts of the world, a modem is called a *data set*.

Modems come in all shapes and sizes: one-way, half-duplex, and full-duplex; synchronous and asynchronous. Originally, modems were a separate component in a network, but nowadays many terminals have modems built in.

Figure 7-3 illustrates a point-to-point connection between a terminal and a computer using a communication line with modems. This picture shows the terminal generating a sharp-edged digital signal that is fed into modem A, which in turn modulates the digital data onto a carrier wave and sends this along the telephone line. At the other end of the telephone line, modem B demodulates the data from the carrier signal and reconstitutes a sharp-edged digital signal that is fed into the computer. Modems can introduce significant time delays into a data transmission sequence, and we now examine the method of operation of a circuit using modems.

Two-wire and four-wire lines

The communication line between modems can be either a *two-wire* line or a *four-wire* line. In Chapter 2 we saw that, in general, two wires are needed to provide one communication channel. This was illustrated in Figs. 2-9 and 2-11. In some cases the modems can electronically manipulate the electrical characteristics of the two-wire communication line and derive two communication channels from the two-wire system. Typical two-wire full-duplex modems are summarized below.

CCITT V.21	300 bps	Bell 103	300 bps
CCITT V.22	1200 bps	Bell 212A	1200 bps
CCITT V.22 bis	2400 bps	Bell 2400	2400 bps
CCITT V.23	1200 bps/75 bps		
CCITT V.32	9600 bps		

These modems are generally used over the public switched telephone network; the actual speed of operation depends on the quality of the particular telephone network. Many common carriers have an upper limit of transmission speed for the dial-up telephone network. Before making extensive use of dial-up commu-

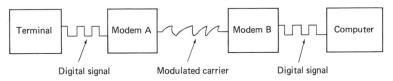

Digital signal   Modulated carrier   Digital signal

Figure 7-3 Data link with modems.

nications, it is always a good idea to check with your common carrier about the availability of different transmission speeds.

If we wish to provide two channels for full-duplex working at higher speeds, we will need to use a four-wire line which, in effect, is 2 two-wire lines in parallel. Due to the nature of the telephone network, we often get four-wire lines because that is the way they come from the system. In other cases we can obtain the lines as two-wire lines. The way they are provided is really a matter of the policy adopted by the common carrier, and for the remainder of this discussion, we will assume that we can get either two-wire or four-wire lines. When you plan your own network, you should find out how your carrier(s) provides lines.

Interfaces

An *interface* can be defined as the line of demarcation between two pieces of equipment. For two pieces of equipment to operate harmoniously, they must each obey a complementary set of interface specifications. There are generally several levels of interface specifications, and we must have compatibility at each level.

Consider the simple computer system illustrated in Fig. 7-4. Two interfaces can be identified, one between the host and the disk control unit, and the second between the disk control unit and the disk. In order that the host and the control unit will operate together, they must each obey a complementary set of interface specifications. If we look at this particular interface in more detail, as in Fig. 7-5, we can illustrate a way in which an interface can be regarded as a number of layers of control sitting one on top of the other.

The very lowest level is the mechanical level, where we have the collection of plugs, sockets, pins, and cables that are used to physically connect together the host computer and the disk control unit. We must have compatibility at this level—the plugs and sockets must match, the correct wires must be connected to the correct pins in the connectors, and so on. If we have mismatch at the level of the sockets or of the wiring of the cable, we cannot expect the host and the disk control unit to operate as a pair. The purpose of the mechanical interface is to provide an electrical communications medium to carry electrical signals from the host computer to the disk control unit. In order that the two devices will

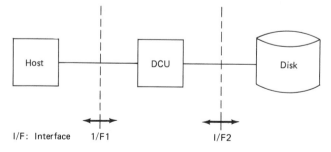

I/F: Interface   I/F1   I/F2   **Figure 7-4** Simple computer system.

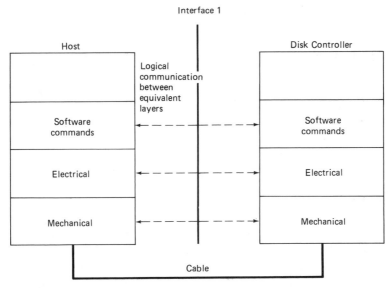

Figure 7-5 Layered interfaces for simple computer system.

operate together, each must use the same electrical signaling convention across the interface. For example, if the host operates at the levels of ± 5 volts (V) and the control unit operates at the level of ± 50 V, something is going to get blown up!

We have thus far established the need for compatibility at two levels: the mechanical level and the electrical level. The purpose of the electrical level is to transfer bits of information from the host to the control unit. The host wishes to transmit a command from a buffer in the host to a buffer in the control unit so that the control unit can execute the command. The command itself consists of a collection of 1s and 0s which must be translated into electrical signals at the electrical interface level. The electrical signals will be transported across the mechanical interface of plugs and sockets and cables to the electrical interface at the other end, where they will be decoded and the corresponding 1s and 0s inserted into the buffer at the disk control unit. Both the host and the disk control unit must speak the same command language if we wish the two devices to operate together. This command language is often referred to as a *protocol*, which defines precisely how data are to be transferred across the interface; of course, we must have compatibility on both sides of the interface.

Hopefully, by now, we have established that for the host and control unit to operate together, we need absolute compatibility at all levels in the interface: the mechanical, electrical, and command language levels. If we have incompatibility at any of these levels, the combination of host and disk control unit will not work.

With the interface that we have been examining, you would find that most of the host computer suppliers have their own interface standards, which means that peripherals from one manufacturer will not operate with the host supplied by another manufacturer. This is fine in the computer industry, where there are a relatively small number of mainframe suppliers. If, however, this principle were to be practiced in the data communications industry, absolute chaos would occur. This is because there are thousands of terminals on the world market, hundreds of modem suppliers, and hundreds of common carriers, and if each did its own thing with interfaces the way mainframe computer suppliers do, it would be very difficult to interface terminals, modems, and so on, to each other.

Consider the simple modem/terminal/network diagram shown in Fig. 7-6. In this diagram three interfaces can be identified. The first, between the host and front-end processor, falls into the category described earlier, in that it is peculiar to the mainframe supplier. The second interface, between the front-end processor and the modem, happens to be the same as the interface between the modem and the visual display terminal. Similarly, the third interface, between the modem and the communication line, is the same at each end of the line. As you can imagine, if all the different suppliers of modems, terminals, and communication lines set up their own standards, chaos would reign supreme. There are therefore standards that have emerged to identify what happens between a modem and a terminal, or between a modem and the communication line.

The interface between the modem and the terminal or between the modem and the front-end processor is usually called the *digital interface*, because this is where the sharp-edged digital signals are transmitted. The interface between the modem and the telephone network is often called the *analog interface*, because this is where the voice-like signals are transmitted.

The following sections identify some of the more common electrical interfaces. Some of the higher-level interface protocols are described in detail in Chapters 12 to 20.

Analog Interfaces. If the carrier supplies the modems and lines as a working end-to-end unit, the user does not need to know much about the electrical char-

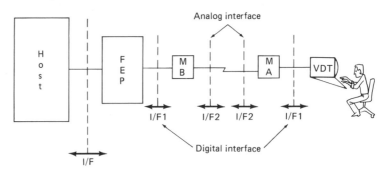

Figure 7-6 Communications network interfaces.

acteristics of the interface. Usually, it is sufficient to know only whether it is a two-wire or a four-wire line, because this gives us an indication of how we can operate the link.

Remember the "rule of thumb": Two wires give us one channel, unless we are using two-wire full-duplex modems. So if you want to run full duplex, you need either a four-wire line or a two-wire line with special modems. Typical two-wire FDX modems are:

CCITT V21	300 bps	Bell 103	300 bps
CCITT V22	1200 bps	Bell 212A	1200 bps
CCITT V32	9600 bps		
CCITT V22 bis	2400 bps	Bell 2400	2400 bps
CCITT V23	1200 bps/75 bps		

If you supply your own modems, it is your responsibility to ensure that the modems and the line will operate as an end-to-end unit. The common carrier supplies lines which have electrical or transmission characteristics which meet a published specification. Matching these modems to these specifications can be a problem, and it is a job best handled by someone with engineering qualifications. In most cases, it is a good idea to arrange to have the modem supplier assume the responsibility for making the end-to-end link work properly.

modulation techniques

Before we look at how modems modulate, we should define some pieces of terminology that frequently crop up in discussions with engineers. These terms are "frequency" and "bandwidth." Engineers drop these words all the time and expect everybody to know exactly what they mean.

Frequency

Take a dry battery, such as that shown in Fig. 7-7(a). If we were to measure the voltage between the terminals of the battery we would find that the voltage is 9 V and stays at this voltage for the lifetime of the battery. If we were to plot a graph showing the voltage of the battery as a function of time, we would find a picture like that shown in Fig. 7-7(b) showing that the voltage is 9 V for the lifetime of the battery.

We call this battery a source of direct-current power. This is because if we were to connect a wire between the two terminals on the battery, electric current would flow through that wire in the same direction until the battery was depleted.

Direct current is the primary power source for most electronic appliances, such as computers, television sets, tape recorders, and so on. The electricity supply authorities, however, find that it is not a good idea to transmit direct current

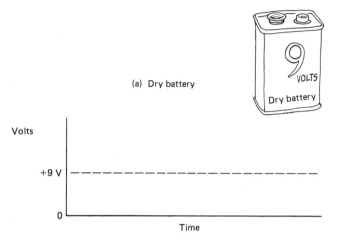

(a) Dry battery

Volts

+9 V — — — — — — — — — — — — — — — — —

0

Time

(b) Direct-current power source—a dry battery

Figure 7-7 (a) Dry battery; (b) direct-current power source—a dry battery.

through the streets from the power station to our homes/offices, because first, it is difficult to change the voltage level of direct-current power, and second, it is unsafe when faults develop.

The mains power is not direct current and, in fact, varies with time in a sinusoidal manner, as illustrated in Fig. 7-8. The mains power is called alternating current because it cycles back and forth starting from zero volts up to a positive maximum, back down to zero, down to a negative maximum, and back to zero again. Each of these excursions from zero to positive back to zero, and negative back to zero, is called one cycle of the sine wave. The repetition wave of these cycles is 60 cycles per second in North America and 50 cycles per second in Europe.

If you were to look up the word "frequency" in a dictionary you would find that the frequency of something is the rate of repetition of that something. In the case of electric power, therefore, the repetition rate of the cycles is either 60

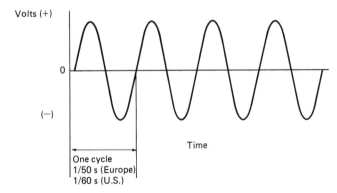

Volts (+)

0

(−)

Time

One cycle
1/50 s (Europe)
1/60 s (U.S.)

Figure 7-8 Alternating current.

cycles per second or 50 cycles per second, depending on whether you are in North America or Europe. This is called the frequency of the electric mains power supply.

Engineers do not like to name their units in such simple terms as "cycles per second." They prefer to name them specially, often after famous people. A certain Mr. Hertz did some work on electromagnetic wave theory and he is honored by having frequency named after him. Therefore, the frequency of the mains power is often said to be 60 hertz, often appreviated to 60 Hz.

Sound Waves. When a human being speaks, he or she produces signal frequencies in the range 30 to 15,000 Hz. The exact range varies from person to person. When it is designing the telephone network, the telephone company does not design the network to carry the full range of signal frequencies that are generated when a person speaks. It would be uneconomical to do so and they find that most of the signal energy generated when a person speaks lies within the range 300 to 3400 Hz, as shown in Fig. 7-9.

Bandwidth

The telephone network is engineered around carrying signals within this range, and we say therefore that the telephone network has a nominal bandwidth of 3000 Hz. Bandwidth is the difference between the upper and lower frequency ranges that the circuit is designed to carry. Although the bandwidth is 3100 cycles, we usually say that the bandwidth is a nominal 3000 Hz.

A bandwidth of 3000 Hz provides sufficient fidelity so that we can recognize the person at the other end of the line. (The more bandwidth we have, the higher the quality or fidelity of reproduction.) Compare the announcer on talk-back radio, who has about a 10,000-Hz bandwidth, with the person on the telephone, who has a 3000-Hz bandwidth.

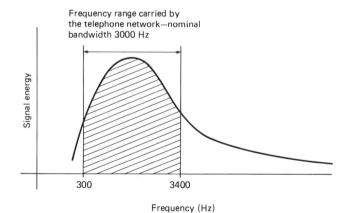

Figure 7-9 Frequency distribution of human speech.

modulation methods

If we modulate one bit of digital information for each cycle of the carrier, this gives the maximum bit rate for a voice channel of about 3000 bps. In reality, we achieve faster bit rates than this because modems can modulate more than one bit per cycle. For example:

2400 bps	V.26	2 bits/cycle at 1200 Hz
4800 bps	V.27	3 bits/cycle at 1600 Hz
9600 bps	V.29	4 bits/cycle at 2400 Hz

As I have indicated before, a modem works by generating a carrier which you can regard as a sine-wave-like signal. Digital data are modulated onto this carrier for transmission along the voice channel. Let us now have a look at how we might modulate digital data onto a sine wave.

The sine wave has three basic characteristics: amplitude, frequency, and phase. The amplitude of a sine wave is a measure of the size of the sine wave measured from the positive peak to the negative peak. This is illustrated in Fig. 7-10, where we see that one signal has a large amplitude and another signal has a smaller amplitude.

Frequency is a measure of the rate of repetition of the cycles of the carrier. As shown in Fig. 7-11, one signal has a high frequency and the other signal has a low frequency. This can be seen when you consider that Fig. 7-11 has a horizontal time scale.

Phase is a measure of the relative timing of the sine wave. In Fig. 7-12 the sine wave drawn with a solid line has a particular amplitude and a particular frequency. The sine wave drawn with a dashed line has the same amplitude and frequency as the first sine wave, but it has a different phase. That is, it goes through its peak at a different time than does the first sine wave. The time difference between the two sine waves going through that peak is a measure of the phase difference between them. This phase change can be expressed in terms of

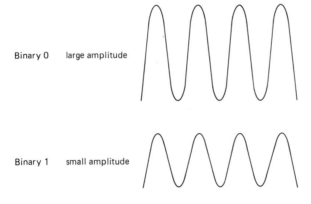

Binary 0   large amplitude

Binary 1   small amplitude

Figure 7-10 Amplitude modulation.

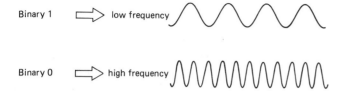

Time

Figure 7-11 Frequency modulation.

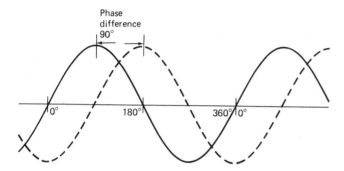

Figure 7-12 Phase modulation.

degrees because one cycle of the sine wave is said to contain 360°, and we can measure the degree of phase shift between the two sine waves. For the sine waves shown in Fig. 7-12 the phase shift between them is 90°.

A modem modulates digital data onto a sine wave by changing one or more of these basic characteristics of the sine wave in sympathy with the incoming digital bit stream. Referring to Fig. 7-13, the transmitting modem takes the incoming digital signal at point 1 and modulates the carrier at point 2 in sympathy with incoming digital signals. Receiving modems detect the changes in characteristics of the carrier at point 3, and reconstitute the digital signal at point 4. Some basic approaches to the modulation of digital signals onto analog sine-wave carriers are described next.

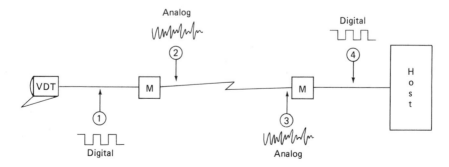

Figure 7-13 Modem operation.

Amplitude modulation

In amplitude modulation systems, the amplitude of the sine wave is varied depending on whether we have a binary 1 or a binary 0 coming into the modems. For example, a binary 1 on the digital side could give a small-amplitude signal on the analog side, and a binary 0 on the digital side could give a large-amplitude signal on the analog side, as shown in Fig. 7-10. The receiving modem can tell the difference between large and small amplitudes and therefore regenerate the signal.

One problem with amplitude modulation is that as the signals pass through the telephone network, they are reduced in size (or attenuated) and at the receiving end, the receiving modem needs to be able to work out whether an incoming small signal is really a small signal or whether it is a large signal that became small. The receiving modem therefore needs to be able to measure the relative amplitudes of the signals rather than the exact amplitudes. Because amplitude modulation is so susceptible to variations in line conditions, it is not often used for data transmission services.

Frequency modulation

Frequency-modulated modems [often called frequency shift keying (FSK) modems] operate by varying the frequency of the analog sine wave in sympathy with the incoming digital signal. For example, an incoming binary 1 could give a low frequency and an incoming binary 0 could give a high frequency, as shown in Fig. 7-11. The receiving modem has a discriminator which allows it to recognize the incoming frequencies corresponding to the 1s and 0s.

Frequency modulation gives much better performance than amplitude modulation because the amplitude of the incoming signal is of no great consequence to the receiving modem as long as it is above a certain threshold. As a comparison, consider the quality of reception of amplitude-modulated radio broadcast compared with the quality of FM radio broadcasts, particularly if there is a thunderstorm while you are listening. You would find that the AM radio suffers badly due to the interference from lightning, whereas FM radio is relatively immune to the lightning strikes because the frequency of the signal is not altered by the lightning. Frequency modulation is most commonly used for low-speed modems at speeds up to 1200 bps.

Phase modulation

Phase modulation modems [often called phase shift keying (PSK) modems] operate by shifting the phase of the analog sine wave in sympathy with the incoming digital signal. The frequency of the sine wave does not change; only the phase is changed as the 1s and 0s come in. In a simple system, for example, a binary 1 may produce a 180° phase shift relative to the preceding phase of the sine wave, whereas a binary 0 will not produce a phase shift at all. This is illustrated in Fig. 7-14, where we see the analog sine-wave signal generated for a digital signal consisting of alternate 1s and 0s. Phase modulation is typically used at 2400 and 4800 bps, and it is also used at 1200 bps in two-wire full-duplex modems.

Capacity of Communications Lines: Bits per Second and Bauds. In computer literature, the terms *bits per second* and *bauds* are often used synonomously. This would not create a problem if everyone used the terms consistently, but communication engineers use the term *baud* differently. I now describe briefly the relationship between bits per second and bauds as seen by a communications engineer. (This description is not absolutely correct technically, but it is a useful way to communicate the idea to nontechnical people.)

The data-carrying capacity of a communications line can be expressed in terms of the maximum amount of information that can be transmitted along that line under ideal conditions. The smallest unit of information that we use is the bit, so it is convenient to express channel capacity in terms of the number of bits per second that the channel can handle. When we send this information down the telephone line, we modulate these data onto a sine-wave-like carrier.

There is a limit to the frequency of sine wave that we can successfully transmit down a normal telephone circuit, and this limit is in the vicinity of 3000 cycles per second (hertz). (A cycle is shown in Fig. 7-8 as being the distance between two contiguous equivalent points on the wave.) In the early modems, the modulation techniques effectively modulated one bit per cycle of the fundamental carrier frequency. Thus a 1200-bps modem used a 1200-Hz carrier. As better modulation techniques were developed, it became possible to modulate more than one bit per cycle of the carrier. Thus a series of 2400-bps modems use a 1200-Hz carrier by modulating two bits per cycle of the carrier. A range of 4800-bps modems modulates three bits per cycle on a 1600-Hz carrier. A range of 9600-bps modems uses a 2400-Hz carrier with four bits per cycle.

Strictly speaking, the baud rate refers to the carrier frequency. Thus the purist would say that the 9600-bps modem referred to previously really uses a 2400-baud carrier. In computer literature, you would see that modem being described as a 9600-baud modem. Because confusion can arise, and because the

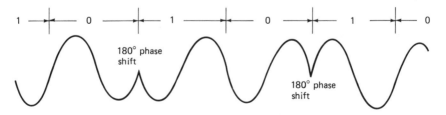

Figure 7-14 Simple phase modulation.

term *bps* is more meaningful, I try to discourage the use of the term *baud*, and it does not appear again in this book (except in the index!).

How Do We Modulate More Than One Bit per Cycle? The 2400-bps modem handles bits in pairs, which are called *dibits*. There are four possible dibit combinations and the modem shifts the phase of a 1200-Hz analog signal in sympathy with the dibits that are being transmitted. These phase shifts are relative to the current phase of the analog signal. The phase shifts for the dibits vary; the following are used only as an example.

Dibit	*Phase shift (deg)*
00	0
01	+90
11	+180
10	+270

If the incoming data stream were

01 11 10 00

the analog signal would be modulated as shown in Fig. 7-15. This shows that the first dibit, 01, requires a phase shift of +90° relative to the preceding phase. The second dibit, 11, requires a phase shift of +180° relative to its preceding phase, and the dibit 11 requires a phase shift of +270° in relation to its preceding phase. The final dibit, 00, requires a 0° phase shift. The resulting analog waveform is also shown.

Those of you who know a little bit about electronics will recognize that high-frequency components will be generated during the abrupt phase shifts of 90, 180, and 270°. These high-frequency components do not survive transmission along the line and the signal becomes distorted by the time it arrives at the other end;

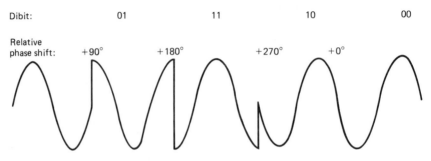

Figure 7-15 Modulating two bits per cycle.

however, the receiving modem has a relatively long time to detect the relative phase shift. It has almost one complete cycle of a sine wave in which to work out that the phase shift has changed from the preceding cycle, and in electronic terms this is an incredibly long time.

Modems rated at 4800 bps operate by handling data bits in threes, called *tribits*. There are eight possible tribit combinations and the modem shifts the phase of the analog signal in 45° increments relative to the preceding phase. A diagram is not given, but you can imagine what it would look like.

Other forms of modulation

Quadrature amplitude modulation (QAM), which is a combination of amplitude modulation and phase modulation, is typically used on 9600-bps modems and on 2400-bps two-wire full-duplex modems. The 9600-bps modem handles bits four at a time. Pure phase modulation is not used because this would require 16 phases, which would necessitate relative phase shifts of 22.5°. Such phase shifts are rather hard to detect, and therefore a technique was evolved that used eight phases and four amplitudes, giving us a combination of amplitude modulation and phase modulation. The resulting waveform is too complicated to draw, so you will just have to believe that it works.

Trellis coded modulation

Trellis coded modulation is a technique used on 14,400-bps and 16,800-bps long-haul modems. This technique involves the modems sending redundant information that allows the effect of some line errors to be minimized. The trellis technique is also too complicated to explain in a book of this nature and the interested reader is referred to the many technical papers available in the engineering literature.

modem/terminal interface—CCITT V.24/RS-232

In Fig. 7-6 we can identify an interface between modem A and the terminal and another between modem B and the computer. The interface between the terminal and the modem consists of a number of wires that carry the various data signals and control signals.

On the world market, there are hundreds of terminal models and also a wide range of modems. To avoid incompatibility problems, some standardized interface specifications have been produced. Perhaps the best known of these is the CCITT V.24 interface specification, which is for speeds up to 20,000 bps, which covers most of our requirements. In the United States, a functionally similar interface is known as the EIA RS-232 interface.

The V.24/RS-232 specifications define the number of wires that are used to connect a modem to a terminal, the electrical signals that are sent along these wires, and the signal levels that are used. We do not go into the operation of the V.24/RS-232 interface in complete detail, but in the following descriptions, we identify the more commonly used signals. We use CCITT terminology, and where the RS-232 terminology is different, it is placed in brackets after the CCITT terminology.

CCITT V.24 and/or EIA RS-232 are the most commonly used modem/terminal interfaces. They are functionally equivalent and cover operation at speeds up to 20,000 bps. CCITT V.35 specifies the modem/terminal interface at 48,000 bps. Newer standards—RS-449, RS-422, and RS-423—are covered later.

Other interfaces that you will see identified on terminal specification sheets include Military Standard 188 and 20-mA current loop. (MIL-STD-188 is similar to the V.24/RS-232 interface, but it is not fully compatible with it. This is a military standard specification and is not normally used in the commercial world.)

Standards

The following are notes on the V.24/RS-232 interface standards. The source for the notes is the relevant standards documentation intended to provide a brief description of the purpose of the individual standards and their relationship to each other.

CCITT V.24. CCITT Recommendation V.24 provides an operational description for a set of interchange signals to allow transfer of serial binary data between data terminal equipment (DTE) and a modem. DTE is a term used in the communications industry to describe anything that is connected to a modem, such as a terminal or a computer port. V.24 makes no attempt to define the electrical characteristics (see V.28) or other physical aspects, such as plug type, pin configurations, cable lengths, and operational speeds. V.24 is a general recommendation that leaves the detailed application to other standards, such as V.28 and RS-232C.

CCITT V.28. CCITT Recommendation V.28 defines the electrical characteristics of the V.24 interface. It is valid up to a speed of 20,000 bps. V.28 defines the electrical characteristics in terms of equivalent circuits, impedances, capacitance, and so on. It is essentially a very technical description of the interface and mades no mention of cable lengths, plug types, pin configurations, and so on.

EIA RS-232C. The EIA standard RS-232C is the complete description of a V.24 interface in practical operation. It is a combination of V.24 and V.28 and adds everything else needed for a practical implementation. As for V.28, it is valid for speeds up to 20,000 bps. The electrical characteristics defined in RS-232C generally reflect those found in V.28.

RS-232 defines 25 circuits as a working group and assigns pin numbers. It does not define the physical plugs and sockets. In fact, the plug and socket type is not defined anywhere; the common 25-pin (DB25) type is standard only by default.

This standard allows for cable lengths of up to 15 meters at up to 20,000 bps. However, it also comments generally that at lower speeds and/or with low-capacitance cable, longer lengths are permissible. It does not give any further assistance in this matter. Not all the wires in the V.24/RS-232 interface are used at any one time; typically, 12 to 16 wires may be used. A complete list of the V.24/RS-232C interface circuits is shown in Table 7-1.

Figure 7-16 illustrates the more important component parts of the V.24/RS-232 interface. On the left of this diagram is shown the *data terminal equipment* (DTE), which is a generic name for the terminals or computers that are connected to the modem. The modem is shown on the right. The eight interface lines shown on the diagram carry the following signals.

- *Data Set Ready—DSR*. This is a control signal from the modem to the DTE which indicates that the modem is switched on and is connected to the line. In other words, the modem is ready to go.
- *Request to Send—RTS*. This signal goes from the DTE to the modem, and as the name implies, it is a request from the DTE for permission to transmit data.
- *Ready for Sending—RFS (Clear to Send—CTS)*. This signal from the modem informs the data terminal equipment that it can start to transmit data.
- *Transmitted Data*. This wire from the DTE to the modem carries the digital data that are to be modulated onto the carrier.

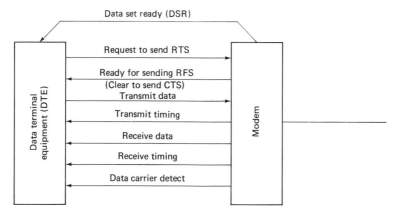

Figure 7-16 Main components of V.24 RS-232 interface.

TABLE 7-1　TYPICAL V.24/RS-232C INTERFACE CONNECTOR PIN ASSIGNMENTS

25-way connector	CCITT circuit numbers	RS-232C equivalent	Circuit name	To or from modem
1	—	AA	Not connected	
2	103	BA	Transmitted Data	To
3	104	BB	Received Data	From
4	105	CA	Request to Send	To
5	106	CB	Ready for Sending	From
6	107	CC	Data Set Ready	From
7	102	AB	Signal Ground or Common Return	Common
8	109	CF	Data Channel Received Line Signal Detector	From
9	—	—	+12 V, 20 mA; available only on some switched network modems	From
10	—	—	−12 V, 20 mA; available only on some switched network modems	From
11	126	—	Select Transmit Frequency	To
12	122	SCF	Backward Channel Received Line Signal Detector	From
13	121	SCB	Backward Channel Ready	From
14	118	SBA	Transmitted Backward Channel Data	To
15	114	DB	Transmitter Signal Element Timing (synchronous service only)	From
16	119	SBB	Received Backward Channel Data	From
17	115	DD	Receiver Signal Element Timing (synchronous services only)	From
18	—	—	Not connected	
19	120	SCA	Transmit Backward Channel Line Signal	To
20	108.1	—	Connect Data Set to Line	To
	108.2	CD	Data Terminal Ready	To
21	110	CG	Signal Quality Detector	From
22	125	CE	Calling Indicator (A/A service)	From
23	111	CH	Data Signaling Rate Selector	To
24	113	DA	Transmitter Signal Element Timing (synchronous service only)	To
25		—	Not connected	

- *Transmit Timing*. This signal from the modem to the data terminal equipment provides timing signals to the terminal so that the data are clocked out of the terminal at the correct speed. As discussed later in the chapter under the heading "Timing Considerations," this signal is not always used.
- *Receive Data*. This wire carries the digital data from the modem to the data terminal equipment. These are the data that the modem has demodulated from the carrier.
- *Receive Timing*. This signal from the modem to the data terminal equipment accompanies the data so that the terminal equipment knows when to sample the incoming received data stream to correctly interpret the bits. The receive timing is derived from the carrier by the modem. As discussed later under the heading "Timing Considerations," this signal is not always used.
- *Data Carrier Detect*. This signal from the modem to the DTE advises the DTE that the modem has locked onto the received carrier and that it is ready to demodulate data.

Speed and distance limitations for V.24/RS-232C

As indicated earlier, there are limitations on both the speed and distance at which these interfaces can work. CCITT defines the maximum speed as being 20,000 bps, and the distance for the interface as being 15 m, equivalent to 50 ft. In reality, the relationship between speed and distance is nonlinear, as illustrated in Fig. 7-17. For operation at the maximum speed of 20,000 bps, the distance of 15 m (50 ft) would apply. For operation at lower speeds, much longer distances can be achieved.

The actual distance that can be achieved on a particular V.24 interface is related to the design of the interface electronics, which may vary from supplier to supplier. Also, the distance/speed ratio depends on the quality of the cable used in the interface. If a low-capacitance cable is used, much longer distances can be achieved between a modem and a terminal on the V.24 interface. Later

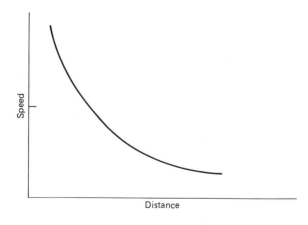

Figure 7-17 Relationship between speed and distance for digital signaling.

we will identify some newer interfaces (RS-423, RS-422, RS-449) which allow us to achieve higher-speed, longer-distance operation than can be achieved with the V.24/RS-232C.

modem operation on a two-wire line

We now examine the sequence of events that takes place in an inquiry and re- sponse transaction using the equipment configuration shown in Fig. 7-18. We assume that the line is a two-wire line and that the terminal is buffered. In this case the operator enters a transaction and then transmits it down the line. The computer receives the message, processes it, and generates a response that is in

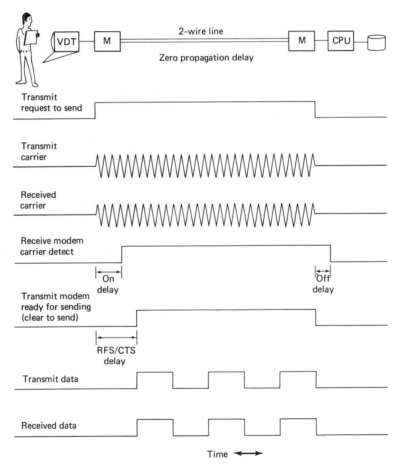

Figure 7-18 Modem timing for two-wire operation—zero propagation delay.

turn transmitted along the same communication channel back to the terminal. If we have only one communication channel between the modems, only one modem can be transmitting at any time. This means that the mode of operation of the modem must be controlled by some means, and this control is exercised, via the interface, by the terminal or computer. While reading the following detailed description of this operation, refer to the timing diagram in Fig. 7-18.

With a buffered terminal, the operator enters transaction data into the terminal, and when he has completed this to his satisfaction, he hits his transmit button. If the terminal is freewheeling, this will cause the terminal to raise its Request-to-Send signal on the V.24/RS-232 interface. If the terminal is controlled, the Request-to-Send will not be raised until the terminal is polled. (Polling is described in Chapter 15.)

The Request-to-Send signal advises the modem that the terminal wants to transmit, and the modem gets ready for transmission by sending the carrier wave down the telephone line. On a short communication line, the carrier wave will appear immediately at the input of the receiving modem. (For longer lines, we encounter a propagation delay, defined later in this chapter.) After a short time, the receiving modem realizes that there is a carrier on the line, and it locks onto the carrier and synchronizes itself to the signal. The receiving modem is now in a condition whereby it can demodulate data from the carrier. The receive modem signals this to its DTE by raising the Data Carrier Detect (DCD) signal. The DCD *On* delay in Fig. 7-18 is effectively the time it takes the receive modem to recognize the presence of the incoming carrier.

To give the receiving modem time to lock onto the carrier, the transmitting modem has a delay built into it. This delay is set to be longer than the DCD *On* delay, and, after it has timed out, the transmitting modem returns a signal called *ready-for-sending* (*clear-to-send*) to the transmitting terminal. This signal tells the terminal that it can proceed to transmit data. The terminal sends its block of data, which is modulated onto the carrier wave by the transmitting modem. The modulated carrier travels along the line and is demodulated by the receiving modem, and the data are passed through to the receiving terminal.

When the sending terminal has finished transmitting the data block, it removes its Request-to-Send signal. This causes the transmit modem to drop both the carrier wave and the Ready-for-Sending (Clear-to-Send) signal. At the receive end, the receiving modem sees both the data and the carrier disappear. After a short delay, the receive modem drops its Data Carrier Detect signal. This delay, known as the DCD *Off* delay, is incorporated to allow the receive modem to coast through a momentary carrier dropout without notifying the DTE that there has been a loss of carrier.

At some stage, perhaps immediately, perhaps after some milliseconds (or longer) have elapsed, the computer will realize that it has received a message that must be processed. This time is called the *computer reaction time*. The computer then processes the message and prepares a response for the terminal. The total time from when the reaction time has elapsed until the computer initiates the transmission of the response message we call the *processing time* (or *computer turnaround time*).

To get the response back to the terminal, the whole process is repeated in the opposite direction. The roles of transmitter and receiver are reversed, and the computer now requests permission to transmit by raising its Request-to-Send signal. This in turn causes the carrier to be sent down the line, the receiving modem locks on and synchronizes itself, and, in order to give the receiver time for this to happen, the transmitting modem waits before returning the Ready-for-Sending (Clear-to-Send) signal. When it receives the Ready-for-Sending (Clear-to-Send) signal, the computer transmits the data, and at the end of the data block, it removes the Request-to-Send, which in turn drops the carrier and drops the Ready-for-Sending (Clear-to-Send). At this point, the terminal has received the response message.

The time delay built into the transmitting modem is called the *ready-for-sending* (*clear-to-send*) delay and is often merely called the *modem turnaround time*. The entire sequence, as described, included *two* modem turnaround times for each transaction.

In real-life systems, we would most likely have some form of automatic error detection and correction mechanism built into the system so that each data block that is transmitted is acknowledged after it is correctly received. This means that the sequence of events would be similar to the following. The operator enters a transaction into the terminal and hits the transmit button, which causes the data to be transmitted down the line after the modem turnaround time has elapsed. When the computer receives the message, it checks it out for validity and responds with an acknowledge signal, which is transmitted after the modem turnaround time has elapsed. In the meantime, the computer is "thinking"—that is, processing the transaction and preparing an output message. When the output message is ready, it is transmitted after the modem turnaround time has elapsed. When the message has been correctly received by the terminal, it responds with an acknowledgment to advise the computer that the message was correctly received. (The mechanism for supervising the flow of data along a line is covered in detail in Chapters 12 to 20.)

If the computer processing time is longer than the modem turnaround time, we would probably be able to overlap the two functions so that the performance of the system with acknowledgments would not be markedly different from the performance of the simple system outlined initially with no acknowledgments.

block-by-block data transfer

It is quite common for remote data entry systems to transmit large numbers of blocks of data from one point to another. In this case, under error-free conditions, the sequence of events is as follows. The transmitting site sends a block of data that is checked out for errors by the receiver; if it passes the test, it is acknowledged. This tells the transmitter that it can transmit the next block, and the sequence of events proceeds with a block being transmitted and acknowledged, the next block being transmitted and acknowledged, and so on.

Over a two-wire communication network, you can see that we would be faced with two modem turnaround times for each block that is transmitted. Depending on the length of the blocks and the length of the modem turnaround times, we may or may not get efficient data transmission. The efficiency of the data transmission can be affected by the modem turnaround time and by other delays in the system, because all the delays reduce the ratio of time spent actually transmitting a data block to the time it takes to send a block and receive its acknowledge. Some of the other delays that can be encountered are listed in the following.

- *Propagation delay* is the time it takes to get the signal from one end of the line to the other. It takes a finite length of time for the electrical signals to travel along a communication line. On terrestrial lines, this delay is about 10 to 15 microseconds (μs) per mile (depending on the type of communication bearer used), and, on satellite links, it is approximately 250 to 300 milliseconds (ms) per satellite hop.

  Figure 7-19 shows what would happen to the sequence of events in Fig. 7-18 if the line has an appreciable propagation delay. In this diagram the propagation delay (T_p) must elapse before any signal fed into the line at one end appears at the other end. You can see how the receive carrier is delayed by T_p with respect to the transmit carrier.

  The diagram shows Ready-for-Sending (Clear-to-Send) being returned to the transmitting terminal before the carrier has reached the receive terminal. This does not present a problem as long as the receive modem can synchronize itself in less time than the Ready-for-Sending delay. In other words, the receive modem will be synchronized by the time the data reach it.

- *Modem delay* is the time from when the digital signal is presented to the V.24/RS-232 interface until the modulated carrier appears on the line. There is a similar delay while the receiving modem demodulates the incoming signal. The value of the delay varies depending on the type of modem used. Unless we know the exact figure for a particular pair of modems, we generally assume a figure of 10 to 15 ms per modem pair for the modem delay.

- *Reaction time* of the terminal equipment or the computer at each end of the line is the time it takes for the terminal (computer) to realize that it has received some data and that an acknowledgment has to be sent or that some other action has to be taken on the data.

- *Other delays* can be encountered in the communication network due to the physical nature of the components used in setting up a network. These delays should be established and used in any analyses that are performed.

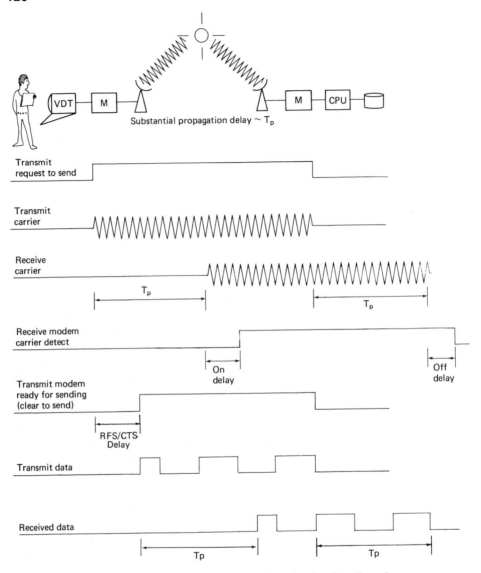

Figure 7-19 Modem timing—two-wire operation showing the effect of propagation delay (T_p).

Example 7-1: Throughput Efficiency of a Simple Point-to-Point Link

Let us examine a situation in which we are transmitting data blocks that take 1 s to transmit over a distance of 500 miles with a modem turnaround time of 250 ms. The total time it would take to send a block and acknowledge it could be computed as follows:

	Elapsed time (ms)
Modem turnaround time	250
Block transmission time	1000
Modem delay	10
Propagation delay (at 1.5 ms/100 mi)	7.5
Receiving terminal reaction time	2
Modem turnaround time	250
ACK transmission time	50
Modem delay	10
Propagation delay	7.5
Transmitting terminal reaction time	2
Total	1589

Solution   The *throughput efficiency* can be calculated by comparing the time spent transmitting data to the total time it takes to send a block and receive its acknowledgment:

$$throughput\ efficiency = \frac{1000}{1589} = 63\%$$

This, of course, assumes error-free transmission. In real life we would get some errors that would cause retransmission, which would reduce the efficiency slightly. The normal situation is error-free transmission with less than 1% of data blocks being corrupted, so that we can generally ignore the effect of errors on throughput efficiency.

The modem turnaround time varies depending on the style of the modem, the speed of the line, and so on. The figure of 250 ms used in the example referred to one of the earlier 1200-bps modems, which was quite widely used.

modem operation on the dial-up telephone network

Figure 7-20 shows an artist's impression of one end of a dial-up telephone network connection. On the right we have the communication line, which in the case of the dial-up network is a two-wire line. Then we have the modem, which has a transmit modulator and a receive demodulator, and notice that there is a switch in front of the modem which allows either the modem or a telephone instrument to be connected to the telephone line. On the left of the diagram is the terminal connected to the modem via the V.24/RS-232 interface.

For the time being, let us assume that the terminal is a buffered freewheeling device. The buffered part means that as the characters are entered onto the terminal keyboard, they are stored in the terminal and not transmitted until the operator hits the transmit button. The freewheeling part means that there is no

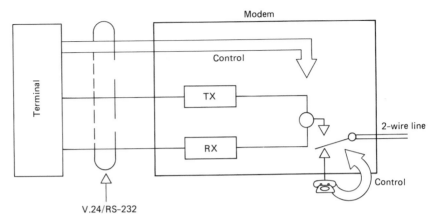

V.24/RS–232

Figure 7-20 One end of a switched network line.

communication protocol employed in this particular terminal, so that when the operator hits the transmit button the terminal tries to send the data immediately.

Let us now examine the operation of the V.24 interface across this link between the terminal and the modem. The quiescent state of a modem is that it is in "receive" mode. If you were to take a modem out of its packing container, connect it to a communication line, plug it into the wall, and switch it on, the modem would come up in receive mode. We need to do something to it to turn it into "transmit" mode. This is the purpose of the Request-to-Send signal.

To set up a call, the operator takes the telephone and dials the number (Fig. 7-20). The telephone is connected to the communication line, so it can be used like a conventional telephone. When the number answers, the operator has to activate a control function to flick the switch that will disconnect the telephone and connect the modem to the communication line. This control function in the

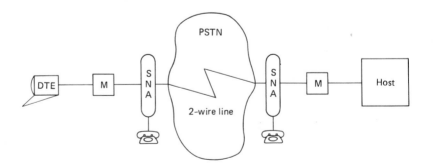

SNA: switched network adapter
PSTN: public switched telephone network

Figure 7-21 Another switched network configuration.

V.24 interface is called Connect Data Set to Line or Data Terminal Ready and is activated on pin 20 of the 25-pin connector. Connect Data Set to Line can be activated in a number of ways. First, some modems have a pushbutton; when you push the button, the switch is flicked automatically. Some terminals have a pushbutton that will activate the Connect Data Set to Line signal through the V.24 interface and operate the switch. Finally, the telephone itself may have a pushbutton or the telephone may be sitting on a little box that has pushbuttons and also contains the switch. Regardless of where the switch is, we must find it and press it. This activates Connect Data Set to Line, flicks the switch, and disconnects the telephone.

At this point we have the modem connected to the telephone line, and assuming that the modem is plugged into the wall and switched on, the modem will then send a signal called Data Set Ready across the interface to the terminal. Data Set Ready means that the modem is switched on and connected to the line. In the case of a leased-line modem, Data Set Ready automatically comes up when the modem is switched on.

The terminal operator can now enter data into the terminal and hit the transmit button. When he hits the transmit button, Request-to-Send is activated across the interface, which switches on the transmit modulator, which sends carrier down the line. At the other end we have an equivalent arrangement of modem and terminal, and the receiving modem detects the presence of carrier and synchronizes and gets ready to demodulate data. In the meantime, we receive Ready-for-Sending back at the terminal, the terminal transmits the data across the digital interface, the data get modulated onto the carrier, it goes down the line, and at the other end it is demodulated. When the terminal finishes transmitting data, it knows that it is finished and removes Request-to-Send, which switches off the transmit modulator and we lose Ready-for-Sending. The modem is now in receive mode and if a carrier were to appear from the other end of the line, the modem would synchronize to it and get ready to demodulate data.

In the situation we described, the switch that allows the telephone or the modem to be connected to the line is contained within the modem. In many cases the switch is outside the modem, as illustrated in Fig. 7-21. Here we have a device known as a *switched network adapter* (SNA), which sits between the modem and the communications network. The SNA contains the switching equipment, which allows either the telephone or the modem to be connected to line. In addition, the SNA may have automatic answering equipment built in so that the modem can answer the telephone automatically when a call comes in.

four-wire point-to-point operation

Modem turnaround time can have a significant effect on data throughput and on system response time. To minimize these effects, we can build our network using a *four-wire* communication line, as shown in Fig. 7-22. The four-wire line effec-

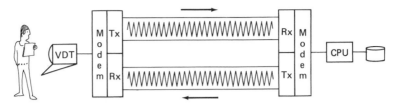

Figure 7-22 Four-wire line configuration.

tively gives us *two* communication channels, which means that we can transmit along one channel and receive on the other. This means that each modem can have its carrier running at all times because the carriers, being on different channels, will not interfere with each other. In this situation, when the terminal wishes to transmit data, it can send the data straight into the modem. The data will go through the modem down the line without getting involved in modem turnaround times. Similarly, when the computer is ready to transmit, it can send the data straight out without encountering the modem turnaround time.

It is a very common practice to configure networks this way because it so happens that, owing to the nature of the telephone network, most long-haul lines come out of the network as four-wire lines. So given that we have four-wire capability in the network, we should use it to the utmost efficiency. (In some systems, the computers or terminals cannot tolerate what is effectively an instantaneous modem turnaround. They like to go through the request-to-send/ready-for-sending sequence, and sometimes a fake delay is built in to satisfy the terminal equipment even though the modem may have its carrier running all the time.)

There are two basic approaches to achieving a state where we have the modem carrier running all the time. First, we can strap up Request-to-Send internally within the modem, in which case we say that the modem is running with *permanent carrier*. Alternatively, we can activate Request-to-Send from the computer or from the terminal, and just keep the Request-to-Send up all the time. Although functionally this provides us with continuous carrier just as in the permanent carrier case, this situation is called *controlled carrier operation*. In other words, the carrier is being controlled via the V.24 interface.

Although permanent carrier and controlled carrier operation seem to be very similar, there are some differences between these two modes of operation. Some modems actually talk to each other in relation to their own status. For example, consider a four-wire point-to-point line running permanent carrier. When we first switch on the modems, they go through what is known as a *training sequence*. The training sequence is a particular startup process that the modems go through to allow the receiving modem, first, to synchronize itself to the incoming carrier, and then to set its automatic equalizer (if it has an equalizer). Typically, the synchronization and equalization take place by the transmitting modem sending out a predetermined set of signal frequencies so that the receiving modem can tune itself to the incoming carrier, and then the transmitting modem sends out a predetermined bit pattern so that the receiving modem can determine from the received bit pattern how to set its equalizer to correct for any errors that have occurred on the line.

Once the receiving modem has synchronized and equalized itself, it will stay in synchronization for the rest of the call. However, disturbances on the line can cause carrier dropouts and, if the carrier dropout lasts for a relatively long time, when the carrier finally returns, it could be that the receiving modem will have lost synchronization and will not be able to reestablish synchronization. Generally speaking, to reestablish synchronization, we need to initiate a new training sequence from the transmitting modem. The transmitting modem, of course, is unaware of the fact that the receiving modem has lost sync and it continues merrily on its way transmitting the normal carrier.

Some modems talk to each other, such that when the receiving modem detects the fact that it has lost synchronization, it can transmit a signal on the other channel, which is often called a "cry for help." The cry for help is typically a particular bit pattern contained within the main data stream, and that is interpreted by the transmitting modem as meaning: "Hey, I've lost synchronization; please retrain me." The transmitting modem then sends out the training pattern to resynchronize the receiving modem.

This conversation takes place between the modems and it is generally unknown to the operators. One problem, of course, is that when the cry-for-help routine is a bit pattern within the data stream, it is possible for the normal transmit data to look like the cry-for-help routine, which will cause a retraining sequence to happen on the reverse channel. If this happens while we are transmitting data on the reverse channel, the data will be corrupted. Quite often the modems talk to each other for other reasons, so before buying your modems, it is worthwhile investigating what conversations, if any, take place between them.

Typically, the cry-for-help routine operates with permanent carrier operation only. When running under controlled carrier, the cry for help does not work because normally under controlled carrier the Request-to-Send will be switched on and off quite frequently. Every time Request-to-Send is switched on, the modem will automatically send out a training sequence so that the receiving modem can retrain itself properly.

The four-wire line shown in Fig. 7-22 gives full-duplex capability in the line. This means that the combination of modems and the four-wire line is capable of transmitting and receiving data simultaneously. However, the entire system, comprised of terminals, modem/line/modem, and computer, would be a full-duplex system only if the terminal and computer were capable of transmitting and receiving simultaneously. It is very common to have half-duplex terminals connected to computers with four-wire lines, and in this case the entire system is a half-duplex system.

To compare the efficiency of transmission of this type of network with the previous one, let us reexamine the time delays for the same data transmission.

The time it would take to transmit a block and receive an acknowledgment would be computed as follows:

	Elapsed time (ms)
Block transmission time	1000
Modem delay	10
Propagation delay	7.5
Receiving terminal reaction time	2
ACK transmission time	50
Modem delay	10
Propagation delay	7.5
Transmitting terminal reaction time	2
Total	1089

$$\textit{throughput efficiency} = \frac{1000}{1089} = 92\%$$

This is a significant increase in performance over the system with the modem turnaround time involved.

four-wire multipoint networks

Another way of improving the utilization of expensive communications lines is to put more than one terminal on the line. One method of achieving this is to use a *multipoint* or *multidrop* line. A line with three drops is shown in Fig. 7-23. In this case, the computer can be called the *central site* or the *instation*, and the terminal equipment can be called the *remote sites* or *outstations*. The instation modem is connected to the outstation modems by a four-wire line. (A two-wire multipoint network can be set up, but the most common arrangement is the one shown.)

The two-wire circuit connecting the transmit side of the instation modem to the receive sides of the outstation modems is called the *outbound* or *broadcast channel*. The two-wire circuit connecting the receive side of the instation modem and the transmit side of the outstation modems is called the *inbound channel*.

On the broadcast channel, the instation modem can have its carrier running all the time. This is because there is only one source of carrier on this channel. All the outstation modems will be synchronized, and each remote terminal will see all the messages that go along the broadcast channel. A given terminal will recognize or accept only a message that has its own address—that is what *polling* and *selecting* are all about (see Chapter 15).

On the inbound channel, there are many potential sources of carrier, because any of the outstations can transmit data to the central site. If we had a situation

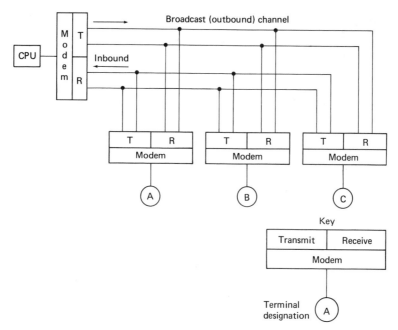

Figure 7-23 Four-wire multidrop line.

in which two remote sites were transmitting at the same time, the signals from the modems would collide on the lines. This would "garble" the signal so that the instation modem could not recognize it. This is a *contention* situation, which can be defined as a situation that arises on a channel when two or more stations attempt to transmit at the same time. To resolve contention, we use the technique known as *polling*, which (as described in Chapter 15) allows us to maintain an orderly flow of data on the line with only one terminal transmitting at a given time. A typical exchange sequence on such a line is as follows.

The computer wishes to solicit information from terminal A, so it sends out a polling sequence containing A's address. All outstations see the message, but all except A ignore it. After the terminal *reaction time* has elapsed (i.e., after the terminal works out that it has received a message and must do something about it), the terminal decides to respond. The response could be a data message or a *no-traffic response*, depending on whether the terminal has data to send. The terminal raises its Request-to-Send, and the modem goes through the sequence of events as described earlier for the two-wire point-to-point network. It raises its carrier, which ultimately appears at the instation modem, which then proceeds to synchronize itself and perhaps also to *equalize* itself (equalization is discussed in Chapter 10).

After the Ready-for-Sending (Clear-to-Send) delay, the outstation modem tells the terminal that it can transmit. The terminal sends the message, which is then received by the central site. After its reaction time, the central site will probably respond with an acknowledgment. This will go straight out because the carrier is already running on the broadcast channel. This sequence of events is repeated every time a terminal is polled.

The mode of operation of the line is highly dependent on the polling logic employed; some of these approaches are discussed in Chapter 15. To estimate the performance of the network, we need to establish potential sources of time delays and the size of these delays and incorporate these into any calculations that we make.

Line splitters for multipoint operation

Leased lines can be point-to-point or multipoint. By using suitable line-splitting equipment, we can extend the one line to a number of locations to set up a multipoint line. Figure 7-24 shows such an arrangement. The line splitter usually resides in a telephone exchange. As shown in the figure, on the outgoing

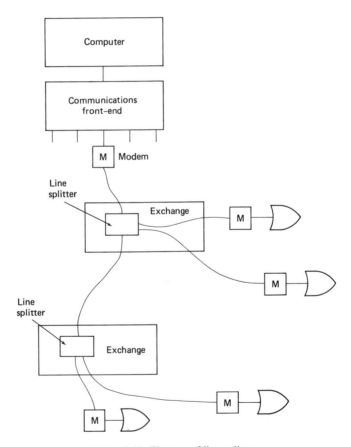

Figure 7-24 The use of line splitters.

route from the computer, it splits the line into three at the first exchange to pick up two terminals and to send the line on the second exchange, where it is split into two to pick up the remaining two terminals. On the inbound channel, the second line splitter would combine the channels from the two modems into one, and the first line splitter would combine the three channels into one to go back to the computer. A line splitter is one of the components that can introduce a delay into the communication process; if possible, the value of this delay should be established with the carrier.

Digital splitters for multipoint operation

A digital splitter, or modem sharing unit, is a device that allows a number of terminals to share a single modem port. In effect, this allows us to set up a multipoint configuration as shown in Fig. 7-25. The diagram shows four terminals connected to a modem via a modem sharing unit. The modem sharing unit allows any one of the terminals to have access to the modem for data transfer, and during this operation the other terminals are excluded. Normally, the way the modem sharing unit works is as follows. The terminals typically have addresses A, B, C, and D, and the computer polls the terminals under the control of the link protocol. The computer may poll terminal A, which wishes to respond, and it first must raise the Request-to-Send signal in the V.24 interface. The Request-to-Send is passed through the modem sharing unit to the modem and a Clear-to-Send signal from the modem is passed back to terminal A. Terminal A can now transmit data. While the combination of Request-to-Send and Clear-to-Send exists between terminal A and the modem, the other terminals are excluded from operation. When terminal A finally removes Request-to-Send, one of the other terminals could transmit data if it wished.

Generally, digital splitters are used in a polled environment; however, they could be used in a contention mode environment, in which case the terminal that brings up Request-to-Send first is the one that will get access to the modem; other terminals will have to wait until the first terminal has finished transmitting data and removes Request-to-Send.

Other configurations for the use of digital splitters allow us to set up multipoint lines as indicated in Fig. 7-26. Here we have a point-to-point line from a

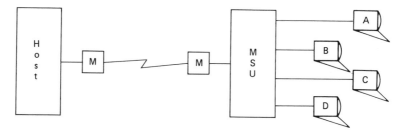

Figure 7-25 Modem sharing unit, or digital splitter.

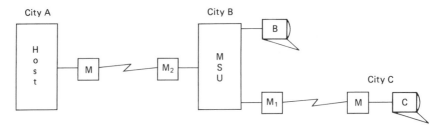

Figure 7-26 Digital splitter (modem-sharing unit) used in multipoint network.

host to location A, where we have a digital splitter which allows us to pick up a single terminal B, and also a modem tail going off to location C. Either terminal B or C could be communicating back to the central site, with contention between the two devices being resolved by the digital splitter. If terminal B wishes to communicate, it will bring up Request-to-Send, which will be passed through to the modem, and the Clear-to-Send from the modem will be returned to terminal B. Terminal B can now transmit. Later, if terminal C wished to transmit, it would bring up Request-to-Send into its modem and would receive Clear-to-Send back from the modem. In the meantime, modem M1 at the other end of the tail going out to terminal C would send Carrier-Detect into the modem sharing unit, which would be presented to modem M2 as Request-to-Send. Terminal C can now transmit and terminal B would be excluded.

two-wire multidrop lines

For economic reasons, some networks have two-wire multidrop lines, as shown in Fig. 7-27. Unless the modems are capable of deriving two channels from the two-wire line, we have only one channel. This means that only one modem can have its carrier running at any instant, which in turn means that the carriers on

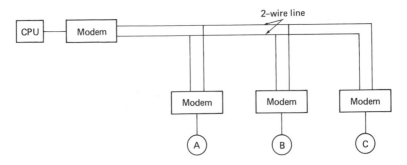

Figure 7-27 Two-wire multidrop line.

all modems must be controlled. We therefore encounter a Ready-for-Sending (Clear-to-Send) delay every time the computer wishes to transmit, as well as when a terminal wishes to transmit.

RS-449/422/423 interfaces

As indicated earlier, the V.24/RS-232C interface has speed and distance limitations. Newer standards that allow higher-speed, longer-distance operation are the RS-422, RS-423, and RS-449. These are standards produced by the American Electronics Industries Association. CCITT has equivalent recommendations: V.10 and X.26 are equivalent to RS-423, and V.11 and X.27 are equivalent to RS-422.

The following table summarizes this equivalency. (The distances in meters refer to the CCITT recommendations; the distances in feet refer to RS-423/422.)

Distance (m)	RS-423 V.10 X.26	RS-422 V.11 X.27	Distance (ft)
1,000	1,000	100,000	4,000
100	10,000	1,000,000	
10	100,000	10,000,000	40

Standards

EIA RS-423 (CCITT V.10 and X.26). The RS-423 standard defines the "electrical characteristics of unbalanced voltage digital interface circuits." "Unbalanced" refers to the fact that, like RS-232, it uses only one wire per interface signal plus a common return. In this respect, then, it is much more compatible with RS-232C. To effect a conversion is almost simply a matter of accommodating the different plug sizes.

As for RS-422, this standard does not define signals, pin configurations, or plug types. It is merely a description of the electrical characteristics of the interface.

The cable length/speed performance trade-off is given in graphical form in the standard. This shows that the maximum speed is 100 kbps. At speeds up to 1000 bps, 4000 ft of cable can be used. Above this speed the cable length drops off, until at the maximum speed (100 kbps), only 40 ft of cable is allowed. Although these speeds are considerably less than those of RS-422, they still represent a major improvement over RS-232. As mentioned before, RS-422 and RS-423 can coexist on different wires (or wire pairs) within the same cable sheath.

TABLE 7-2 RS-449A, RS-232C, AND CCITT V.24 EQUIVALENCY CHART

RS-449A function	37-pin	Abbr.	25-pin	Abbr.	Code	V.24 number Shd.	Dir.	RS-232C/V.24 function
Shield	1	—	1	RG	AA	—	—	Protective Ground
Signaling Rate Indicator	2	SI	12	—	CI	112	To DTE	Data Signal Rate Selector (CH or CI)
—	3	Spare	—	—	—	—	—	
Send Data	4	SD	2	TD	BA	103	To DCE	Transmitted Data
Send Timing	5	ST	15	TC	DB	114	To DTE	Transmit Clock (DCE source)
Receive Data	6	RD	3	RD	BB	104	To DTE	Received Data
Request to Send	7	RS	4	RTS	CA	105	To DCE	Request to Send
Receive Timing	8	RT	17	RC	DD	115	To DTE	Receive Clock
Clear to Send	9	CS	5	CTS	CB	106	To DTE	Clear to Send
Local Loopback	10	LL	—	—	—	141	To DCE	
Data Mode	11	DM	6	DSR	CC	107	To DTE	Data Set Ready
Terminal Ready	12	TR	20	DTR	CD	108	To DCE	Data Terminal Ready
Receiver Ready	13	RR	8	DCD	CF	109	To DTE	Carrier Detect
Remote Loopback	14	RL	—	—	—	140	To DCE	
Incoming Call	15	IC	22	RI	CE	125	To DTE	Ring Indicator
Select Frequency/ Signaling Rate Selector	16	SF/ SR	23	—	CH/ CI	111/ 112	To DCE/ To DTE	Data Signal Rate Selector/ Data Signal Rate Selector
Terminal Timing	17	TT	24	TC	DA	113	To DCE	Transmit Clock (DTE Source)
Test Mode	18	TM	—	—	—	142	To DTE	
Signal Ground	19	SG	7	SG	AB	102	—	

Name	Pin	Abbr.						Description
Receive Common	20	RC	7	SG	AB	102	To DTE	Signal Ground
—	21	Spare	—	—	—	—	—	
RS-422 Return Lead	22	SD	—	—	—	—	To DCE	
RS-422 Return Lead	23	ST	—	—	—	—	To DTE	
RS-422 Return Lead	24	RD	—	—	—	—	To DCE	
RS-422 Return Lead	25	RS	—	—	—	—	To DCE	
RS-422 Return Lead	26	RT	—	—	—	—	To DTE	
RS-422 Return Lead	27	CS	—	—	—	—	To DCE	
Terminal in Service	28	IS	25	—	CN	135	To DTE	Busy out
RS-422 Return	29	DM	—	—	—	—	To DCE	
RS-422 Return	30	TR	—	—	—	—	To DTE	
RS-422 Return	31	RR	—	—	—	—	To DCE	
Select Standby	32	SS	—	—	—	116	To DTE	
Signal Quality	33	SQ	21	SQ	CG	110	To DCE	Signal Quality Detector
New Signal	34	NS	18	NS	—	136	To DCE	New Sync
RS-422 Return	35	TT	—	—	—	—	To DTE	
Standby Indicator	36	SB	—	—	—	117	To DCE	
Send Common	37	SC	7	SG	AB	102	To DCE	Signal Ground

9-Pin Common

Name	Pin	Abbr.						Description
Shield	1	Shd.	1	FG	AA	Shd.	—	Frame Ground
Secondary Receiver Ready	2	SRR	12	—	SCF	122	To DTE	Secondary Carrier Detect
Secondary Send Data	3	SSD	14	—	SBA	118	To DCE	Secondary Transmitted Data
Secondary Receive Data	4	SRD	16	—	SBB	119	To DTE	Secondary Received Data
Signal Ground	5	SG	7	SG	AB	102	To DCE	Signal Ground
Receive Common	6	RC	7	SG	AB	102B	To DTE	
Secondary Request to Send	7	SRS	19	SRS	SCA	120	To DCE	Secondary Request to Send
Secondary Clear to Send	8	SCS	13	SCS	SCB	121	To DTE	Secondary Clear to Send
Send Common	9	SC	7	SG	AB	102A	To DCE	

EIA RS-422 (CCITT V.11 and X.27). RS-422 is the EIA standard that defines the "electrical characteristics of balanced voltage digital interface circuits." It is a standard that allows higher speeds, up to 10 Mbps, and longer distances, up to 4000 ft, on the DTE/DCE interface. In practical application, the cabling difference is that each signal uses two physical wires, in contrast to RS-232, where each signal uses a single wire plus a common return. By some electrical/electronic magic, this allows better top-end performance.

It should be noted that this standard does not define interface signals, plug types, or how the interface should transfer and control data. Like CCITT V.28, it is simply a description of the electrical characteristics of the interface. The standard provides a graph of cable length versus data rate which shows that up to 100 kbps a maximum length of 4000 ft is allowed. This then drops off until at 10 Mbps the allowable distance is 40 ft—a substantial improvement over RS-232 operation.

RS-422 was developed together with RS-423, and it is permissible for interchange circuits operating at each of these standards to be located in the same cable sheath. RS-422 is not compatible with RS-232 except through a specially constructed interface converter.

EIA RS-449. We have seen the purpose of RS-422 and RS-423, but do we put it into effect? RS-449 provides the missing information, such as signal descriptions, plug types, pin configurations, and so on. In this respect, then, RS-449 is the umbrella standard for RS-422 and RS-423. It is, in effect, analogous to the relationship between RS-232/V.24 and V.28. RS-449, which provides for data rates up to 2 Mbps, defines 30 interface signals and describes their operation on the interface.

The combination of RS-449, RS-422, and/or RS-423 was originally intended to eventually replace RS-232C operation. Given the enormous current investment in RS-232, however, this is not going to happen overnight, but the speed/distance performance under the new standards is greatly enhanced.

Some of these circuits have no RS-232 equivalent, but most can be seen to be analogous to RS-232 signals. All the names have been changed to avoid confusion.

Ten of the RS-449 signals are defined as category 1 circuits. These include all the major data and timing signals, such as Send Data, Receive Data, Terminal Timing, and so on. These are the signals that suffer most from signal degradation with speed, cable length, and so on. For Category 1 circuits at speeds of up to 20,000 bps, either RS-422 or RS-423 can be used. At speeds above 20,000 bps (2 Mbps is the maximum), RS-422 must be used.

The remaining 20 circuits are classified as category 2 and all use the RS-423 standard. These signals tend to be those whose binary state is not altered at a high rate and are therefore not as susceptible to the capacitance effect of long cables. Category 2 circuits include such signals as Signal Quality and Signaling Rate Selection.

RS-449 defines in detail the physical plug and pin connections (unlike RS-232C) (see Table 7-2). The connectors used have 37 pins for the primary channel and a 9-pin connector for secondary channel operation. The connectors used are similar to those of RS-232 fame.

balanced and unbalanced voltage digital interfaces

When sending electrical signals along a cable we need two pieces of wire: one for the signal to go out and along, and the other for the signal to return. These wires are often called the "go" and "return" wires. In interfaces such as V.24 and RS-423, each interface cable has one wire and they all use a common return wire, often called the *signal ground*. A simplified diagram is shown in Fig. 7-28. A digital signal being transmitted from the terminal to the host changes the voltage of transmit wire relative to the ground, depending on whether you have 1s or 0s being transmitted, and at the receiving end the host measures the relative voltage between the incoming receive wire and the signal ground. Theoretically, the signal ground should be at the same voltage level at each end, and it should never change. When interference occurs, the signal on the transmit lead fluctuates in sympathy with the interfering electrical signal, while the signal ground lead stays at the same voltage level as it was before. The result is that we get a noisy signal that can be misinterpreted by the host.

In a balanced voltage interface signal, as shown in Fig. 7-29, we actually used two separate wires for each signal so that the Go and Return wires were dedicated to the one signal. In this case the signaling used on the wires is called a *differential mode*, where we measure the voltage change between the two wires. The 1s and 0s being transmitted from the terminal change the voltage on the wires, and at the other end the host detects the difference in voltage between the two wires. Typically, the two wires are twisted together so that they are in close proximity, and if electrical interference occurs, it interferes with both wires at the same time and in the same manner. This means that the voltage level on both wires changes together and the relative voltage difference between them stays

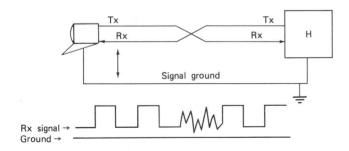

Unbalanced: V24/V28, RS–423

Figure 7-28 Unbalanced signaling.

Balanced: RS–422, V35

Figure 7-29 Balanced signaling.

the same. This gives a higher degree of noise immunity to circuits using balanced voltage signaling. The result is that circuits can be run at much higher speeds and achieve longer distances than can be achieved with unbalanced signaling.

It is possible, and in fact recommended, that both balanced and unbalanced voltage circuits be mixed within the same cable. For example, signals that change frequently, such as transmit data, received data, transmit clock, and receive clock, can be transmitted using the balanced mode of signaling, whereas signals that change infrequently, such as request-to-send, clear-to-send, and carrier detect, can be transmitted adequately using unbalanced signaling. This mixture reduces the physical bulk, and thus the cost, of the interface cable.

multistream modems

As described in Chapter 4 some presently available modems have enhancements such as built-in *time division multiplexers* (TDMs). A time division multiplexer allows the modem data stream to be split into a number of data streams running at slower speeds. For example, it is quite common for a 9600-bps modem to enable the data to be split into multiples of 2400 bps as follows:

$$1 \times 9600 \text{ bps} = 2 \times 4800 \text{ bps, } or$$

$$= 1 \times 4800 \text{ bps} + 2 \times 2400 \text{ bps, } or$$

$$= 1 \times 7200 \text{ bps} + 1 \times 2400 \text{ bps, } or$$

$$= 4 \times 2400 \text{ bps}$$

In most countries it is generally less expensive to install one 9600-bps line than it is to install four 2400-bps lines or any other multiple of 2400 bps. Multistream modems can therefore save us money by allowing us to make more efficient use of the available communication resource.

An example showing two solutions to the same problem is given in Fig. 7-30. Suppose that an organization has a computer in one city and a requirement for two clusters of terminals each operating at 4800 bps in another city; the old approach to solving this problem would be to install two 4800-bps lines, as shown in Fig. 7-30(a). Using multistream modems, one 9600-bps line can be run between the two cities, and the TDM feature in the modems can split the 9600-bps bit stream into two 4800-bps streams, as shown in Fig. 7-30(b), which would provide the same facility as shown in Fig. 7-30(a) but at a lower cost. The user may elect

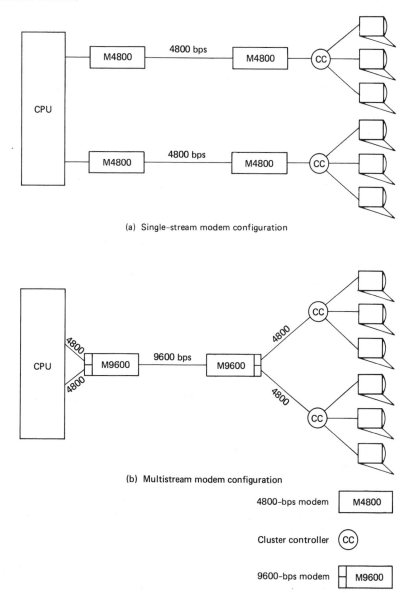

(a) Single–stream modem configuration

(b) Multistream modem configuration

4800-bps modem   M4800

Cluster controller   CC

9600-bps modem   M9600

Figure 7-30 (a) Single-stream modem configuration; (b) multistream modem configuration.

to go for the configuration in Fig. 7-30(a) because of the increased reliability it may offer. In this case, the user should specifically ask the common carrier to route the lines over physically separate paths. This is because if they go over the same physical route, a single cable fault caused by a shovel or bulldozer could take both circuits out of service.

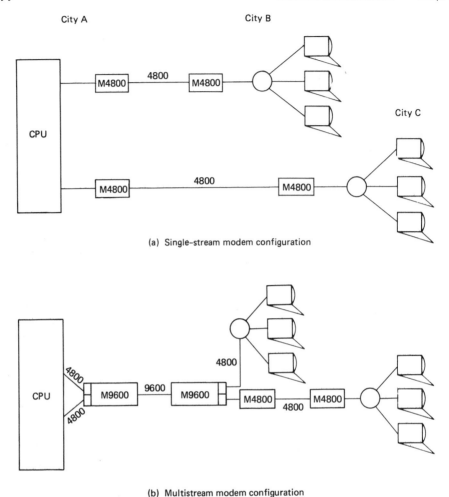

(a) Single–stream modem configuration

(b) Multistream modem configuration

Figure 7-31 (a) Single-stream modem configuration; (b) multistream modem configuration.

Another example, shown in Fig. 7-31, shows the case in which we have a computer in one city, a cluster of 4800-bps terminals in another city, and a cluster of 4800-bps terminals in a third city that is beyond the second city. The old approach would have been to run two separate 4800-bps lines, as shown in Fig. 7-31(a). The new approach shown in Fig. 7-31(b) allows us to run a 9600-bps line between the computer and the second city and to split this data stream into two 4800-bps lines—one to serve the local terminal cluster and the other to go on at 4800 bps to the third city. Once again, this approach is likely to be a lot less expensive than the previous approach. There are many variations on this theme that can be exploited by the ingenious network designer.

intelligent modems

Many modern modems incorporate microprocessors to assist in performing equalization. This intelligence in the modem can also be used to monitor the status of the modem and the status of the incoming analog and digital signals so that this information can be reported back to the network management team at a central site. These modems can be incorporated into a centralized network management system which gives operators at the network control center complete control over the modems in the network from the central site. One class of network management system uses "intelligent" modems while the other class uses conventional modems in conjunction with an electronic "wraparound" box, which adds the necessary functionality to the modem.

These network management systems require that a secondary communication channel be derived together with the primary data channel. Typically, the primary data channel operates at normal speeds up to, say, 19.2 kbps, while the secondary channel operates in the range 75 to 150 bps. As shown in Fig. 7-32, the primary channel is used for the main data transfer, while the secondary channel is connected back to the network management system computer, which allows commands to be sent out to the network and the status of the network to be monitored. The modems communicate with each other along the secondary channel and can exchange information which, as indicated, can be sent back to the network management system. As illustrated in Fig. 7-33, the secondary channel occupies a small slice of the available bandwidth in the voice channel, and the primary channel occupies the rest of the available bandwidth.

The functions of the network management system include the following:

1. Monitoring of analog parameters. The incoming analog signal parameters, such as signal-to-noise ratio, can be monitored by the intelligence in the modem. This information can be transmitted back to the central site, either as a result of a command requesting status or as an alarm if the incoming analog parameter drops below a certain preset threshold level.
2. Monitoring modem characteristics such as power supply and voltage, V.24

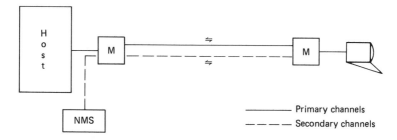

Figure 7-32 "Intelligent" modems for network management.

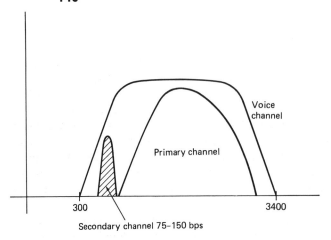

Figure 7-33 Derivation of primary and secondary channels from voice-grade line.

interface status, and the configuration of multistream modems (i.e., which ports are running at which speeds).

3. Recording faults, threshold violations, and so on.

4. Switching modems on and off.

These network management systems give great power to the network control center operator in that complete network status can be monitored from a central point, and tests can be initiated quite easily in the event of failures in the network. The electronic wraparound boxes used in systems using conventional modems fit into the system as shown in Fig. 7-34. The wraparound box electronically derives the secondary communication channel on the telephone line for setting up communication back to the network management system computer. It should be noted that this configuration requires that the basic modems do not use all the available voice bandwidth on the circuit, so that there is some room left for the wraparound box to derive the secondary channel. In many ways the electronic wraparound box provides more functionality than the built-in intelligence in a modem, in that the wraparound box can be used to switch in a second modem as a backup.

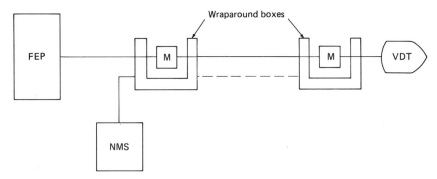

Figure 7-34 Modem-independent network management system.

timing considerations

Bit synchronization

When discussing the V.24/RS-232 interface, we identified transmit and receive timing signals. The purpose of these signals, when used, is to maintain bit synchronization on a line by allowing us to propagate timing signals.

When discussing asynchronous transmission in Chapter 2 we saw that the receiving terminal had its own clock, which was resynchronized by the start pulse at the beginning of each character. Figure 7-35 shows the terminal being connected to the host over a data link, with modems using asynchronous transmission and frequency modulation. In asynchronous systems we have independent clocks at each end of the line. The transmit clock in the terminal determines the basic bit rate at which the data will be transmitted, and the receive clock in the host determines how often the host interface hardware will sample the line to extract the bits from the incoming data. In Fig. 7-35 100 bps is the basic bit rate being generated by the transmit clock in the terminal. The modem uses frequency modulation, which in this case generates a low-frequency signal for an incoming binary 1 and generates a higher-frequency signal for an incoming binary 0. The receiving modem detects the difference in frequency between the high and low frequency values and regenerates the digital signal in accordance with its interpretation of the incoming frequency.

Although the receive clock is running at the same speed as the transmit clock, it will not be running in phase with the transmit clock. It needs to be pulled

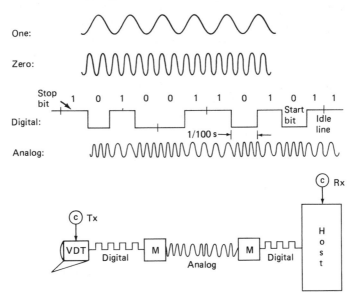

Figure 7-35 Point-to-point line, asynchronous transmission.

into step with the transmit clock if we are to sample the bits properly. Typically, a receiver samples a bit by taking a snapshot of the bit at or about the middle of the bit, and based on the instantaneous reading it obtains, decides if the bit is a 1 or a 0. The question is: How do we find the middle of the bit?

This is where the *start bit* comes into the act. As indicated in the discussion on asynchronous transmission, each character is preceded by a start bit, which is formed by switching the line from the idle state (all 1s) to the 0 state for one bit time. The receiver detects the transition from the idle line condition to the 0 condition, and this pulls the receive clock into step with this transition. The receive clock waits for half a bit time and samples the line to verify that the status of the line is indeed a 0. If the line is in the 0 condition, it assumes that is a start bit, and thereafter it samples the line at one-bit intervals. If the original sample had indicated a binary 1, that would have meant that the transition from 1 to 0 was a noise impulse. The receiver would, in that case, not bother sampling the line any further and we would avoid receiving a garbled character.

If the receive clock is running at exactly the same speed as the transmit clock, the system described above will allow the receive clock to sample each bit exactly in the middle. In reality, the clocks will be running at slightly different speeds. Let us assume that the receive clock is running slightly faster than the transmit clock. As shown in Fig. 7-36(a), the receive clock is pulled into step by the leading edge of the start bit, and it samples half a bit time later as determined by the receive clock. This means that we sample the incoming bit slightly ahead of its center. We again sample the following bits at one-bit time intervals, the bit-time interval being determined by the receive clock, which means that we sample progressively earlier in each bit until finally we sample one bit twice.

On the other hand, if the receive clock had been running slightly slow, as illustrated in Fig. 7-36(b), the clock would have been pulled into step at the leading edge of the start bit and it would then have sampled half-a-bit time later as determined by the receive clock. Because the receive clock is slow, the sample would be slightly after the middle of the start bit and then we sample at one-bit time intervals as determined by the receive clock, which means that we sample

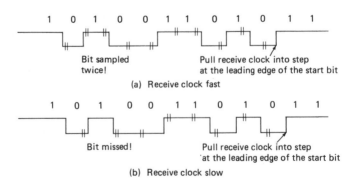

Figure 7-36 Effect of different clock speeds.

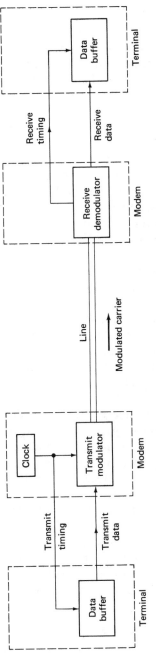

Figure 7-37 The propagation of timing signals.

the bits progressively later and later until finally we reach the point where we miss one bit completely.

This indicates that the clocks need to be reasonably accurate in order to sample the data properly. For asynchronous data transmission the clocks do not need to be too accurate because the clocks get resynchronized at the beginning of each start bit. This means that the clocks only need to be accurate enough to stay in step with each other for one character time, which is typically a maximum of 12 bits.

In synchronous systems, however, we may have very long blocks, and small differences in speed between the transmit and receive clocks could result in data being misinterpreted. For example, if the transmit clock runs at 2400.01 bps and the receive clock runs at 2400 bps, the receiver could get into trouble very quickly. If the receiver started to sample bits in the middle, as time went on it would be sampling closer and closer to the trailing edge of the bits. Eventually it could sample during a bit transition, or perhaps an incoming bit could come between two samples because the incoming bits are slightly shorter than the time between samples.

It is, of course, possible to resynchronize the receive clock on every 1/0 or 0/1 transition, but it is more usual to propagate the transmit timing so that the receiver can be precisely in step with the transmitter. This is illustrated in Fig. 7-37, which shows a one-way transmission system.

The transmit modulator in the transmitting modem requires data to be presented to it at precisely the right time to be modulated onto the carrier. We therefore use the same timing source to drive the transmit modulator and to clock the data out of the data buffer in the terminal. As long as the same clock is used, it does not matter in this simple case where the clock comes from. In Fig. 7-37, the clock is in the modem, and the timing signals are sent across the V.24/RS-232 interface to the terminal. At the other end of the line the receiving modem synchronizes itself to the incoming carrier and, in the process, produces a receive clock that is exactly in step with the incoming carrier. As the carrier itself was directly related to the transmit clock, the receive clock will be exactly the same speed as the original transmit clock.

Alternatively, we could use a clock in the terminal and send it across to the modem to drive the transmit modulator. There is another transmit-timing lead in the V.24/RS-232 interface that can carry this signal. Needless to say, if the terminal clock is being used as the timing source, the modem clock must be disabled.

Finally, in some cases, we use an external clock to drive both the terminal and the modem. In this instance, both the terminal clock and the modem clock are disabled.

Time division multiplexers

In systems using time division multiplexers, timing is very important. Consider a multistream modem that is configured to take four 2400-bps data streams and combine them into one 9600-bps stream. The modem does this by taking one bit from each 2400-bps stream and modulating them onto one cycle of the carrier. For the modulation process to work properly, the bits must all be available at precisely the same time. If one of the 2400-bps streams differ from the others by, say, 0.01%, its actual bit rate would be 2400.24 bps. Very quickly this line would supply one bit too many. If the line had been slower by 0.01%, then very soon it would provide one bit less than the others. If each 2400-bps line does not supply precisely the same number of bits over a period, the multiplexing system will not work. Short-term fluctuations in speed can be absorbed by buffers within the multiplexer, but if the bit rates differ over a long period, an overflow or underflow situation will ultimately arise. To cater to this situation, it is usual practice to have one master timing source, or clock, to control the speed of transmission of all lines entering and leaving the multiplexer.

To illustrate the principles involved, let us first examine a simple point-to-point line without multiplexers. Figure 7-38 shows a point-to-point line connecting a terminal to a computer. The modem nearest the computer is the master timing source. The send clock of this modem is used to time the data out of the computer and to drive the transmit modulator. At the other end of the line, the second modem demodulates the incoming signal and derives its receive clock from this signal. The derived receive clock will be running at precisely the same speed as the master modem's send clock. The receive clock is given to the terminal so that it can sample the incoming bit stream. At the same time, the receive clock is turned around and used as a transmit clock for both the terminal and the modem. The terminal's data are then modulated onto the carrier and sent down the line to the master modem, which demodulates the received signal and extracts its receive clock. This receive clock will also be running at exactly the same speed as the master clock. Thus, in this simple system, all clocks are exactly synchronized with the master clock.

We can now extend this principle to a multiplexer system. Figure 7-39 shows two 4800-bps data streams being combined into a 9600-bps stream through multistream modems. To simplify the diagram, only the timing signals are shown. The 9600-bps modem (M1) nearest the computer is the master timing source. This clock provides transmit timing to the computer on the two 4800-bps channels. These are multiplexed into a 9600-bps stream, which is modulated on to the line. Modem M2 derives its receive clock from the signal on the line and produces two 4800-bps clocks, which are therefore synchronized to the master clock. These receive clocks become send clocks for modems M3 and M5 on the 4800-bps tail circuits. At the far end, modems M4 and M6 derive receive clocks that are used

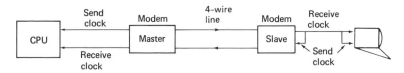

Figure 7-38 Synchronization of clocks on a point-to-point line.

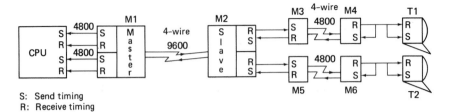

S: Send timing
R: Receive timing

Figure 7-39 Synchronization of clocks in a network.

as both receive and send clocks for the terminals, and they are also turned around
to become send clocks for modems M4 and M6. These modems modulate the
terminal data onto the carrier, which after demodulation by M3 and M5, provides
receive clocks for those modems. These receive clocks become send clocks for
the 4800-bps ports of modem M2. These clocks are still synchronized to the master
clock. The resulting 9600-bps data stream from M2 is synchronized with the 4800-
bps streams, as are the 4800-bps streams derived from modem M1. All the data
streams in this network are speed synchronized so that the multiplexing and demultiplexing operations will always operate correctly.

compounded delays

Most delays encountered in a network are additive, and some are additive in quite
a subtle way. Consider the situation depicted in Fig. 7-40. This diagram shows a
two-wire multidrop line connected back to the computer via time division multiplexers. The carrier on the instation modem on the two-wire line must be controlled by the computer, and the request-to-send and ready-for-sending (clear-to-
send) signals can be propagated by the TDMs. There will be a delay encountered
as the request-to-send signal traverses TDMs, modems, and the four-wire line,
and there will be a similar delay encountered by the ready-for-sending (clear-to-
send) signal on the way back. These delays must be added onto the modem turnaround time for the instation modem.

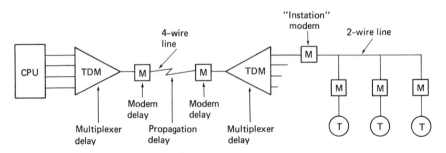

Figure 7-40 Potential sources of delay for control signals.

digital data network interfaces

The new digital data networks described in Chapters 3 and 23 do not require the use of modems. They do, however, require network terminating units to be used between the computer or terminal and the network. The data networks provide full-duplex facilities on point-to-point or multipoint lines, and, in many cases, they provide a switched service.

CCITT Recommendations X.20 and X.21. A simplified interface has been recommended by CCITT for these digital networks. Recommendation X.20 defines the interface between asynchronous terminals and the network terminating unit; Recommendation X.21 defines the interface for synchronous operation. These recommendations define procedures for setting up and clearing calls on a switched network, and they also define the operation of the interface during the data transfer phase.

Because the network is a full-duplex facility, there is no need for delays such as the ready-for-sending (clear-to-send) delay we encountered on the V.24 interface. Also, owing to the nature of the network, there is no need to switch the carriers on and off at the outstations on a multipoint line. This results in improved performance over that of a conventional multipoint line with modems.

CCITT Recommendations X.20 bis and X.21 bis. Because there are hundreds of thousands of terminals that have a modem-compatible interface, CCITT has devised a mechanism that allows them to be connected into a digital data network. Recommendations X.20 bis and X.21 bis provide the general facilities of X.20 and X.21, but they allow the terminal to think it is talking to a modem. If the request-to-send signal is used, there will be a delay before the ready-for-sending (clear-to-send) signal is returned. However, owing to the full-duplex nature of the network, there should be no need to switch the request-to-send on and off during the data transfer phase. This applies to both point-to-point and multipoint lines.

acoustic couplers

Another device for interfacing terminals to communication lines is the *acoustic coupler*. An acoustic coupler enables a normal telephone to be used as the interface between a terminal and a line by converting the digital data signals into audible tones that can be transmitted along a telephone line via a telephone handset. Communications are established by dialing the computer center on the telephone; when the computer answers, the handset is plugged into the acoustic coupler. Many terminals have acoustic couplers built in so that the telephone handset can be plugged into a special receptacle on the terminal to enable the transfer of the audible tones from the handset of the telephone to the terminal. Other acoustic couplers have a V.24/RS-232 interface on one side so that it can interface readily to a terminal; on the other side, it has an acoustic interface that will enable the audible tones to be transferred into the telephone handset.

Acoustic couplers have many uses, primarily for traveling salespeople or for occasions when a temporary connection to a computer is needed. Acoustically coupled devices are not really designed for permanent operation in a fixed location, owing to the design of the telephone handsets. Many telephone handsets contain carbon granules in the microphone, and when we talk the voice vibrates the carbon granules, which modulates a signal to send down the telephone line. As the conversation progresses, the carbon granules get compressed, with the result that the generated signal becomes noisy. In normal voice communication, the person holding a telephone usually shakes the telephone about while talking, which keeps the granules loose and enables a clear signal to go through. When a telephone is fixed into an acoustic coupler, the granules do not get shaken about, with the result that distortion can result.

8
Local Area Networks

A local area network (LAN) is a short-haul, high-speed network which can be shared between a number of users. LANs have achieved prominence due to developments in the automated office and personal computer fields as well as developments in satellite and other forms of communications that can deliver high-speed digital data to your premises.

In the "automated office" it is desirable that practically every piece of office equipment have the capability to communicate with any other piece of office equipment. This requires a switching facility to enable communications channels to be established, on demand, between different pieces of equipment. There are two major classes of local area networks: the PBX and the cable-based local area network.

PBX networks

The "sleeping giant" of office communications is the private branch exchange (PBX). You must have a PBX for voice communications, and the newer machines can switch data as well as voice, as indicated in Fig. 8-1. Most office buildings are already wired for PBXs, and this wiring can be used for data.

The new digital PBXs allow us to eliminate modems and can switch data at

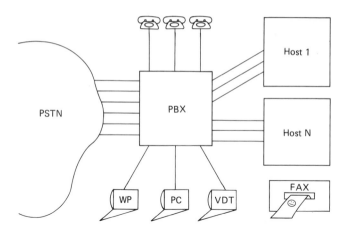

Figure 8-1 A PBX can switch data as well as voice.

64 kbps, which is the "natural" operation speed of the PBX. This is fast enough for a good many applications in the office. Evidence of the importance of the PBX as an office communications controller is the fact that many of the mainframe computer suppliers have formed relationships with PBX suppliers. A more detailed description of the PBX as an office communications controller is given in Chapter 9.

LANs for personal computers

With personal computers it is often desirable to interconnect the PCs so that they can either communicate with each other or share expensive resources between them. Alternatively, the driving force behind the implementation of the LAN may be to allow the PCs to share application programs and data. Many of the peripheral units attached to a personal computer, such as hard disks and high-quality printers, cost as much as, if not more than, the personal computer itself. In this case it is often desirable to share the expensive resource among a number of personal computers rather than dedicating one per unit.

A typical LAN consists of a file server or disk server connected to a number of PCs. The idea is that the file or disk server is the expensive resource shared by the PCs. A *disk server* is based on a hard disk with associated software that manages the available capacity on the disk so that each PC can use the disk in such a way that it thinks it is its own exclusive property.

A *file server* is based on a disk with software that manages the files on the disk and in the process, may or may not (depending on the implementation) allow files to be shared between different users. In any case, we have a disk being shared between a number of users and as the number of users increases, the demand for the disk will increase with it. As the disk is relatively slow compared to other parts of the computer, it can generally become a bottleneck and substantial queuing delays can be encountered by the user PCs. This is probably the major reason why, in real life, most LANs seem to give up the ghost with a relatively small number of PCs in operation, even though, in theory, the LAN may be able to support hundreds of PCs. Of course, the loading on the disk is going to depend on how compute bound or disk bound are the applications. It is possible to have quite satisfactory performance with a large number of PCs on a LAN if they make only sporadic references to the disks. A program that requires a lot of disk activity, such as one written for a database processor, tends to be *disk bound*. This means that the program spends more time accessing the disk for information than it spends processing. On the other hand, a program that requires a lot of processor time and has not much disk activity is said to be *compute bound*. An example is a spreadsheet processor.

cable-based LANs

Cable-based local area networks typically run either on a twisted-pair wire, a coaxial cable, or on optical fibers. Generally speaking, the twisted-pair wiring is used for relatively low speed, inexpensive baseband local area networks, while coaxial cables are used for higher-speed broadband or baseband systems. The optic systems can, of course, provide extremely high capacity.

LANs come in three basic configurations: star, ring, and bus. The network structure also has an impact on how a LAN behaves. Star LANs consist of point-to-point connections from the individual PCs back to the disk/file server. On point-to-point lines, the PCs have unrestricted access to the line, so queuing should occur only at the disk/file server.

Ring and bus networks need a protocol of some kind to control the operation of the network. Ring networks generally use a technique called *token passing*, which means that the PCs take turns at having access to the network. As the load on the network increases, queuing problems can arise as the PCs wait for the network.

Whether the network or the disk/file server is the main problem depends on the relative speed of the network and the disk. It may look as though the disk is the bottleneck, but when it is upgraded to a faster unit, it may become apparent that there is also a problem in the network.

A typical bus configuration provides a single high-speed communications channel that is shared by all the devices connected to the channel. User devices are connected to the LAN by interface units that perform the required signal translations.

This single channel can be on the only communications channel on the cable, which is the situation with *baseband systems*, or it may be one of a number of channels which are electronically derived from the communications medium, as in a *broadband system*.

In a baseband system, a single signal is sent along the cable and all interface units connected to the cable can receive or transmit this signal. In a broadband system, a number of communications channels are electronically derived from the available communications capacity in the cable. Interface units connected to the cable tune into a particular channel and communications can be established with other devices using that particular channel. Regardless of how the channel is derived, the capacity of the channel must be shared between the devices connected to that channel. Some networks use token passing, while others use a contention method called CSMA/CD (Carrier Sense Multiple Access with Collision Detection).

Bus configuration CSMA/CD

A common structure for a local area network is shown in Fig. 8-2. Here we have a bus-structured local area network with a number of personal computers sharing a hard disk and a letter-quality printer. The local area network normally operates at a relatively high speed compared to the natural operating speed of the devices attached to the network. In our case, personal computer A is communicating with hard disk D, perhaps reading or writing a file. In Fig. 8-2(b) and (c), we see bursts of data being carried along the local area network, representing the transmissions from A to D.

While this is going on, personal computer B may be sending data to printer C. To control the flow of data along a local area network in an orderly fashion, some form of protocol is needed. This protocol should either prevent collisions from occurring or if they do occur, it should resolve the problem without losing any data. A commonly used protocol is CSMA/CD. A CSMA/CD bus operates

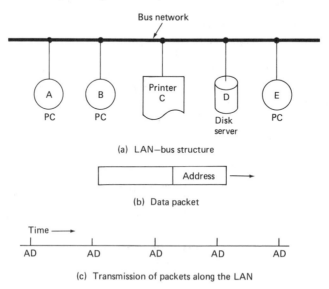

(a) LAN—bus structure

(b) Data packet

(c) Transmission of packets along the LAN

Figure 8-2. (a) LAN—bus structure; (b) data packet; (c) transmission of packets along the LAN.

at high speed, say 10 Mbps, which is very fast compared to the natural operating speed of the devices connected to the bus.

Consider a pair of devices communicating at 2400 bps. The user devices are connected to intelligent interface units which buffer a number of bits and then transmit them in a burst along the cable at 10 Mbps. The receiving interface takes the burst and retransmits the data at 2400 bps to the receiving terminal device. Considering the ratio of the speeds (2400 bps:10 Mbps), the user data will not consume very much time on the channel. The delays in such a system can be very small—it is related primarily to the number of bits that are sent in each burst.

The CSMA/CD approach allows the devices to transmit at random. With random transmission, collisions can occur so that the intelligent interface unit handles the bus protocol, which is aimed at detecting collisions and recovering from them. Basically, the interface unit listens before it talks. This is the "carrier sensing." If there is a signal on the channel, as in Fig. 8-3(a), it waits until the channel is free and then it transmits.

If two units are waiting to transmit, as shown in Fig. 8-3(b), a collision can occur when they do finally transmit. By "listening while they are talking" the interface units detect the collision, cease transmission, and wait a random time before retransmitting. This is illustrated in Fig. 8-3(c). Hopefully, there are no collisions the second time. If a collision occurs, the process repeats itself but usually with a longer time delay before the retransmission. All of this happens so fast compared to the natural operating speed of the user devices that in most cases it is imperceptible to the user devices.

The CSMA/CD control operates at the local interface between the interface unit and the LAN communications channel. There is no protocol, as such, between the interface units, and any communications protocol that is desired must be exercised between the user devices. Generally, the LAN provides the services of the lowest one or two layers (depending on the implementation) of the ISO seven-layered model for open systems interconnection.

A variation on the theme is called CSMA/CA, where the "CA" means "collision avoidance." The interface units "listen before talk," as before, but do not detect collisions. An acknowledgment is returned from the receiving interface unit and if an acknowledge is not received, the transmitting interface assumes that a collision occurred and after a random time delay, it retransmits.

One drawback of the CSMA/CD system is that it is theoretically possible for retransmissions to go on and on forever. This is because when a collision occurs the interface units wait a random time interval before retransmitting. Under heavy-traffic conditions it is possible that the retransmit itself will collide with another transmission. In this event the interface unit increases the random time interval and then has another attempt at retransmitting. Once again, this retransmit could collide with another message, and so on ad infinitum. Thus it is theoretically possible that the message may never get through the system.

Many people do not like CSMA/CD systems because of this possibility that a message may never get through. On the other hand, other people point out that,

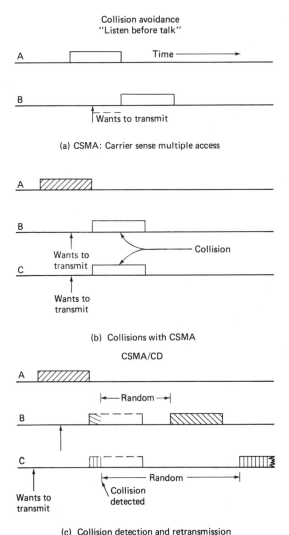

Figure 8-3 (a) CSMA (carrier sense multiple access); (b) collisions with CSMA; (c) collision detection and retransmission.

generally speaking, these networks are used with relatively light loads and it is highly unlikely that a message would get hung up in the system forever.

If you are in a situation where it is possible that due to heavy traffic on the network, the message may never get through, perhaps you should be looking at another form of protocol on the link, such as token passing. Token passing is described under the heading "Ring Configurations."

The communications aspects of a LAN present no major problems today. To make the network behave in a useful manner, we need a network operating system that will manage the flow of information between the devices and provide network services, such as file sharing and printer sharing.

If you want to support more than one PC, you need to have software that is capable of handling more than one PC at one time. This is where many PC-based systems come to grief because they have only single-user operating systems and/or single-user application packages.

If multiuser software is available to you, you are exposed to potential problems due to queues developing within the system. Queues will develop for the disk(s) as different users attempt to read and write to the disks. Apart from problems that can be caused by different users accessing the same file (or worse, the same record), some run into the non-linear queuing delays, which, from the point of view of the individual user, can really make system performance go through the roof.

Ring configurations

A ring network is configured as shown in Fig. 8-4 and the signals on the ring pass *through* the terminal interface units rather than *past* the interface units as on a bus. This means that an interface unit can intercept a signal on the loop and either modify it or prevent it from propagating further.

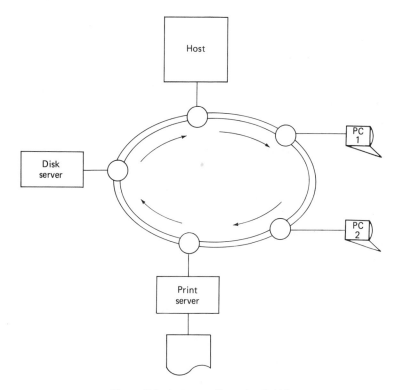

Figure 8-4 A ring-configuration LAN.

Two types of ring are in general use: the slotted (Cambridge) ring and the token ring. In a *slotted ring* system, the ring can be regarded as consisting of a continuous stream of time slots that circulate on the ring. Each time slot has a header which can contain the address of an interface unit and may contain data for the addressed unit.

If an interface unit has received data from its terminal and wants to send it through the ring, it waits until it sees an empty time slot. It puts data in the slot and sets the address of the receiving interface unit in the header. If more time slots are required for the data, the transmitting device waits until vacant slots arrive.

The receiving device recognizes its own address in the incoming time slot, removes the data, and sets a flag indicating that it has received the data. When this time slot arrives back at the transmitting unit, it can tell that the data has been received. To prevent one device from monopolizing the network, the returning time slot should not be reused by the same device.

In a token ring, a bit pattern called a *token* circulates on the ring. An interface unit cannot transmit unless it has the token. A device wishing to transmit waits until it sees the token and removes it from the ring. It can then transmit without fear of collision because there is only one token. When the transmission is finished, the transmitting device can append the token to the end of the message.

A variation on the theme is one in which the token is addressed to a particular interface unit which gives that device permission to transmit. If this device does not wish to send, it can pass the token on to another device, and so on. In this manner we can establish a priority system for transmission over the network if we so desire. Another variation on token passing is to use a bus rather than a ring. In this case the network can be called a *token bus*.

LANs as multiplexers

Many LANs use "Terminal Servers" that allow messages from a number of terminal devices to be multiplexed onto the LAN. A common class of Terminal Server handles simple asynchronous character-oriented terminals in a manner similar to that used by a PAD in a Packet Switching Network. Fig. 8-5 shows Terminal Servers in use on a LAN. This LAN is a bus structure and it could be either baseband or broadband.

The terminal server communicates with the terminals in accordance with their own native protocol rules and converts the messages from the terminal into packets suitable for transmission along the LAN. At the host end, there are two readily available options. One is to use another terminal server that takes the incoming data packets from the LAN and converts them into their original native protocol. This means that host number 1 is presented with individual data streams on individual ports corresponding to the ports on the distant terminal server. In other words, the host and the terminals think that they are connected on individual

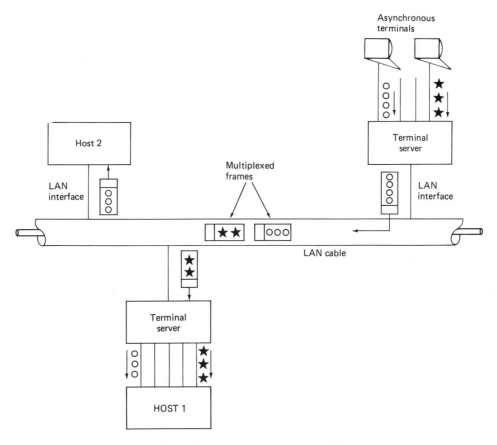

Figure 8-5 Terminal servers on a LAN.

point-to-point lines. In this configuration, the combination of terminal servers and the LAN is acting like a Statistical Multiplexer.

The second option is to present the data packets from the LAN directly to host number 2 on a conventional LAN interface. This configuration is rather similar to a host connected to a Packet Switch under the X.25 protocol communicating with terminals connected to the packet switch via a PAD.

packet radio systems

Local area networks are generally used within your own building. They can, however, be extended beyond your own building by using fiber optic links, cable television techniques with broadband local area networks, or they can be extended via packet radio systems. The packet radio concept was first proposed by Xerox Corporation in the 1970s for use in the proposed XTEN communication network. The aim was to provide a 10-Mbps digital communication channel over a limited distance within a city, which would enable the network to bypass the local telephone networks. There were two reasons for wishing to bypass the local telephone network: first, because it was owned by a competitor, and second, because the wires in the local telephone network were generally not capable of high-speed data transmission. Packet radio provided a solution.

Packet radio operates in a manner similar to satellite communications, except that being on the ground it has practically zero propagation delay. A radio transmitter/receiver is located on a tall building and users have transmitter/receivers pointing toward the central site. A user transmits a block of data in a packet with an address in front and an error-detecting mechanism at the rear. The packet is picked up by the central site and broadcast out where it can be picked up by all other sites. At the remote sites, users look at the incoming data packets and only accept those which have their own address. In effect, the packet radio system is a point-to-multipoint microwave system.

9
Digital PBX

The digital PBX plays an important part in data communications, office auto-mation, and general business telecommunications. In addition to its traditional role of handling voice communications, it is able to operate with other services, such as data switching, local area networks, electronic mail, and electronic mes-sage services. Many people regard the digital PBX as the "sleeping giant" of computer-communications systems.

The importance of the PBX in computer-communications system develop-ment is evidenced by the fact that the mainframe computer suppliers have an-nounced mergers or joint ventures involving the well-established PBX suppliers.

so, what is a digital PBX?

The private branch exchange is your telephone switchboard. Every office has one—it is the hub of your business telecommunications network and it provides the interface between people in your organization and the rest of the world. Until recently, the PBX merely allowed people to originate and receive telephone calls. The range of SPC (stored program control)/PBX introduced in the 1970s extended the range of facilities available to individual extension users, but the basic switch-ing mechanism tended to stay the same. These facilities, such as abbreviated dialing, follow me, camp on busy, last number redial, and so on, made the telephone into a more interesting and more efficient tool. The digital PBX not only offers the facilities provided by computer control, it also provides a switching and transmission mechanism closely related to those used with computer systems. This means that computer data and other digital signals from communicating word processors and other office machines can also be easily handled.

The applicability of the digital PBX arises because:

1. It is there; every office must have a PBX, and new or replacement machines will be digital.
2. The wiring is there; buildings are already wired for telephones and it is not a major operation to extend this wiring.
3. The PBX is a transparent switch.
4. The new breed of telephones incorporate a data terminal or an executive workstation.
5. The PBX has redundant processors, and the spare computer(s) can perform many office functions.
6. The PBX can be a network node.
7. The new PBXs are compatible with the Integrated Services Digital Network (ISDN).

Let us now examine each of these items a little more closely.

It Is There. This goes without saying. Every office needs a PBX and a high proportion of existing PBXs need replacement. The new digital PBX may well reside in the computer room rather than in a special back room. The PBX works by converting voices to a 64-kbps data stream for switching. This is in contrast with the conventional approach whereby we use modems to make data look like a voice so that they can go through the telephone network. In years to come, the common carriers will turn the public network into an ISDN and thus digital transmission can go straight through the PBX and the network. That is in the near future. In the meantime, the PBX provides a 64-kbps digital transmission path between any two ports.

Refer to Fig. 9-1. This PBX has 1000 ports. Of these, 60 go to the public network, 700 go to telephone extensions, 40 go to the computer, and the other 200 go to terminals, word processors, workstations, and facsimile and other office machines.

The PBX allows a 64-kbps transmission path to be set up on demand between any two ports. One instant the terminal can access the computer, the next instant the word processor, the next instant another terminal. By means of a little electronic trickery, it can also communicate with terminals or computers in other locations. An executive with a telephone/workstation can talk on the telephone and at the same time use the intelligent terminal for local processing or, via the PBX, access files in the computer(s), word processors, and so on.

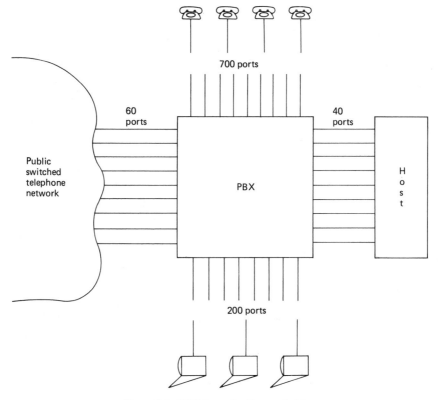

Figure 9-1 PBX for voice/data switching.

In short, the PBX provides a powerful, flexible switching and control function. The natural transmission speed of 64 kbps is more than enough for most office applications. You do not need to operate at the full 64 kbps; you can operate at lower speeds. If you do need faster speeds, say for computer file transfer, you may have a problem which requires the use of a local area network (LAN) or other specialized facility. As time goes on, we can expect to see higher speeds being incorporated into the PBX.

The Wiring Is There. All buildings are wired for telephone and usually there is more capacity installed than is actually in use. Wiring buildings is very expensive and this is one of the drawbacks of coaxial-cable LANs. With telephone services, the backbone of the wiring is already there: the block cabling that goes up and down the building to provide service to each floor; the distribution frames that allow the wires to be tapped off and distributed around the offices on each floor. Adding new circuits is relatively easy. The existing wiring can usually carry quite high digital transmission speeds, say 300 kbps, and this can be exceeded in most cases.

The PBX Is a Transparent Switch. This means that the PBX will provide a transmission path capable of operating at up to 64 kbps but that the PBX is not interested in the format or protocols of the data flowing through it. This means that virtually any piece of office equipment can communicate through the switch; it only needs to worry about the characteristics of the device at the other end, not about the characteristics of the switch.

Telephones Can Incorporate a Computer Workstation. Executive workstations incorporating a personal computer and a telephone instrument are available. The digital PBX allows simultaneous voice and data operation so that the computer can be used as a terminal as well as a personal computer. It can be used to access other computers, terminals, and word processors while the executive is on the phone. The application possibilities opened up by such a telephone work station are immense.

Redundant Processors Perform Office Functions. The computer control for PBX switching and facilities management is exercised via one or more computers, and for reliability purposes, we need to have redundant processors. The spare processors can be used to provide enhancements such as packet switching, electronic message services, voice messaging, and store-and-forward facilities for services such as electronic mail.

The executive workstations mentioned earlier will be used to access the electronic mailboxes that allow us to minimize the effects of "telephone tag." Voice messages can be left for people who do not answer their telephones. Digitized voice can be stored on disk and the recipient can play the message back as if it were on an answering machine.

The PBX as a Network Node. Companies with many locations often install private tie-line networks between the various PBXs for voice communications. Due to the nature of voice traffic, the tie lines are idle most of the time. During this idle time they could be used to carry computer data, electronic mail from communicating word processors, facsimile, and other forms of nonvoice traffic. The switching capability and the intelligence of the digital PBX make it an ideal mechanism for integrating voice and data onto a common network.

the PBX and the ISDN

As described in Chapter 23, the PBX can have a pure digital interface to the ISDN enabling 64 kbps data to be switched to remote sites with a fast call setup time of less than 2 seconds.

the role of the PBX

The traditional role of the PBX has been to provide a mechanism for connecting extension telephones within a company into the public telephone network. A typical PBX configuration is shown in Fig. 9-1. This organization has several hundred extension telephones and the PBX allows any telephone to be connected to any other telephone as a result of the extension user dialing a three- or four-digit number. Also, extension users wish to get access to the public telephone network, and there are exchange lines connecting the PBX into the public telephone network. We do not need the same number of exchange lines as we have telephones or extension telephones because, on average, each extension telephone is used for a very small portion of the time. It does not make sense, therefore, to dedicate one exchange line to each telephone.

The PBX allows the small number of exchange lines to be shared between the large number of extension users. The basic job of the PBX has been to enable any telephone extension to communicate with any other telephone extension, or to enable any telephone extension to gain access to an exchange line for making outgoing calls, or to allow any telephone extension to receive an incoming call that comes through an exchange line.

The traditional switching function within the PBX has been performed by what is known as a *crossbar switch*. A crossbar switch is illustrated in Fig. 9-2, where we have the extension telephones coming in on one side of the switch and exchange lines coming in on the other. By activating the cross points, that is, the

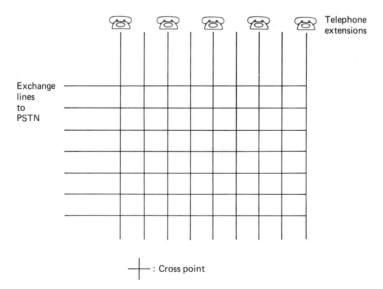

Figure 9-2 Simple crossbar switch.

points at which the line from the extension and the exchange line intersect, we can connect any telephone to any exchange line. In a similar way, the crossbar switch can enable any telephone to communicate with any other telephone.

The first crossbar switches were electromechanical, and they have been replaced in later years by electronic cross points. Electronic cross points were better in that they were faster and were noise-free. The electromechanical switch, as indicated in Chapter 10, generates sparks whenever the switches are activated, and these sparks generate electromagnetic radiation which is picked up in the surrounding wires as noise. With the use of electronic switching, no sparks and thus no noise are generated.

The new range of PBXs operate on a pure digital basis. The incoming analog signal from the telephone instrument is converted into a 64,000-bit data stream at the interface on PBX. This conversion is performed by a device known as a *codec*, which is a contraction of the words ''coder/decoder.'' The codec is actually an analog-to-digital converter and in the other direction it is a digital-to-analog converter. It converts the analog voice signal into a 64-kbps data stream in one direction, and in the other direction it will receive a 64-kbps data stream and turn it back into an analog signal.

The switching matrix itself is a time division switch which is illustrated in Fig. 9-3. This shows a simplified time division switching matrix with three communication lines coming in on each side. Normally, line A on the left would be connected to line A on the right, line B on the left to line B on the right, line C on the left to line C on the right. A voice signal coming in on line A would be digitized to 64 kbps, combined with the others to be transmitted over the composite link and then demultiplexed at the other end. It would be output on line A, where it will be fed through a codec to be turned back into an analog signal. The control function is exercised, via the computer, which can determine the configuration of the multiplexer and demultiplexer arrangement. It is possible for the data that come in on line A on the left to be demultiplexed and output on line B on the right. Therefore, it is possible, by manipulating the time slots within the multiplexers, to allow any input port to communicate with any output port.

On a larger scale this is the principle of operation of the digital PBX. As you can see, the time division multiplexer switch itself can switch either voice

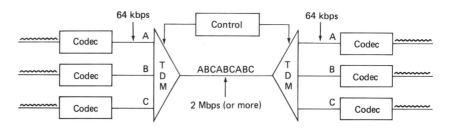

Figure 9-3 Time division switching.

or data; it would not know whether a particular 64,000-bps data stream was, in fact, a voice or a data or digitized facsimile or anything else.

The terminology of PBXs is rather different from that of data communications in that within PBXs people talk about space division switches and time division switches. A space division switch is one like the crossbar switch, where the calls are set up by physically operating switches to connect the calls together. That is, the physical space within the PBX is divided up and allocated to two telephones on a per call basis.

In a time division switch, the same physical path is used for all calls, that is, all calls go over the composite link between the multiplexers. However, the time on the composite link is important and calls can be differentiated from each other by sampling that composite link at different times. So we say that in the digital PBX we use a time division switch rather than a space division switch.

There are, of course, variations on the theme. We can have what is known as a time-space-time switch, one where we have two or more stages of time division switching that are physically separated in space.

PBX networks

Consider an organization that has offices in two cities, as shown in Fig. 9-4(a). In each office we have a PBX that is connected into the public switched telephone network. Naturally, there will be a lot of traffic between employees in the offices

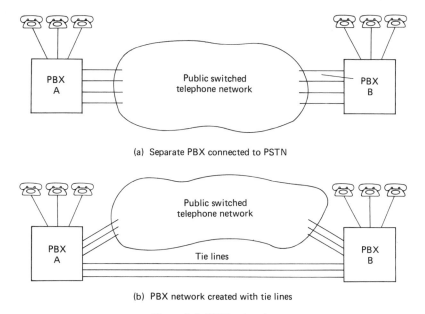

(a) Separate PBX connected to PSTN

(b) PBX network created with tie lines

Figure 9-4 PBX network.

in the two cities, and these calls would normally go through the public switched telephone network. If there is a long distance between the two cities, we will be paying toll charges.

As the traffic builds up it gets to the point where it would perhaps be cheaper to lease a telephone line from the telephone company to connect the PBXs together permanently so that calls could go over this line rather than going through the dial-up telephone network. This situation is shown in Fig. 9-4(b). As the traffic increases further, we get to the point where we may have a number of tie lines interconnecting the two PBXs.

The idea is that whenever a person in the organization in one city wants to call a person in the other city, the call would be switched through the tie-line network. If all the tie lines happen to be busy, a decision needs to be made as to whether the call should wait or whether it should overflow through the dial-up telephone networks. The digital PBXs with computer control are capable of making these decisions, and typically the decision would be based on the importance of the person within the organization. For example, if the president of the company wishes to call the other office and the tie lines are busy, the call would overflow through the dial-up network so that he gets through quickly. On the other hand, if the office boy wanted to call an office boy in the other city, it is quite likely that his call would be placed in a queue for the tie lines so that when the tie line finally becomes free, he can make his call.

This queuing is not a major problem because the office boy does not have to hold onto the telephone waiting for the line to become available. He can put the telephone down and the PBX will call him when the line is available.

The tie-line network is normally dimensioned to provide an adequate grade of service during the peak hour. *Grade of service* is a piece of telephone technology which relates to the probability that a call will be unsuccessful. Therefore, a telephone system with a grade of service of 5% means that there is a 5% chance that when you try to make a call you will not be able to get through. Consider the diagram in Fig. 9-5, which shows a typical loading pattern for the traffic

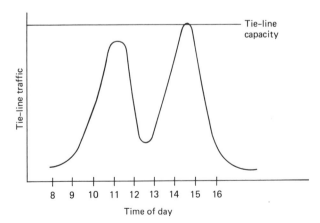

Figure 9-5 Tie-line traffic distribution.

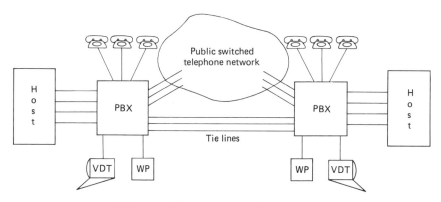

Figure 9-6 Simple voice/data PBX network.

between the two branch offices. Notice the peaks and troughs. This is fairly typical; there is usually a morning peak perhaps between, say, 10 and 11 A. M. and an afternoon peak between perhaps 2:30 and 3:30 P. M. These peaks tend to last for about one hour and are generally referred to as the *busy hour*. The tie-line network is normally designed to give an adequate grade of service, say 5%, during the busy hour. This means that during the nonbusy periods the tie-line network is going to be relatively idle.

It makes sense, therefore, to see if we can use this idle capacity for some other purpose, because tie lines are available 24 hours a day, and as we have said, the telephone traffic peaks generally last for only an hour in the morning and an hour in the afternoon, so we have 22 hours during the day when the tie-line network is relatively idle.

Because it is capable of handling both voice and data, the digital PBX can manage the use of the tie-line network so that when the lines are not in use for voice, they can be used for data transmission. The PBX can provide a connection for terminals, computers, word processors, and other office equipment. It can provide a switching capability so that any piece of office equipment can be connected to any other within the same building, or, through the tie-line network, to any other piece of office equipment within that company's PBX network. The network shown in Fig. 9-6 is quite simple, but complicated networks can be developed as indicated in Fig. 9-7, where we have many PBXs interconnected in a mesh arrangement, some PBXs being used purely for transit switching of a call. For example, a call from a telephone in PBX A to PBX C needs to be switched through PBX B. We say that in this case PBX B is a transit switch and it switches the call, but it comes from one incoming trunkline or exchange line and goes out on to another trunkline or exchange line; it does not go to an extension. Networks of this nature can be programmed so that they have a lot of redundancy. Alternate routing can be made available so that if one particular route in the network is busy, the calls can automatically overflow to another route. In the ultimate sit-

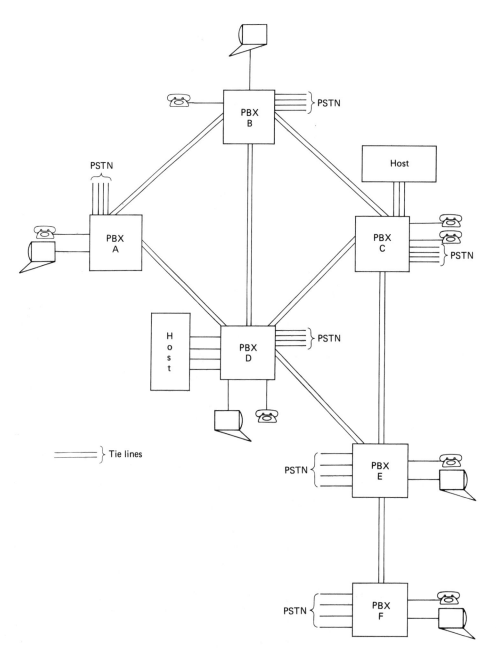

Figure 9-7 PBX voice/data network (mesh configuration).

uation, of course, if all the routes in the network are busy, the calls can overflow to the public telephone network.

Networks such as this offer the hope of great utility and economy as time goes on because the common carriers are upgrading their telephone networks so that they can operate on pure digital transmission. This is the concept of the ISDN (Integrated Services Digital Network). The ISDN will be a network consisting of computer-controlled time division switches interconnected with digital transmission links running at speeds 1.5 or 2 megabits and greater, and under these circumstances the 1.5 or 2-megabit data streams from the ISDN can connect directly into a PBX and provide the equivalent of 30 voice channels. The actual speed of operation varies from country to country. For example, in the United States the standard digital transmission speed is 1.544 megabits, which is equivalent to 24 voice channels running at 64 kilobits; in Europe the CCITT standard is 2.048 megabits, which is equivalent to 30 voice channels running at 64 kilobits. The ISDN is discussed in Chapter 23.

10
Error Detection

We have all had telephone conversations that have had to compete with a background of clicks and splutters on the line and even with crosstalk, where we can hear another conversation. In Chapter 2 we classified all of these unwanted disturbances as *noise*.

The various noises heard on a telephone line are caused by switching transients in telephone exchanges or by outside influences such as lightning strikes, power failures, line repair work, and electrical and magnetic forces associated with other lines or equipment.

Figure 10-1 shows a man talking to a woman through the public switched telephone network. Each person's telephone is connected to the nearest central office or telephone exchange by a two-wire telephone line. The central offices themselves are connected by a cable which the common carriers usually call a *junction cable*. The call itself is switched through the switching equipment in the first central office along the junction cable, through the switching equipment in the second central office, and out to the receiving party. Most of the noise within the telephone network arises within the telephone exchange itself. Most telephone exchanges in the world use electromechanical switching equipment, and mechanical contacts are opened and closed to set up the circuits. Whenever a mechanical contact opens or closes, it generates a small spark that radiates electromagnetic energy which is picked up in the surrounding wires as noise. A typical

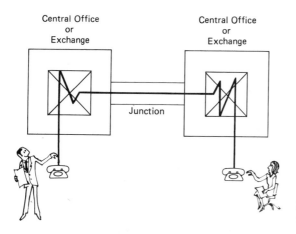

Figure 10-1 Dial-up telephone network.

telephone exchange can have thousands, or perhaps tens of thousands, of these contacts opening and closing at different times. There is therefore a constant background of noise generated within the telephone exchange. Noise impulses on telephone lines generally come in bursts, and the bursts themselves tend to occur at random. [Errors can occur systematically (i.e., at regular time intervals) or in some other predictable manner such as a hardware failure, always causing a particular error pattern to occur. Because of their predictable nature, systematic errors are more easily dealt with than random errors.]

As telephone exchanges are upgraded to use electronic switching and digital control, the noise generated within the telephone exchange will be greatly reduced because with electronic switching no sparks are generated and therefore these switches should produce little noise. Most common carriers around the world are upgrading the telephone networks to incorporate electronic switching and computer control. However, due to the scale of the task, it is going to be 20 to 30 years before we have full electronic switching penetration.

The human brain is a very good computer, and it can adapt itself to the changing conditions on the line and minimize the effect of the noise. For example, if a click on the line obliterates a word, we can usually replace the word in context without asking the other person to repeat the word. If the line condition deteriorates, we can ask the other person to speak more slowly or perhaps to speak more clearly. Each of these actions is an example of the transmitter and receiver modifying characteristics to adapt to changing conditions on the telephone line.

Because most data communication systems use telephone lines as the communication medium, they are subject to the same types of noise that we encounter in a telephone conversation. Unfortunately, the computers we use in data communication systems are not as smart as the human brain, and if a computer is receiving a raw data stream and one or more bits of data are obliterated, it has no way of knowing what they were. It cannot detect errors unless it is given redundant information that will enable it to do so.

In most commercial systems, errors should be detected as well as corrected.

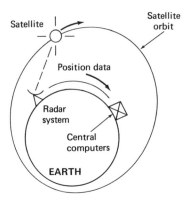

Figure 10-2 Satellite tracking system.

Error detection is discussed in this chapter; error correction is discussed briefly at the end of this chapter and is treated in more detail in Chapters 12 to 20.

In many continuous monitoring or continuous control systems, it is sufficient to detect the occurrence of an error without correcting it. This is illustrated in Fig. 10-2, which shows a satellite tracking system keeping track of a satellite in orbit around the earth. The radar system keeps track of the position of the satellite by taking several readings of its position every second. These readings are then transmitted along a communication line to the central computing system. If, on the way, one of the blocks of data is corrupted by noise, it is sufficient for the receiving computer to detect the error and reject the erroneous data. It does not need to correct the error, because a satellite orbit is relatively stable, and the true value of the erroneous point can be calculated by the receiving computer based on the correct points that have been received. This situation is generally true for continuous control systems.

If the data being transmitted had been commercial data such as payroll information, not only would we need to detect the error but we would need to be able to correct it. (We could not correct it merely by interpolating between adjacent blocks of data, because in commercial systems there is not necessarily any relationship between the content of one block of data and the content of the next.)

rate of occurrence of errors

The rate of occurrence of errors in data transmission systems varies with the transmission speed. Figure 10-3 shows the effect of a noise burst of 2 ms on data being transmitted at different speeds. If we are transmitting data at the rate of 50 bps, each bit will last for 20 ms. The receiving hardware samples each bit as near as possible to the center of the bit to determine whether it is a 1 or a 0. It effectively takes a snapshot of the bit to determine its status. If the noise burst occurs while the receiver is sampling the bit, we may or may not get an error, depending on the instantaneous condition of the noisy bit. At a transmission rate of 50 bps, it

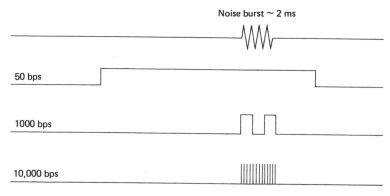

Figure 10-3 Effect of noise on data at different transmission speeds.

is quite unlikely that a noise burst of 2 ms would affect the data, because there is only 1 chance in 10 that the noise burst will occur at the instant that we are sampling the bit.

If we raise the transmission speed to 1000 bps, each bit lasts for 1 ms, and the 2-ms noise burst would span two bits. It is quite likely that one or both of the bits would be corrupted. If we increase the transmission speed to 10,000 bps, 20 bits will be contained in the 2-ms noise burst, and it is almost a certainty that one or more of these bits would be corrupted.

The moral of the story is that on a given line, we are more error-prone at high transmission speeds. This is compounded by the fact that high-speed modems use complex modulation techniques, and it is possible for a single noise impulse to corrupt a string of bits, because it can throw out the demodulation process in the modem.

It is difficult to obtain error rates from communication carriers, because they were not particularly concerned with instantaneous noise impulses until we started using their networks for data communications. Table 10-1 gives an indication of types of error rates that could be expected if we were to select a line at random from an average telephone network and transmit data along it at different speeds. The range of values given for 9600-bps transmission is an indication of the fact that in telephone networks quite a wide variety of circuits are in use.

TABLE 10-1 TYPICAL ERROR STATISTICS FOR
A RANDOMLY SELECTED
TELEPHONE LINE

Transmission speed (bps)	Random bit error rate
1200	1 in 200,000
2400	1 in 100,000
9600	1 in 1000 to 1 in 10,000

There are open pairs of wires on poles; there are multicore twisted-pair cables buried beneath the streets of our cities; there are high-capacity, high-quality coaxial cables; and there are microwave radio and satellite communications links. Depending on whether we happen to get a high-quality or low-quality circuit component when we make a telephone call, we get errors in the low-error-rate or high-error-rate end of the range given. At lower transmission speeds, the systems are relatively insensitive to variations in the quality of the cable.

Tests carried out in various countries have indicated that there is an enormous variability in error rates on different lines. The variation between lines can be as much as three or four orders of magnitude, so the figures in Table 10-1 should be taken with the proverbial grain of salt—they are the figures we would hope to get from a telephone network that has been engineered in accordance with CCITT recommendations.

Table 10-1 shows why some countries have an upper speed limit of 1200 bps for data transmission over the switched telephone network. This is because error rates greater than about 1 in 100,000 to 1 in 200,000 are generally unacceptable for data transmission. Nevertheless, many networks can survive on lines with higher error rates. This is because errors tend to occur in bursts (i.e., bit errors are not randomly distributed; rather, bursts of errors are randomly distributed).

When we transmit data in blocks, we find that this works to our advantage, because a block with one erroneous bit is usually just as useless as a block with 10 or 15 erroneous bits. Thus, if we have, say, 100 noise impulses of one bit length randomly distributed over a given period, we could conceivably corrupt 100 blocks of data. If the same number of noise impulses are clustered in a number of bursts over the same period of time, significantly fewer blocks will be corrupted. You can visualize the situation for block transmission systems and see that at high error rates, smaller data blocks have a better chance of getting through than large blocks.

leased-line conditioning

When we lease a line and have it permanently connecting our terminals and computers, it is possible for the common carrier to bypass the switching equipment in telephone exchanges, and this substantially reduces the amount of noise on the line. Figure 10-4 shows a typical configuration for a leased line joining two computers. In addition, the carrier can measure the performance of the selected line and can add electrical components to alter its characteristics. This process, known as *conditioning*, improves the characteristics of the line and therefore reduces the basic error rate. This allows us to use the line at higher speeds such as 16,600 bps while achieving acceptable error rates.

The process of conditioning can be applied only to leased lines. Owing to the random selection process involved in the switched telephone network, we never know exactly which particular network components will be linked together

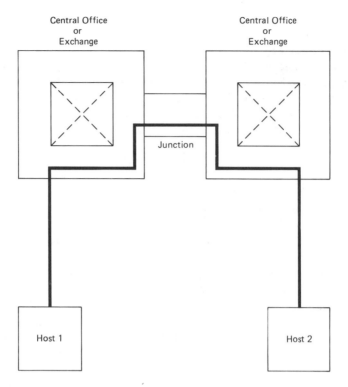

Figure 10-4 Leased-line configuration.

to set up a communications path, so we do not apply conditioning to switched lines.

equalization

Modern modems are capable of monitoring the condition of the line and the incoming signal and automatically counteract certain variations from normal behavior. This process is known as *equalization,* and these days it is usually an automatic process. So far, equalization has not been able to produce the same results as line conditioning, but it has reached the point where transmission at 9600 bps over the normal switched telephone network is quite feasible.

Equalization is often used in conjunction with line conditioning on multidrop lines. From the point of view of the instation modem on a multidrop line, the characteristics of the line will look different depending on which outstation modem is transmitting. The process of line conditioning on the multidrop line can bring the quality of the line up to a particular standard; then the adaptive equalization process in the instation modem can compensate for the different characteristics of the outstation lines.

detection of errors

The simplest way to handle errors is not to detect them at all. We noted that this is usually unacceptable, but in systems where written text is the only type of data being handled, it may be cheaper and easier to let the human operator interpret the intended message. The human brain has a complicated method of manipulating language, so a garbled sentence can often be sorted out by the syntax and the general context of the message. For example, the sentence

TXE WEAQUER FORECASS IS FOR RANN

can be correctly interpreted by us as

THE WEATHER FORECAST IS FOR RAIN

Provided that there are not too many errors, erroneous text can usually be handled adequately by most people. Telegraph systems and Telex systems generally rely on this capability. Significant information such as numerics are often repeated at the end of a telegram because we cannot usually reconstruct numerical information intuitively.

Error detection in data communication systems involves the use of redundancy (i.e., adding additional information above and beyond that merely required to transmit the text). The more redundancy, the more reliable the method of error detection. However, the redundant information uses up some of the transmission capacity that could be used for data transfer, so most error detection systems are a compromise between the amount of redundancy required and the percentage of errors detected.

Echo technique

The *echo technique* (sometimes called *echoplex*) is a simple form of error detection often used in interactive situations (i.e., when a human operator is entering information into a computer using a teleprinter or a simple visual display terminal). Figure 10-5 shows a typical situation with a human operator entering data into a visual display terminal that is connected to the computer by a communication line.

The operator thinks about the character that he wishes to enter and keys it into the terminal. The terminal transmits the character to the computer, where it is received and probably stored on mass storage. The computer then retransmits (or echoes) the character back along the communication line to the terminal. When the character is received by the terminal, it is displayed, and the operator can tell by looking at the displayed character whether it is the same character that he thought about in the first place. If a communication error had occurred on the way, it is likely that the character would have been corrupted; therefore, the character that was echoed back and displayed on the screen would not match the

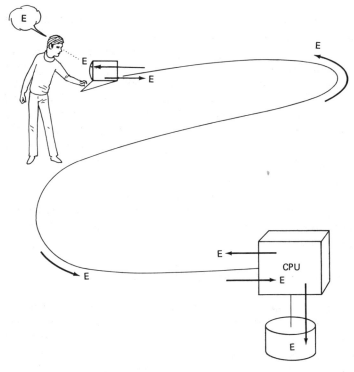

Figure 10-5 Echo technique.

character that the operator entered. In this case the operator can detect the error and correct it.

On rare occasions, the corrupted character can itself be hit by noise and transformed back into the character that the operator thought about in the first place. In this event we would have an undetected error because the computer would have the corrupted character stored away and the operator would think that everything was all right. Statistically, it is highly unlikely that this kind of undetected error will occur, and in most interactive situations, we live with this low probability.

The echo technique is used on most terminals connected to most minicomputers in the world. It is the communication technique used by so-called "dumb" terminals, and it is also widely used on personal computers when they emulate a dumb terminal.

automatic error detection techniques

In modern computer systems, it is desirable to make the detection and correction of errors as automatic as possible. This minimizes operator intervention and im-

proves system performance, because it removes the relatively long reaction times
that are involved with human beings.

There is a general approach to automatic error detection that is the basis of
two commonly used methods. The general approach illustrated in Fig. 10-6 shows
that the data are put through a mathematical process (or algorithm) to produce a
frame check sequence (FCS). The data are sent down the line with the FCS
appended. At the receiver, the data taken from the line are put through the same
algorithm to produce a computed FCS. When the received FCS comes off the
line, it is compared with the computed FCS, and if they match, the data are
declared valid. If there is a mismatch, the data block is declared erroneous and
corrective action can be taken.

The trick lies in picking the algorithm such that it is highly unlikely that
corrupted data or FCS would pass the test. We now describe the two most commonly used approaches: the *two-coordinate parity check* and the *cyclic redundancy check*.

Two-coordinate parity checking

In Chapter 2 we saw that the simple character parity check was of limited
use on its own because it only allows us to detect odd numbers of bit reversals
within a character. When transmitting data in blocks from a computer or from a
buffered terminal, we can extend the power of this simple parity check by adding
a *block check character* (BCC) to the end of the block of data. Figure 10-7(a)
shows a block of data being transmitted, each character having its own parity bit;
in addition, the block check character is appended to the end of the block. This
block check character gives us a cumulative parity check on all the preceding
characters. This is illustrated further in Fig. 10-7(b).

In Fig. 10-7 we have a block of 14 characters, each with its own parity bit,
and at the end of the block is the block check character. Bit 1 of the block check
character is a parity check on bit 1 of all the preceding characters. Bit 4 of the
block check character is a parity check on bit 4 of all the preceding characters,
and so on. Any bit in this block of data has two parity checks being performed
on it: one in the horizontal direction being carried out by the character parity bit,
and the other in the vertical direction being carried out by the block check
character.

The *character* parity bit is often called the *horizontal* parity bit, the *trans-
verse* parity bit, the *lateral* parity bit, or the *row* parity bit. A block check character
parity bit is often called the *longitudinal* parity check, the *column* parity check,
or the *vertical* parity check. In fact, some people use the term *longitudinal redundancy check character* (LRCC) instead of *block check character*.

The transmitting device appends a block check character to the end of the
data stream and transmits the data down the line. The receiver accumulates its
own block check character based on the data it receives, and then it compares

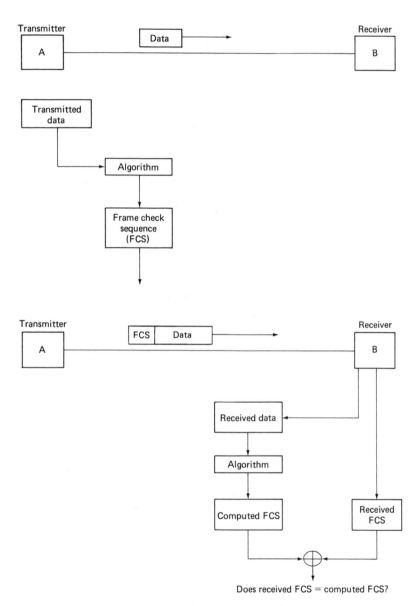

Figure 10-6 Generalized approach to automatic error detection.

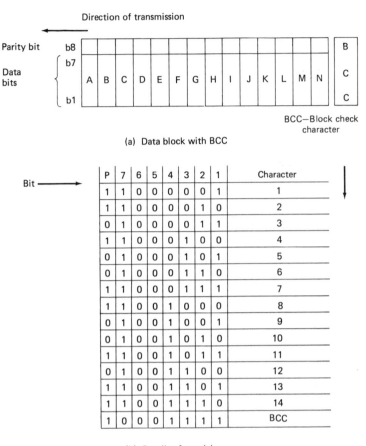

(a) Data block with BCC

P	7	6	5	4	3	2	1	Character
1	1	0	0	0	0	0	1	1
1	1	0	0	0	0	1	0	2
0	1	0	0	0	0	1	1	3
1	1	0	0	0	1	0	0	4
0	1	0	0	0	1	0	1	5
0	1	0	0	0	1	1	0	6
1	1	0	0	0	1	1	1	7
1	1	0	0	1	0	0	0	8
0	1	0	0	1	0	0	1	9
0	1	0	0	1	0	1	0	10
1	1	0	0	1	0	1	1	11
0	1	0	0	1	1	0	0	12
1	1	0	0	1	1	0	1	13
1	1	0	0	1	1	1	0	14
1	0	0	0	1	1	1	1	BCC

Bit ⟶

(b) Details of part (a)

Figure 10-7 Two-coordinate parity check.

the computed block check character with the received block check character; if they match, the receiver declares the block valid.

If there is only one bit in error in the block, the exact bit could be located, because both the character parity and the block parity for that bit will be incorrect. If there are two compensating errors in a character, the character parity bit will be correct, but the block check character for the erroneous bits will be incorrect, and an error would be detected in the block, although it would not be possible to locate the erroneous character. Similarly, if there are two compensating errors in the same bit position of two characters, the error will not show up in the block check character, but the parity of each of the erroneous characters will be incorrect, and the errors will be detected. The two parity calculations, horizontal and vertical, act as complementary checks on each other to increase the overall error detection capability of the system. If compensating errors occur in the same bit positions in two characters in the same block of data, the errors will not be detected, but the probability of this occurring is very small.

Figure 10-8 illustrates some of the error patterns that can occur. The single bit error in character 2 would be detected by both the horizontal and the vertical parity check; the double bit error in character 9 would be picked up by the vertical parity check, whereas the four-bit error in characters 6 and 7 would get through undetected. As a general rule, any error pattern in which the erroneous bits lie on the four corners of a rectangle would get through undetected.

The situation can be analyzed mathematically, and for a given line with a given error rate, an optimum block length can be computed that will give maximum throughput for a desired undetected error rate.

The two-coordinate parity check is easy to implement in either hardware or software, although these days it is most commonly performed in hardware. The block check character is formed merely by performing an EXCLUSIVE OR on all preceding characters; depending on whether we start out with all 1s or all 0s when we begin accumulating the block check, we would then end up with either odd parity or even parity. The rules for accumulating the block check character are illustrated in Fig. 10-9, which shows two typical message formats being used in a synchronous transmission system. The transmitter generates a block check character in the following manner. The block check accumulation is initiated by the first appearance of either SOH or STX. This first character is not included in the block check accumulation, and the system performs an EXCLUSIVE OR

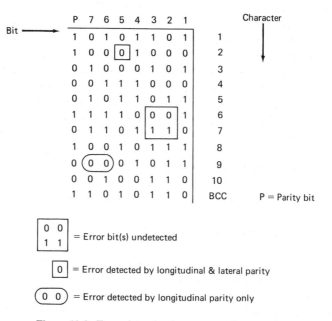

Figure 10-8 Error detection by two-coordinate parity.

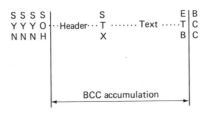

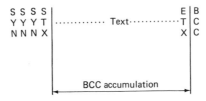

Figure 10-9 BCC accumulation.

on all the remaining characters up to and including the first occurrence of either ETB or ETX. After the ETB or ETX, the block check character is transmitted. At the receiving end, the receiver scans the data to locate the first appearance of either SOH or STX. As soon as this starting character is received, the receiver begins to accumulate its own block check character by performing an EXCLU-SIVE OR on all the characters after the SOH or STX up to and including the first appearance of either ETX or ETB. By this time, the receiver has accumulated its own block check character, and the next character that is received from the line is the received block check character. If the two characters match, the block is declared valid. If they do not match, it is flagged as being in error. (The character parity bit on the block check character is, incidentally, a parity check on the block check character; it is not a parity check on all the preceding parity bits.)

SYN characters can be embedded in the data stream after the block check character has been accumulated. Some systems insert SYN characters as a time fill if they are unable to get all the characters out to line quickly enough to maintain synchronization between the characters. Embedded SYNs are not included in the block check character; in fact, most systems strip SYNs from the data stream and do not pass them through to the user programs.

Cyclic redundancy checking

The two-coordinate parity check is useful for character transmission systems, but it involves a reasonable amount of overhead in the form of one bit for each character plus an extra character at the end of the block. There is a growing trend in the industry toward pure binary transmission, in which we do not necessarily break the data stream up into individual characters. In this case, we cannot easily apply a check, such as the two-coordinate parity check. The *cyclic redundancy check* (CRC) is becoming more widely used, owing to recent advances in hardware circuitry. Also, it is relatively simple to implement with modern large-scale integrated circuits.

If we treat the data we are transmitting as one long binary number, regardless of whether they are a string of characters or a pure binary bit stream, we can divide them by another binary number that we call a *constant*. This is, in fact, a modulo 2 division, not a normal arithmetic division. The process of dividing the *data* by the *constant* will yield a *quotient* and a *remainder*. The remainder is transmitted down the line immediately after the data, and at the other end, a similar operation is performed on the received data. The receiving system takes the received data, treats them as a pure binary number, divides the received data by the same constant, and produces a computed remainder and a computed quotient. The quotient is discarded, and the computed remainder is compared with the received remainder. If they match, the data are declared valid; if they do not match, the data are declared erroneous.

As illustrated in Fig. 10-10, the process is performed fairly simply in hardware. The binary number (i.e., the data) is transmitted down the line to the receiver and at the same time is fed into a hardware divider. The hardware divider accumulates the remainder, and after the data, the contents of the divider are transmitted down the line; at the other end, the computed remainder is compared with the received remainder.

There are many cyclic redundancy tests used in different systems around the world. In the commercial data processing world, however, most CRCs are 16 bits long. However, there is a trend toward the use of 32-bit CRCs, which obviously would be much more powerful.

The performance of different error detection techniques

As I have indicated earlier, it is possible to have undetected errors on a communication line even though we are using a two-coordinate parity check or a cyclic redundancy check. People often ask how often undetected errors are

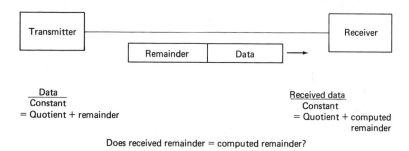

Does received remainder = computed remainder?

Figure 10-10 Cyclic redundancy check.

likely to occur and are also interested to know how often detected errors are likely to occur. The answers to these questions are similar to the question "How long is a piece of string?"; but I will give you some guidelines.

For a typical communication line running through the telephone network we would expect to have a raw bit error rate of about 1 in 100,000 (10^{-5}). If we are transmitting data in blocks for typical block sizes, we would expect the block error rate to be less than 1%. This figure can be checked if you have an existing computer system which keeps error statistics in the front-end processor. You can check the error rate on lines and if the block error rate starts to get beyond 1%, there is a reasonable indication that something is wrong in the network. The probability of getting an undetected error (i.e., the undetected block error rate) is typically about 1 in 100 million (10^{-8}) for two-coordinate parity check systems, and the undetected block error rate for CRC systems is one order of magnitude better at 1 in 1 billion (10^{-9}).

It should be noted for digital transmission systems, the basic error performance of the line is already about two orders of magnitude better than the lines from telephone networks. If a typical bit error rate from the telephone network is 1 in 100,000 (10^{-5}), the typical bit error rate from a digital line is in the order 1 in 10 million (10^{-7}). Clearly, this will give much better block error rates and undetected block error rates than the figures quoted above. The error rates for CRC check systems are typical error rates for systems with a 16-bit CRC.

Noise Comes in Bursts. If you are mathematically inclined, you may try to calculate block error rates and similar rates based on the bit error rate of 10^{-5} for voice lines. If so, you would get the wrong answer. This is because bit errors occur in bursts rather than at random. This tends to work to our advantage because as shown in Fig. 10-11, with bursty noise we tend to get the errors concentrated in relatively few blocks other than having single-bit errors scattered throughout

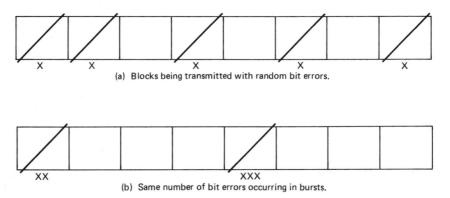

(a) Blocks being transmitted with random bit errors.

(b) Same number of bit errors occurring in bursts.

Figure 10-11 Noise comes in bursts.

a number of blocks. In Fig. 10-11(a) you see a number of blocks being transmitted with random bit errors occurring, and each random bit error will effectively wipe out one block of data. In Fig. 10-11(b) we have the same number of blocks of data with the same number of bit errors, but the bit errors occur in bursts, and in this case we can see that fewer blocks are taken out. Clearly, bursty noise works to our advantage because from our point of view a block of data with one bit in error is just as bad as a block with several bits, so if we get all the bit errors in one block, we are ahead.

error correction

Once an error has been detected, it is desirable to take some action that will correct the error or at least minimize its effect. There are three main ways in which transmission errors can be handled:

- Symbol substitution
- Forward error correction
- Retransmission

Symbol Substitution. For many cases in which the data are intended to be read by a human operator, we use a simple parity check; if a character parity error is detected, we can substitute for the erroneous character with some other character. The ASCII character set has the communication control character SUB, which, when printed or displayed, comes out either as a reverse question mark (ς) or as a sequence of three vertical lines (|||). If this character appears in the message, it stands out and the human operator can usually correct the error just by looking at it.

Forward Error Correction. Forward error correction involves the use of special transmission codes that contain sufficient redundant information so that any detected errors can also be corrected at the receiving end. There are a number of codes that permit this type of operation, but they are not widely used in commercial applications. This is because the overheads involved can be relatively large and because, in general, less than 1% of messages are corrupted. Under these circumstances, it turns out to be more efficient for the receiver to request that the data block be retransmitted.

Forward error correction is also used to improve the basic error rate on a line. This improvement is achieved at the expense of line speed. For example, in Fig. 10-12, the basic error rate on the line is 10^{-3} at a speed of 16,800 bps. The modem has forward error correction built in that enables an error rate of 10^{-5} to be achieved at a speed of 9600 bps.

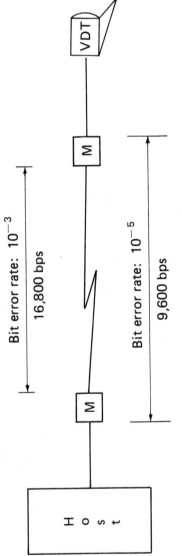

Figure 10-12 Forward error correction can improve bit error rate.

Retransmission. Retransmission is by far the most common means of error correction. Simply speaking, when the receiver detects the block of erroneous data, it asks the transmitter to retransmit it; hopefully, the second time around, it will arrive with no errors. Retransmission implies that there must be some dialogue between the source and the receiver, and this interaction between the two terminals is controlled by a set of *line control procedures*, which are examined in more detail in Chapters 14 to 20.

11
Network Delays: Loop Delay

When calculating network performance, an important component to consider is the effect of the various time delays encountered as the message transits the network. The concept of loop delay is a convenient method of handling these time delays. *Loop delay* is defined as the sum of the round-trip delays encountered going through the network from the computer out to the terminals and back to the computer again.

components of time delay

The various components of time delay encountered in a network are described next.

Propagation delay

Propagation delay is the time it takes for an electrical signal to get from one end of the communication line to the other. In the case of a radio wave, such as in a satellite link or a microwave radio link, the radio wave travels at the speed of light. If we send an electrical signal over wires, however, it travels at less than the speed of light. The actual speed of propagation depends on a number of factors, such as the size of the wires used in the cable, whether the cable is coaxial or twisted pairs, and so on. Also, in the case of microwave and cable links, we have repeaters at various distances along the link, and these repeaters have the effect of slowing down the propagation speed of the signal. For satellite circuits, the propagation delay is generally in the range 250 to 300 ms per satellite hop. A hop is a one-way transition from an earth station up to the satellite and back down again. In a satellite circuit, therefore, we would normally expect to have two hops in the round trip, so the minimum round-trip delay is going to be in the range 500 to 600 ms.

In the case of terrestrial lines, that is, communication lines on the ground, because of the wide variety of transmission media in use, we normally say that the propagation delay is in the range 6 to 10 μs/km. If you happen to know the propagation delay on a particular link, you can use this figure in any design calculations. You may have measured the delay or may have obtained a figure from a common carrier or from another user. On the other hand, if you do not know the real propagation delay, it is usually a good idea to assume the worst case and take a figure of 10 μs/km for the line-of-sight distance between the two centers.

Modem delay

Modem delay is the modulation/demodulation delay encountered through a pair of modems. Modulation is not instantaneous; it takes a certain length of time from when the digital signal appears at the digital interface of the modem until the modulated carrier appears on the line. Similarly, in the other direction there is a time delay from when the receiving modem receives an incoming analog signal until a digital signal is presented on V.24 interface. The value of this delay varies depending on the type of modem used, and generally speaking, the slower the modem, the shorter the modem delay. In high-speed modems, not only is the modulation process more complicated than in low-speed modems, but we also tend to have automatic adaptive equalization built into the high-speed modems, which tend to make the modem delay longer. It is good if you can establish, by measurement, the modem delay for the particular modems that you are using. If you are unable to do this, then assuming a figure in the range 10 to 15 ms per pair of modems is a reasonable approximation. We normally express the modem delay in terms of so many ms per pair because we always go through modems in pairs. We never ever go through an odd number of modems.

Reaction time

Reaction time is the length of time that it takes a terminal or a computer to realize that it has just received a message. Reaction time varies dramatically from machine to machine. In the case of the hardware-based terminal, the reaction time might be virtually instantaneous, whereas in the case of the software-controlled terminal, such as a personal computer, the reaction time can be quite long.

This is because the processor in the terminal may be busy handling one of the screen processing commands, such as erasing the screen or scrolling the screen, when a message comes into the terminal. The processor may not realize that a message has been received until it finishes handling the screen control; therefore, the reaction time can be quite long. The best way to determine reaction times is to measure them using suitable test equipment, such as a serial data analyzer, which is capable of measuring time delays.

Multiplexers and statistical multiplexers

Time delays are introduced by these multiplexers and statistical multiplexers. In the case of time division multiplexers, typically a time delay of one or two character times is encountered. In the case of a statistical multiplexer, not only do we have a time delay of one or two characters but we can have nonlinear time delays caused by queuing within the statistical multiplexer. These time delays are generally best established by measurement or by liaison with the supplier of the statistical multiplexer.

Other components

Any other component used in the network is a potential source of time delay. Components such as line splitters, which are used to set up multipoint lines, can cause a small time delay of, say, 1.5 ms. Any other component in the network is a potential source of time delay and should be examined closely to see whether it does contribute a time delay and, if so, how much.

Example 11-1: Calculation of Loop Delay

Loop delay is the sum of the round-trip delays encountered when a message goes through the network from the computer to the terminal and back to the computer. Consider the network shown in Fig. 11-1(a). Here we have a point-to-point line connecting two computers, A and B, via a satellite communication link which is running at 4800 bps. We are transmitting blocks of data of 480 characters, which is the complete size of the block, including all the synchronizing characters and message framing characters. Acknowledgment messages contain six characters and the various components of time delay in the network are summarized as follows:

	Elapsed time (ms)
Propagation delay (one-way)	250
Reaction time (each end)	2
Modem delay per pair (in each direction)	10

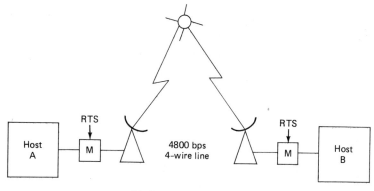

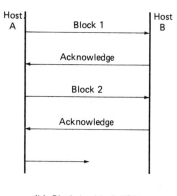

(a) Network configuration

(b) Block-by-block HDX
protocol sequence

Figure 11-1 Half-duplex point-to-point network.

There may also be time delays associated with the earth stations; however, in this particular example let us assume that any such time delays are included in the 250-ms propagation delay.

Solution   A basic calculation is to work out how long it takes to send one block and receive an acknowledgment. Let us assume that we are using a half-duplex protocol, as illustrated in Fig. 11-1(b). To calculate the time to go through one complete sequence of sending a block and receiving an acknowledgment, we have three components of time that need to be considered. First, we need to calculate the message transmission time; second, the acknowledgment transmission time; and third, the loop delay.

A message transmission time is calculated quite simply by considering the size of the message and speed of the line. The message length is 480 characters and assuming that we are using ASCII code with synchronous transmission, we will then have eight bits per character transmitted. The message transmission time, therefore, using the laws of physics, is

$$\text{transmission time} = \frac{\text{message length}}{\text{line speed}}$$

$$= \frac{480 \text{ char} \times 8 \text{ bits/char}}{4800 \text{ bps}}$$

$$= 0.8 \text{ s}$$

$$= 800 \text{ ms}$$

Similarly, the acknowledgment transmission time is

$$\text{transmission time} = \frac{\text{message length}}{\text{line speed}}$$

$$= \frac{6 \text{ char} \times 8 \text{ bits/char}}{4800 \text{ bps}}$$

$$= 0.01 \text{ s}$$

$$= 10 \text{ ms}$$

Next we need to calculate loop delay, which is the sum of the round-trip delays. The various components of loop delay were given above, and we now itemize the components of loop delay going from computer A out to computer B and returning to computer A.

Note: In this particular case we would not expect to have come across modem turnaround time because it is a four-wire point-to-point line, and on this type of line we would expect to be running permanent carrier on both modems, so that we can eliminate the effect of modem turnaround time.

The first component of time delay we encounter is *modem delay*. The second component of time delay is *propagation delay* encountered in going from computer A to computer B. Then we have *reaction time* at computer B while this computer realizes that it has just received a message. When computer B responds with the acknowledgment message, this message first encounters modem delay in the reverse direction, followed by propagation delay, and finally reaction time at computer A. The components of time delay can therefore be summarized as in the following table.

	Elapsed time (ms)
Modem delay A–B	10
Propagation delay A–B	250
Reaction time at B	2
Modem delay B–A	10
Propagation delay B–A	250
Reaction time at A	2
Total	524

The total time to send the block and receive an acknowledgment can therefore be summarized as follows:

	Elapsed time (ms)
Message transmission time	800
Acknowledgment transmission time	10
Loop delay	524
Total	1334

The calculation of loop delays is normally quite straightforward provided that one thinks clearly about what is going on in the network. Careful consideration needs to be given to whether we are running permanent carrier or controlled carrier on the modems, and if so, where the modem turnaround times are likely to be encountered. Similarly, careful consideration needs to be given to all the other components in the network to determine which components, if any, are likely to cause time delays.

Once we have worked out loop delay we find we can use this figure over and over again. When we begin the analysis of protocols, particularly half-duplex protocols, it will become evident that loop delay is encountered many times when going through the protocol sequences.

PART TWO
PROTOCOLS AND ARCHITECTURES

12
Introduction to Network Protocols

network protocols

Network protocols are sets of rules that govern the flow of data in a network. The aim is usually to ensure that data are transferred quickly and correctly from one point to another. This involves automatic error detection and correction as well as recovery procedures so that we can handle contingencies in an orderly fashion.

There may be several levels of protocol in a network, as shown in Fig. 12-1. This diagram shows a network with a concentrator; the computer is transmitting a series of multisegment messages to a *remote job entry* (RJE) terminal attached to the concentrator. A message may consist of a number of blocks of data, and each block must travel over 2 data links and through a concentrator to reach the RJE terminal. The network protocols ensure that the messages do reach the RJE terminal. In this example we would need to identify at least three levels of protocol.

The lowest-level protocol is actually at the hardware level, for which we need a set of rules to tell us how to get the individual bits of data onto and off of the communications line. This protocol includes items such as identifying the type of hardware interfaces to be used, such as the CCITT V.24 interface between the computer and the modem, or the X.21-series interfaces if we are using a digital network. As we saw in Chapter 7, there can be extended "handshaking" se-

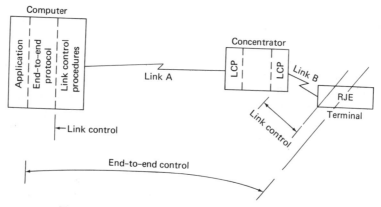

Figure 12-1 Multilink network showing protocol layers.

quences at this level, such as raising the request-to-send signal when we wish to transmit and waiting for the ready-for-sending (clear-to-send) signal before we start transmitting. In most systems these low-level protocols are transparent to the user, who needs to be aware that they are there because of the time delays that can be introduced but usually does not have to implement them. In short, the lowest-level hardware protocols ensure that bits can be put onto a communications line and that they can be taken off again at the other end.

These low level protocols, however, do *not* give any protection against transmission errors. A bit could become corrupted, but the low-level protocol would not know about it. To handle this and other contingencies, we incorporate a higher-level protocol called a *line control procedure* (or *link protocol* or *line discipline*). This protocol is a set of rules that ensures that a block of data gets from one end of a data link to the other and also that it gets there correctly. This implies automatic error detection and correction. To perform automatic error detection and correction, we first must specify the format of the data blocks and the type of error detection method used. The error detection mechanism is incorporated at each end of the link, and we use a series of supervisory messages to inform the transmitting device of the progress of a transmission. If an error is detected, the receiving device can ask for a retransmission. A line control procedure strictly defines the format and use of all the supervisory messages, so that, theoretically, any contingency encountered on the line can be handled.

The terms *line control procedure* and *link protocol* are used interchangeably; the latter is probably more appropriate. The term *line control* implies that we are supervising the flow of data along the communications line itself, whereas we are really doing more than that. We are supervising the flow of data along a *data link*, which can be described as a logical point-to-point connection between two terminals (or computers) consisting of the following components: the communications line, the modems, the communications interface hardware on the terminal (computer), and that part of the terminal (computer) hardware and/or software that is used to house the link control procedures.

The idea is that a block of data given to a link control procedure at one end of a data link will be correctly output by the link control procedure at the other end, or if it is completely lost on the way, the link control procedure will initiate suitable recovery action. The concept of a data link as a logical point-to-point connection can be applied to multidrop lines because, in any single data transfer operation, we are sending data from one point to another even though there may be many terminals on the line. In the network in Fig. 12-1, we would have link control procedures operating on links A and B. Each link control procedure ensures that individual blocks of data transit their links correctly.

To ensure that a message traverses the series of links and the concentrator and reaches its destination, we have a higher-level protocol, which is identified in Fig. 12-1 as an *end-to-end protocol*. This protocol is another set of rules related to message flow. A message may consist of a number of blocks, and the computer is interested in knowing whether the complete message was correctly received. The end-to-end protocol, after giving all the segments of the message to the first line control procedure, can send out a special message asking the receiving terminal to verify that it has indeed received the complete message. If it has not been completely received, the end-to-end protocol can initiate recovery action. Another function of the higher-level protocol is *flow control*. Flow control means ensuring that the data flows smoothly through a network without flooding a terminal or concentrator.

A link protocol usually attempts to deliver data as fast as it can, but there may be some restriction imposed by the rate at which the receiving device can accept data. An RJE terminal, for example, may be double buffered so that it can be receiving one block of data while it is printing another block. If the communications line can deliver data faster than the RJE printer can print it, we could flood the system unless some control is built in.

One approach uses *pacing* messages, which flow from the final receiver to the source. With our RJE system, the first two blocks can be sent as fast as the network can handle them. The RJE terminal will not be able to handle the third block until it has finished printing the first, so it will not send a pacing response until the first block has been printed. Upon receipt of the pacing message, the source will send the next data block, and so on. The end-to-end protocol at the source has to know the characteristics of the terminal; in this case it knew it could send out the first two blocks quickly, but thereafter, it had to wait for a pacing response before sending the next block.

As illustrated in Fig. 12-2, there can be several levels of pacing in a network. This diagram illustrates message pacing without showing all the link-level, message-exchange sequences. The concentrator, for example, may have four buffers allocated to the RJE terminal. This means that it can always have a queue of messages waiting for the RJE terminal so that the terminal can be driven at its

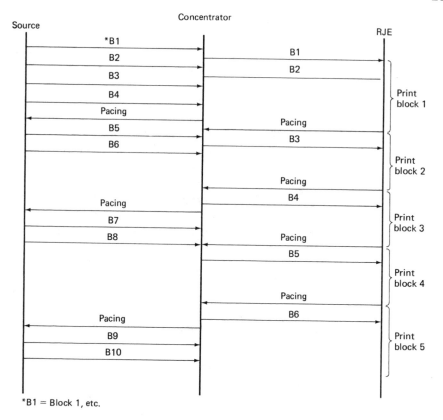

Figure 12-2 Flow control for RJE terminal in network of Fig. 12-1.

maximum speed. Flow control between the concentrator and the RJE terminal can proceed as described previously. Between the source and the concentrator, a different set of rules can apply. Because we have four buffers in the concentrator, the source can send out the first four blocks as fast as it can and then wait for a pacing message from the concentrator. The concentrator, after delivering the first two blocks to the RJE, sends a pacing message to the host, which then sends the next two blocks. After the next two blocks have been sent to the RJE, the concentrator is ready for the next two, so it sends a pacing message, and the sequence goes on.

Using the flow control techniques outlined above, it is possible to have several remote job entry devices attached to the concentrator, each with independent flow control being exercised by the pacing messages. This is a very elegant method of controlling the flow of data to a number of devices with minimal cross impact between the flow control on the different devices.

network architectures

Most computer manufacturers have their own set of network protocols incorporated into some form of *network architecture*. One of the main aims of these network architectures is to give users the tools for setting up a network and for performing flow control and related functions without the application programs needing to be concerned about the intricacies of doing so.

Until fairly recently, the interface between the application programs and the communications-handling systems was somewhat hazy, as shown in Fig. 12-3. The application program had to know the characteristics of the terminal at the other end of the line and had to know how the terminal liked to receive its data. For example, one visual display terminal may accept a 1024-character block of data, whereas another may require the same data in four blocks of 256 characters, so changes in network components were reflected in changes in the application programs.

Over the years, computer manufacturers have been advancing toward several layers of network protocols with clearly defined interfaces between them. This is illustrated in Fig. 12-4. Here we have a *link handler* (link control procedure), which ensures that a block of data gets from one end of the link to the other. Above this is the *network handler*, which knows the configuration of the

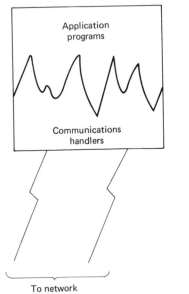

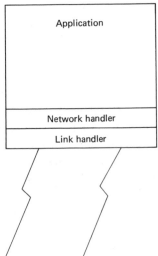

Figure 12-3 The interface between application programs and communication handlers has been very hazy.

Figure 12-4 Layered protocols.

network and the characteristics of the terminals. It knows how fast a given terminal can handle data and what size blocks it can consume. Above this is the *application program*, which knows that it wants to send data to, or receive data from, a terminal but does not need to know the minute details of how this is done. It does need to know how big the screen is on a visual display terminal or how long the print line is on an RJE terminal, but it does not become involved with message segmentation and flow control.

With clearly defined interfaces between the various protocol layers, it is easier to make changes in one layer without affecting the adjacent layers and, in particular, without affecting the application programs. For example, the link control module could be changed from basic mode to high-level data link control, and the application program should be unaffected by the change.

Figure 12-4 does not include the lowest-level (hardware) protocol and some higher-level protocols that may be present.

higher-level protocols

With the increasing use of intelligent terminals, there is a trend toward dispersing the application programs around the network so that part of the application processing can be performed at the terminal location and part at the central site. There may be several application segments residing in a terminal, so we may need to have a higher-level protocol to handle communication between applications in various parts of the network. It is important for the system designer to understand the function of the various protocols, which, owing to the nature of their operation, can have a marked effect on system performance.

Higher-level protocols vary from manufacturer to manufacturer, and we do not describe them in detail. We do, however, take a detailed look at some typical link protocols because these are quite similar from manufacturer to manufacturer. Once you are familiar with the basic mechanics of information interchange at the link level, you should have little difficulty in familiarizing yourself with the higher-level protocols supplied by your manufacturer.

13

The International Standards Organization's Open System Interconnection

The International Standards Organization has developed an architectural model which it calls *open system interconnection* (OSI). The OSI model is a seven-layered model which if implemented by all the computer suppliers, would allow any computer to communicate with any other computer. In fact, the OSI model would allow any terminal connected to any computer to access any application on any other computer provided that the computers were connected by some form of common network. Clearly, this is a highly desirable goal, and just as clearly, achieving it is a very tall order. Let us have a broad look at the overall concept of the OSI model.

Consider the simple connection of two computers shown in Fig. 13-1. Here we have a point-to-point line connecting two computers and we wish to transfer data from computer A to computer B. The data in computer A are in a buffer ready to be transmitted along the point-to-point line to the buffer which is waiting in computer B. In the simplest case we would send the block of data using pure asynchronous transmission with no form of error detection. In a slightly more complicated case we would use a communications protocol across the point-to-point line to enable us to detect any errors and correct them before the data are declared valid in the receiving buffer.

From the communications point of view, the situation is very simple. In reality, the computers may need to perform translations on the data, particularly

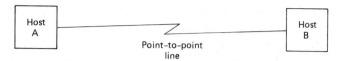

Figure 13-1 Simple point-to-point network.

if the computers are a different brand, because internally in the computers they may use different character sets, different data formats, different file structures, and so on, so some translation will be necessary.

If we take the two computers and connect them via a network such as a packet-switching network, we would have a configuration of equipment such as shown in Fig. 13-2. This diagram is also a very simple one, as it shows a simple packet-switching network with only four packet-switching exchanges. The first computer is connected into the nearest packet-switching exchange over a point-to-point line consisting, in this case, of a telephone line with modems. The link could indeed be a digital data network line with network terminating units, and it would logically behave the same as a telephone line with modems. Internally, in the packet-switching network we have connections between the packet-switching exchanges, which may be telephone lines or digital lines, and finally the connection from the distant packet-switching exchange to the distant host is also a point-to-point line with modems or a digital line with network terminating units.

As we have seen, the function of the physical communication line consisting of the lines, modems, and line interfaces is to transmit bits of information from

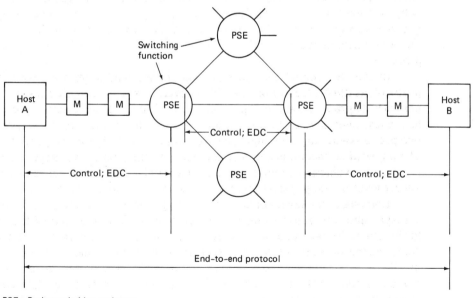

PSE: Packet switching exchange
EDC: Error detection and correction

Figure 13-2 Simple packet-switching configuration.

one end of the line to the other. Errors can occur at this level, and to detect and then correct the errors, we exercise a link protocol across the data link. Thus we have three separate link protocols being exercised across the links as illustrated in Fig. 13-2. Each link control has but one purpose—to ensure that a block of data crossing the interface to the link control at one end of the link will emerge quickly and correctly at the other end of the link. Having performed that task, the link control's job is over and what happens next is of no consequence to link control.

We, of course, are interested to make sure that the block of data gets from host 1 to host 2 and is not switched out to some other machine. This implies that a switching function must take place within the packet-switching exchanges. As the block of data is delivered from the first data link to the first packet-switching exchange, the switching software within that exchange would examine the header of the data to determine the destination address and thus select the appropriate data link for forwarding the data. Similarly, at the other end of the second data link, the packet-switching exchange would examine the destination address and the header of the packet to determine which particular data link should be used to forward the data out to the receiving terminal. We have thus identified three levels of control within the packet-switching network: the lowest level, the *physical level*, carrying the bits of information across the physical data link; the second level, the *link control level*, which is responsible for delivering blocks of data across the data links; and the third level, the switching function or the *network control level*, which is responsible for routing the data through the network. Finally, we may have a fourth level of control operating end to end between the two hosts to ensure that the blocks of data do in fact get from the first host all the way through the network to the second host. We call this an *end-to-end protocol*.

In the ISO model for open system connection, there are seven levels of protocol, as illustrated in Fig. 13-3. This diagram is related to the packet-switching network diagram shown in Fig. 13-2. At each end of the diagram we have the host with seven levels of protocol and the two intermediate blocks represent the two packet-switching exchanges, each of which have only three layers of protocol. The physical connections between the host and the packet exchange and between the packet exchanges themselves are illustrated on this diagram, and that is the lowest level or the physical level of the seven-level interface.

Looking at the layers of control, starting from the bottom, the *physical layer* is responsible for transporting bits of information from one end of the data link to the other. Errors occur at this level, and the physical interface is incapable of detecting the presence of errors. Error detection is performed at the next level— the *link control layer*—and when an error has been detected, a retransmission request is sent to the other end of the link so that the block of data can be retransmitted and hopefully will arrive without error on the second occasion.

Sitting above the link layer is the *network layer*, which, as we have seen, performs the switching function which will route the data through the packet-

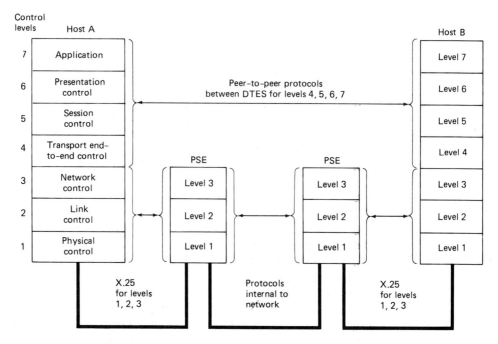

Figure 13-3 ISO architectural model for open system interworking.

switching exchanges out to the correct destination. On top of this is the fourth layer of the protocol, called the transport end-to-end protocol. Among the jobs of this protocol is checking the end-to-end integrity of the data transmission, to make sure that blocks of data do indeed transit the network and arrive safely at the required destinations. Another function of the end-to-end protocol would be to select the most appropriate network to use for a particular application transaction. As you know, there are many different forms of computer networks: packet-switching networks, digital data networks, telephone networks, local area networks, satellite communication networks, and so on. In a modern computer system we may have many of these different networks connecting the computers and we will find that each network has its own pricing and performance characteristics. One network will be suitable for one application while a second will be suitable for another. For example, a packet-switching network is ideally suited for short transactions of the on-line inquiry type, where we have one packet in/one packet out, whereas for high-speed file transfer, a local area network or a satellite network could be more appropriate.

The fourth layer in the network architecture should be capable of identifying the most appropriate network to use for a particular transaction, and it would route the file transfers through a high-speed network and perhaps the sporadic application transactions through a packet network.

The fifth layer is called *session control layer*, which handles the data flow and major error recovery. The session layer controls whether the communications should be FDX or HDX and it handles major error recovery by restarting the process or by backing off to a resynchronization checkpoint. The link level handles minor error recovery of a few blocks but the session layer handles the kind of recovery that is necessary after a link failure or a failure in the interconnecting network.

The next layer above session control is called the *presentation control*. This control layer is involved in presenting data to the layers above in a form which that layer can understand. With different brands of computers connected through the network we would find that internally they have different conventions for data handling. They may use different character sets, have different data formats, different file structures, and so on, so that for communication between dissimilar computers we need translation to take place so that the receiving device can understand the messages. This code conversion, format conversion, and so on, would take place in the presentation layer, which, as we have seen, is so called because it is involved with "presenting" the data to the next higher level in the architecture in a form which that higher level can understand.

The top layer, the *application layer*, is not the application program but rather the application service layer. The application programs actually sit above the application layer. The application layer is concerned with initiation of the overall interconnection of one application and another; it is concerned with the termination of this interconnection. It is also involved with resource allocation as necessary, job accounting, task synchronization, and so on.

As can be seen from the diagrams and from the preceding description, the bottom three layers of the architecture have what is known as *local significance*; that is, they operate across the immediate boundary between the hosts and the packet-switching node, or between the packet-switching nodes, or between the packet-switching node and the hosts. The four upper layers have *end-to-end significance*; that is, they are above the network and operate from one host to another. To this extent one can see that the network itself is transparent to the four upper layers. That is, the upper layers would operate largely the same way regardless of whether the network interconnecting the computers was a packet network, a digital network, a satellite network, or a local area network.

The ISO model is an admirable approach to computer networking. In the long term, computer suppliers will implement the protocols; in the meantime, they have to be fully defined before they can be implemented. At the time of writing, the bottom three layers have been specified in quite some detail for a number of different network types. Probably the best known is CCITT Recommendation X.25, which specifies the network access protocols for a packet-switching network. Recommendation X.25 is, in fact, a particular implementation of the bottom three layers. Other implementations have been specified for digital data networks and local area networks.

The upper four layers are still in the process of being specified, and when they are finally agreed upon, it will take some time for computer suppliers to have products on the market which do, in fact, incorporate the full range of facilities specified. In the meantime, specialized implementations of the seven layers are emerging.

A good example of a specialized implementation of the seven layers is the Teletex protocols which have been developed for communicating word processors. These protocols allow different brands of word processors to communicate in such a way that we can exchange an exact copy of a page of information from one machine to another. This involves all the levels of the ISO seven-layer model. We should emphasize, however, that this is a very specific implementation. It could be viewed as a narrow vertical slice of the model. Other applications are emerging that can also be regarded as a narrow vertical slice of the model but it will be a long time before we see widespread implementation of a generalized seven-layer model that truly allows any terminal on any computer to access any application on any other computer.

14
Introduction to Line Protocols: Half-Duplex Point-to-Point

As indicated earlier, the existing high-level protocols vary dramatically from manufacturer to manufacturer. In the long term the ISO model will be implemented by most suppliers, but until that happy day we must live with the architectural models that are put out by the different suppliers. My approach is to describe line control procedures in some detail, which will then enable the reader to study his or her own suppliers' architectures and high-level protocols. You will be in a good position to read their manuals and attend their courses, and although their protocols tend to be complicated, you should have no great difficulty in understanding how they work.

line control procedures

Line control procedures are one of the lower-level network protocols. Their aim is to control the flow of data on a communication line to ensure that data are transferred quickly and correctly from one point on the line to another. The orderly flow of data on a line generally means ensuring that only one terminal is transmitting at a time. Note the situation illustrated in Fig. 14-1, where we have a point-to-point line connecting two computers. If the line consists of a single channel, it is only capable of half-duplex operation, and if both computers attempt to

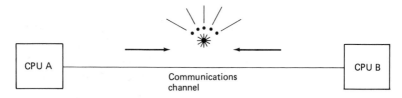

Figure 14-1 Contention on a point-to-point line.

transmit at the same time, the data collide on the line and become garbled and unrecognizable. Similarly, on the multidrop line in Fig. 14-2, if two of the remote terminals attempt to transmit at once, the data collide on the line and are unrecognizable. These situations are known as *contention*, which is defined as a situation arising on a channel when two or more stations try to transmit at the same time. To prevent contention, we need some type of control in the network, and this is one of the jobs of the line control procedure.

An obvious way to prevent contention is to put one terminal (computer) in charge of the line so that no terminal transmits unless the controlling terminal gives it permission. (The mechanics of this approach are covered in detail in Chapter 15 under the heading ''Polling.'') If one terminal controls the line, there is continual overhead involved while that terminal asks the other terminal(s) if it has anything to transmit.

In modern computer systems such as those running SDLC or HDLC protocols, this is, in fact, the approach that we take. However, in the older computer systems we found that the overhead involved was too great and we are always on the lookout for ways of reducing the overheads. The reason the overhead was too great was that one processor was handling both the link control and the application processing. The overhead involved at the link level, by continually asking the other terminal if it had data to send, reduced the amount of time available in the host for batch processing, and therefore we were on the lookout for ways of reducing this overhead. In modern computer systems with front-end processors, the front end really has nothing better to do than sit there asking the other terminal for data, so there is no overhead on the host itself.

To avoid this overhead, many point-to-point systems are arranged so that when data transmission is not taking place, neither terminal is in charge of the

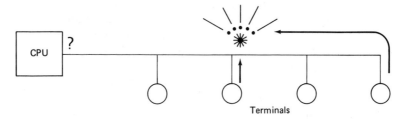

Figure 14-2 Contention on a multipoint line.

link. When a terminal wishes to send data, it can contend for the right to transmit and then take charge of the link for the duration of that transmission. It then relinquishes control, and thereafter either terminal can contend for the right to transmit. If both terminals should contend for the line simultaneously, different timeouts built into the terminals would ensure that one of them retried before the other, thus resolving the contention situation.

The terminology used to describe the various states of the terminals and the line varies somewhat. For the older-style half-duplex *basic mode* line procedures, of which the well-known binary synchronous (BSC or Bi-Sync) line procedure is an example, we talk about master/slave relationships. In the point-to-point case, the line is said to be in the *neutral* condition when it is not in use. A station wishing to transmit contends for *master* status, the other station becomes the *slave*, and data are transmitted from the master to the slave. In this situation, data messages are only transmitted from the master to the slave, and the flow of data is supervised by *supervisory* messages. Either terminal can assume master status for a given data transmission sequence. For example, if terminal A wishes to transmit to terminal B, it can assume master status and designate B to be a slave station for that transmission; terminal A will therefore control the flow of data along the line. Similarly, if terminal B wishes to transmit to A, it can assume master status and designate A to be the slave for that particular data transfer; terminal B will therefore control the flow of data along the line.

If both terminals should attempt to assume master status at the same time, a contention situation arises. This is resolved by building a timeout into each terminal and by making one timeout longer than the other; when the shorter timeout has elapsed, the terminal will get in first and seize master status.

typical message-exchange sequences

Let us now examine a number of typical message-exchange sequences on point-to-point and multipoint lines, under both *basic mode* procedures and *HDLC-style* procedures:

Block-by-block transmission: basic mode point-to-point

We often need to transfer large amounts of data from one point to another. We may wish to transfer files from one computer to another, or we may perhaps be operating a remote data-entry system based on an intelligent terminal or personal computer or, having collected a day's data, we may wish to transmit these data to the central computer.

We normally segment the data into blocks, and these are transmitted one after the other. A simple line control procedure involves handshaking between the two terminals transferring the data. After each block is transmitted, the receiver sends an acknowledgment to advise whether the transmission was received correctly. If the transmission was received without any error being detected, the receiver sends a *positive acknowledge* (ACK); if transmission errors were detected, the receiver sends a *negative acknowledge* (NAK).

Half-duplex block-by-block transmission

A common line control procedure in use today is a half-duplex procedure whereby the source waits for an acknowledgment from the receiver before transmitting the next block of data. If the source receives ACK, it is free to continue with the next transmission, but if NAK is received, the source retransmits the last block of data. There is usually a defined limit to the number of times the block is retransmitted because if the same data have been retransmitted many times, it is likely that there is a fault on the line or in the transmitter or receiver. This fault condition can be signaled to a human operator for action.

The half-duplex block-by-block data transmission operation may be performed on either two-wire or four-wire lines. The use of a four-wire line enables greater throughput to be achieved due to the reduction of modem turnaround time.

Figure 14-3 illustrates a typical block-by-block message-exchange sequence. This diagram is a method of showing the message sequence on the line. Computer A is on the left, computer B is on the right, and the arrowed lines represent the data and supervisory messages that are being transmitted, with the arrows indicating the direction of the transmission. You can imagine a time scale running vertically from top to bottom.

Figure 14-3(a) illustrates the effect of network delays on the transmission and reception of messages. Figure 14-3(b) illustrates the same sequence of events with a distorted time scale. For most of the diagrams in this chapter, the illustration of sequence is more important than the illustration of time, because timing is calculated separately. We therefore use the method of representation of Fig. 14-3(b) unless the proper illustration of timing is important.

The block transmitted from A is received a short time afterward at B. It takes a certain amount of time to transmit the data, and this time is a function of the size of the block and the transmission speed. The propagation delay is largely a function of the length and nature of the communication line. For satellite circuits, the propagation delay is in the vicinity of 250 to 300 ms per satellite hop; for terrestrial lines, the propagation delay is in the range 6 to 10 μs/km (10 to 15 μs/mi).

The block of data is transmitted complete with error-detecting envelope, and when it is received by B, it is checked for transmission errors. If the block is received correctly, B will acknowledge it with a positive acknowledgment (ACK), which will encounter the propagation delay on the way back. Upon receipt of the ACK, A transmits the second block of data. Under ideal conditions, when no data or acknowledgments are corrupted, the time taken to transmit each block of data and to receive the acknowledgment is the time from the transmission of the

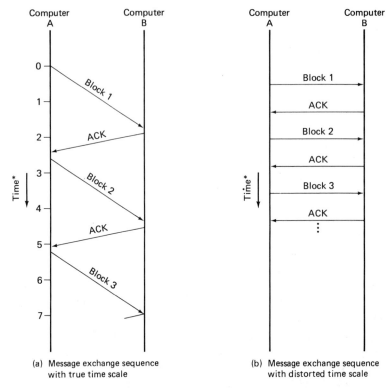

(a) Message exchange sequence
     with true time scale

(b) Message exchange sequence
     with distorted time scale

Note: Diagram (a) is a more accurate representation of message exchange sequences
because it illustrates the time delays involved in data transfer. Diagram (b) shows
the sequence of events involved in message exchange but it does not give an accurate picture of the time involved. As timings need to be calculated separately
and, for the purposes of this book, the pictorial representation of sequence is usually
more important than an accurate representation of time, the diagrams will usually
be drawn in the form of Diagram (b). The form of Diagram (a) will be used if it
is absolutely necessary to show the time relationships. This situation arises with
full–duplex message exchange sequences.

Figure 14-3 Error-free half-duplex block-by-block transmission.

first character of the data block from A until the reception of the last character
of the acknowledgment at A. Knowing this time, one can compute the maximum
throughput of the link in message blocks per second.

Example 14-1: Throughput of a Point-to-Point Line

In Chapter 11 we examined various sources of delays that may be encountered
in block-by-block transmission systems. Let us once again compute the efficiency
of transmission for such a system. Consider the satellite circuit illustrated in Fig.
14-4. If we are transmitting at the rate of 4800 bps, the circuit has a theoretical
throughput of 600 ASCII characters per second using synchronous transmission.
The various delays that may be encountered in such a system include propagation
delay, modem turnaround time, reaction time of the computers at each end of the
link, the delay as the signal passes through a modem, and perhaps some other delays

introduced by particular components in the transmission system. We cannot always accurately identify these component delays, but wherever possible we should attempt to determine the delays introduced by the various transmission components of the system.

Solution   The propagation delay (T_p) for a satellite circuit is approximately 250 ms. If the line is a four-wire line, we should not be faced with modem turnaround time, so we can disregard this component. For the purpose of analysis, we assume that the reaction time of the computers is 2 ms. The delay introduced as the signal passes through modems varies with the type of modem, and we assume a figure of 10 ms for the pair of modems. This delay will be encountered in each direction.

Let us assume that we are transmitting blocks of data that contain 240 ASCII characters (including synchronizing characters) and that the acknowledgment messages consist of a total of six characters including the synchronizing characters. The components of time required to transmit and acknowledge one block will therefore be as follows:

1. Message transmission time
2. Acknowledgment transmission time
3. Loop delay

As indicated earlier, *message transmission time* is the time it takes to physically send the message at the line speed. The message transmission time of 240 characters with ASCII code using synchronous transmission is calculated as follows: Transmission time equals 240 characters × 8 bits per character divided by 4800 bits per second equals 400 ms.

Acknowledgment transmission time for six characters assuming ASCII code is calculated as follows: 6 characters × 8 bits per character divided by 4800 bits per second equals 10 ms.

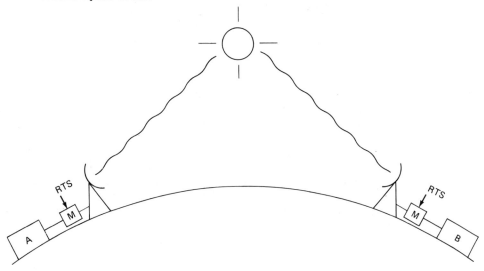

Figure 14-4 Satellite communications.

In this network with a point-to-point four-wire line, the major components of *loop delay* would be as follows;

- *Modem delay* would be encountered in each direction.
- *Propagation delay* would be encountered in each direction.
- *Reaction time* would be encountered at each end of the line.

Modem turnaround time should not be encountered in this network because, with a four-wire point-to-point line, we would expect to be running the modems with permanent carrier. The loop delay is therefore calculated as follows;

			Elapsed time (ms)
Modem delay	2 × 10 ms	=	20
Propagation delay	2 × 250 ms	=	500
Reaction time	2 × 2 ms	=	4
Total loop delay			524

The total time to send a block and receive an acknowledgment therefore consists of the following components;

	Elapsed time (ms)
Message transmission time	400
Acknowledgment transmission time	10
Loop delay	524
Total	934

This simple calculation shows that it takes a total of 934 ms to transmit one block of data and to receive an acknowledge. We can determine the efficiency of transmission by taking the ratio of the time spent actually transmitting data (400 ms) to the total time it takes to transmit and acknowledge the block (934 ms). This gives an efficiency of 400/934 = 43%.

An obvious way to improve the throughput on such a system is to increase the size of the message blocks. If the block transmission time is larger compared to the loop delay (the combination of propagation delay, reaction times, turnaround times, and so on), we can make better use of the available system capacity. However, the problem with long message blocks is that they are more prone to errors being introduced by noise. For a given line with given speed, error rate, and loop delay, it is possible to calculate an optimum block size that will give maximum throughput efficiency.

The Effect of Increasing Line Speed   What happens if we increase the speed of transmission on the communication line? Many people think that if we double the line speed on a given link, we will double the throughput. Let us see if this is true. In the following table we show the equivalent timings for operation on this network at speeds of 4800 and 9600 bps.

Component of loop delay	Elapsed time (ms) at:	
	4800 bps	9600 bps
Message transmission time	400	200
Acknowledgment transmission time	10	5
Loop delay	524	524
Total	934	729

Calculating the throughput for each of these cases, the throughput for 4800 bps in terms of blocks per hour will be as follows:

$$\text{throughput} = \frac{3600 \text{ s/h} \times 1000 \text{ ms/s}}{934 \text{ ms/block}}$$

$$= 3854 \text{ blocks/h}$$

For the second case,

$$\text{throughput} = \frac{3600 \text{ s/h} \times 1000 \text{ ms/s}}{729 \text{ ms/block}}$$

$$= 4938 \text{ blocks/h}$$

It can be seen that the overall improvement in throughput by doubling the line speed is a mere 28%. This relatively small increase in throughput is caused by the fact that the half-duplex protocols require an acknowledge from the other end before the block can be transmitted. This, in turn, invokes the long loop delay and causes severe overheads on the system performance.

Satellite circuits are being used more often for data transmission. This is especially true for international data transmission and in those countries that are using domestic satellite systems. The long propagation delays on these systems can seriously reduce the efficiency of data transmission, so we must look for other methods of improving the throughput. These improved methods involve either full-duplex transmission, as discussed in chapters 17 to 20, or systems whereby we send multiple blocks of data and return a single acknowledgment for many blocks. This means that we increase the amount of time spent transmitting data and reduce the amount of time required to turn the line around to acknowledge the blocks of data. This is the principle of operation of newer line control procedures, such as HDLC/SDLC (high-level data link control procedure and synchronous data link control procedures). These line procedures are described in detail later in chapters 18 to 20.

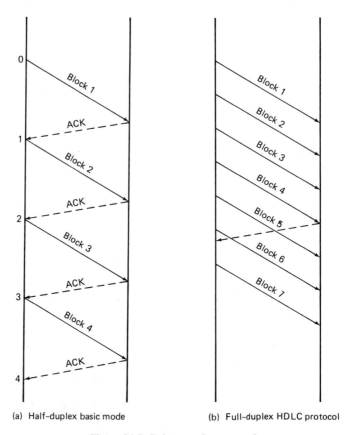

(a) Half-duplex basic mode   (b) Full-duplex HDLC protocol

Figure 14-5 Point-to-point protocols.

Although these line procedures are described in detail in later chapters, the following is a brief illustration of the throughput that can be achieved with a protocol such as HDLC.

Example 14-2: Throughput of Point-to-Point Line under HDLC Full-Duplex Protocol

Figure 14-5 shows the basic protocol sequences for basic mode half-duplex point-to-point and full-duplex HDLC protocols. Under the basic mode protocols each block of data is separately acknowledged and a subsequent block of data cannot be transmitted until the acknowledgment for the preceding block is received. Under HDLC, the blocks are numbered and the blocks can be transmitted one after the other without waiting for an acknowledgment. Finally, a response is received from the other end of the line which, in effect, acknowledges a number of blocks of data at once. As long as there are no errors on the line, it is possible to approach 100% throughput on the link. This can be seen in the diagram.

Solution   In the example that we have been using with blocks of data of 240 characters being transmitted at 4800 bps each block takes 400 ms to transmit. As soon as one block has been transmitted the next can follow, so that the transmission time of one block overlaps with the propagation delay of the preceding block. In this case we transmit one block every 400 ms, which is equivalent to 2.5 blocks per second, which in turn is equivalent to 9000 blocks per hour. Compare this 9000 blocks per hour under full-duplex protocol with 3854 blocks per hour which we achieve with a half-duplex protocol, and we see that the HDLC style protocol has an improvement of 234% over the half-duplex protocol in this particular case.

Contingencies

In real life, perfect message exchange does not always happen. A noise hit can corrupt a message or an acknowledgment, or, perhaps, complete messages and acknowledgments can be lost. Figure 14-6 shows the sequence of events that takes place if a noise hit corrupts the data in a message block during transmission. Computer A transmitted a message block. During transmission, noise caused the data to be corrupted, and, when the message was received at B, an error was discovered within the block. Computer B then transmitted an error response, which would be a negative acknowledgment (NAK). When the NAK is received

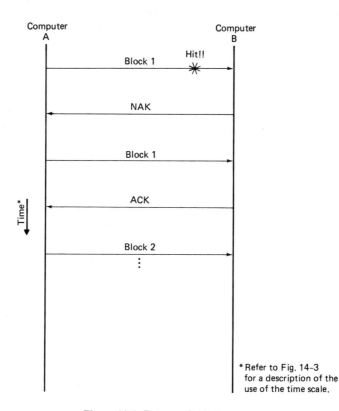

Figure 14-6 Retransmit block sequence.

by A, it knows that it must retransmit the message block. If this message block is successfully received by B, an ACK is returned to A, which, upon receipt of this acknowledgment, can transmit message block 2.

Figure 14-7 shows another problem that can occur with this kind of message-exchange sequence. In this case, the message block was transmitted from A to B, where it was successfully received and an acknowledgment transmitted. The acknowledgment was hit on the line, and it was not detected by A. Computer A does not know what has happened. However, A would have expected a response of some kind within a short period after the transmission of the last character of the message block. Because it did not receive an acknowledgment, A can assume that a problem has occurred, but it does not know whether the problem was a hit on the acknowledgment (or perhaps a hit on the message block) or whether the line is down or B is out of action.

A simple way to find out what happened is to issue a *reply-request* sequence, which is a signal asking B to retransmit its last message. Figure 14-8 shows the reply-request being sent after a timeout; upon its receipt, B checks to see what it last sent and discovers that its last message was an ACK. It then retransmits the ACK, which is received at A. A then knows that the data block was received in one piece, and it then transmits the second block.

At first glance, this looks like a good system, but it turns out that it is possible to lose data under some circumstances. For instance, consider the situation illustrated in Fig. 14-9. Block N − 1 was transmitted, successfully received, and acknowledged by B. Block N was transmitted from A, and it was hit on the way in such a manner that it was totally unrecognizable. Computer B therefore does not acknowledge the message; after a timeout, A issues a reply-request. Upon receipt of the reply-request, B checks to see what it said last time and retransmits

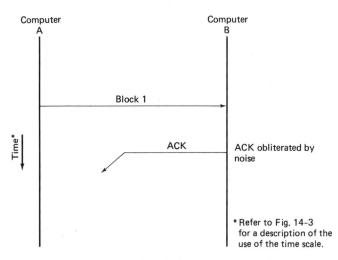

Figure 14-7 Acknowledgment lost in transit.

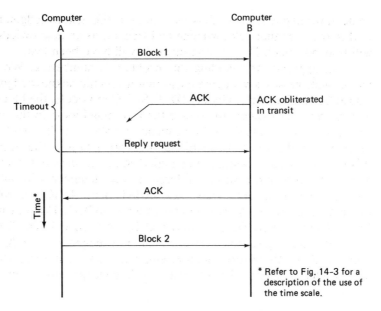

Figure 14-8 Reply-request sequence.

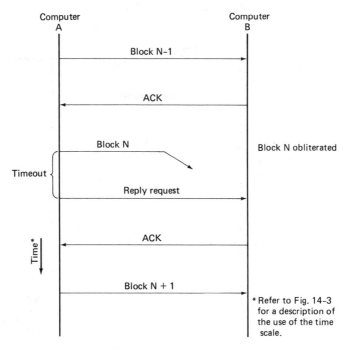

Figure 14-9 Repeat block sequence—data are lost.

an acknowledgment to A. This was, in fact, the acknowledgment to block N −
1. If A receives that acknowledge and treats it as an acknowledge to block N, it
will transmit block N + 1, and block N will have been lost.

An approach to avoiding this problem is numbering. We can number the
blocks and the acknowledgments so that a specific acknowledgment is related to
a specific block of data. Under HDLC/SDLC protocols, the blocks are numbered
and the receiver expects to receive the incoming blocks in the correct sequence.
When it detects a break in the sequence numbers, as it would when it receives
block N + 1, the receiver can initiate recovery action. In the early days, however,
this was regarded as being too complicated and it turns out, that a simple way to
handle this problem is to use different acknowledgments for alternate blocks of
data. Instead of having a single acknowledgment (ACK), we will have two, one
of which is known as ACK-0 and the other as ACK-1. The transmission sequence
for ACK-0 is usually DLE 0 and for ACK-1 it is DLE 1. The first message block
received following station selection is acknowledged with ACK-1 and the second
with ACK-0. Alternating acknowledgments are sent thereafter. Figure 14-10
shows what happens with alternating acknowledgments when the data block is

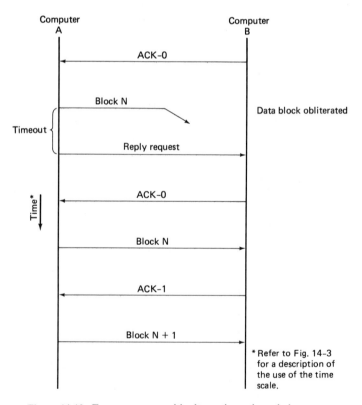

Figure 14-10 Error recovery with alternating acknowledgments.

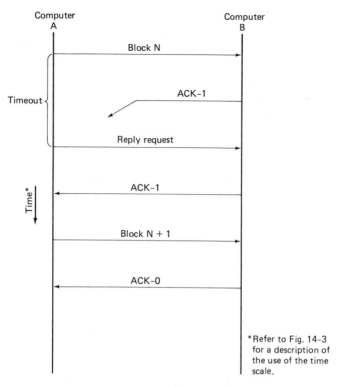

Figure 14-11 Error recovery with alternating acknowledgments.

destroyed, and Fig. 14-11 shows what happens when the acknowledgment is destroyed. In each case, we can recover the situation without losing data.

Typical basic mode half-duplex message-exchange sequences

Having examined the theory behind half-duplex block-by-block data transmission, let us now look at some specific sequences to get a feeling for what happens during a data interchange. The following represents the mainstream of a common set of line control procedures. You will find differences in detail between these and the procedures used by particular manufacturers, but if you can follow this line procedure, you should have no difficulty in analyzing the line control procedures offered by particular vendors.

In this example, we assume that computer A wishes to transmit eight blocks of data to computer B. Alternating acknowledgments are used, and these are designated as ACK-0 and ACK-1. Figure 14-12 illustrates the sequence of events during this operation.

To initiate the data transmission, A must seize master status by sending a station-selection sequence to B. The station selection sequence commonly con-

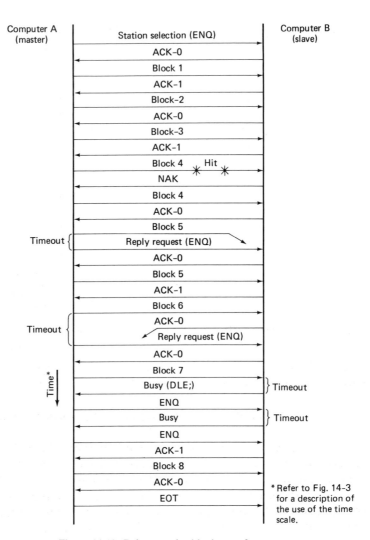

Figure 14-12 Point-to-point block transfer sequence.

sists of the *enquiry* transmission control character (ENQ), which says, in effect, to B, "Hello, are you there, do you wish to accept data?" Assuming that B is ready and willing to accept data, it will respond with a "positive reply to station selection," which is the ACK-0 sequence. Upon receipt of the ACK-0, computer A transmits the first block of data surrounded by an error-detecting envelope.

The block arrives without errors, and B responds with ACK-1. A sends block 2, and B responds with ACK-0. Computer A transmits block 3, and B responds with ACK-1.

During the transmission of block 4, noise corrupts the data, and B detects an error, so it responds with a negative acknowledge (NAK). This causes A to retransmit block 4, and when it arrives in one piece, B transmits ACK-0. Upon receipt of ACK-0, A transmits block 5, which is obliterated by noise and does not arrive at B. After a timeout, during which computer A received no reply, it initiates a reply-request sequence, which also consists of the enquiry character (ENQ). The reply-request causes B to retransmit the last sequence that it sent to A. In this case, it was DLE-0. This tells A that the last block correctly received by B was block 4, so A retransmits block 5. If block 5 arrives without errors, B will respond with ACK-1, which will then cause block 6 to be transmitted. Block 6 draws an ACK-0 response, which in this case is obliterated and does not arrive at A. After a timeout, A initiates the reply-request sequence, which causes B to retransmit its last message, which was ACK-0. That tells A that block 6 did indeed arrive correctly, and A sends block 7.

At this point, B has become busy and is unable to accept any more data, so it temporarily slows down the process by responding to block 7 with a *busy* signal (often called *wack*), which is represented in Fig. 14-12 by the DLE; sequence. The busy signal is an acknowledgment to the block that was received and is a request that A should not transmit any more data. A delay can be built into the system, and in this case the delay is built in at B. So after reception of block 7, B waits a short time before sending the busy signal. Upon receipt of the busy signal, A initiates an enquiry sequence (ENQ), which says, in effect, "Are you ready yet?" If B is still busy, it will allow a timeout to elapse before responding with the busy sequence (DLE;). Upon receipt of the busy signal, A will again initiate the enquiry and this sequence of events continues until such time as B is ready to accept data; at that time, B will respond to the enquiry with DLE-1. This is the acknowledgment that would have been given to block 7 if B had not been busy at the time. This tells computer A that B is ready for more data. A transmits block 8, B responds with DLE-0, and, because it was the last block, A sends an *end-of-transmission* sequence (EOT), which tells B that that is the end of the transmission. The line is then returned to the neutral state.

The preceding examples illustrate the mechanism for transferrring data in the face of noise on the lines. Other problems can occur, and some of these are illustrated in Figs. 14-13 and 14-14. Figure 14-13 shows a situation in which the slave station will not accept data. In this case, the master is on the right and the slave is on the left. The master is attempting to initiate a data transmission by sending a selection sequence (ENQ). The slave does not wish to indulge in data transmission, and it responds with a *negative reply to selection* (NAK). After a suitable time delay, the potential master tries again by sending out the selection sequence, which again draws the negative reply. If this goes on and exceeds a preset retry counter, the master initiates an EOT sequence to return the line to the neutral state and exits to a recovery routine, perhaps to inform its operator that the other computer will not talk to it.

Figure 14-14 shows what happens when the slave does not respond to a station selection. In this case, the master is on the left, and the slave is on the right. The master is attempting to initiate a data transfer by selecting the slave with the enquiry sequence. The slave does not respond. At this point, the master has no way of knowing what happened. Perhaps the slave is out of action; perhaps the line is out of action; perhaps the ENQ was received and the slave responded

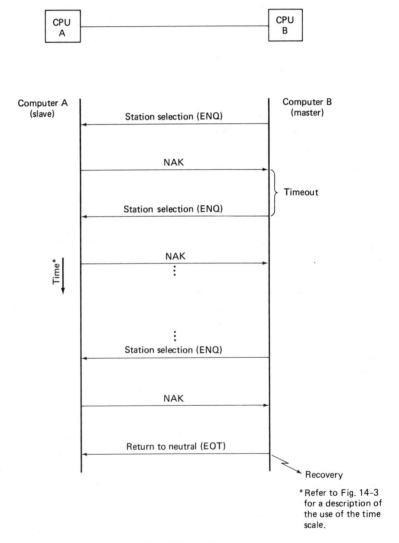

Figure 14-13 Slave will not accept data.

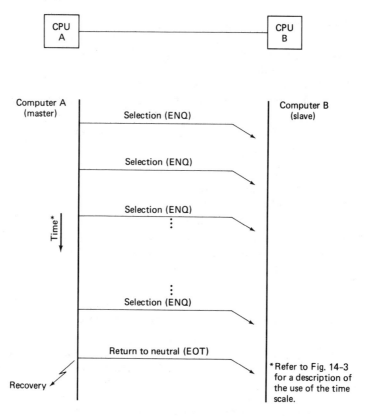

Figure 14-14 Slave does not respond to selection.

with a positive reply to selection, and this was obliterated by noise. After a timeout, the master initiates another enquiry sequence (you can regard this as either a station-selection sequence or a reply-request sequence—it really does not matter), and once again, no response is received. After a number of retries, the master station issues an end-of-transmission sequence (EOT) to reset the slave and return the line to neutral, and it exits to a recovery routine. The EOT sequence is sent out just in case the slave was alive and well and was responding with a *positive reply to selection* (ACK-0) every time the master station sent out the selection sequence (ENQ).

The efficiency of half-duplex data transmission

When analyzing the efficiency of data transfer with a half-duplex line control procedure (or for that matter any other kind of line procedure), one first must understand the logic involved in order to correctly lay out the transmission sequences. Second, one needs to establish the size of the various messages, both data and supervisory messages, so that the transmission times for the messages can be calculated. Third, one needs to determine the loop delay—that is, all the components of delay that can be encountered. The following is a list of the major sources of delay in a system. Not all of them are encountered in every system, and, in fact, some systems may have other sources of delay that are not in this particular list. It is extremely important for the system designer to understand the logic and therefore be able to identify any potential sources of delay in the system. The following are potential sources of delay:

- Propagation delay
- Modem turnaround time
- Modem delay
- Reaction time of computers and terminals
- Delays through other systems components, such as multiplexers, concentrators, line splitters used by communication carriers to split a line out into a multipoint line, and so on

Example 14-3: File Transfer from Sydney to Singapore

This example is extracted from an actual analysis that was performed for one of our clients. Our client wished to transfer files from Sydney, Australia, to Singapore by transmitting blocks of 500 ASCII characters over the international switched telephone network. The line procedure was to be basic mode half-duplex. To determine the length of time (and hence the cost) required for the data transfer, it was necessary to calculate the time required to transmit one block and receive an acknowledgment.

The known loop delays were identified as follows:

- Modem turnaround time was measured at 250 ms.
- One-way propagation delay was established from the international carrier as being 250 ms for a satellite circuit or 160 ms for a submarine cable circuit.

The unknown components of loop delay, such as reaction times and delays introduced by the telephone transmission equipment at each end of the link, were lumped together with an estimated value of 500 ms. This sounds high, but we wanted to make sure that any errors in calculations were on the conservative side.

The total two-way loop delay consists of the sum:

$$
\begin{aligned}
2 \times \text{modem turnarounds} \quad &= \quad 500 \text{ ms} \\
2 \times \text{propagation delay (cable)} &= \quad 320 \text{ ms} \\
\text{Reaction times, etc.} \quad &= \quad \underline{500 \text{ ms}} \\
&\quad\;\; 1320 \text{ ms}
\end{aligned}
$$

Message transmission times can be calculated as follows:

time to transmit a 500-character block

at 1200 bps using synchronous transmission

$$= \frac{500 \text{ char} \times 8 \text{ bits/char}}{1200 \text{ bps}} = 3.333 \text{ s}$$

The acknowledgment message will consist of only five or six characters, and its transmission time can be ignored in this example.

Total time to transmit and acknowledge one block

$$= \text{loop delay} + \text{block transmission time} + \text{ACK time}$$

$$= 1320 \text{ ms} + 3333 \text{ ms} + 0$$

$$= 4653 \text{ ms}$$

The efficiency of this data transmission is 3333/4653 = 72%. Based on this calculation, the cost of transmitting a complete file was calculated, and it was decided to go ahead.

When the system was up and running, we found that it actually took 4.29 s to transmit one block and receive its acknowledgment. This indicated that our original estimate of 500 ms for reaction times and other delays was too conservative. Nevertheless, in calculations aimed at determining the economic feasibility of a project, it is better to err on the conservative side.

The system designer may find it more attractive to come up with high and low estimates for each delay in the system. He or she can then perform a series of calculations and produce a range of results from the expected best case to the expected worst case.

15
Half-Duplex Multipoint

multipoint line control

In a multipoint situation, under basic mode procedures, one station is designated as the *control* station, and generally, no other station transmits unless the control station gives permission.

In the newer link procedures, such as high-level data link control (HDLC) and synchronous data link control (SDLC), one station generally is permanently in charge of the line. The control station is called a *primary* station, and the others are called *secondary* stations. Data can flow in either direction, but in general, a secondary never transmits unless told to do so by the primary.

polling (inbound messages)

The technique that the controlling station uses to control the flow of data on the line is called *polling*. Polling can be defined as the process of inviting stations, in an orderly fashion, to transmit data.

In the simplest case, the computer polls the terminals on the line sequentially by asking each one if it has anything to transmit. The terminal will either have a message or will not have a message, which means that the response to a poll will either be data or a *no-traffic response* (NTR).

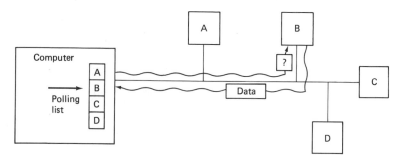

Figure 15-1 Polling on a multidrop line.

Figure 15-1 shows a computer polling a line with four terminals. The computer has a polling list that indicates the sequence in which the terminals will be polled, and in this particular case, terminal B is being polled and is responding with a data message. It is possible to give one terminal priority over the others by including its address in the polling list more frequently than the others. For example, terminal A could be given higher priority by including its address every second time such that the polling sequence would be A-B-A-C-A-D-A-B. Similarly, a terminal can be dropped from the polling list if desired (e.g., it may be unattended, or it may have broken down).

To implement a polling system, we must have terminals that are uniquely addressable. Figure 15-2 illustrates a line with four drops and one terminal at each drop except for the third drop, which has a cluster of three terminals. It is common to use a two-level addressing structure so that the first level of addressing specifies the drop, and the second level specifies the terminal at the drop. In this diagram, terminal address AA means terminal A at drop A, terminal address CB means terminal B at drop C, and so on.

A poll transmitted from the computer is seen by all terminals, but only the terminal whose address is in the poll recognizes it. All other terminals ignore it. The general rule is that if a terminal does not see its own address in a message, it ignores it. The polled terminal can respond either with a message or with a no-traffic response. The usual response to a poll is a no-traffic response, because we

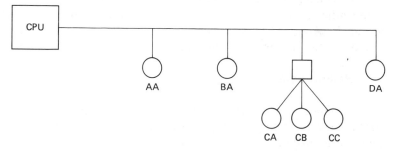

Figure 15-2 Multidrop line—terminal addressing.

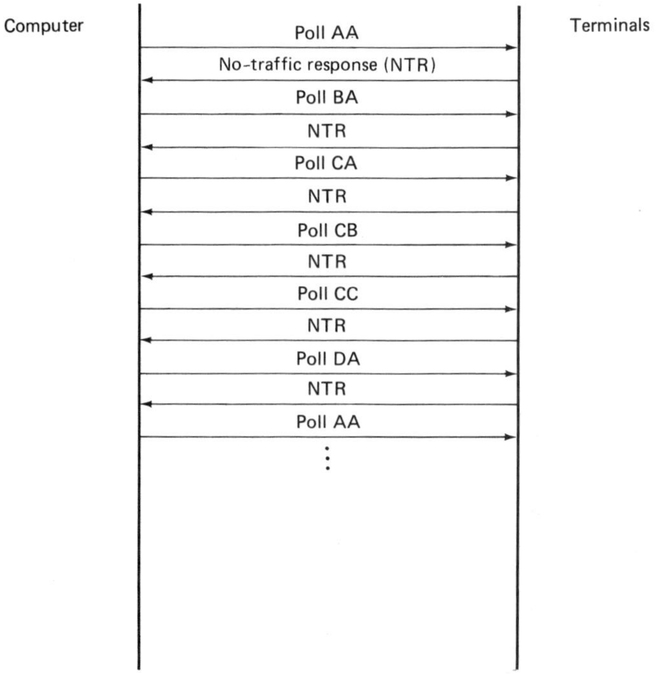

Figure 15-3 Polling on a multidrop line.

generally poll at a much faster rate than that at which messages are generated. A poll that does not draw a message is called an unsuccessful poll. As indicated earlier, most polls are unsuccessful.

Figure 15-3 shows the sequence of events on the line in Fig. 15-2 if there are no messages being generated in the network. This is a method of showing message-exchange sequences. The computer is on the left of the diagram, the terminals are on the right, and we can imagine a time scale running from top to bottom. Figure 15-3 shows the computer polling terminal AA, which responds with a no-traffic response; the computer then polls terminal BA, which also responds with a no-traffic response. It then polls terminal CA, which responds with a no-traffic response, and so on, until finally the computer gets around to polling terminal AA again. This sequence of events takes time. We analyze the timing in more detail on the following pages.

Polling delay

Polling is not instantaneous. It takes time to poll a terminal, receive a no-traffic response, and get ready to poll the next terminal. Let us now calculate the time for an unsuccessful poll for the network shown in Fig. 15-4. If the host was in one city the terminals in another city 1000 km away and the line running at

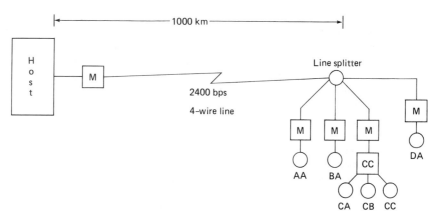

Figure 15-4 Multipoint line.

2400 bps, it would typically take around 150 ms for an unsuccessful poll. This can be calculated as follows.

Example 15-1: Polling Time for a Multipoint Line

The time for an unsuccessful poll has three major components:

1. Poll transmission time
2. No-traffic-response transmission time
3. Loop delay

The *poll transmission time* is the time that it takes to physically send the poll at the line speed. Imagine a buffer in the host containing the polling message; then the poll transmission time is the length of time it takes to discharge the buffer onto the line at the basic transmission speed of the line. In our case let us assume that the polling message is 15 characters in length. If we are using ASCII code with synchronous transmission, we have eight bits per character and the transmission time for the poll will be:

$$\text{Transmission Time} = \frac{15 \text{ ch} \times 8 \text{ bits/ch}}{2400 \text{ bps}}$$

$$= 0.05 \text{ s}$$

$$= 50 \text{ ms}$$

The *no-traffic-response transmission time* can be calculated similarly. Let us assume a NTR of five characters. The transmission time will be:

$$\text{Transmission Time} = \frac{5 \text{ ch} \times 8 \text{ bits/ch}}{2400 \text{ bps}}$$

$$= 0.017 \text{ s}$$

$$= 17 \text{ ms}$$

The final component of time delay is *loop delay*. As we have seen, loop delay is the sum of the round-trip delays encountered by a message going from the computer out to the terminals and back to the computer again. The following are components of time that would be involved in loop delay in this example.

Modem Turnaround. In this network the instation modem should be running permanent carrier, as it is most likely a four-wire multipoint line. On a four-wire multipoint line we can have a permanent carrier on the outbound channel because there is only one source of carrier, which means that we do not need to encounter modem turnaround at the instation modem. On the inbound channel, there are four modems; therefore, we must use controlled carrier on these modems, and whenever a remote terminal wishes to send a message to the computer, it must wait for the modem turnaround time. As we are using 2400-bps modems, we will assume a high time delay from the CCITT recommendations of 40 ms. (In practice you would use the actual modem turnaround on the modems that you are using, and in most cases you would find that this will be substantially less than 40 ms.)

Modem Delay. Modem delay is the modulation/demodulation delay that we encounter going through the modems. We encounter this delay in both directions going from the host to the terminals and again from the terminals back to the host. In our case we will assume that the modem delay is 10 ms per pair of modems in each direction.

Propagation Delay. Propagation delay is the length of time it takes for the electrical signal to get from one end of the communication line to the other. We will assume the figure of 10 μs/km, and as we have 1000 km of line, the propagation delay will be 10 ms.

Splitter/Combiner Delay. The splitter/combiner which is used to enable the line to be set up into a multipoint line will introduce slight time delays. In our case there is only one splitter/combiner (in reality there could be more, depending on the geography of the situation) and we will assume a time delay of 1.5 ms each time we go through the splitter/combiner.

Reaction Times. We will have reaction times at the host and also at the terminals. We will assume a 2 ms reaction time for the host and 6 ms for the terminal. Note that at drop C we have a cluster controller with three terminals. In practice we should endeavor to establish whether there is a separate reaction time for the cluster controller. In our particular case we will assume that it is zero, so that the reaction time for all terminals will be the same.

The loop delay can now be summarized as in the following table:

		Elapsed time (ms)
Modem delay	2 × 10 ms gives	20
Propagation delay	2 × 10 ms gives	20
Splitter/combiner delay	2 × 1.5 gives	3
Reaction time		
Host		2
Visual display terminal		6
Modem turnaround time		<u>40</u>
Total		91

The time for an unsuccessful poll is therefore summarized as follows:

	Elapsed time (ms)
Poll transmission time	50
No-traffic-response transmission time	17
Loop delay	91
Total	158

Poll cycle time

Poll cycle time is the length of time between successive polls to a particular terminal assuming that there is no other traffic in the network.

As indicated in Fig. 15-3, in a typical network the usual response to a poll is a no-traffic response. In our case we had six terminals on the line and each terminal is polled once per cycle. The poll cycle time will therefore be 6 times 158, which is 948 ms. Looking at the situation from the point of view of one terminal as shown in Fig. 15-5, that terminal will receive a poll every 948 ms. Occasionally, a terminal operator will enter a transaction into the terminal and hit the transmit button. If the terminal operator is lucky, he or she will hit the transmit button just before the next poll comes into the terminal and the message will be transmitted immediately. If the terminal operator is unlucky, he or she will hit the transmit button just after the terminal said no traffic to the last poll. Therefore, on average the terminal operator will hit the transmit button midway between polls as shown on Fig. 15-5.

The average time from when we hit the transmit button until we receive the next poll is called the *polling delay*. It should be noted that the polling delay itself is an average, that it will fluctuate from transaction to transaction, and that the definition of polling delay assumes that there is no other traffic in the network.

In reality there will be other traffic in the network. There will be traffic going to or from other terminals on the network and the terminal operator will experience

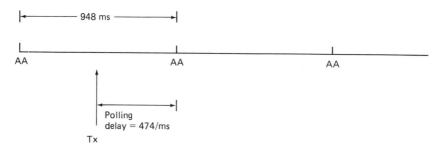

Figure 15-5 Polling delay.

an additional delay caused by interference from other traffic in the network. As shown in Fig. 15-6, this delay can be encountered in the time between hitting the transmit button and the poll being received. Also, depending on the software organization, an interference delay may be experienced prior to the output message being transmitted. In Fig. 15-6 the operator enters the transaction into the terminal and hits the transmit button. We wait for the polling delay; however, when the polling delay elapses, we still may not receive a poll because another operator may have hit the transmit button within the same poll cycle, which means that this other operator may be polled first and we must wait while that terminal's message is transmitted. Alternatively, when we hit the transmit button there may already be a message on the line going into the computer or out to a terminal and polling has been suspended. We must wait for the message or messages to be transmitted before polling can be resumed. This interference time delay is, in fact, a queuing delay and is a nonlinear time delay increasing exponentially as the load on the line increases. After the host finishes processing, we are once again likely to come across an interference time delay. If we are running with a single-thread system (i.e., one in which the transactions are processed strictly one at a time so that we handle the input from one terminal, process it, then send an output to that terminal), we would not have an interference time delay after the host processing. In a multithread system, where we allow inputs and outputs to take place simultaneously with the processing in the host, we will suffer a time delay caused by interference from traffic going to or from other terminals prior to output. When the host is ready to output the response, it could be that there is already a message on the line coming in or going out and that we must wait for that message to be finished before we can get access to the line.

Many variations on the theme can occur. For example, in some systems the host does not attempt to transmit the output message until the host would normally

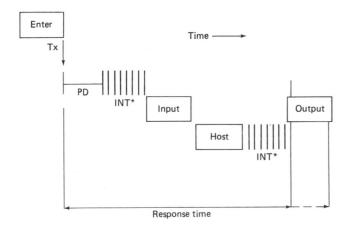

*INT: Interference
PD: Polling delay

Figure 15-6 Block diagram for a simple on-line inquiry system.

have got around to polling that terminal in the normal sequence of events. In this case we would experience an additional time delay between the host and the output which would be the equivalent of a polling delay. The diagram shown in Fig. 15-6 is a typical block diagram of an on-line enquiry. In reality you should examine your own system in some detail to build a model of the way your system operates.

Note: On a particular communication line different terminals may have different polling delays. This is because it is possible to set up the polling sequence so that some terminals are polled more often than others. This means that some terminals will have shorter poll cycle times and therefore shorter polling delays.

Example 15-2: Periodic Polling

There are various approaches to polling. Some systems poll as fast as they can, so that the computer issues a poll to the terminal as soon as it has received a no-traffic response from a preceding terminal. This was the case in the earlier example. In the early days, however, it was found that polling as frequently as possible caused overheads in the host which limited the amount of time left for the host to process other work. In many systems, therefore, polls were issued periodically. For example, if the computer can issue a poll and get a no-traffic response within 158 ms, as calculated earlier, we may decide to poll once every 200 ms. This leaves some time for the host to carry on with other work. In this case if we poll every 200 ms it will take a total of 6 × 200 = 1200 ms for the computer to poll all the terminals in the network of Fig. 15-4 and get around to polling the first terminal again. This 1200 ms is the poll cycle time and the polling delay would be 600 ms.

In modern computer systems, where we have a front-end processor, the front-end has nothing better to do than sit there polling the terminals as fast as it can and, in the process, relieving the host of the load of polling the terminals so that the host can carry on with the business of processing other work. Therefore, with front ends, there is generally no reason why we should not poll at the maximum speed.

Group polls

In the system we have just analyzed, we polled the terminals individually and we call these polls *specific polls*. A specific poll is a poll addressed to a particular terminal, and although it will be seen by all terminals on the line, other terminals will ignore it because they do not see their address in the poll. Only the terminal whose address appears in the polling message will respond to the poll.

If there are many terminals on the line, as in an airline system, where there may be 40 or 50 terminals on the line, it would take an intolerably long time to go around the network if we use specific polls on the terminals. In this situation, it is possible to speed up the polling process by polling all the terminals at a drop simultaneously. This is accomplished by having a *group address*, which is recognized by all terminals at a drop; those terminals that have messages to transmit signal this fact to the cluster controller. This results in a contention situation at

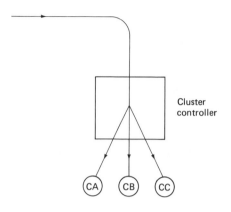

(a) All terminals see the group poll

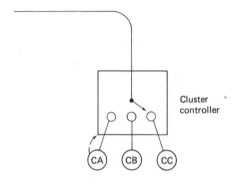

(b) Terminal CA signals that it has a message to send

Figure 15-7 Logical operation of a cluster controller.

the cluster controller, and the cluster controller then resolves the contention by selecting one of the terminals to transmit. (Cluster controllers are also termed *terminal multiplexers, control units, line-sharing adapters*, etc.)

This sequence of events is illustrated in Fig. 15-7. In the outbound direction, the cluster controller sends the messages from the computer to all terminals. All the terminals at the controller recognize the message if it has the correct group address. On the inbound side from the terminals to the computer, a cluster controller has a logical switch, which enables it to connect one and only one terminal through to the line so that that terminal can transmit data to the computer. If two or more terminals have messages to transmit, they will signal to the cluster controller, typically by activating one of the V.24/RS-232 interface signals, which will then switch one of the terminals through to the line to allow it to transmit the message into the computer. If there are 30 terminals at the drop and four of them have messages to send, we can poll all terminals with a group poll, and depending on the implementation of terminal hardware/software, we may collect all the messages with one group poll or perhaps with four, rather than having to issue 30 specific polls to get the same amount of information. This saves a lot of time and so boosts the system performance.

It should be noted that group polling can only be used to poll terminals that are connected to the one cluster controller. If we were to group poll terminals on separate drops, we could have a contention situation because one terminal at each drop may wish to transmit. In this case the transmissions could collide and become unrecognizable.

The implementation of a cluster controller varies from system to system. Some of them are indeed simple hardware devices that perform exactly as shown in Fig. 15-7, whereas others are logical devices built into systems in which the terminals are daisy-chained (or concatenated). Various implementations of cluster controllers are as follows:

Intelligent Terminal Control Unit. This unit contains buffers and flags for each individual terminal's data and control information. Figure 15-8(a) shows such an intelligent terminal control unit. In this case the terminals themselves are little more than picture tubes with keyboards connected, typically, via a coaxial cable back to the control unit. As data are entered on the terminal keyboard they are stored in the buffer in the control unit and the screen is refreshed directly from this buffer. When the terminal operator hits the transmit button, a flag is set in the control unit and when a group poll is received at the control unit, logic in the control unit will scan the available buffers and see which terminals have the messages to send. In the simplest case the first terminal that activated the transmit button will have its message sent in response to the poll, and to get subsequent messages, we need additional polls. In a somewhat more sophisticated situation where several terminals have messages to send, the poll may draw the message from the first terminal and when the acknowledgment comes back to that message, we will then get the second message, which will be acknowledged, then we get the third message, and so on. Finally, in the newer systems which have more intelligence in the control units, it is possible to get all the messages in response to the one poll as follows. A poll is received by the control unit which scans the buffers to see which terminals have messages to send; it then builds up a large message consisting of a number of smaller messages end to end and transmits all these messages in one block down the line to the host.

Daisy Chain. (Concatenated Implementation with Contention Being Resolved at the V.24 Physical Interface). Figure 15-8(b) shows a typical daisy-chain connection where a number of modems are connected via an extended V.24 interface. Typically in this situation the poll is received by the cluster of terminals and recognized by all terminals. If no terminals have messages to send, as a rule the terminal at the end of the daisy chain will transmit a no-traffic response. If a

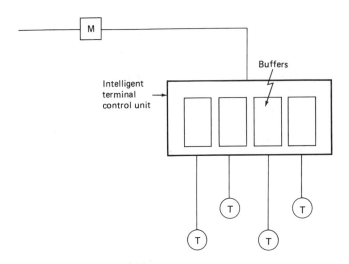

(a) Intelligent terminal control unit

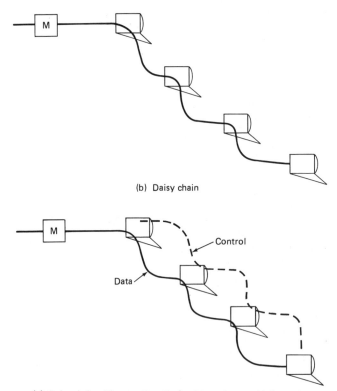

(b) Daisy chain

(c) Daisy chain with separate paths for data and control information

Figure 15-8 Cluster controllers—various configurations.

terminal has a message to send, it will activate request-to-send, which will be propagated up the V.24 interface to the modem. The modem will respond with clear-to-send, which will be captured by the terminal closest to the modem with request-to-send raised. This terminal can then transmit data and, should any other terminals farther down the daisy chain have their request-to-send raised, they will not get to transmit data because the clear-to-send will be trapped by the first terminal and will not be propagated down the line to the subsequent terminals. After a timeout these terminals lower their request-to-send and wait for the next poll.

In this situation we resolve contention at the daisy chain at the V.24 interface level. It may look as though the terminal closest to the modem has priority, and in the situation I just described it does indeed have priority. In the early days this did not cause a problem because the messages were generated by human operators and it was not possible for one operator to generate messages fast enough to take all the polls. This meant that even with fairly active operators, all terminals had a reasonably equal chance of transmitting data.

In new systems with intelligent terminals or personal computers equipped with disks or floppy disks, it is possible for one terminal to take all the polls. Suppose that an operator has built up a file on floppy disk and wishes to transmit it from terminal A. Loading the floppy disk into terminal A and setting up the terminal to transmit the file block by block, it is possible for this terminal to transmit a block of data in response to each poll that comes down the line, which means that the remaining terminals on the cluster would not get a chance to transmit. In this situation it would be a wise idea to use the terminal at the end of the daisy chain for file transfer.

Some manufacturers implement timing mechanisms to avoid this kind of lockout situation as follows. It is possible to have variable reaction times built into the terminals so that each terminal responds to a poll with a random reaction time. This means that all terminals have an equal chance of being the first terminal to bring up request-to-send. Another approach is to have a cycle of reaction times and each terminal cycles through a range of reaction times each time a poll comes, and therefore each terminal has a chance of having a short reaction time or a long reaction time.

Daisy Chain with Separate Paths for Data and Control Information. As indicated in Fig. 15-8(c), the main V.24 interface is extended through the terminals for data transfer, and there is also a second daisy chain extending through the terminals which allows them to exchange control information between themselves. In this case when a poll is received by the cluster, the terminals can indulge in a dialogue to establish which terminal wishes to respond and when it is going to respond. There are many other variations on the theme, but the foregoing should give you a reasonable amount of information with which to be able to analyze your own situation.

selection (outbound messages)

In the reverse direction, if the computer wishes to transmit a message to a terminal, it must *select* that particular terminal to receive the message. This involves preceding each message with an address so that only the terminal whose address is in the message will receive it. As with polling, all terminals on the line see the message, but only the terminal whose address is contained in the message recognizes it.

There are two main approaches to *selection*. One is known as *fast select*, and the other, for want of a better name, I call *polite selection*. In fast-select systems, the message is transmitted preceded by a terminal address, and the terminal has no option but to accept the message. In the case of a visual display terminal, the message will be received and displayed immediately. This is fine for *solicited* traffic, because a solicited message is one that the terminal operator asked for and that is therefore expected to be received. This is the typical situation in *enquiry-and-response* systems, in which the terminal operator has input an enquiry and is awaiting an answer. When the computer has the answer, it addresses it specifically to that terminal, and the message appears immediately on its screen.

Suppose, on the other hand, that the terminal operator had been busily composing a 2000-character message and was entering data at the rate of one or two characters per second. If another terminal operator wishes to send the first terminal operator a message, and the fast-select technique was used, that message would appear immediately on the screen and would perhaps destroy the data that the operator had been entering. This is an *unsolicited* message, which the terminal operator did not ask for, did not know he was going to get, and, most likely, did not want at that particular instant. In this case we would use a special technique for handling unsolicited messages. There are a number of approaches to this, and one is to send out a selection sequence to the terminal. This is similar to a polling sequence in that it asks the terminal if it wishes to receive data. If the terminal is not in a position to receive, it will respond with a negative response, which will cause the computer to hold the message. If the terminal is in a position to receive, it can answer with a positive response, and the computer will then transmit the message using fast select.

Another system is the so-called *message-waiting* system. Some terminals have an indicator light or an audible alarm, which indicates that the computer has a message waiting for it. The alarm or the light is activated by a special supervisory sequence that is addressed to that terminal and informs it that the computer has a message for it. The operator takes note of the alarm or light and, when finished composing the long message and ready to accept the unsolicited message, can press the message-waiting button. The next time the computer polls that terminal, it will transmit a *send message-waiting* sequence, which will inform the computer that the terminal is now ready to receive the message. The computer can then send the message to the terminal using the fast-select sequence.

half-duplex multipoint operation (basic mode)

Now that we have examined the basic principles of polling and selection, we sample some typical sequences of line control on a multipoint line to illustrate the mainstream of operation of a line control procedure. Once again, there are differences in detail between the methods of implementation of these line procedures by different manufacturers, but if you can follow the principles outlined in the following pages, you should be able to analyze any line procedure that you come across in the field.

Figures 15-2 and 15-4 illustrate the type of network that we will look at. This shows a multipoint line with a number of terminals, some in clusters and some with single terminals at a drop. In most cases we would use a four-wire line for this configuration, which will enable us to keep the modem carrier running continuously at the instation modem. This modem will always transmit carrier, and the remote modems will remain locked onto it. In the case of the inbound channel, we will need to switch the modem carriers on and off depending on which terminal is being given the opportunity to transmit.

For this multipoint line to operate, we need an addressing structure so that a terminal can be uniquely identified in a polling or selection message. We also need to use buffered terminals so that the operator at the remote site can enter the data into the terminal at his or her own speed. When the operator is ready to transmit, he or she will press the *transmit* (or *enter*) key. When the terminal is polled, the data from the terminal buffer will be transmitted to the computer at the line speed.

Earlier, when defining terms for basic mode control, we said that, for a particular data transfer operation, we must have a master and a slave. The master transmits data to the slave, and the process is controlled by supervisory messages. On a multidrop line, we either transmit data *to* the control station or *from* the control station. This means that sometimes the control station is a master and sometimes it is a slave. Similarly, the status of the remote station changes from time to time.

The control station can assume master status for itself, or it can designate another station to be a master station. Polling confers master status on a terminal, and the master station can *select* another station to be the slave for that data transfer. The terminal that is polled selects the computer (the control station) to be the slave to receive an input message. (It is logically possible, on a two-wire line, to select another terminal to receive a message.)

Figure 15-9 illustrates a typical error-free sequence of events showing the computer polling a remote terminal and receiving a message in response. The computer first sends out an EOT, which is used to reset the network. This is issued just in case any terminal in the network is hung up in a nonstandard situation, and it will clear the terminal's line control logic and return the line to the *control* situation. The computer then polls the network; this poll will either be addressed specifically to a terminal, or it will be a group poll issued to all terminals

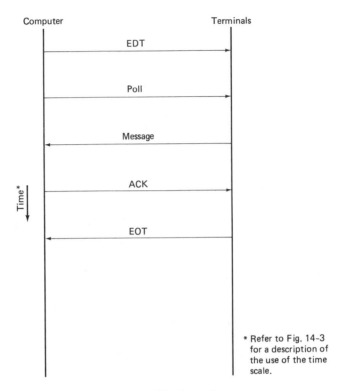

Figure 15-9 Polling for an input message.

at a single drop. Assuming that the terminal has a message, it will send it surrounded by an error-detecting envelope. When the message arrives in one piece, the computer will acknowledge the message. When the acknowledgment is received, the terminal responds with an EOT sequence to signify that that is the end of the transmission and that the line is now returned to the control situation.

In some systems we have multiple blocks of data to transmit from the terminal, in which case the computer will poll the terminal, and, after the first message block is received and acknowledged, the subsequent blocks will be transmitted. We would need to use an alternating acknowledge sequence for the message blocks; otherwise, we could run into the problem we encountered with half-duplex PTP data transmission, whereby it is possible to lose blocks of data.

In Fig. 15-3, we saw the sequence of events when we poll the network and no terminals have any data to transmit. Figure 15-10 illustrates the sequence of events whereby we poll the network and receive no response to the poll. The computer issues an EOT sequence to reset the network and to return the line to the control situation; then it polls the terminal. It gets no response, and the computer has no way of knowing whether the polled terminal did indeed respond with data or perhaps with a no-traffic response; so after a reasonable timeout, it issues another EOT sequence to reset the network just in case the terminal had responded, and then it issues another poll. If the terminal at the other end had tried to transmit a message, it would retransmit the message upon receipt of the poll. In this particular example, there is still no response to the poll, so the computer repeats the sequence of events until it has exceeded a preset number of retries. It then issues an EOT to clear the network down and return the network to the control state. The computer then exits to a recovery routine because in this event there is likely to be a problem with the network.

Figure 15-11 shows how we can recover lost data if a message is corrupted by noise. In the diagram the computer sends the EOT followed by a poll. The polled terminal has a message that it transmits, and, on the way, the message is hit by noise and arrives at the computer with an error in it. The computer detects the error and responds with a negative acknowledge (NAK). Upon receipt of the NAK, the terminal retransmits the message, and, assuming it arrives in one piece, the computer will respond with a positive acknowledgment (ACK). The terminal then responds with EOT to indicate the end of the transmission.

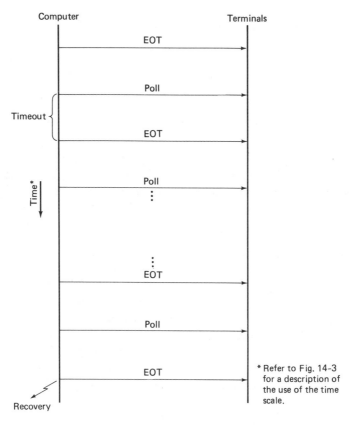

Figure 15-10 Polling with no response from the network.

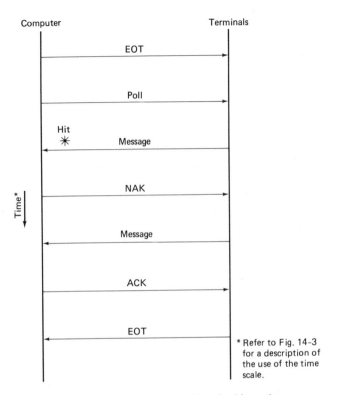

Figure 15-11 Input message transfer with noise hit on the message.

Figure 15-12 illustrates a fast-select sequence, which is used to transmit a message from the computer to a terminal. Initially, the computer sends an EOT sequence that will reset the network; this is followed by the message. The message itself contains an address for the receiving terminal. Although all terminals on the line see the message, only the terminal that recognizes its own address accepts the message. If it is received correctly, the message is acknowledged. After receipt of the ACK, the computer responds with an EOT sequence to return the situation to the control state. If an error had occurred, the message would be retransmitted, as shown in Fig. 15-13. In this diagram the computer issues the EOT to reset the network and then transmits the message. The message is hit by noise and arrives at the terminal with an error, so the terminal responds with a negative acknowledge (NAK). This tells the computer to retransmit the message. When it arrives in one piece, the terminal responds with an acknowledge (ACK), and the computer then terminates the transmission with an EOT sequence.

If the message had been totally obliterated on the way, the computer would issue a reply request, as illustrated in Fig. 15-14. The computer first issues an EOT and then transmits the message using fast select. The message is totally obliterated by noise and does not arrive at the terminal. This means that the

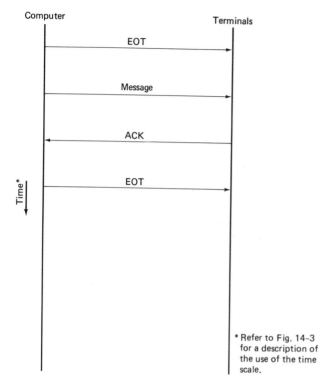

* Refer to Fig. 14-3
for a description of
the use of the time
scale.

Figure 15-12 Fast select for output message.

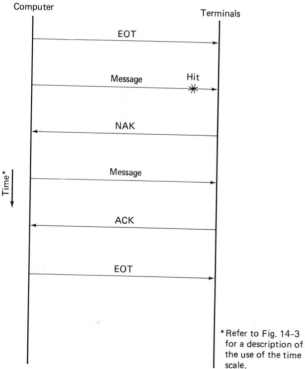

* Refer to Fig. 14-3
for a description of
the use of the time
scale.

Figure 15-13 Fast select with noise hit on message.

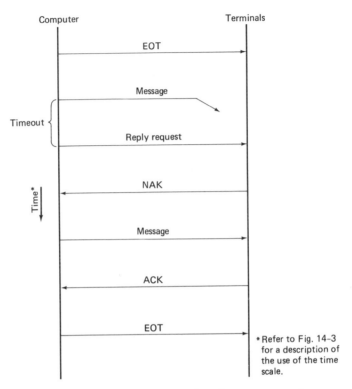

Figure 15-14 The reply-request sequence allows lost messages to be recovered.

terminal does not respond, and after a timeout, the computer issues a reply-request sequence. When the terminal receives the reply-request, it has nothing to say because it had not said anything, and it responds with a NAK. When the computer receives the NAK, it retransmits the message. This is a logical sequence of events, because it could have been that the message had arrived at the terminal with an error in it and that the terminal had indeed responded with NAK and the NAK had been lost on the way back. In that case, the reply-request would have drawn the NAK, which would have achieved the same purpose. When the message is received, the terminal responds with an acknowledge (ACK), and the computer then transmits an EOT to restore the network to the control state.

If the line had been down, if there was severe noise on the line, or, perhaps, if the terminal had been down, then the series of events in Fig. 15-15 would have taken place. In this diagram both the EOT and the message disappear on the way to the terminal. The computer gets no response, and it has no way of knowing whether the message arrived at the terminal. So after a suitable time delay, it issues a reply-request. In this case, the reply-request also disappears, and the computer still gets no response. After a timeout, it issues another reply-request and repeats this sequence of events until it exceeds a preset retry count. The computer then sends an EOT just in case the terminal had been receiving all the messages and had in fact been responding with acknowledgments or negative acknowledgments, as the case may be. The computer then exits to a recovery routine.

Unsolicited messages are handled differently than solicited messages, which can use the fast-select sequence. One method for handling unsolicited messages is illustrated in Fig. 15-16. In this diagram we are assuming that the terminal has a message-waiting indicator, which will sound an alarm or light a lamp upon receipt of a special message-waiting sequence from the computer. This alarm or lamp will draw the operator's attention to the fact that the computer has a message.

When the computer has an unsolicited message for the terminal, it first initiates an EOT sequence and then sends out the special message-waiting sequence to the particular terminal. This will be a control message, which contains the terminal address, and it will cause the message-waiting indicator on the terminal to be activated. The terminal responds with an ACK to acknowledge receipt of the message-waiting signal.

The indicator on the terminal informs the operator that the computer has a message, and the operator continues doing whatever he or she was doing when

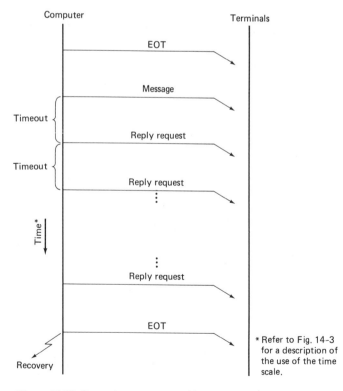

Figure 15-15 Fast-select sequence with no response from the network.

the message-waiting signal came in. When the operator is ready to receive the message, he or she can activate the message-waiting switch. The next time the computer polls that terminal, it will respond with a send-message-waiting signal. This is also illustrated in Fig. 15-16. The computer polls the terminal, and, because the operator has hit the message-waiting button, the terminal responds with a send-message-waiting sequence. The computer immediately drops into the fast-select mode and sends out an EOT followed by the message, which is addressed specifically to that terminal. Assuming that the message arrives in one piece, the receiving terminal acknowledges with ACK, and the computer responds with EOT to return the network to the control state.

An alternative method for handling unsolicited traffic is shown in Fig. 15-17. Here the computer sends out a *select* message, which acts similarly to a poll

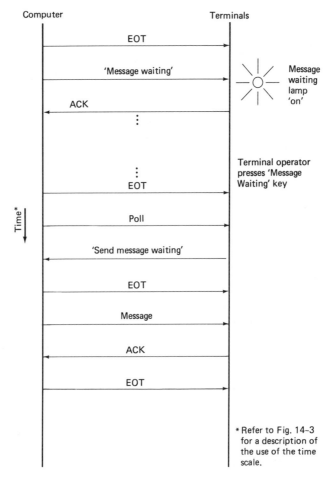

Figure 15-16 Message-waiting procedure for unsolicited message.

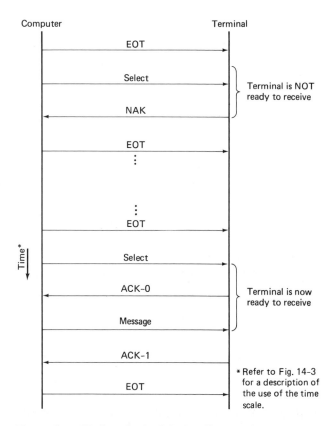

Figure 15-17 "Polite selection" for handling unsolicited message.

in that it asks the terminal if it is ready to receive data. If the terminal is not ready, it can respond with a NAK, which causes the computer to continue with its other activities on the line. Later it will attempt once again to select the terminal to receive data. When the terminal is ready, it will respond to the selection sequence with an acknowledge, which will then cause the computer to transmit the message by using fast-select techniques. The message is acknowledged if it is correctly received, and the computer then sends out an EOT to reset the network to the control state. Note that in this method we need to use alternating acknowledgments to enable us to recover the message if it were completely wiped out by noise.

16
Half-Duplex Performance Analysis: Examples

performance analysis for half-duplex multidrop lines

The performance of a multidrop line is probably best expressed in terms of the amount of traffic the line can handle and the speed with which it handles the traffic. In an enquiry-and-response situation, the terminal operators will be interested primarily in the overall system response time, which can be defined as the time from when the operator presses the transmit or enter key on the terminal until the first character of the response appears on the screen.

The timing for such an operation will have a number of components. The first component is the *polling delay*, which is the time that elapses from when the operator presses the transmit key until the computer gets around to polling that particular terminal. When the network is lightly loaded, it is likely that when the operator presses the transmit key, he or she is the only operator to do so within that particular polling cycle. The polling delay therefore will be, on average, one-half of the time it takes to poll all the terminals in the network.

If the network traffic is fairly high, not only will there be polling messages on the network but there will be data messages going to and from other terminals on the line. In this case, when the operator presses the transmit button, he or she will have to wait not only for the computer to get around to polling the terminal but for other transactions that may be processed from other terminals.

In Figs. 15-9 and 15-12 we saw typical message sequences for input and output messages. Each supervisory or data message takes a certain amount of time to send and may also encounter delays in the network. To analyze the performance of the network, we must identify all these delays.

We now briefly analyze the components of a typical enquiry-and-response transaction on a multipoint line.

Example 16-1: Half-Duplex Multipoint No. 1

A typical multipoint line is illustrated in Fig. 16-1. This shows a system with a computer in city A and a line extending to city B, where a component called a *line splitter* splits off two drops to local terminals and allows the main line to continue on to city C, where a second line splitter splits off the line to two drops in that city.

The line splitters themselves often introduce a time delay of the order of 1.5 ms per transmission through the line splitter in either direction. The delay introduced by line splitters will be different depending on whether we are communicating with terminals in city B or city C; similarly, the propagation delay will be different depending on whether we are communicating with city B or city C.

To accurately determine the polling cycle time, we should analyze the time it takes to poll each terminal individually and add these together. For the sake of simplicity, however, we assume average delays for propagation time and average delays for line splitters.

Let us assume that the terminals are polled cyclically and that no terminal is given priority over the others. We also assume that messages are generated at the same rate by each terminal. If the distance from city A to city B is 500 km, and the distance from city B to city C is 500 km, we can say that the average transmission path will be 750 km. This gives us a propagation delay of 7.5 ms if we assume that the propagation delay is 10 μs per kilometer.

When we poll the terminals in city B, the signals pass through one line splitter, and if we poll the terminals in city C, the signals pass through two line splitters. So, on average, a signal would pass through 1.5 line splitters giving a delay of (1.5 line splitters) $\times$ (1.5 ms per line splitter) = 2.25 ms.

If the line is operating at 4800 bps in synchronous mode, its raw throughput is 600 ASCII characters per second. The modem turnaround time at 4800 bps would

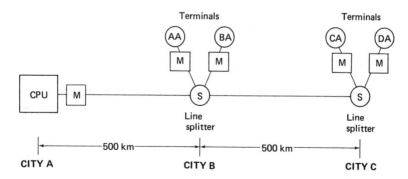

Figure 16-1 Multidrop line for example calculations.

typically be up to 50 ms. We assume this figure, although in real life you should find out the exact turnaround times of the modems that you are using in your network. We also assume that the modems themselves introduce a delay of 10 ms per modem pair when a signal passes through them.

The loop delay can therefore be calculated as follows:

	Elapsed time (ms)
Propagation delay	$2 \times 7.5 \;=\; 15$
Modem delay	$2 \times 10 \;\;\;= 20$
Line splitter delay	$2 \times 2.25 = \;\;4.5$
Terminal reaction time	2
Modem turnaround time	50
Computer reaction time	5
Total	96.5

This figure for loop delay will be used several times in the subsequent calculations.

Calculation of Polling Delay. To calculate the polling delay, we need to take account of three components of time:

1. Poll transmission time
2. No-traffic-response transmission time
3. Loop delay

The polling message is likely to consist of nine characters as follows:

```
P S S       E P
A Y Y X X X X N A
D N N       Q D
```

The PAD character at each end of the polling message is an all -1s character, which is often transmitted to ensure that the receiver correctly interprets the first and last characters. Not all systems require the use of PAD characters—you should check out the requirements of your own equipment. The sequence XXXX is the terminal address, and the addresses are typically transmitted in redundant fashion. For example, to address terminal AB, the address would really be transmitted as AABB.

The no-traffic response (NTR) would typically consist of the following sequence of five characters:

```
P S S E P
A Y Y O A
D N N T D
```

The transmission time for the polling message would be

$$\frac{9}{600} = 15 \text{ ms}$$

and the transmission time for the no-traffic response would be

$$\frac{5}{600} = 8.5 \text{ ms}$$

In this case, the no-traffic-response format is the same as the EOT sequence used to reset the network to the control state.

Figure 16-2(a) shows the sequence of events required to poll one terminal and receive a no-traffic response from it. The EOT message can often be concatenated with the polling message as follows:

```
P S S E P S S       E P
A Y Y O A Y Y X X X X N A
D N N T D N N       Q D
```

In some cases, however, the EOT sequence and the polling message may be concatenated as follows:

```
P S S E       E P
A Y Y D X X X X N A
D N N T       Q D
```

Note that the PAD and two SYN characters after the EOT are missing. The question is: Why would one supplier require that the PAD and SYN characters be embedded in the message while the other supplier can do without?

There are a couple of possible reasons. First, the EOT character may throw the first terminal out of character synchronization and the SYN character may be

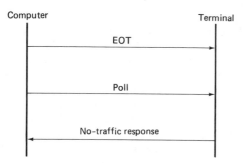

(a) Line control sequence for an unsuccessful poll

Loop delay	96.5 ms
EOT/POLL transmission time	23.5 ms
NTR transmission time	8.5 ms
Total	128.5 ms

(b) Calculation of time required for an unsuccessful poll

Figure 16-2 (a) Line control sequence for an unsuccessful poll; (b) calculation of time required for an unsuccessful poll.

needed to allow the terminal to reestablish synchronization in order that it can recognize the address in the polling message. Alternatively, the terminal may not be thrown out of sync, but it may have a reaction time to the EOT while it does whatever it needs to do after it receives an EOT. In this case the PAD and SYN characters may be inserted as a time fill sequence, to allow the terminal to react to the EOT before the address characters appear.

In our model, the combination of EOT and the poll can be treated as a single message that requires a transmission time of 15 + 8.5 = 23.5 ms. Figure 16-2(b) lists the major components of time that are encountered in polling the network; as closely as possible, these are listed in the order in which they occur. The modem delay, however, is listed as occurring once, whereas in reality half of it occurs at each end of the line as the signal passes through the modems.

When a signal is transmitted along a line, it encounters the propagation delay, modem delay, and line splitter delay. These have a cumulative effect, and for the rest of this discussion, they are added together and called the *transmission delay*. When the poll reaches the terminal, it takes the terminal a certain amount of time to realize that it has been polled and for it to initiate its response. This delay is called *terminal reaction time*, and it can vary significantly from terminal to terminal. In a pure hardware terminal, the reaction time can be virtually instantaneous, whereas in some software terminals, there can be a considerable delay while the system determines that it has been polled. For this example, we use a delay of 2 ms.

The terminal has no traffic to send, so it responds with a no-traffic response. The first thing it must do is turn on the modem carrier, which it does by raising request-to-send; we are therefore faced with a modem turnaround time before we can start transmitting the data. When the ready-for-sending (clear-to-send) signal is returned to the terminal, it can start to transmit the no-traffic response. The no-traffic response encounters all the transmission delays on the way back to the computer. When it is received at the computer, there is likely to be a *computer reaction time* with which to contend while the computer realizes it has received a no-traffic response and gets ready to transmit the next poll. At this point the computer is ready to poll the next terminal. In our model, we are assuming that the computer reaction time is 5 ms. If possible, the real value should be determined for each system.

The total time it takes to poll one terminal will be, on average, the sum of all the delays we have just identified. As shown in Fig. 16-2(b), this turns out to be 128.5 ms. If the computer is polling as fast as it can, it will then take a total of 4 × 128.5 = 514 ms to poll all the terminals on the network. This means that the average polling delay is going to be one-half of the polling cycle time, or 257 ms. This is quite a short time, but, as you know, we only have four terminals on the line. If the line had 10 terminals, it would take 10 × 128.5, or 1285, ms to go around the network for an average polling delay of 642.5 ms.

With a large number of terminals on the line, the polling delay can increase quite substantially unless we can use *group polling* to poll all the terminals at a cluster with one polling sequence.

input message transmission

When a terminal has a message to transmit, the time it takes to poll the terminal and successfully complete an input message transmission can be determined. Figure 16-3(a) illustrates the sequence of events. This shows the computer polling terminal

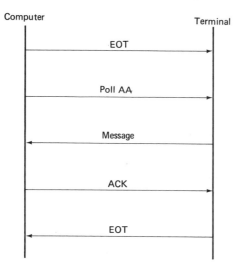

(a) Line control sequence for one input message

2 X Loop delay at 96.5 ms	193 ms
EOT/POLL transmission time	23.5 ms
Message transmission time (100 characters)	167 ms
ACK transmission time	17 ms
EOT transmission time	10 ms
Total	410.5 ms

(b) Calculation of time to receive an input message

Figure 16-3 (a) Line control sequence for one input message; (b) calculation of time to receive an input message.

AA, which then transmits a message that is acknowledged by the computer. The terminal then responds with an EOT sequence. At that point, the computer is ready to poll the next terminal. Figure 16-3(b) lists the message transmission times and the components of time delay that go into determining this overall time. To calculate the message transmission time, we have assumed an input message of 100 characters including synchronizing, control, and error-detecting characters. Note that in the input message exchange sequence shown in Fig. 16-3 we have two loop delays to take account of, the first in the cycle when we poll the terminal and receive the input message and the second loop delay in the cycle when we send the acknowledgment and receive the EOT from the terminal.

output message transmission

When the computer has processed the input transaction and has prepared its response, it will select the terminal to receive a message. The sequence of events involved in transmitting the output message and receiving an acknowledgment from the terminal are outlined in Fig. 16-4a. The computer starts with an EOT to reset the network and follows with the data message containing the terminal address. This is the fast-select mode. Assuming that the message arrives correctly, the terminal responds with an acknowledge sequence, and the computer replies with an EOT.

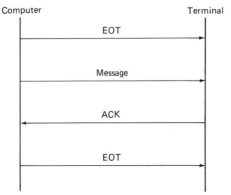

Computer   Terminal

EOT

Message

ACK

EOT

(a) Line control sequence for output message with fast select

Loop delay	96.5 ms
EOT transmission time	10 ms
Message transmission time (200 characters)	333 ms
ACK transmission time	17 ms
EOT transmission time	10 ms
Total	466.5 ms

(b) Calculation of time required to complete an output sequence

Figure 16-4 (a) Line control sequence for output message with fast select; (b) calculation of time required to complete an output sequence.

Let us assume that the output message is a total of 200 characters including synchronizing characters, addressing characters, and error detection mechanism. The transmission time for 200 characters will be 333 ms. The timing for the output message will therefore be as outlined in Fig. 16-4(b).

In the output message transmission sequence, note that we have one loop delay to take account of, that is, from when we send the message to the terminal and receive the acknowledgment. After we have reacted to the acknowledgment and transmitted the EOT we are not interested in any further time delays because the computer could transmit another message straight after the EOT and overlap the transmission time with the propagation time of the EOT.

In many situations it will be found that the trailing EOT on this fast-select sequence is, in fact, the leading EOT on the next poll. In this case we would not even include the transmission times of the trailing EOT when calculating the time required to complete an output sequence because we would have already have counted that EOT in the equivalent input sequence.

line utilization calculation

We need to be able to calculate the line loading in terms of the traffic it is carrying. A convenient method of representing the loading on a line is to speak in terms of the line utilization, which is a measure of the percentage of time that the line is actually in use transmitting data to or from the computer. If the line is fully loaded, it has a utilization of 100%; if it is not loaded at all, it has a utilization of 0%.

Utilization can be expressed in either of the following ways:

• The ratio of the time spent actually transmitting data to the total time available

- The ratio of the actual load on the line to the maximum load that the line is capable of carrying

In Figs. 16-3 and 16-4, we calculated the time required for the line to be able to handle an input message from a terminal and an output message to a terminal. In these cases, the effective line time included not only the time required to physically transmit the data but also included the overhead associated with the line control procedures, transmission delays, terminal delays, and computer delays.

When calculating line loadings using the techniques illustrated in this chapter, we set an upper limit of line loading for acceptable performance of about 50%. If our calculations indicate that the line loading is likely to be greater than 50%, we should resort to more sophisticated methods for analyzing its performance, or perhaps we should redesign the network to produce a lower line loading.

For the purposes of calculation, let us assume that each of the terminal operators on our line is entering one transaction per minute. This means that each terminal generates one input message and receives one output message every minute. With four terminals, this gives a total of $4 \times 60 = 240$ transactions per hour that will be carried by the line. The amount of time the line is occupied in handling these transactions is given by

$240 \times$ (input message-handling time + output message-handling time)

$$= 240 \times (410.5 + 466.5)$$

$$= 240 \times 877$$

$$= 210{,}480 \text{ ms}$$

$$= 210 \text{ s}$$

This means that the line is occupied handling input and output transactions for 210 s per hour, which gives a line utilization of $210/3600 = 5.8\%$. This line loading of 5.8% means that the line is very lightly loaded.

When the operator enters a transaction and presses the transmit key, it is highly unlikely that any other operator will have pressed the transmit key within the same polling cycle, which means that the polling delay is likely to be one-half of the total polling cycle time.

The value of a calculation like this is that it can be performed very simply and quickly and allows us to do a quick reasonableness test on the network. The conclusion that we can draw from this particular calculation is that the line is very lightly loaded. It could, if necessary, support a larger number of terminals than we already have on it. Alternatively, if there was some cost benefit to be achieved by using a slower line such as 1200 or 2400 bps, it is likely that the line would not have any trouble in handling the load at the lower speed.

If the line utilization calculation indicated a loading of approximately 50%, there would be a high probability that when an operator presses the transmit button another transaction will already be in progress. This means that the operator would have to wait not only for the normal polling delay but also perhaps while one or more other transactions on the line were completed. These delays are caused by queuing and they can be analyzed using the techniques outlines in Chapter 23.

If it is difficult to quantify any of the network delays, you may decide to assume a best-case and worst-case value and perform two calculations to determine the expected best-case and worst-case network performance.

the effect of errors on system performance

It should be noted that the calculations which we have been giving for system performance and throughput give answers for transmission under ideal circumstances, that is, when no blocks are retransmitted due to noise hits. It is difficult to get statistics for error rates on lines in many countries, but in general, under good conditions with a good line and good equipment, the retransmission rate ought to be less than 1% of all blocks that are transmitted. This figure is a reasonably good guide for data that are being transmitted over a telephone network that has been designed in accordance with CCITT recommendations, that is, a network with a basic bit error rate in the order of 1 in 100,000 (10^{-5}). In the case of digital networks where the bit error rates are approximately two orders of magnitude better than on telephone lines, that is roughly 1 in 10 million (10^{-7}), the block retransmission rate should be far less than 1%. Therefore, any errors introduced due to ignoring retransmission due to line hits are inconsequential in most cases.

If you happen to live in a country where the telephone network is extremely noisy, you should try to obtain a figure for retransmission rates from the experience of other people in your region and load any calculations that you make with that figure to get a better picture of throughput and performance.

Example 16-2: Half-Duplex Multipoint No. 2

In Example 16-1 we considered the basics of network analysis for multipoint lines. We worked out the line utilization for a simple multipoint line. Let us now examine a more sophisticated calculation wherein not only do we calculate the line

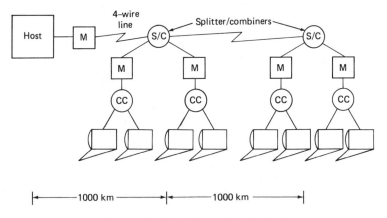

Figure 16-5 Four-wire multipoint line.

utilization for a multipoint line, but we also calculate the response time for transactions entered by the operators.

In the network shown in Fig. 16-5, we wish to provide an on-line enquiry service to branch offices in two distant cities. To simplify the calculations, the cities are exactly 1000 km apart, there are two offices in each city, and each office handles exactly the same number of transactions per hour. In each office we have a cluster controller with a number of terminals. We are using group poll on the terminals, so for the purpose of this calculation the absolute number of terminals at each office is immaterial.

Traffic Statistics   The basic message statistics are as follows:

Host processing time	1 s (this is the processing time at the application level in the host; it is not the reaction time of the host)
Line speed	2400 bps
Input message	200 char (including overhead)
Output message	200 char (including overhead)
Transmission code	ASCII
Transmission mode	Synchronous
Message volume	500 inquiries/hour (i.e., 500 in, 500 out spread evenly between the clusters)

Protocol Sequences   The protocol is a typical basic mode half-duplex protocol. The message formats and message-exchange sequences are shown in Fig. 16-6.

Note: The message formats given in this example are one of a number of typical message formats that you may come across in real life. Although it is unlikely that these exact formats will be reflected in your own system, you should have no trouble

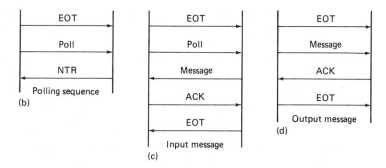

Figure 16-6 Message formats and protocol sequences.

finding out exactly what formats are used in your own system and therefore be able to build a model of that system for analysis. Group poll is used in this network. This means that we issue one group poll for each cluster of terminals and we therefore have four polling points.

Network Delays and Loop Delay   One of the first calculations we perform is to work out the loop delay for the network. In real life we should work out two loop delays, one for each city. The loop delays would be different because the propagation delays depend on the distance involved, and the splitter/combiner delays will be different for the two cities.

For easy calculation, we have made this model a little artificial in that the traffic is shared equally between the clusters of terminals and we have two clusters in each city. We can therefore work out our average loop delay for the network. To help do this we can redraw the network as shown in Fig. 16-7 and locate all four clusters of terminals at a phantom site halfway between the two cities. The phantom site is 1500 km from the host. Note that the phantom site has $1\frac{1}{2}$ splitter/combiners because when we poll the first city, we go through one splitter/combiner; when we poll the second city, we go through two splitter/combiners, so, on average, we go through $1\frac{1}{2}$ splitter/combiners.

The delays can therefore be summarized as follows:

	First city	*Second city*	*Average*
Propagation distance (km)	1000	2000	1500
Number of splitter/combiners	1	2	1.5

Delays

Propagation delay	1500 km at 10 µs/km = 15 ms
Splitter/combiners	1.5 splitters at 1.5 ms each = 2.25 ms
Modem delay	10 ms per pair
Modem turnaround	40 ms (toward upper CCITT limit)
Reaction times	CPU 2 ms
	Terminal 6 ms

Note: These reaction times are arbitrary. Once again, they will vary dramatically from system to system, and they are best established by measurement with appropriate test equipment.

Multithread Operation   Assume that the system is running multithread (as opposed to single thread). In a single-thread system, transactions are handled one at a time, that is, the communications line is held during the host processing time so that the line is immediately available to the output message. Single thread is illustrated in Fig. 16-8(a). In the single-thread system, we take an input message from transaction 1 and process it in the computer, look up the disk, process the transaction further, and then send the output to transaction 1. Then we take the input from transaction 2, process it, and send the output. By looking at Fig. 16-8(a) you can see there is a lot of idle time within the system. While the line is handling input and output mes-

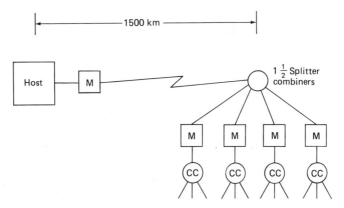

Figure 16-7 Phantom network for analysis.

sages, the computer is idle, and similarly, while the computer is processing, the line is idle.

In a multithread system, operations on the line and in the host are overlapped as shown in Fig. 16-8(b). This enables better utilization of the available resources and allows greater throughput to be achieved. In the multithread system, once we accept input from transaction 1, we release the line while that transaction is processed, so that while transaction 1 is processed, we can handle other inputs and/or outputs on the line. As you can see, we are overlapping operations on the line and on the processor, thus getting better throughput.

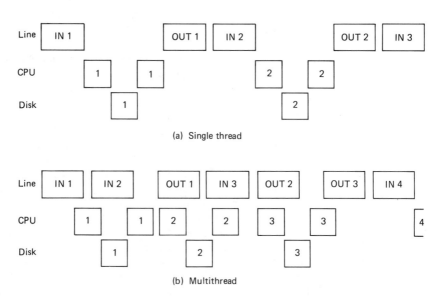

Figure 16-8 Single-thread and multithread operation.

The Problem to Be Solved
    Find the answer to the two questions that the boss should ask:

1. Will it work?
2. How well will it work?

These questions may look rather strange, but when you think about it, they are quite logical. When presented with a network design, apart from being concerned about the cost of the network, the first question you should ask yourself is: Will this network work? The answer to that question is going to be either "yes" or "no." If the network does not work, there is no point proceeding further. If the network does work, we ask the next question: How well will it work? The criterion that determines whether the network will work or not is simply this: Will the network carry the load that we intend to impose on it? If the network will not handle the amount of traffic that is going to be generated by the system, then, clearly, it will not work.

    If the network will not carry the load that we intend to impose on it, there is no point in proceeding further until we redesign the network so that it will carry the load. Once we know that the system will carry the load, we want to know how well will it work, and in our particular case, with an on-line inquiry system, the criterion that will determine how well it will work is going to be: What is the response time of the system? Therefore, in our example we wish to work out what the line utilization is, and if the line utilization is less than 100%, we can assume that the network will carry the load. Then we work out the response time, look at it, and reach a conclusion as to how good that response time is likely to be in our system.

Method
    The following is a guide to the approach that can be used to solve this problem:

1. Build a model, a bar chart showing the time sequence of events involved with a single transaction.
2. Work out the loop delay.
3. Work out how long the line will be occupied for an input message sequence and for an output message sequence.
4. Find the line utilization for 500 transactions per hour.
5. Find the polling cycle time and the polling delay.
6. Work out the response time. *Note:* This really involves the use of queuing theory to work out the interference delay. An approximate figure for interference will be presented based on the queuing graphs in Chapter 28.

Solution   A good starting point is to draw a block diagram showing the time sequence of events encountered by a single transaction in the system. Such a diagram is shown in Fig. 16-9. This bar chart has a horizontal time scale and it shows, first, that the operator enters the transaction into the terminal. This means that the operator is keying the characters into the keyboard and they are being held within the memory of the buffered terminal. When the operator is ready, he or she hits the transmit button to initiate the transmission of the message down the line to the computer. We first experience a polling delay while we wait for the poll to be received. Polling delay, you will recall, is the average time from when the operator hits the transmit button until the poll is received, assuming that there is no traffic in the network. In

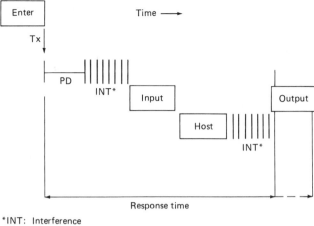

*INT: Interference
PD: Polling delay

Figure 16-9 Block diagram for on-line inquiry system.

reality there will be traffic in the network and we will encounter another time delay caused by interference from traffic going to or from other terminals in the network. For example, two operators may hit the transmit button within the same poll cycle and that means that one operator must wait while the other terminal transmits the input message, and polling is suspended while this takes place. Alternatively, it could be that when the operator hits the transmit button there is already a message on the line going to or from the compluter, and that polling has been suspended while this message travels along the line. When the interference time delay has elapsed, the transaction then gets the line for input and the message is transmitted down the line to the computer in accordance with the protocol sequences shown in Fig. 16-6(c). The host then processes the message and prepares an output. When the host is ready to respond, it could be that there is already a message on the line going in or out, and that we have to wait until that message is completed before we transmit the message down the line. Also, there could be other output messages in front of our output response, but we have to wait for these to be handled. In other words, we have another time delay caused by interference from traffic going to or from other terminals on the line. Finally, we get the line for output and the output message is transmitted in accordance with the message exchange rules shown in Fig. 16-6(d).

This model is typical of the type of model we would have for an on-line enquiry system. There may, of course, be variations on the theme, and these are best established by closely examining the operation of your own system. For example, in some systems when the host is ready to transmit the output message, it will not attempt to transmit until the computer would normally have gotten around to polling the terminal in the normal sequence of events. In this case we would have another time delay equivalent to a polling delay after the host processing time.

The boxes labeled "in" and "out" contain the complete message exchange sequences given for the input message and output message sequences. The delays labeled "INT" are delays caused by interference due to the presence of traffic to or from other terminals on the line. These delays are nonlinear and can be estimated by using queuing theory as described in Chapter 28.

The first question to answer is: Will it work? The answer to this question will be either "yes" or "no." If the answer is "yes," the question "How well will it work?" must be answered. In other words, what response time will be experienced? It is possible that the system will work but that it will have terrible response time. The decision as to whether the response time is satisfactory is very subjective—it depends on the application and the level of service that you wish to supply to your users. In other words, only you and your users can really decide on a satisfactory response time.

Will It Work?

In other words, will the line carry the load? You need to work out the line utilization of the system. If the line utilization is less than 100%, the line will carry the load and therefore the system will work. Line utilization can be calculated using the following equation:

$$\text{line utilization} = \frac{\text{time occupied}}{\text{time available}}$$

$$= \frac{(\text{input time} + \text{output time}) \times \text{message rate}}{1 \text{ hour}}$$

As usual, the first calculation will be that of working out the loop delay.

Loop Delay

The components of loop delay are:

	Elapsed time (ms)
2 × modem delay at 10 ms	20
2 × propagation delay at 15 ms	30
2 × splitter/combiner delay at 2.25 ms	4.5
Remote modem turnaround	40
Reaction time	
Host	2
Terminal	6
Total loop delay	102.5

Then we can work out the time for the input and output message exchange sequences. In other words, how long will the line be occupied for an input sequence, and how long will the line be occupied for an output sequence?

Let us consider the input sequence first. Referring to the protocol diagram in Fig. 16-10, we can see that the line first becomes occupied from the point of view of handling an input message sequence when the computer is ready to transmit the leading edge of the first bit of the EOT sequence which precedes the poll. From this instant the line is occupied until the computer reacts to the EOT received as response to the acknowledgment at the end of the sequence. The total time the line is occupied can therefore be calculated by considering the transmission time of all the messages

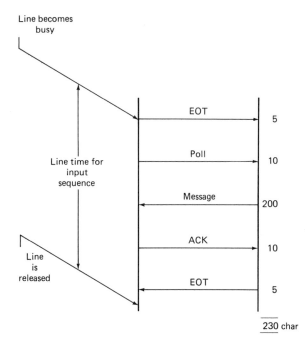

Figure 16-10 Calculating line time for an input message sequence.

and by taking into account the appropriate number of loop delays. In the input message exchange sequence we can identify two occurrences of loop delay. The time for an input sequence can therefore be worked out as follows:

	Elapsed time (ms)
EOT/POLL transmission	50
INPUT message transmission	667
ACK transmission	33
EOT transmission	17
2 × loop delay	205
Total Input time	972

Using a similar approach, we can calculate the length of time the line will be occupied for an output message sequence. Referring to Fig. 16-11, we can see that the line becomes occupied from the point of view of an output sequence when the computer is ready to transmit the leading edge of the first bit of the EOT which precedes the message. The point of time in which the line becomes available for use after the output sequence, however, will vary from system to system.

Let us consider the options. One option is that the line may not be considered to be available for use until the terminal reacts to the trailing EOT. Upon careful consideration, however, this can be seen to be false because the computer is in charge

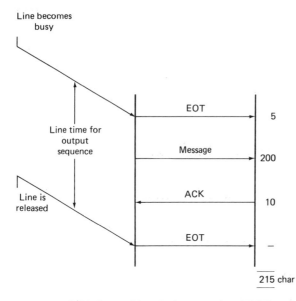

Line becomes busy

Line time for output sequence

Line is released

EOT — 5

Message — 200

ACK — 10

EOT — —

215 char

Figure 16-11 Calculating line time for an output message sequence.

of the line, and once it transmits the EOT, it can do what it likes. The computer is not really concerned as to whether or not the EOT does in fact reach the terminal. Once the computer has transmitted the trailing EOT, it could start transmitting other messages along the line. So one option, therefore, is that the line becomes available for use after the computer transmits the EOT message.

Another option is that the computer waits a predetermined time before it initiates the next action on the line. In this case, the line must be considered to be busy until the next action is initiated by the computer.

Yet another option, however, is that the trailing EOT on the output sequence, could in fact be the leading EOT on the next input sequence, or, if you like, on the next poll. This is quite common where we share an EOT between an input and an output sequence. In this case the line would become available for use at the beginning of the trailing EOT.

Let us assume that in our model the EOT is, in fact, shared between the output message sequence and the next input message sequence or the next poll, and therefore the line becomes available for use at the beginning of the trailing EOT. We can then calculate the total length of time the line will be in use for an output sequence by considering the transmission time of the messages (ignoring the trailing EOT), and by taking into account one loop delay as follows:

	Elapsed time (ms)
EOT transmission	17
OUTPUT message transmission	667
ACK transmission	33
Loop delay	102.5
Total Output time	819.5

Having calculated the input time and the output time, we are now in a position to calculate the line utilization because we know the message volume. The equation given earlier is repeated now:

$$\text{line utilization} = \frac{(\text{input time} + \text{output time}) \times \text{message rate}}{1 \text{ h}}$$

Let us substitute the figures for the input time and output time in this equation:

$$\text{line utilization} = \frac{(0.972 + 0.8195) \text{ s/transaction} \times 500 \text{ transactions/h}}{3600 \text{ s/h}}$$

$$= 0.25 \text{ or } 25\%$$

Will It Work?

It would appear so because the line utilization is less than 100%. Therefore, the line will carry the load and the system will work. The next question is:
How Well Will It Work?

We now add up all the components of response time. We will assume in this example that the terminal does not display the characters on the screen until it receives the ETX in the output message. Therefore, adding up all the components of time will give us an answer that will be quite close to the average response time.

Polling delay can be worked out to be an average of 339 ms (4 drops on the line; 169.5 ms for an unsuccessful poll to one drop; poll cycle time = 4 × 169.5; polling delay = $\frac{1}{2}$ poll cycle time = 339).

Interference delays will be approximately 310 ms each. You can check this after you have studied queuing theory in Chapter 28. (The method of calculation is outlined in the following pages.)

Adding up all of the time components gives a response time of 3.75 s. That may look fine but bear in mid that this figure is an *average* response time.

Most of our network performance calculations lead us toward average results, that is, average response time and average line utilizations. This is because the message lengths themselves are usually average message lengths, the processing times are usually averages, polling delay itself is an average, and interference time delays are also averages. In other words, the response time is going to vary from transaction to transaction.

If you measure the response time of every transaction during a day and plot a frequency distribution curve, you will get a picture like that shown in Fig. 16-12. The curve in Fig. 16-12 shows that there is a minimum response time that we cannot get below. This is related to loop delays, message lengths, and so on. We see the average response time of around 3.75 s. However, toward the right of the diagram we see that the curve tapers off toward infinity, which shows that it is possible to get extremely long response times. This can happen; for example, if every operator in the network hits the transmit button within the same polling cycle, some of the response times are going to be very long indeed. It is often regarded as being more useful, therefore, to consider a 90th percentile or perhaps a 95th percentile response time. The 90th percentile response time is the time below which 90% of all transactions come in, while the 95th percentile response time is the time below which 95% of all transactions come in.

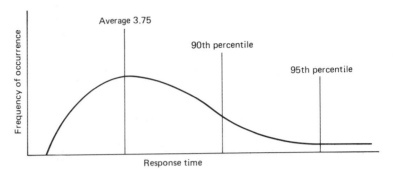

Figure 16-12 Response-time distribution.

The relationship between the average response time and the 90th percentile or 95th percentile response times will vary from system to system depending on the shape of the response-time distribution curve. However, there is a rough rule of thumb which states that the 90th percentile response time is likely to be twice the average, and that the 95th percentile response time is likely to be three times the average response time. On this basis, therefore, if 3.75 s looked okay for an average response time, how does the thought of 10% of transactions having response times of greater than 7.5 s sound? Or, alternatively, how about the probability that 5% of transactions will have response times greater than 11.25 s?

Example 16-3: Calculation of Delays Caused by Queuing

The interference delay is actually the average waiting time $E(t_w)$ experienced by a transaction in the line queue. There is only one queue because there is only one facility (the line) providing the service, and each transaction enters this queue twice, once for input and once for output.

An approximation to the interference delay (waiting time) can be obtained as follows. The line holding time for input is 0.972 s and for output is 0.82 s. The average line holding time is therefore

$$\frac{\text{input} + \text{output}}{2} = \frac{0.972 + 0.82}{2}$$

$$= 0.9 \text{ s}$$

A model of the line queue would be as shown in Fig. 16-13.

As indicated above, the interference delay or the average waiting time for the communication line is going to be the same for input and output transactions. This is assuming that the protocol gives equal priority to inputs and outputs. It is possible by manipulating the protocol sequences to give priority to either inputs or outputs, but in our case we will assume that we have equal priority. Therefore, the average waiting time for the communication line is going to be the same for inputs and outputs.

If we calculate the average line queuing time, we can estimate the average waiting time, which is the interference delay. At a line utilization of 25%, look up

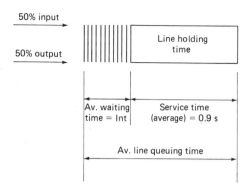

Figure 16-13 Model of the line queue.

the single server, worst case curve on Fig. 28-4 and find that

$$\frac{E(t_q)}{E(t_s)} = 1.35$$

So

$$E(t_q) = 1.35E(t_s)$$

which means that

queuing time = 1.35 (service time)

average queuing time $E(t_q) = 1.35 \times 0.9 = 1.21$ s

So

average waiting time $E(t_w) = 0.31$ s

This is the average waiting time, or interference time delay, for both the input and output queues.

Comment: The above assumes equal priority for input and output messages. In reality, the relative priorities can be manipulated by software to alter the relative sizes of the queues. For further details, refer to *System Analysis for Data Transmission* by James Martin (Englewood Cliffs, N.J.: Prentice-Hall, Inc., 1972).

Example 16-4: Half-Duplex Point-to-Point Line with Printers and a Cluster of Visual Display Terminals

This example illustrates the dramatic effect that relatively small time delays can have on system performance. In the network shown in Fig. 16-14, we have a cluster controller with four terminals and two printers at a single location. The aim of the game is to drive the printers at maximum speed but at the same time allow the visual display terminals to be used for on-line inquiries. The application is that the terminals and printers are at a warehouse where trucks are being used to deliver products to shopkeepers around the city. The printers are being used to print out delivery dockets, run sheets, packing slips, and invoices for the truck drivers. The terminals are used for on-line order entry on the rare occasion when the shopkeeper brings his own truck in to place an order and take away products. Because it takes something like 20 minutes to pick an order and load the truck, response time for the

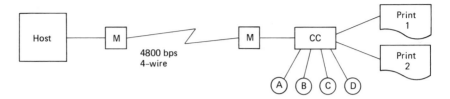

Figure 16-14 Half-duplex point-to-point network.

on-line order entry terminals is immaterial. The main application, therefore, is to drive the printers at maximum speed but to allow the inquiries to take place when a shopkeeper comes in.

There are a number of problems with the terminal equipment which has an impact on the way the system can perform. In the network, four visual display units and two printers are connected to a cluster controller, which is, in turn, connected to the host via a point-to-point four-wire line running at 4800 bps. The terminals and the host are in the same city. Despite the fact that the line is point to point, the modems are running in controlled carrier mode with the turnaround time set at 20 ms! On a point-to-point line we would expect the modems to be running permanent carrier. There is, therefore, scope for improving the performance of the network by strapping up the modems so that they do run permanent carrier.

There is also a problem in relation to the reaction time of the terminals and the printers. The printers and the terminals have a reaction time of 20 ms! The terminals were, in fact, third-party terminals, that is, they were made by a supplier other than the computer mainframe supplier. The third-party supplier attempted to emulate the mainframe protocols and in the process erroneously built the terminals with a long reaction time of 20 ms. The terminals and printers are software controlled, that is, there are microprocessors in the terminals that are used to implement the protocol and it is possible to reduce the reaction time to 2 ms by rewriting the software in the terminal. Assume that any delays in the cluster controller are included in the terminal/printer reaction time. CPU reaction time is 2 ms. Because the host and the terminals are in the same city, we can assume that the propagation delay is zero. Although connected via a cluster controller, the terminals do *not* have group polling implemented. This is because of another mistake in the protocol implementation. The third-party supplier did implement group poll and identified a particular protocol sequence for the group poll. The problem is, however, that in implementing the group poll capability, the supplier did not build in any mechanism for resolving contention if more than one terminal had a message to send. This meant that we could not use group poll in the network. There is capability, however, of modifying the hardware and the software in the cluster so that we can implement group poll properly. Fast select is used for printing and the message exchange sequence used on the line is shown in Fig. 16-15.

Let us now work out the performance of the sytem, first, as described, and then by starting to implement improvements to the system by changing the modems to permanent carrier, by reducing the reaction time in the terminals and the printers, and by implementing group poll properly, and we will see what effect this has on system performance.

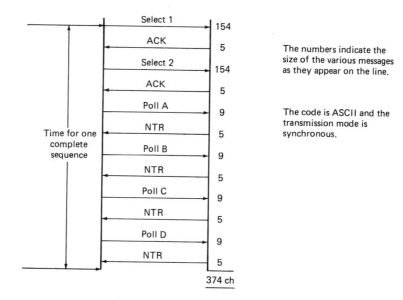

The numbers indicate the size of the various messages as they appear on the line.

The code is ASCII and the transmission mode is synchronous.

Figure 16-15 Protocol sequence for network in Fig. 16-14.

Question 1

For the system as described, determine the theoretical maximum throughput of the communications line in terms of print lines per minute. That is, what is the combined throughput of the two printers?

Question 2

Strap up request-to-send in both modems so that they are running permanent carrier. Determine the combined throughput of the printers.

Question 3

As well as running permanent carrier, spend some money and have the terminal reaction times and the printer reaction times reduced from 20 ms to 2 ms (they are microcomputer controlled, so you can do this). Determine the combined throughput of the printers.

Question 4

As well as permanent carrier and a 2-ms reaction time, spend more money on terminal software and implement group poll. Determine the combined throughput of the printers.

Question 5

As well as everything in Question 4, you discover that the printers can buffer three print lines. You now transmit 434 characters to each printer each time you select it. What is the combined throughput of the printers?

Solution To find the throughput of the communications line, we must work out how long it takes to go through one complete sequence as shown in Fig. 16-15. Once we know how long it takes to go through one complete steady-state sequence on the communication line, we can calculate the throughput by considering the number of print lines contained in the steady-state sequence. In the first question, for example, there are two print lines in each steady-state sequence, so that we can easily calculate the throughput of the communication line. In going through the steady-state sequence we encounter loop delays six times. To calculate the total time to go through the steady-state sequence, we need to calculate the transmission time of all the messages and then add in six loop delays.

Loop Delay

	Elapsed time (ms)
2 × modem turnaround	40
2 × modem delay	20
Reaction time	
Terminal or printer	20
Host	2
Loop delay	82

Message Transmission Time

The transmission times for the individual messages (Select, Ack, Poll, NTR) can be calculated and added together or, alternatively, the number of characters in the individual messages can be added together and the transmission time calculated for the total. The latter approach gives a more accurate result because it minimizes the errors caused by rounding the results of calculations.

The total number of characters to be transmitted in one complete sequence is 374. Therefore,

$$\text{message transmission time} = \frac{\text{length}}{\text{speed}}$$

$$= \frac{(374 \text{ char}) \times (8 \text{ bits/char})}{4800 \text{ bps}}$$

$$= 623 \text{ ms}$$

$$\text{time for one complete sequence} = (\text{message transmission time})$$

$$+ (6 \times \text{loop delay})$$

$$= 623 + 6 \times 82$$

$$= 1115 \text{ ms}$$

Question 1

The throughput of the system, in terms of print lines per minute is determined as follows: ,

$$\text{throughput} = (\text{no. sequences/min}) \times (2 \text{ print lines/sequence})$$

$$= \frac{60 \text{ s/min} \times 2}{1.115 \text{ s/sequence}}$$

$$= 108 \text{ print lines/min}$$

Question 2

Running the modems with permanent carrier rather than controlled carrier reduces the loop delay by 40 ms. Loop delay is now 42 ms. Using the same approach as in Question 1 gives a throughput of 137 lines/min.

Question 3

Reducing terminal reaction time (and printer reaction time) to 2 ms reduces loop delay by a further 18 ms to 24 ms. Using the same approach as in Question 1, we can calculate that the throughput now becomes 156 lines/min.

Question 4

Loop delay is still 24 ms and, due to the proper implementation of group poll, the sequence changes to that shown in Fig. 16-16. The group poll draws a single NTR from the terminal cluster, indicating that no terminals have messages to send. The number of characters involved is reduced to 332 and, of course, loop delay is now encountered only three times in each sequence. The calculation shows a throughput of 192 lines/min.

Question 5

The sequence is as in Question 4, the difference being that the number of characters in each sequence has been increased to 892 and there are six print lines per sequence. The calculation shows a throughput of 231 lines/min.

Comment: The calculation is quite straightforward once the protocol sequences have been identified. The results are quite accurate even though error-free transmission has been assumed. The error introduced by ignoring errors ought to be less than 1% in *most* cases. Perhaps the most outstanding feature of this example is that it illustrates the dramatic effect that seemingly small delays (e.g., 20 ms) can have on system performance. Another outstanding feature of this example is that it shows how easy the calculation really is. The mathematics involved is very simple, and once the protocol sequences have been identified, the calculation, as indicated earlier, is quite straightforward.

Flow Control

So far we have assumed that the printers are capable of handling all the print lines that we can send to them. In real life, the printers had a maximum throughput of 75 lines/min each and the system was being operated under the conditions described in Question 5.

Clearly, the system is capable of flooding the printers. We are faced with the problem of flow control. *Flow control* can be crudely defined as throttling the flow of data through the network so that the data arrive at the receiving device at just the right rate for the receiving device to be able to handle it properly.

There are various approaches to flow control and the method used in this

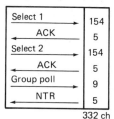

Figure 16-16 Message exchange sequence for group poll Question 4.

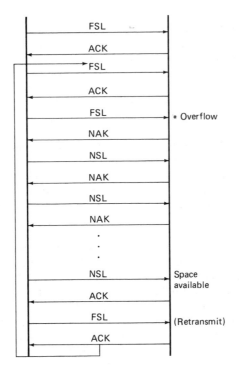

Figure 16-17 Exercising flow control at the link level.

example involved manipulating the protocol sequences, at the link level, to achieve the desired result. The printers were actually buffered with about 3000 characters of buffer space. The principles of flow control used in this system can be illustrated simply as in Fig. 16-17 if we consider a case with a single terminal on the line.

Using fast select (FSL), the host can deliver data to the printer at the maximum rate allowed by the line. Eventually, the buffer will overflow and the FSL that causes the overflow will draw a NAK. This puts the host into Normal Select (NSL) mode. The NSL effectively says "Are you ready for more data?" and until the printer is ready, the NSL messages will draw NAK responses. Ultimately, there will be space for a block of data, the NSL will draw ACK, and the block will be sent down using FSL. The host stays in FSL mode until another overflow occurs and the sequence repeats itself.

This method of flow control looks very inefficient but, in our example, this inefficiency does not really matter because, if we have time to go through the NSL/NAK sequence it means that we have nothing better to do! Think about it.

Questions

1. What would be the impact of running this system over a satellite communications link?
2. What is the line utilization in each of the cases considered in the example?
3. What is the response time for terminal operators likely to be? Assume an inquiry/response situation with 50 characters input and 250 characters output.

Flow control for character-oriented terminals

"Dumb" terminals, those which do not have a protocol (e.g., TTY), can exercise flow control using techniques such as XON/XOFF or V.24 flow control. The XON/XOFF technique requires the use of a full-duplex line so that the terminal can send control information back to the host while the host is sending data to the terminal. A typical configuration is shown in Fig. 16-18. A terminal sending "XOFF" is asking the host to cease transmission on the outbound channel. When the terminal sends "XON," the host can resume transmission on the outbound channel.

For example, the host is transmitting data out to the dumb printer and the printer experiences a paper jam. In the past the host would have been totally unaware of this and would have continued sending data, which would have resulted in the printing of a very black line on the printer which is difficult to read. Using XON/XOFF flow control, however, when the paper jam occurs, the printer can transmit XOFF to the host and when the XOFF is recognized by the host, the host will cease transmission on the outbound leg of the circuit. When the paper jam is finally cleared, the printer transmits XON, which enables the host to recommence transmission. Clearly, in order that this will work properly, the printer needs to have some buffer capacity so that characters which are received between the time the paper jam occurs and the XOFF being recognized by the host can be temporarily stored without being lost.

Visual display terminal flow control

XON/XOFF flow control is used in many other situations apart from the one described. Many of the functions performed at a VDT take a relatively long time, for example, erasing the screen or scrolling the screen. In many cases, when a command to erase or scroll the screen is issued, the terminal will send an XOFF to stop transmission temporarily while it executes the command. When it has finished executing the command, it will transmit XON to the host so that the host can resume transmission. This prevents the terminal being flooded with data during the time it takes to perform the extended command sequence.

Also, when personal computers are emulating dumb terminals, if the computer is sending files of data to the personal computer, the PC can get overloaded

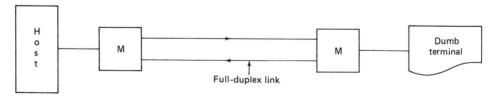

Figure 16-18 Typical "dumb" terminal on point-to-point line.

accepting the data and writing them out to disk. It may not be able to do this fast enough to keep up with the incoming data stream, and in this situation, the PC may transmit XOFF to stop the flow of data temporarily while it stores the data it has just received, and then send XON to allow the computer to recommence transmission of data.

V.24/RS-232 flow control

Many terminals do not use XON/XOFF for flow control. Instead, they manipulate signals in the V.24 interface. For example, Data Terminal Ready may be switched on/off or clear-to-send may be switched on/off to temporarily stop the flow of data from the computer to the terminal. This technique is often used in systems where printers are directly connected onto computers, and the V.24 interface can be activated directly. In other cases the computer is set up to recognize XON/XOFF, whereas a terminal is set up to handle V.24 interface flow control, and in these situations it is possible to obtain "black boxes" which will handle the conversion from V.24 flow control to XON/XOFF.

Flow control with statistical multiplexers

Systems with statistical multiplexers (statmuxes) can handle flow control by propagating the XON/XOFF signals through the network to the host. Typically, statmuxes also respond to the XON/XOFF commands.

Figure 16-19 illustrates a typical statistical multiplexer configuration where we have four dumb terminals each running at 2400 bps being statistically multiplexed onto a single 2400-bps line. The four terminals would be using asynchronous transmission, while on the composite link between the statistical multiplexers we would be using synchronous transmission.

In our system we have one printer and three terminals. If we experience a paper jam on the printer, it will transmit XOFF to the slave statmux, which will recognize the XOFF and immediately cease transmission to the terminal. In the meantime, the XOFF command is propagated back to the host, and when it is received, the host also ceases transmission to the terminal. By the time the XOFF

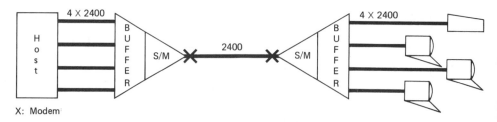

Figure 16-19 Typical statistical multiplexer configuration.

is received at the host, we will have a number of characters in transit which will be stored temporarily in the buffers in the statistical multiplexers. When the paper jam is cleared, the printer transmits XON, which releases the blockage at the slave statistical multiplexer and the XON is also propagated back to the host, which releases the blockage back at the host. In this situation we therefore have two stages of flow control.

The statistical multiplexers themselves can actually exercise flow control on their own behalf in a number of ways. One technique is illustrated as follows. Let us assume that the host transmits three large screenfuls of data out to the visual display terminals. The instantaneous data rate going into the master statmux is now $3 \times 2400 = 7200$ bps, while the composite link can discharge only 2400 bps. To handle this overload situation, we need buffering in the statistical multiplexer to store the data temporarily until they can be sent down the line to the other statmux. The statistical multiplexer has a flow control algorithm built in such that when the buffer reaches a certain percentage of its maximum capacity, say 87%, it will transmit XOFF commands on each of the ports into the host, thus stopping all transmission from the host. In the meantime, the statistical multiplexer can discharge the contents of the buffers down the line to the slave statmux and then send it to the terminals. When the buffer capacity reaches some other percentage, say 65%, of its capacity the statistical multiplexer can transmit XON on all the ports into the host, thus releasing the ports so the transmission can resume. There are many variations on the theme of statistical multiplexer; some allow individual flow control of the buffers attached to each line.

17
Introduction to Full-Duplex Protocols

full-duplex protocols

Point-to-point

On a point-to-point line, the line and modems are typically capable of full-duplex operation, while the protocol often constrains us to half-duplex operation. As illustrated in Fig. 17-1 we have a point-to-point four wire line, which as we know, contains two communication channels. Also, the modems are capable of transmitting and receiving simultaneously, so the telecommunications part of the network is capable of full-duplex operation. However, when we are running a half-duplex protocol in the two hosts, the overall operation of the system is constrained to half-duplex.

It is possible to run either half-duplex or full-duplex over this network as illustrated in Fig. 17-2. With half-duplex, when message A is going from host 1 to host 2, it is transmitted over channel A in the four-wire line. As we are running half-duplex, then *by definition* channel B in the four-wire line is idle. Similarly, when message B comes from host 2 to host 1, it travels along channel B and *by definition* channel A will be idle.

Because we have two independent communication channels in the link, it is possible to run full-duplex, and if we had suitable protocols in the hosts, we

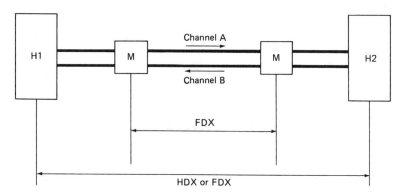

Figure 17-1 A four-wire PTP line can be operated either full-duplex or half-duplex.

could achieve the situation illustrated in Fig. 17-2(b). Here we can see messages going from host 1 to host 2 on channel A while messages are being transmitted from host 2 to host 1 on channel B. The messages overlap and this is possible because the channels are independent and the messages do not collide on the line.

Clearly, the throughput in the full-duplex system is far superior to that which

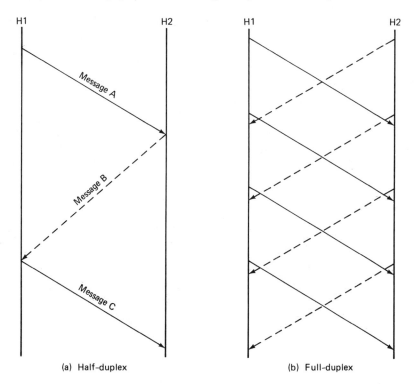

Figure 17-2 Sequence diagrams for a four-wire PTP line.

is achieved in the half-duplex system. In the half-duplex system, loop delay has a serious effect on system throughput, whereas in the full-duplex system, theoretically at least, loop delay should have no effect on system throughput. What this means is that as long as there are no errors in the system, the throughput that we can achieve with a full-duplex system is the same regardless of whether the loop delay is zero or a large number. Of course, when errors do occur, we need to recover them, and in that event the loop delay will have an effect on system throughput. Fortunately, in most systems the error rate is relatively small; that is, less than 1% of all blocks of data should be subject to errors. We can generally say that in practical terms, the throughput of a full-duplex link is independent of the loop delay.

Multipoint

As we have seen, most multipoint lines are four-wire lines and it is possible to make use of the full-duplex capability of the line by simultaneously transmitting to one terminal and receiving from another. Consider the line illustrated in Fig. 17-3. In the past, we have usually operated such lines half-duplex, but newer systems do allow us to run full-duplex, and as with the point-to-point case, we can achieve better throughput.

Consider the two systems illustrated in Fig. 17-4(a) and (b). In Fig. 17-4(a) we have a typical half-duplex protocol. We are attempting to drive the printer at maximum speed and at the same time to allow inquiries to be input from the visual display terminal. A typical message-exchange sequence is illustrated in Fig. 17-4(a). Here we send a print line to the printer, which immediately acknowledges. When the acknowledgment is received by the host, we can then poll the terminal, which responds with "No Traffic." We send another print line to the printer, which is also acknowledged; we can then poll the terminal, receive a message, acknowledge it, and then receive EOT.

The thing that turns the protocol into half-duplex is the fact that we get automatic responses from the printer. When the print line is received by the printer, the printer automatically acknowledges. We must wait for the acknowledgment to be received at the host before we can do anything else. This is because if we did poll before the acknowledgment came back, we could have the ac-

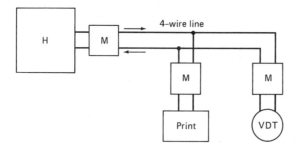

Figure 17-3 Four-wire multipoint line.

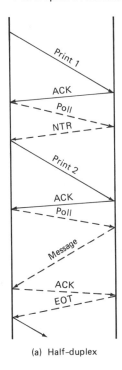
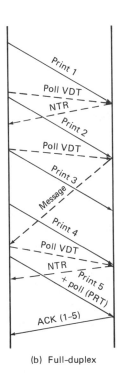

(a) Half-duplex   (b) Full-duplex

Figure 17-4 Protocol sequences for a four-wire multipoint line.

knowledgment from the printer overlapping with the response from the visual display terminal and both messages would be corrupted. Therefore, with half-duplex multipoint protocols, we must complete a conversation with one device before we can enter into a conversation with the next.

If we eliminate the automatic responses from the printers, we can then achieve full-duplex operation, as illustrated in Fig. 17-4(b). Here we send the print line to the printer, which accepts the block of data and presumably begins printing it. The printer does not acknowledge the block. The host immediately polls the terminal, which responds with a no-traffic response on the inbound channel of the four-wire line. While the no-traffic response is coming in, we are transmitting another print line on the outbound channel and thus achieve a full-duplex operation on the four-wire line. Having sent the second print line, we poll the terminal, and this time the terminal sends an input message on the inbound channel. While this message is being received, we send two more print lines on the outbound channel, again overlapping operation on the four-wire line.

As you can see, we are achieving full-duplex operation and getting far better throughput. In the equivalent time, for the half-duplex system we sent two print lines and received one message, while in the full-duplex system we sent four print lines and received a message. You will note that we have not yet acknowledged the print lines in the full-duplex system. The way that this is typically done is that one of the print lines would contain a poll, perhaps print line 5, which would ask the printer for an acknowledgment. The printer would then acknowledge the correct reception of all the blocks up to and including print line 5, as illustrated in Fig. 17-4(b).

full-duplex block transmission: point to point

As shown earlier, the half-duplex block-by-block transmission system has a potential drawback due to the effects of loop delay on the message throughput. One solution to that problem is to transmit longer messages, but this causes another problem owing to the fact that long messages are more error-prone than short messages. Another method of solving this problem is to use a full-duplex circuit and to transmit messages without waiting for acknowledgments. This is illustrated in Fig. 17-5, which shows blocks of data being transmitted from A to B on one leg of the full-duplex line. Acknowledgments are being returned on the second leg of the line. Depending on the length of the message blocks and the loop delay, several message blocks may be transmitted before any response is received for the first block that was transmitted. This causes a displacement between the message block and its response. This in turn means that we need to number the message blocks and also number the acknowledgments so that a particular acknowledgment can be related to a particular block of data.

　　　　Under error-free transmission conditions (which is hopefully the norm for most data transmission systems), we can achieve nearly 100% data throughput on the outbound channel. If a block is received with an error, the receiving computer can transmit a negative acknowledgement; upon receipt of the NAK, the transmitting computer has two options available to it. In simple systems, we would retransmit the erroneous block plus all the blocks that had been transmitted since

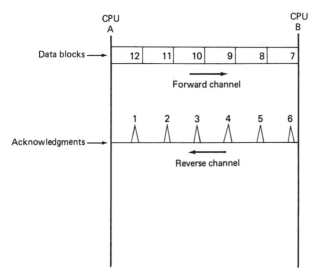

Figure 17-5 Full-duplex block transmission.

the erroneous block. If we have a more complex system, we can retransmit only the erroneous block and rely on the receiving computer to reinsert that block in the correct sequence.

This full-duplex system makes very efficient use of one channel of the circuit; the other channel is very lightly loaded and can also be used for data transmission in the opposite direction. Then both channels will have data messages alternating with supervisory messages. This allows us to achieve a full-duplex data-flow situation. This system is obviously going to become much more complex than our simple half-duplex block-by-block technique, but, considering the cost of long-distance data circuits, it can be sensible to spend the money on software/hardware for a full-duplex line control procedure to allow for greater throughput on the circuits. As time goes on the full duplex protocols, such as SDLC and HDLC are gaining more of a foothold and thus more users are able to make better use of their expensive lines.

18
Introduction to HDLC/SDLC (High-level Data Link Control/Synchronous Data Link Control)

HDLC/SDLC line procedures

There are a number of line control procedures that operate broadly as described in Chapter 17. Two of the better-known procedures are those specified by the International Standards Organization (ISO) and by IBM. The ISO procedure is called *high-level data link control* (HDLC), and the IBM procedure is called *synchronous data link control* (SDLC).

As the latter name implies, these line procedures use synchronous transmission. All of the bits in a message are precisely timed, and the beginning of a message must be detected by using a unique synchronizing pattern in a similar manner to that outlined in Chapter 2 for obtaining character synchronization. The structure of the synchronizing pattern is described shortly under the heading "F: Flag Field."

Various names used for line procedures similar to HDLC and SDLC are: Burroughs Data Link Control (BDLC), Universal Data Link Control (UDLC), Advanced Data Communications Control Protocol (ADCCP), and Digital Data Communications Message Protocol (DDCMP). All of these procedures are similar from the fundamental point of view, although they differ in points of detail.

As usual, we deal with the basic principles of operation, and you can obtain the detail applicable to your installation from your supplier. For the remainder of this book, we refer to the line procedure as HDLC.

HDLC link structures

HDLC can be used on point-to-point or multidrop lines. Whereas in the simple half-duplex procedures we had temporary *master/slave* relationships for controlling data flow, in HDLC we have permanent *primary/secondary* relationships.

In general, one station on a data link is given *primary* status. This station controls the data link and supervises the flow of data on the link. All other stations on the link are called *secondary* stations and respond to commands from the primary station. Only the primary can generate *commands*; the secondaries generate *responses*. Figure 18-1 illustrates various primary/secondary relationships. Note the relationship in Fig. 18-1(c), where station B is a secondary in relation to primary A on link 1 and is a primary in relation to secondary C on link 2. (*Note:* Under the heading "Asynchronous Balanced Response Mode," we see that on some links we can have two stations with equal status, each having both primary and secondary functions.)

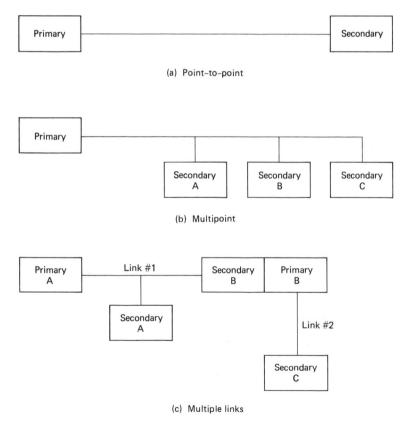

Figure 18-1 HDLC link structures.

binary data transmission: HDLC frame structure

HDLC-style line procedures are based on the transmission of pure binary data streams. This introduces problems in the area of synchronization and in determining where a message starts and where it finishes. We examine the solution to these problems shortly.

The vehicle for carrying messages on an HDLC link is called a *frame*, and it has the general format illustrated in Fig. 18-2. The various fields that comprise the frame are as follows:

F	Flag
A	Address
C	Control
I	Information
FCS	Frame Check Sequence
F	Flag

A frame will not necessarily contain an information field, and the minimum number of fields in a frame are the F, A, C, FCS, and F fields.

The content and purpose of the various fields are summarized in the following paragraphs.

F: Flag field

In character transmission systems, we had individual transmission control characters to identify the start of header (SOH), the start of text (STX), the end of text (ETX), and so on. With binary transmission systems, we do not have separate characters, and an approach has been developed that allows one unique bit pattern to be used to identify the beginning and ending of a message and also to act as a frame-synchronization pattern. This bit pattern is called a *flag*, and it consists of the sequence 01111110. Referring to Fig. 18-2, note that the message with its frame check sequence (the cyclic redundancy check) is surrounded by two flag fields.

A communication link, as shown in Fig. 18-3, consists of a computer and its communications controller joined via a communications line to another communications controller and its associated computer. The transmitting computer

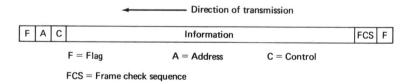

Direction of transmission

| F | A | C | Information | FCS | F |

F = Flag   A = Address   C = Control

FCS = Frame check sequence

Figure 18-2 HDLC frame format.

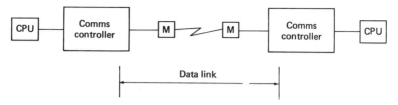

Figure 18-3 Typical data link.

sends the message to the communications controller, which computes the FCS and puts the flags on each end of the combination of message and FCS.

Because it is possible for the message itself to contain a bit pattern that looks like a flag, we must ensure that the data, as transmitted on the line, contains no such bit pattern. This is accomplished by using a technique known as *zero insertion* (sometimes called *bit stuffing*). The transmitting communications controller monitors the bits between flags as they go to the line. If it sees five contiguous 1s, it inserts a 0 bit after the fifth 1. This prevents a data pattern of six 1s appearing on the line and therefore being mistaken for a flag. Figure 18-4 shows that if the data field originates in the computer as 111111, it appears on the line as 1111101. Similarly, if the data pattern consisted of 1111101, the communication controller would insert an additional 0 after the five 1s so that the data on the line would consist of 11111001. At the receiving end, if the receiving communications controller receives six 1s in a row, it recognizes this as a flag; if it receives five 1s followed by a 0, it will assume that the 0 has been inserted and will remove (*pull*) the 0 and thus reconstitute the original data stream. This means that an incoming data stream consisting of 1111101 would be passed through to the computer as 111111, and an incoming data stream consisting of 11111001 would be passed through to the computer as 1111101. This is a simple but effective scheme for organizing the flow of binary data.

A: Address field

The address field is an eight-bit pattern that identifies the *secondary* station that is involved in the data transfer. The primary has no address. When the primary sends to the secondary, it identifies the secondary in the A field. When the secondary sends to the primary, it identifies itself in the A field.

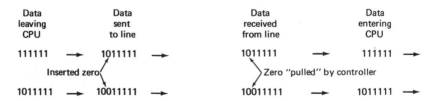

Figure 18-4 Zero insertion procedure.

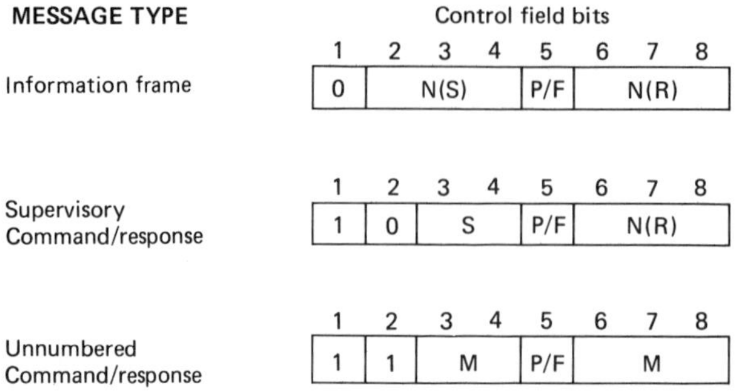

MESSAGE TYPE   Control field bits

Information frame

1	2	3	4	5	6	7	8
0	N(S)			P/F	N(R)		

Supervisory
Command/response

1	2	3	4	5	6	7	8
1	0	S		P/F	N(R)		

Unnumbered
Command/response

1	2	3	4	5	6	7	8
1	1	M		P/F	M		

N(S) = Send sequence count
N(R) = Receive sequence count
S   = Supervisory function bits
M   = Modifier function bits
P/F = Poll/final bit

Figure 18-5 Control field formats.

C: Control field

The control field is normally an eight-bit field, although HDLC makes allowances for the use of a 16-bit field. The eight-bit control field has one of the general formats shown in Fig. 18-5.

The first bit of the C-field identifies the frame as either an *information frame* (I-frame) or a *command/response frame*.

Information frames (I-frames)

An I-frame is the only frame that can be used for information transfer. The remaining bits in the control field perform the following functions: The N(S) and N(R) counts are send and receive sequence counts, which are maintained by each station for the I-frames sent and received by that station.

The send sequence count is incremented by one for each I-frame transmitted. The receive sequence count is incremented by one for each I-frame that is successfully received in the correct sequence.

Each secondary station on the line maintains its own N(S)/N(R) count in relation to messages sent to and received from the primary. The primary, however, maintains a separate N(S)/N(R) count for *each* secondary on the link.

With an eight-bit C-field, the N(S)/N(R) counts can each range from 0–7, whereas with a 16-bit C-field, they can range from 0 through 127. The purpose of the receive sequence count is to advise the other station of the *expected* sequence number of the next received frame. N(R), therefore, acts as an acknowledgment to indicate that the station has correctly received all I-frames numbered up to $N(R) - 1$. We will shortly see how useful this can be.

The remaining bit in the C-field is the *poll/final* (P/F) bit. The P/F bit is used as a *poll* by the primary (when set to the 1 condition) to solicit a response from a secondary station. The response may consist of a single frame or may be a number of frames. The maximum number of frames will be either 7 or 127 depending on whether the C-field contains 8 or 16 bits.

A secondary station generally uses the P/F bit as a *final* bit (when set to 1) to indicate the last frame of a sequence of frames. There are various other uses, but describing them is beyond the scope of this book.

The P and F bits are always exchanged as a pair. On a link, only one poll can be outstanding (unanswered) at a time, and a second poll cannot be transmitted until the previous poll has been accounted for (i.e., until it has been matched with an F bit). In addition, the receive sequence count [N(R)] of a frame with a P/F bit set to 1 can be used as an acknowledgment to help to detect frame sequence errors. The N(R) count of a frame received with the P/F bit set to 1 should acknowledge *at least* all of the I-frames transmitted up to and including the last frame transmitted with the P/F bit set to 1.

Command/response frames

Command/response frames are used to help control the flow of data along a link. *Commands* can only be generated by a primary station, and the secondary stations generate *responses*. There are two classes of command/response frames: *supervisory frames* (S-frames) and *unnumbered frames* (U-frames). Control frames do not contain an N(S) count as this relates only to information messages. The S-frames, which contain an N(R) count, are used for functions such as acknowledging I-frames, requesting retransmission of I-frames, and requesting a temporary suspension of I-frames.

The U-frames are unnumbered and hence provide five bits (modifiers), which can be used to give up to 32 additional command functions and up to 32 additional response functions. The U-frames can be used to extend the number of link control functions (e.g., for link startup or shutdown or to specify that in the future the extended control field of 16 bits will be used).

The basic command is a poll, which consists of *any* kind of message with the P/F bit set to 1. The secondary will reply either with one or more I-frames or a response frame; in addition, it must match the poll bit with a final bit before ending its transmission.

The most commonly used commands and responses are the supervisory sequences (S-frames) shown in Fig. 18-6. Each of these command/response formats contains an N(R) receive sequence count, which enables the message to acknowledge the successful receipt of all information frames with a send sequence count N(S) up to and including N(R) − 1. Each format has a P/F bit that acts as a poll in the case of a command and a final bit in the case of a response.

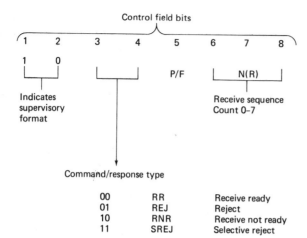

Figure 18-6 Supervisory frame control field formats.

The four commands/responses are defined as follows:

- *RR: Receive Ready.* The RR frame indicates that the station sending it is ready to receive information frames.
- *REJ: Reject.* The REJ frame is used to request retransmission of all input frames starting with the frame numbered N(R).
- *RNR: Receive Not Ready.* The RNR frame indicates that the station is temporarily unable to receive information frames. In other words, the RNR indicates a busy condition. The busy condition can subsequently be cleared by the transmission of an RR, REJ, SREJ command/response or a valid information frame with the P/F bit set to 1.
- *SREJ: Selective Reject.* The SREJ enables a station to request retransmission of a specific block numbered N(R). Theoretically, the SREJ allows for more efficient operation on links where several blocks may have been transmitted by the time the erroneous block is detected and its SREJ is returned.

Many systems do not implement the SREJ command on the grounds that errors occur infrequently (hopefully, less than 1% of the time), and therefore the absolute gain in efficiency achieved by SREJ over REJ is usually small. On systems with long loop delays and extended numbering (up to 127), one could expect to achieve more efficient operation by implementing SREJ.

I: Information field

This field can be of any length, and it can contain any information. The contents of this field are treated as though they are pure binary data even if they are indeed characters such as ASCII or EBCDIC.

FCS: Frame check sequence

Because the I-field is treated as pure binary information, the FCS employed is generated using a *cyclic redundancy check* (CRC).

general principles of data exchange

There are two operational modes specified for HDLC: *normal response mode* (NRM) and *asynchronous response mode* (ARM). Normal response mode is the more usual mode of operation. In this mode, a secondary can *only* transmit in response to a poll. When polled, a secondary can transmit any number of frames, in succession, up to 7 or 127 (depending on the size of the C-field), and it must indicate the last frame by setting the F-bit. *In NRM, a secondary cannot transmit under any circumstances if it has not been polled.*

In asynchronous response mode, the secondary can initiate transmission at any time without being polled by the primary, although it will always reply if polled. This can, of course, lead to contention on the line. As long as we are aware that contention can arise, we can take steps to ensure that we can recover from such a situation.

A variation of the asynchronous response mode is a balanced or symmetrical asynchronous response mode known as *asynchronous balanced response mode* (ABRM) or *asynchronous balanced mode* (ABM). In this case, both stations on a point-to-point link are both a primary and a secondary. Either of the two stations can initiate transmission without receiving permission from the other. This mode can be used when the main aim is to achieve high efficiency on full-duplex point-to-point links. Asynchronous balanced response mode is discussed further under the heading "HDLC Two-Way Simultaneous Data Flow."

In Chapters 19 and 20, we refer to normal response mode (NRM) unless otherwise stated.

19
HDLC Data Transfer

data transfer under HDLC

The following pages contain an outline of the kind of messages exchanged on typical data links. There are many variations on the theme, and these examples represent some typical exchanges. In all cases, we are assuming that the link is up and running, and we look at the mainstream of its operation; we do not cover system startup and shutdown or all of the contingencies that can occur.

In the message-exchange-sequence diagrams, we show the primary on the left and the secondary (or secondaries) on the right. The arrows represent messages, and there is a time scale running vertically. Thus all message transmissions are represented by a downward-slanting arrow. The length of the arrow is related to the length of the message (i.e., to its transmission time) and to the delays encountered in the link. Contrary to the convention we adopted with half-duplex exchange-sequence diagrams, these diagrams have a linear time scale, because the relative timing of transmissions on the full-duplex link is important.

In the exchange-sequence diagrams, messages are identified as follows:

TYPE, N(S), N(R), P/F

In our examples, message type will either be I for information or RR, REJ, RNR, or SREJ if it is a supervisory frame. N(S) and N(R) are the send and receive sequence numbers [remember that supervisory frames do not have N(S)], and P/F indicates whether the poll or final bit is set.

Thus, I,2,4,P indicates an information frame with N(S) = 2, N(R) = 4, and the poll bit set; I,2,4 would be the same message without the poll bit. Similarly, RR,,4,F would represent a receive-ready response with N(R) = 4 and the final bit set.

Half-duplex point-to-point data transfer

Although HDLC is designed as a full-duplex procedure, it can be used in half-duplex mode. Whereas with basic-mode half-duplex procedures we acknowledge each block separately, HDLC gives us the opportunity of sending a number of blocks and then acknowledging them as a group. This considerably reduces the number of line turnarounds required and consequently increases the efficiency of transmission.

Figure 19-1(a) shows a sequence of four frames being transmitted before an acknowledgment is required. In this diagram, the one-way delay is one-third of the information frame transmission time, and we have assumed an instantaneous line turnaround.

In Fig. 19-1(b), the same sequence is transmitted using the basic-mode half-duplex procedure. In comparing Figs. 19-1(a) and (b), you can see the increased efficiency achieved through the use of HDLC.

If an error had occurred—block 1 had been hit by noise—the message-exchange sequence would be as shown in Fig. 19-2. This shows the four blocks being transmitted, and the poll draws the response RR,,1,F, which indicates that the last successfully received, in-sequence, block was block 0 [N(R) − 1]. The primary then retransmits blocks 1, 2, and 3 and continues with block 4.

In addition to the previous examples on the one-way transmission of information, there is the capability of two-way alternate exchange of information frames, as shown in Fig. 19-3. The primary station sends two blocks with the poll bit set in the second block. This causes the secondary to begin transmission, and it sends three blocks with the final bit set in the third block. This indicates that the secondary has finished its message and the primary can now turn the line around. It does so and sends block 3 with the poll bit set, the secondary responds with two blocks, and so on.

Full-duplex point-to-point data transfer

If the link, primary, and secondary are capable of full-duplex operation, then the message exchange sequence could be as shown in Fig. 19-4. In Fig. 19-4(a), we have a one-way data transmission over the full-duplex line; in Fig. 19-4(b) we have the same data exchange with a noise hit on a block. Notice that the primary continues to send data after the poll has been transmitted. Note also that the send

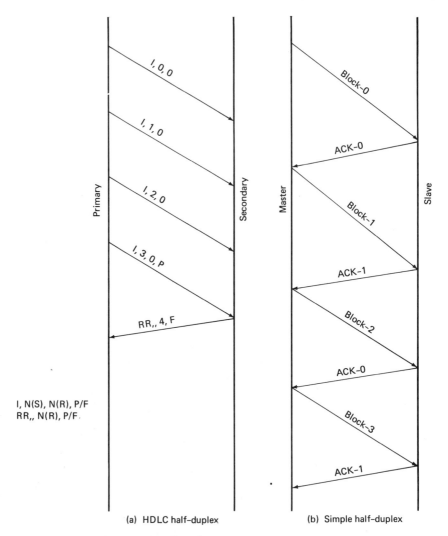

I, N(S), N(R), P/F
RR,, N(R), P/F.

(a) HDLC half–duplex   (b) Simple half–duplex

Figure 19-1 Half-duplex operation, HDLC and simple.

sequence count reverts to zero after block 7. In this system the maximum number of blocks that could be transmitted before an acknowledgment is required is 7.

The sequence in Fig. 19-4(b) shows a noise hit on block 1. When the poll is received, the secondary indicates that the next in-sequence block it expects to receive is block 1, and this causes the primary to initiate a retransmission. The secondary could have replied with REJ,,1,F, which would have achieved the same result.

We saw earlier that the maximum number of blocks we could transmit before we require an acknowledgement is 7. (If we had an extended control field, it would be 127.) *What is the minimum number?* If we transmit the data as fast as we can get the bits onto the line, the blocks will go out as shown in Fig. 19-5. This shows a contiguous stream of frames in which the flag fields are shared by adjacent frames. Thus the end-of-frame flag on block 0 is also the start-of-frame flag for block 1. With this arrangement, the minimum number of blocks that could be in transit at any time is two. There is no way that a poll can be issued with

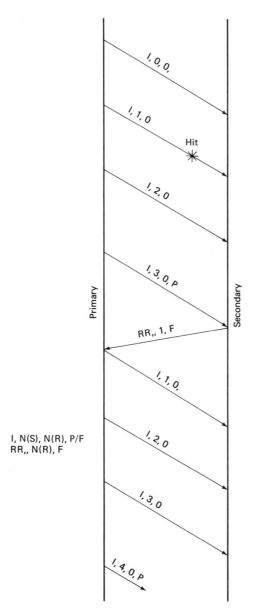

Figure 19-2 Half-duplex exchange with hit on message block.

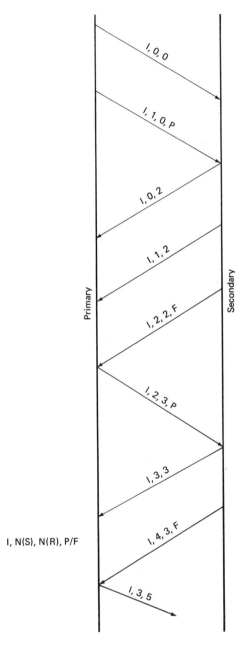

Figure 19-3 Two-way alternate exchange of information frames.

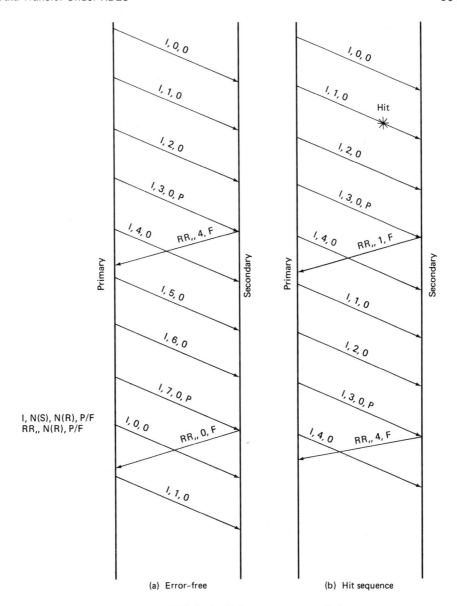

Figure 19-4 Full-duplex link, one-way transmission.

Figure 19-5 A flag can be shared by two data blocks.

each data block, because a response with the final bit set would not be received before the next poll went out. One of the HDLC rules is that we can only have one outstanding poll on a link at any time. In practice, the minimum number of blocks between polls is determined by the message length and the round-trip loop delay.

Figure 19-6 shows a message-exchange sequence with short messages and a long loop delay. If a poll is issued with block 0, the earliest a matching final bit can be received is after block 3 has been transmitted.

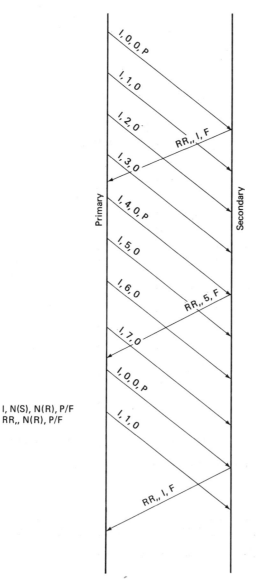

Figure 19-6 Minimum distance between polls.

HDLC two-way simultaneous data flow: normal response mode

If the secondary has messages to send to the primary, they can be sent while the primary is sending messages, as shown in Fig. 19-7. At this stage of your reading, Fig. 19-7(a) should be virtually self-explanatory. The primary sends a sequence of blocks, and it sets the poll bit in the first block. The secondary has data to send, so it starts to transmit information frames. Both primary and secondary are transmitting at full speed with the interframe flags serving as end-of-frame indicators for one frame and as start-of-frame indicators for the next. In the diagram, the secondary messages are shorter than the primary messages.

In response to the poll contained in primary block 0, the secondary sends three blocks with the final bit set in block 2. While this is happening, the primary is continuing with its data transmission so that we have true full-duplex data flow.

Note how the send and receive sequence numbers are incremented. Each station increments its N(S) count by one every time it sends a new block, whereas the N(R) count always indicates the expected number of the next block to be received. Thus the primary, when it sends block 2, has received no blocks, so its N(R) count is zero. By the time the primary is ready to send block 3, it has received two blocks, so the N(R) count on block 3 is updated to 2 to indicate that blocks 0 and 1 have been successfully received. After the primary receives the final bit in block 2, it can issue another poll, which it does in block 4.

If a transmission error occurred, we could encounter the sequence of events shown in Fig. 19-7(b). Here, primary block 1 is hit by noise and is therefore discarded by the secondary. When primary block 2 arrives, the secondary detects the break in the sequence number and it therefore knows that an error has occurred. By the time primary block 2 arrives, the secondary is nearly ready to send its block 2. A quick way to recover the situation is for the secondary to send a REJ supervisory frame as shown. The REJ,,1 frame tells the primary to start retransmitting from block 1. The secondary then continues with its data transmission while the primary receives and acts upon the REJ message. As shown in Fig. 19-7, by the time the REJ message is received, the primary has transmitted block 3.

This means that it must retransmit three blocks of data. If the secondary had implemented the selective reject (SREJ), as shown in Fig. 19-8, the primary would have transmitted only block 1.

Reject versus Poll/Final Checkpoint Recovery. People often wonder what the difference is between initiating recovery based on a reject message and initiating a message based on the poll/final checkpoint. In Fig. 19-7(b), where we use the reject, we had to retransmit three blocks of data, I,1,X I,2,X and I,3,X. The question is: If we relied on the poll/final checkpoint, where would we initiate recovery? This situation is illustrated in Fig. 19-9, where we see once again the reject recovery in Fig. 19-9(a) and poll/final checkpoint recovery in Fig. 19-9(b).

Initially, people expect the recovery to begin at the first poll/final checkpoint

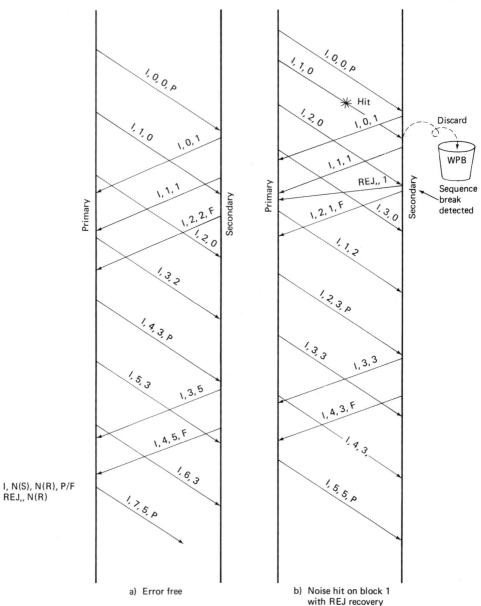

Figure 19-7 HDLC two-way simultaneous data flow.

indicated at (A), whereas in reality it cannot commence until the poll/final check-point at (B). This is because the first poll/final checkpoint can really only expect to checkpoint all the messages up to and including the message that contained the first poll, which was frame I,O,O,P. That means that we cannot detect the error at the first poll/final checkpoint; we can only detect the error at the second poll final checkpoint down at (B), so we begin recovery at the point shown. This means that we must retransmit six frames of data in this particular case where we rely on the poll/final checkpoint, compared to two frames of data where we use the reject command.

Efficiency. Referring to Fig. 19-7(a), note that we may reduce the efficiency of transmission from the secondary to the primary if we poll by setting the P-bit in an information message. Remember that a P must be matched with an F before

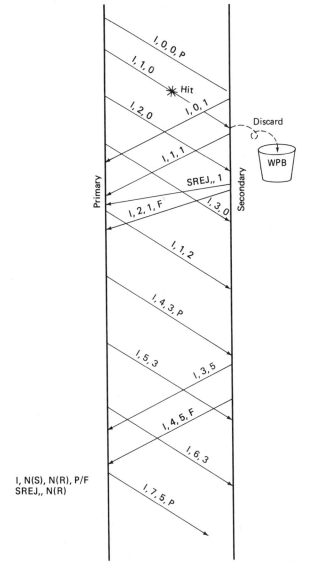

Figure 19-8 HDLC two-way simultaneous data flow with SREJ recovery.

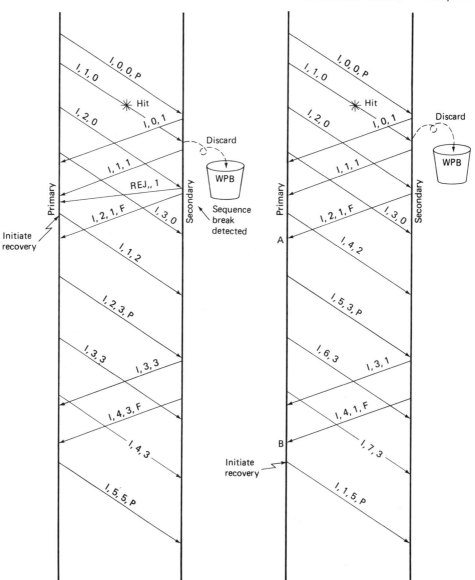

Figure 19-9 Comparison of REJ and Poll/Final recovery.

we can send the next poll. In the diagram, after I,2,2,F is received by the primary, it polls the secondary with I,4,3,P. The secondary cannot respond until the message has been received, which means that the secondary-primary channel is idle for some time. This time is the combination of message transmission time and network delays. If the secondary has a lot of data to send, the overall throughput

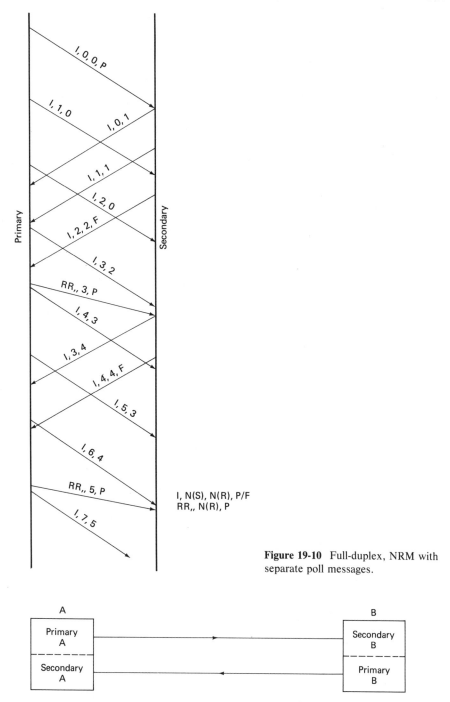

Figure 19-10 Full-duplex, NRM with separate poll messages.

I, N(S), N(R), P/F
RR,, N(R), P

Figure 19-11 Asynchronous balanced mode (ABM) configuration.

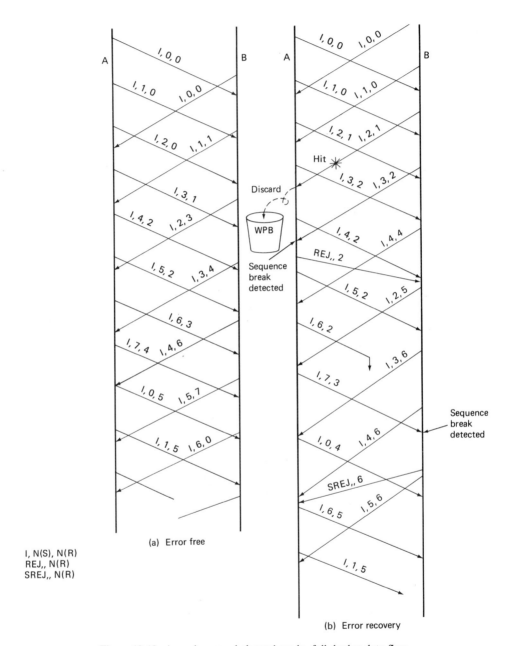

(a) Error free

(b) Error recovery

I, N(S), N(R)
REJ,, N(R)
SREJ,, N(R)

Figure 19-12 Asynchronous balanced mode, full-duplex data flow.

efficiency on that channel will be less than that which could be achieved on the primary–secondary channel.

We can improve the secondary–primary channel throughput by issuing separate poll messages at the first opportunity after an F-bit is received. Figure 19-10 shows an RR,,3,P being issued as soon as I,2,2,F is received. This means that the secondary sends its next block earlier than if it received the poll in the next I-frame I,4,3.

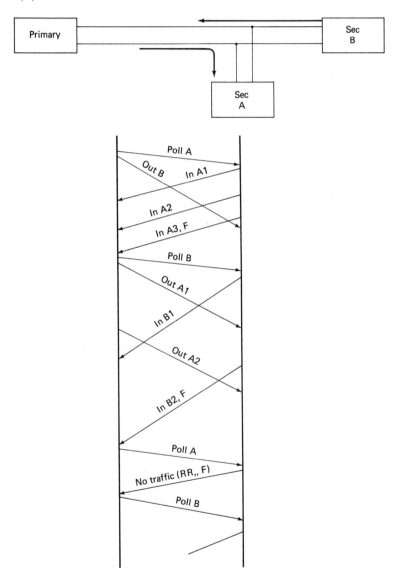

Figure 19-13 HDLC multidrop line operation (NRM).

Asynchronous balanced mode (ABM)

If we are looking for highly efficient two-way simultaneous data flow, we can use ABM. In this mode, which is for point-to-point operation only, each station has both a primary and a secondary. Figure 19-11 shows this arrangement. On the A–B channel, primary A sends data to secondary B, while, on the B–A channel, primary B sends data to secondary A. The N(R) and N(S) counts work in the usual way. Under ABM, either station can transmit whenever it wishes, and we therefore do away with the idle time on the secondary–primary channel that we had in Figs. 19-7 and 19-10.

Under error-free circumstances, we can achieve the maximum throughput rate on each channel, as shown in Fig. 19-12(a). If the N(S) count of an incoming block is out of sequence, recovery can be initiated by using either REJ (reject) or SREJ (selective reject), as shown in Fig. 19-12(b).

ABM is useful in dial-up situations. Because each station has equal status, it is not necessary to have preassigned primary–secondary relationships.

ABM is used as the Level 2 protocol in the X.25 packet switching network interface protocol. This level 2 protocol is sometimes called LAP-B, which means "Link Access Protocol-Balanced."

Multipoint line operations under HDLC

The basic nature of HDLC allows us to indulge in more efficient data exchanges on a multidrop line than can be achieved under the simpler half-duplex line procedure. On a line using the basic-mode half-duplex procedure, we could communicate with only one terminal at a time. With HDLC, it is possible to be communicating with two terminals at a time (assuming, of course, that the line is full-duplex). This is because we could be transmitting to one terminal at the same time as we are receiving from the other terminal.

Figure 19-13 illustrates this facility. The diagram shows a line with two terminal clusters A and B. The exchange sequence diagram shows the primary polling cluster A and then sending an output message to cluster B. In the meantime, cluster A has started to transmit an input message in response to the poll. The input and output messages can be overlapped because they are on different channels.

20
HDLC Network Examples

Example 20-1: HDLC Network No. 1—Point-to-Point Line with Printers and Terminals

Let us consider a system similar to one we have analyzed using half-duplex protocols. Figure 20-1 illustrates a system that was used earlier in Example 16-4, where we have two printers and four terminals on a cluster controller connected on a point-to-point line back to the host. To run full-duplex protocols, however, we must run with permanent carrier on the modems so that we have request-to-send permanently applied so that we can have true two-way simultaneous data flow. Apart from the fact that we are running permanent carrier, it does not really matter what the loop delays are in this system, because as we will see, the throughput of the system will be independent of loop delay as long as there are no errors in the system. The following is an overview of the operation of the terminal/printer network using HDLC protocols.

Assume that the system is running with permanent carrier on each of the modems. Assume error-free transmission, which will allow us to eliminate the effects of loop delay as far as throughput is concerned. A message-exchange sequence may be set up as shown in Fig. 20-2. A steady-state situation can be established whereby the host sends a print line to printer 1, a print line to printer 2, and then group polls the terminals. This sequence is repeated continuously. Although it is not shown on the diagram, it will be necessary to checkpoint the printers at least every seven frames. This should have no effect on the system throughput if it is performed regularly.

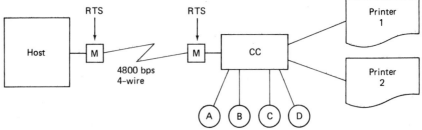

Figure 20-1 Network for Example 20-1.

To determine the throughput we merely work out how long it takes to go through one steady-state sequence and from that, calculate how many sequences we can execute every minute. We can then work out the throughput because each steady-state sequence contains two print lines.

Message Sizes

The print line frames will contain 146 characters. This is made up of 6 characters of HDLC overhead, 132 print characters, and 8 characters for printer control functions. (In the HDX example, the framing overhead was 14 characters.) The group poll is 6 characters. The steady-state sequence is made up of:

	Characters
Print frame 1	146
Print frame 2	146
Group poll	6
Total	298

At 4800 bps, the transmission time for 298 characters is:

$$\text{time for one steady-state sequence} = \frac{298 \text{ char} \times 8 \text{ bits/char}}{4800 \text{ bps}}$$

$$= 0.497 \text{ s}$$

$$\text{throughput} = \left(\frac{60 \text{ s/minute}}{0.497 \text{ s/sequence}}\right) \times 2 \text{ print lines/sequence}$$

$$= 241 \text{ print lines/min}$$

The comparable figure for the half-duplex example would have been 192 lines/min, which is the result obtained using group poll in Example 16-4, Question 4.

Example 20-2: HDLC Network No. 2—With Remote Concentrators, Remote Job Entry, and On-Line Inquiry Terminals

The following is an outline of a reasonableness test analysis that was carried out on a network belonging to one of our clients.

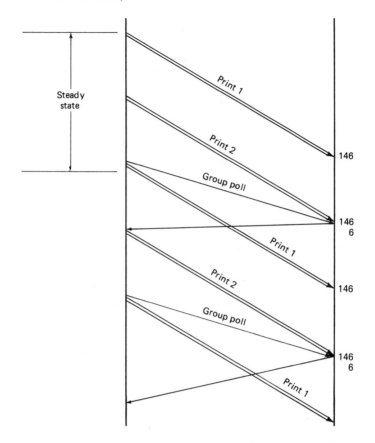

Figure 20-2 Protocol sequence of Example 20-1.

The network. The client has a large host computer with a front-end processor controlling the network. The network is quite widespread, and the bulk of the traffic originates at a point several thousand kilometers away. Because of the high cost of communication lines, a concentrator was installed at the remote site in order to optimize the flow of messages on the long haul line. All the lines in the network are running at 9600 bps.

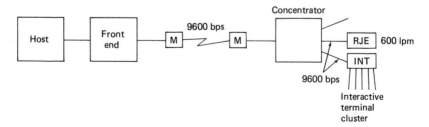

Figure 20-3 HDLC network for analysis.

The major components of the network are illustrated in Fig. 20-3. Not shown on this diagram are a number of very lightly loaded lines that connect into either the concentrator or the front-end processor. The RJE terminal is capable of printing at the rate of 600 lines per minute, with each print line containing the equivalent of 50 characters from the communication line. The data are sent from the host in blocks of 512 characters, so each block contains an average of 10.24 print lines. The overhead characters associated with HDLC and the network end-to-end protocol add an extra 19 characters to the block. So on the link, the RJE output blocks contain 531 characters. The message-exchange sequences for the RJE output traffic are as shown in Fig. 20-4. The pacing messages contain 25 characters.

The interactive traffic originates from a cluster of visual display terminals. The terminals are used for on-line program development, the average input message size

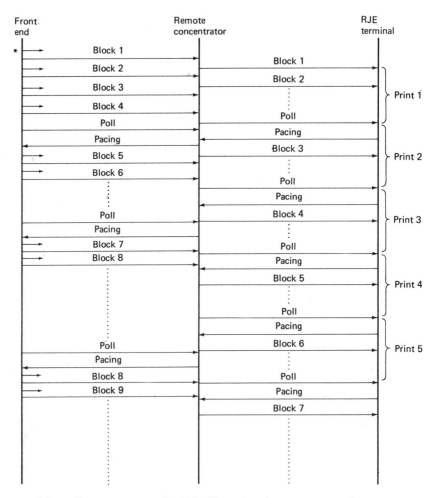

*The small arrows represent polls which will precede each output message unless there is a poll outstanding.

Figure 20-4 Message-exchange sequence for RJE.

is 60 characters, and the average output message size is 400 characters. The terminals handle data in 256-character blocks, so the output message would consist of a block of 256 data characters followed by a block of 144 data characters. The message is displayed on the screen in 256-character segments after the segment has been completely received.

The number of overhead characters used on the main link (between the front end and the concentrator) and on the local link (between the concentrator and the interactive terminals) are different. The block sizes, as seen on the links, are as follows:

		Message size	
	Data size	*Main link*	*Local link*
Input	60	79	71
Output 1	256	275	267
Output 2	144	163	152

The message-exchange sequence for the interactive traffic is shown in Fig. 20-5.

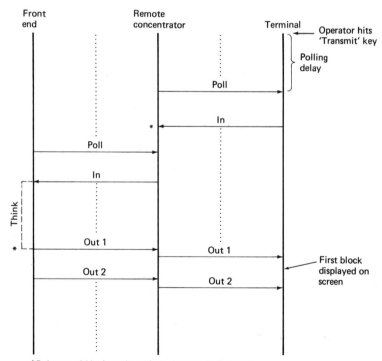

*Delays could be introduced here due to a RJE output block being transmitted.

Figure 20-5 Message-exchange sequence for interactive terminals.

Regarding the interactive message rate, the interactive messages initially will be generated at the rate of 900 per hour. The network, however, must be capable of handling three times this load simultaneously with the RJE traffic and with adequate response time.

The RJE and interactive messages will be mixed on the link between the front end and the remote concentrator. Interactive messages will be given priority over RJE messages. This means that if the host has both an interactive output block and an RJE output block to send, the interactive block will go first. If an RJE block is in the process of being sent, the interactive block will wait until the end of the RJE block. This delay could be encountered at the indicated points on Fig. 20-5. If an interactive message is delayed, the average delay it will encounter is one-half of the transmission time of an RJE output message. The probability of this delay being encountered is equal to the component of output channel utilization owing to RJE output messages. Knowing this probability of delay and the average delay we will encounter if we are delayed, we can calculate the overall average delay that will be encountered by interactive messages. We can then use these figures when estimating the response time that will be achieved by interactive messages.

Network delays. The following sources of delay were identified:

	Elapsed time (ms)
Front-end reaction time	1
Modem delay (9600 bps)	15
Propagation delay	25
Front-end or remote concentrator transit time (time from when a message is received until it is queued for output)	6
Terminal controller reaction time	2
Concentrator reaction time	1
Local link propagation delay	0
Terminal display delay (time from receipt of first 256-character segment until it is displayed on the screen)	100

Method of analysis. The first thing we need to know is whether the system has any chance of working, and, if so, what response times we are likely to get. We therefore first calculate the utilization of the link between the front end and the concentrator. If that looks reasonable, we proceed to work out the expected response time for interactive traffic. We can then determine whether the response time will be adequate.

The approach we use will give us a reasonably accurate figure for both line utilization and response time. The response time predictions will be such that although we will not be able to forecast whether the response time will be 2.2 or 2.35 s, we will be able to tell whether it is likely to be 2.2 or 6.2 s.

This is a *reasonableness test.*

Line utilization. To find the utilization of the main link, we calculate the time required for each activity shown on both Figs. 20-4 and 20-5.

RJE traffic. For the RJE traffic, we consider the steady-state situation, which is what we see after block 4 has been sent. If we calculate the appropriate times for poll/pacing/block 7/block 8, we can then multiply by the number of times this sequence is repeated every hour to calculate line utilization owing to RJE.

The polling messages have six characters.

RJE timings	Input channel (ms)	Output channel (ms)
Poll transmission	5[a]	5
Modem delay	15	—
Propagation delay	25	—
Concentrator reaction time	1	—
Pacing transmission	21	—
Output of block 7	—	442
Output of block 8	—	442
Total	67	889

[a] See the text.

In the foregoing table, propagation and modem delays and reaction times are included for the poll transmission on the input channel, but not for the output channel. This is because under normal circumstances the poll would not be transmitted unless the input channel were idle. There is no traffic on the input channel during the poll transmission and traffic cannot commence until the poll is received by the concentrator. Thus the input channel is effectively busy during this time and the transmission delays therefore contribute to input channel utilization. The poll transmission time is included in both the input and output channels because, by definition, the input channel cannot be used for anything else while a poll is being transmitted.

Message rate. The RJE printer operates at 600 lines/min and we assume that we can drive it at full speed. (In real life it may be somewhat slower than full speed depending on the interference that is caused by the interactive messages.) If each message block contains 10.24 lines, we will have

$$\frac{600 \text{ lines/min} \times 60 \text{ min/h}}{10.24 \text{ lines/block}} = 3516 \text{ blocks/h}$$

on the main link.

The utilization of the input and output channels due to this traffic is calculated as follows. The timings calculated earlier were for two blocks, so

$$\text{input channel utilization} = \frac{0.067}{2} \text{ s/block} \times \frac{3516 \text{ blocks/h}}{3600 \text{ s/h}}$$

$$= 0.033$$

$$= 3.3\% \text{ (very lightly loaded)}$$

$$\text{output channel utilization} = \frac{0.889}{2} \text{ s/block} \times \frac{3516 \text{ blocks/h}}{3600 \text{ s/h}}$$

$$= 0.43$$

$$= 43\%$$

Interactive traffic. A similar calculation is performed for the interactive traffic. Referring to Fig. 20-5, the following time components can be isolated for the main link:

	Input channel (ms)	Output channel (ms)
Poll transmission	5	5
Modem delay	15	—
Propagation delay	25	—
Concentrator reaction time	1	—
Input message transmission time (79 char)	66	—
Output of block 1 (275 char)	—	229
Output of block 2 (163 char)	—	136
Total	112	370

The utilization of the input and output channels at the base load can be calculated as follows:

$$\text{input channel utilization} = \frac{0.112 \text{ s/trans} \times 900 \text{ trans/h}}{3600 \text{ s/h}}$$

$$= 0.028$$

$$= 2.8\%$$

$$\text{output channel utilization} = \frac{0.37 \text{ s/trans} \times 900 \text{ trans/h}}{3600 \text{ s/h}}$$

$$= 0.09$$

$$= 9\%$$

These line utilizations are very low. By adding the components of line utilization owing to RJE and interactive traffic, we can determine the total line utilization:

	Input channel (%)	Output channel (%)
RJE component	3.3	43
Interactive component	2.8	9
Total	6.1	52

This shows that the line is capable of carrying the load. *Note:* It is not strictly correct to find total line utilization by adding the utilization components due to RJE and interactive traffic. This is because the polls are common to both types of traffic. The error introduced in this example is, however, negligible.

Increased interactive traffic. The system is required to handle three times the base interactive load. This will increase the interactive component of line utilization by a factor of 3 to give the following:

$$\text{input channel utilization} = 3 \times 2.8 = 8.4\%$$

$$\text{output channel utilization} = 3 \times 9 = 27\%$$

The overall utilization with both RJE and three times the base interactive load is

	Input channel (%)	Output channel (%)
RJE component	3.3	43
Interactive component	8.4	27
Total	11.7	70

The system can operate under these conditions. The output channel utilization seems high, but we must remember that the interactive traffic has priority and that the RJE traffic is carried as a background load. With a 43% output channel utilization owing to RJE traffic, there is a very good chance that the interactive messages will be delayed by an RJE output. We consider this in the following analysis of response times.

Response time for interactive traffic. To determine the response time, we go to the message-exchange-sequence diagram in Fig. 20-5, trace through the steps shown on the diagram, and put times on each. When the operator hits the transmit key, nothing happens until the next poll comes in. With only one cluster of terminals on the line, the concentrator can poll quite fast (say, every 100 ms), so that the average polling delay will be one-half of this (i.e., 50 ms). We should also evaluate the probability of more than one operator hitting the transmit button during the same polling cycle.

If the transaction rate is 2700 per hour (three times the base load), then we generate, on average, one transaction every 1.3 s. It is highly unlikely that more than one operator will hit transmit buttons during the same polling cycle. Even if they did, there would be very little delay, because all of the messages would be input in response to the one poll.

Once the message is received in the concentrator, it must transit the concentrator and wait for a poll on the main link. There is a 43% chance that an RJE output message will be on the line; if it is there, the interactive input message will be delayed by an average of 221 msec (one-half of the transmission time for one RJE block). The overall average delay that will be encountered will therefore be $0.43 \times 221 = 95$ ms. The input message then goes down the line and is processed by the host computer after it transits the front-end processor. The host takes 1 s to process the transaction and prepare a response.

The host then outputs the message, which is queued for the line in the front end. The front end has two queues for the line: the high-priority queue for interactive traffic, and the low-priority queue for RJE. The interactive messages take precedence over the RJE, but they must wait until the current RJE output block is finished. The probability of delay and the average delay due to RJE is the same as calculated earlier (i.e., 95 ms). The queue of high-priority messages has a nonlinear behavior depending on the component of line utilization owing to the interactive messages.

The student of queuing theory can look up a graph (Fig. 28-4) to determine the average delay introduced by the queue on the output channel.* With an output channel utilization of 27%, the average delay introduced by queuing is one-half of the average time taken to transmit an interactive output message. The total transmission time for the two interactive output blocks is 365 ms, so the average additional queuing delay will be $0.5 \times 365 = 182$ ms. The output messages should then go straight through the network, encountering the normal delays on the way.

Because response time is usually defined as the time from when the operator hits the transmit key until the first character on the screen is seen, we calculate the time until the first block is displayed on the screen. Allowing for terminal display delay time, this will be approximately 100 ms after the last character of the first block is received at the terminal.

The main components of response time can then be listed as follows:

	Elapsed time (ms)
Polling delay (average)	50
Terminal reaction time	2
Input transmission time (local link) (71 char)	59
Concentrator transit time	6
Delay due to RJE	95

* Refer to Chapter 28 for a discussion on the use of Queuing Theory.

	Elapsed time (ms)
Input transmission time (main link) (79 char)	66
Modem delay	15
Propagation delay	25
Front-end transit time	6
Host turnaround	1000
Front-end transit time	6
Delay due to RJE	95
Delay due to queuing on main link	182
First output block transmission time (main link: 275 char)	229
Modem delay	15
Propagation delay	25
Concentrator transit delay	6
First output block transmission time (local link: 267 char)	222
Terminal display delay	100
Total	2204

This is the average response time we could expect. In practice, the response time will vary because of variations in input and output message sizes, instantaneous line loadings, and for other reasons, but the foregoing calculation gives us a useful idea of the approximate response times we can expect.

As we indicated earlier, this style of calculation is very useful as a quick method of finding out if a system is likely to work. It tells us that the response time will be around 2 s; it does not tell us whether it will be 2.204 or 2.304 s, but it does indicate that it is not likely to be 4.204 s.

21
Network Design Summary

The approach used for network design can be summarized as follows:

- Work out the physical configuration of the network and establish all the components of time delay which may be incorporated in the loop delay for the network.
- Determine all the logic processes of the line protocol.
- Build a model, which may be a bar chart, showing the time sequence of events encountered by a single transaction going through the network. Alternatively, the model may, in fact, be a protocol sequence itself.
- Analyze the model using the techniques outlined in this book.

Calculations can be performed in a number of ways; for example, they can be performed manually using the queuing charts indicated in this book. Alternatively, they could be performed by using spreadsheet programs on personal computers. We find this to be a very convenient method of solving the equations because it allows the equations to be solved over and over again for various input parameters; also, the graphical representation allows us to draw charts showing polling delays, queuing delays, response times, and so on. Alternatively, if the mathematics becomes too difficult, which happens sometimes, then using simulation packages on mainframe computers is another method that can be used to perform the network calculations.

In the long run it does not really matter how the calculations are performed. The key to the whole analysis is the model. If the model is no good, it does not matter how you perform the calculations, the results will be no good. An accurate model is essential if we wish to be able to accurately predict the performance of the network. The key to establishing an accurate model is clear thinking. There are many sources of delays in the network, and there are many idiosyncrasies built into the various protocols and various hardware components. These parameters need to be identified accurately for each system and you will find that they vary dramatically from system to system. For a particular application running on two different computers with two different types of terminals, it is likely that the network models are going to be quite different.

I find that clear thinking and a systematic approach are the key to designing a good model. I generally find that it is not possible to build a good model in one sitting and I normally like to design a model and then put it away for a few days before coming back to look at it. On reviewing the model it is likely that I will find that I have made a mistake somewhere and I can rectify this mistake, put the model away, and have another look at it. As you can see, what I am advocating is that you iterate in toward a solution. I generally find that I get a feeling when the model is right and can then analyze it with a reasonable degree of confidence.

A good way of building up your confidence in your own ability to design networks is to apply the theory given in this book to an existing network that you may already have. Analyze this network considering the time delays, the protocol sequences, and so on, build a model, and compare the performance of the real network with the performance predicted by your model. One of two things will happen—either the predictions will agree with the real performance or they will not agree. If the predictions agree, you can congratulate yourself for building a good model and boost your own confidence in your ability to build these models. If the predictions and the real performance do not agree, either you have made a mistake or the original network designer has made a mistake.

In either case you can profit from the exercise by finding out either where your mistake is or where the original designer's mistake was, and once again boost your own confidence in your ability to perform network calculations and accurately predict network performance. After you have done these calculations a number of times, you will find that they become second nature to you and that there is less likelihood that your model is inaccurate.

PART THREE
COMMON CARRIER NETWORKS

22
Communications Carrier Facilities

An organization that provides telecommunications facilities to the public is called a *communications carrier* (or *common carrier*). In most countries, domestic communication facilities usually are provided by the same governmental department that is responsible for the postal service. In Europe, the generic name for the carrier is *PTT*, which is an acronym for Posts, Telephone, and Telegraph. In some countries, the communications carrier is not a governmental department although it is subject to strict government regulations. This is because most carriers are monopolies. In some countries, more than one carrier provides domestic services.

Having a single common carrier has both advantages and disadvantages. An advantage is that one body controls the standards that must be maintained in the use of the communications system; also, in theory, it enables one point of contact to be maintained between the user and the carrier. A disadvantage is that the user must accept whatever terms and conditions the carrier offers. Often, particularly in the field of data communications, the users feel that the common carriers do not supply sufficient facilities and that they impose too many restrictions on the use of their facilities. In general, we find a wider range of data transmission facilities in those countries where there are competing carriers.

Many countries use different carriers for the handling of domestic and international communications. The main difference between domestic and international communications is greater distances for international communications. Intercontinental communications are normally handled either by satellite links or by undersea coaxial or fiber-optic cables, both of which provide extremely high-quality channels.

telephone networks

The main resource of a domestic communication carrier is an extensive telephone network. Depending on the size of the country, the telephone network may consist of hundreds or perhaps thousands of telephone exchanges (switching offices) linked together in a mixture of mesh and hierarchical networks. Subscribers' telephones are connected into a nearby telephone exchange by physical pairs of wire. The telephone exchanges themselves are large switching units that enable subscribers to set up point-to-point connections between telephones. As illustrated in Fig. 22-1, the telephone exchanges switch the call through the network from the calling telephone to the receiving telephone.

The telephone exchanges themselves range from manual plugboard exchanges, where calls are physically switched by human operators, through step-by-step uniselector exchanges, through the more modern crossbar exchange, to the latest telephone exchanges, which are completely electronic and computer controlled.

Telephone exchanges are connected by various forms of communications media. Around the local metropolitan area, they tend to be connected by cables consisting of hundreds of pairs of wire. Over longer distances, coaxial cables, optical fibers, satellites, and microwave radio systems are used.

Because of the wide range of transmission media employed in a telephone network, a particular telephone call may have several different qualities of medium in use. The quality of the overall connection will be determined by the quality of the poorest component in the link. This is particularly true with intercontinental communications systems because, although the satellite or submarine cable portion of the link is of very high quality, the tail ends could be of poor quality, therefore limiting the overall performance of the link. For example, in many of our cities, some of the twisted-pair cables have been buried for half a century, and the quality of these cables is deteriorating.

The communication channels that can be derived from the telephone network can be used for many purposes. The biggest single class of user is the average person with a telephone in his house or in his business. This user demands an efficient, reliable, cheap telephone service. In the developed countries, the telephone market is almost saturated, and the growth of the service in terms of the number of telephones installed more or less follows the population growth of the country.

Figure 22-2 illustrates a typical development curve for the installation of a new communications facility. This S-shaped curve shows that (1) when the service is initially introduced, demand is somewhat slow; (2) as people get used to the facility, the demand increases at a higher rate; and (3) as the market becomes

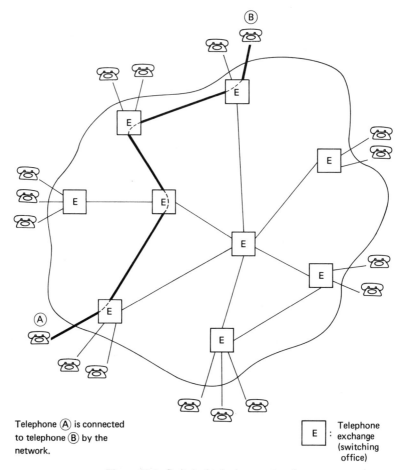

Telephone (A) is connected
to telephone (B) by the
network.

| E | : | Telephone exchange (switching office) |

Figure 22-1 Switched telephone network.

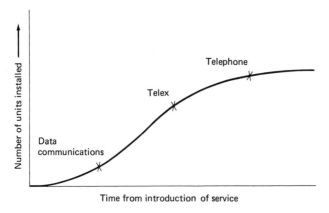

Figure 22-2 Growth curve for telecommunications facilities.

saturated, the demand tends to fall off. In most developed countries, the telephone service would be on the upper right part of the curve in the area of low rate of increase of demand.

Most countries have subscriber trunk dialing facilities so that a telephone subscriber can automatically establish a point-to-point telephone connection with any other telephone in the country. This facility is extended for international subscriber dialing, so it is possible for residents of many countries to dial directly to residents of other countries without operator assistance. This facility is taken for granted today, and few people stop to think how life as we now know it would be impossible without such a communications facility.

Communication lines from the telephone network can be used for many purposes other than the familiar telephone system. Some of these other applications are discussed later in this chapter.

coaxial cable

A *coaxial cable* is a broadband communications facility that can carry thousands of simultaneous telephone conversations. The capacity of a particular cable depends on the way the system has been engineered.

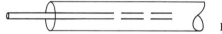

Figure 22-3 Coaxial cable.

A coaxial cable is actually a two-wire line that has been constructed in a special way with one conductor inside the other. The outer conductor is a cylinder and and the inner conductor runs down the axis of the cylinder as shown in Fig. 22-3. When a cable is constructed in this way, you can send an extremely high frequency signal along the cable, and this signal can be split up into a number of smaller frequency bands, each of which can be assigned to one voice conversation. As the signal goes through the cable, it deteriorates in size and it needs to be fed through an amplifier or repeater to boost it to drive it along the next piece of cable. The closer together the repeaters are placed, the more communication channels can be derived from the cable. As an example, if the repeaters are spaced at approximately 1-km intervals, thousands of communication channels can be derived from the coaxial cable about as thick as your little finger.

microwave radio

A *microwave system* is a broadband facility providing line-of-sight radio communications via a very high frequency radio signal which is transmitted from one microwave tower to another. Because the curvature of the earth limits the distance

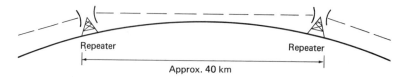

Figure 22-4 Line-of-sight microwave communications.

we can communicate line-of-sight, repeater stations are installed approximately every 40 km along the route, as shown in Fig. 22-4.

The quality of transmission varies with the type of medium and the distance involved. Physical wire pairs provide quality communications over short distances, whereas the coaxial cable and microwave systems can provide high-capacity, high-quality communications over longer distances.

satellite communications

Many countries use satellite communications for domestic purposes. The advantage of satellite communication is that the satellite can provide very wide coverage on the ground, and within the view of the satellite, we are able to set up an earth station and immediately get very high quality communications with other earth stations. This is of great value to developing countries and in areas where long terrestrial distances are involved.

As shown in Fig. 22-5, a communications satellite is a radio relay unit up in the sky. The job of the satellite is really very straightforward, that is, to receive a signal that has been transmitted up from an earth station, amplify it, and then broadcast it down again so that it can be received by another earth station. In the process, the satellite provides a communication link between the two earth stations and thus between the two users connected into the earth stations. To act

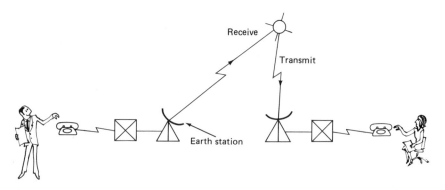

Figure 22-5 A satellite is a radio relay in the sky.

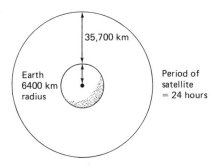

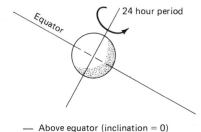

— Above equator (inclination = 0)   **Figure 22-6** Geostationary orbits.

as a radio relay unit, the satellite must be in a special position. First, as illustrated in Fig. 22-6, it must be in a circular orbit approximately 37,000 km above the equator, at which height it takes exactly 24 hours for the satellite to go around once in its orbit. If the orbital plane of the satellite coincides exactly with the equatorial plane, we have a special situation because both the satellite and the earth are rotating once every 24 hours around the earth's polar axis. This means that from our point of view on the ground, the satellite is always in the same position. This orbit is called a geostationary orbit; that is, the satellite is stationary in relation to the earth.

From the geostationary orbit we have a field of view of roughly one-third of the surface of the earth, as shown in Fig. 22-7. The satellite can receive a signal

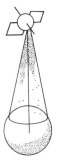

Figure 22-7 Field of view approximately one-third of the surface of the earth.

transmitted from any earth station within the field of view and broadcast it down to where it can be received by any other station within the field of view of the satellite.

You have no doubt seen earth stations; some are large and some are very small. The size of an earth station is really related to the received signal strength on the ground at the point where the earth station is located. The aim of domestic satellite systems is generally to minimize the size and therefore the cost of the earth stations, to enable more people to use them.

Although the physical field of view of the satellite is about one-third of the earth's surface, the electronic field of view can be made smaller by shaping the radio beam so that it falls onto a smaller area. This is desirable for domestic satellites so that the radio energy falls on the target country rather than being wasted in areas where it will not be used.

As shown in Fig. 22-8(a), if the satellite is sitting up in orbit radiating radio energy like a light bulb, the radio energy goes in all directions, and the only useful energy is that which falls on the target countries. All the other energy is wasted. We therefore shape the radio beam in a similar manner to the way in which we can shape a light beam, so that we direct all the radio beam on to the target countries.

A radio wave can be shaped just like a light beam, as shown in Fig. 22-8(b). With a flashlight [Fig. 22-8(b)] we use a parabolic reflector and put the light bulb at the focus of the parabola. This means that light waves from the bulb go into the parabola and are reflected out as a more-or-less parallel beam and we therefore get a concentrated beam of light. The same thing happens with satellite earth stations using a parabolic reflector to shape the radio wave more-or-less into a parallel beam, so that we get the concentrated beam going onto the target countries. By distorting the antenna and positioning the feed correctly, it is possible to obtain radio beams of various shapes so that they can correspond roughly with the shape of the target countries. Consider Fig. 22-9, where we show the beam patterns of the Australian domestic satellite. There is a national beam that covers the entire country, enabling communications between any points within the coun-

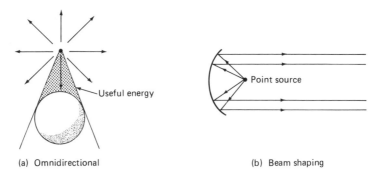

(a) Omnidirectional   (b) Beam shaping

Figure 22-8 Radio beam shaping.

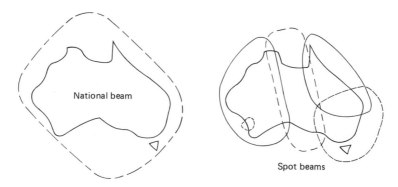

Figure 22-9 Domestic satellite beam patterns.

try via that beam. Also, there are four spot beams which are used for television broadcasting. As can be seen from the diagrams, the spot beams are approximately one-fourth the size of the national beam, which means that the signal strength within a spot beam should be approximately four times the signal strength of the signal within the national beam. This means that smaller earth stations can be used to receive signals from the spot beams. Therefore, people who are watching television can have a small antenna which is relatively inexpensive, whereas business users who require to use the national beam need to have larger antennas.

The general characteristics of satellite communications, from the point of view of data communications, are as follows:

- Long loop delay
- Cost relatively independent of distance
- High speed
- Broadcast capability
- Security needed
- High reliability

A brief examination of these characteristics follows.

Long Loop Delay. Probably the most outstanding characteristic of satellite communications is the long loop delay (in excess of 1/2s for the round-trip delay). This delay can cripple data communication systems that use the old-style half-duplex communication protocols. To obtain effective use of satellite communications with data communication systems, we need to use full-duplex protocols because in these cases the throughput on a point-to-point link can be relatively independent of the loop delay as long as there are no errors in the system.

Cost. The cost of establishing a link through the satellite is relatively independent of distance. What this means is that the cost of installing an earth station is approximately the same regardless of the location.

High Speed. The communications capability of a satellite depends on the design of the satellite transponders, but most satellites are easily capable of handling 60 Mbps or perhaps even double this speed, and although nothing like the speeds that can be obtained over fiber-optics systems, these speeds are in excess of most of the communication speeds readily available over terrestrial networks. This will change with the advent of widespread digital networks.

Broadcast Capability. Because any earth station within the field of view of the satellite can receive the signal, it is possible to update multiple databases at the same time with one transmission.

Security. Because any earth station within the view of the satellite is capable of intercepting a signal, you can be reasonably sure that somewhere, sometime, someone will intercept your signals. Because you probably value your data in regard to their confidentiality, it would be a good idea to encrypt the data prior to transmission so that unauthorized users cannot gain access to your data.

High Reliability. Satellite links are extremely reliable. This may sound funny because the satellite is up there in the sky and it is difficult to get there with a screwdriver to fix it. On the other hand, over our 20-year history with satellites, they have proven to be extremely reliable once they reach orbit. If a satellite is going to fail, it seems it fails on the way up to orbit rather than failing once it has reached orbit. Once in orbit the satellites tend to last their lifetime, and although parts of the satellite fail, they are designed for reliability with lots of redundant equipment, and generally speaking, we do not seem to have catastrophic failures in the satellites once they reach orbit.

Between two terrestrial locations, there are only three major components in the link: the earth stations at each end and the satellite up in the sky. Compare this with going through the terrestrial network, where you may have microwave towers every 40 km or so going across the country. In the terrestrial network there is more equipment to go wrong.

fiber optics

Optical fibers are probably the most promising medium for carrying high-speed digital datastreams. An optical fiber is a strand of very fine glass thinner than a human hair. The glass is so clear that a window 1 km thick would be as easy to see through as a normal window. The fibers are flexible, and if a light source is placed at one end, the light will appear at the other end even if the fiber is twisted or coiled. By properly manufacturing the fiber, it is possible to confine the light within it so that none is radiated externally. If the light is flashed on and off, a pulse of light travels through the fiber which can be detected at the other end and turned into an electronic digital pulse. If the light source is a laser, it can be flashed on and off millions of times per second, thus enabling a very high speed digital pulse stream to travel through the fiber, where it can be detected at the other end and turned into an electronic digital data stream. Speeds of thousands of millions of bits per second can be reached with suitable light sources and fibers. The light source is either a light-emitting diode or a laser diode, both of which can be switched on or off at high data rates. Laser diodes are capable of producing a light beam modulated with data at the rate of thousands of millions of bits per second.

A fiber-optic cable is much smaller and lighter than its conventional counterpart. For example, a cable with several hundred pairs of copper wires may be 2 or 3 inches in diameter. A fiber-optic cable of equivalent capacity may be less than 5 mm in diameter, of which the fiber itself would typically be about 5 to 50 micrometers.

Telex/TWX networks

The Telex network operates similarly to the telephone network except that the terminals are teleprinter devices rather than telephone handsets. The Telex network allows for any two users connected to the Telex network to establish temporary point-to-point connection between their teleprinters that they can exchange messages. Traditionally, the Telex networks around the world have offered a pure switched service such that if the called party was busy, the calling party would have to keep trying until the called party was available. This is just like the telephone network.

Newer facilities, however, are being introduced into the Telex network such that many Telex networks now have store-and-forward capability, which means that if the called party is unavailable, messages can still be sent and will be stored internally within the Telex network and forwarded on to the called party when the called party's machine is available for service. This greatly increases the throughput of the system from the point of view of individual users because the users no longer have to spend time attempting to establish connections with terminals that are either busy or out of action. Also, the use of computer control in the Telex network allows services such as abbreviated call establishment by using a smaller acronym for the called party's name rather than the full Telex number, and automatic conference calls can be set up.

Telex networks operate at 50 bps using Baudot code, and the American TWX network uses ASCII code at 110 bps. Internationally, many countries' Telex networks are interconnected with over 1,500,000 Telex sets in use around the world. The Telex service is still growing at a fairly high rate, and it would be somewhere toward the upper middle of the growth curve shown in Fig. 22-2.

Teletex

While Telex and TWX networks have many advantages, disadvantages are the very low speed of communication and the very poor quality of the printed outputs. These days, word processors with letter-quality printers are capable of communicating with each other and providing very high quality printout at reasonably high speed. For example, transmitting at a rate of 2400 bps, it is possible to send an entire A4-size page of paper in under 10 s. At Telex speeds this would take several minutes, and the quality of the printout would be nowhere near as good as that provided by the word processor. One problem with word processor communications is that all manufacturers' equipment operates in a different way using perhaps different character sets, different control functions, and different communication protocols, making it difficult, if not impossible, to communicate between different brands of word processors.

In the early 1980s, CCITT came out with a new international recommendation for Teletex communication which defines all the communication rules, the protocols, the character sets, the control functions, and so on, that are required to transmit an exact copy of a page of information from one machine to another. If the various word processor suppliers implement the Teletex protocols into their machines, it would be possible to have communication between different brands of processors. The Teletex protocols are, in fact, a specific implementation of the seven layers of the ISO open system interconnection architecture model. Common carriers in different countries are implementing Teletex networks specifically to carry traffic from communicating word processors, and these networks generally interface via a conversion facility with the existing Telex network. This means that it is possible for Telex users to communicate with Teletex users, and vice versa.

The public network for Teletex differs in different countries. In some countries the packet switch is used, while in others the public switched telephone network is used or even special dedicated-circuit switched Teletex networks.

Perhaps the easiest way to visualize Teletex is as a super-duper Telex network operating at high speed and providing very high quality output. This means that we can use the Teletex network to bypass, to a certain extent, the postal service and courier services.

videotex

Videotex is an information retrieval service that makes databases available to subscribers via a relatively simple terminal. Public videotex services are generally provided by a common carrier, while there are many private services provided by service bureaus or by individual organizations for use within that organization or by its customers.

A simple terminal is usually connected to their service via a 1200/75-bps modem. The 75-bps channel is used to handle keyboard data entered by the user while the 1200-bps channel is used to transmit data to the terminal. The terminals usually have only 40 characters per line and they fill the screen relatively quickly at 1200-bps.

Data are stored on the databases in the form of pages where one page is equivalent to a screenful of data. Each page has a number and its user selects the appropriate page by keying in its number. A 75-bps channel is therefore more than adequate to handle this form of input.

Facilities are often provided for the user to add information to the database; for example, he or she can make theater bookings or airline reservations or perform banking transactions through a videotex service. Most videotex services also provide an elementary computer messaging service and an interface to the telex network.

telegram networks

The PTT usually provides some form of telegram network, which also uses the communication lines derived from the telephone network. Instead of using the conventional telephone exchanges for switching, it uses different switching equipment that is often computer-based.

public message-switching systems

Many carriers provide an automatic message-switching service to their customers. Message switching is perhaps the oldest established application for data communications, and we describe it by means of an example.

Figure 22-10 shows an organization with five offices in different cities. These offices need to be able to communicate with each other for the purpose of sending administrative messages in hard copy form. One method of achieving this aim

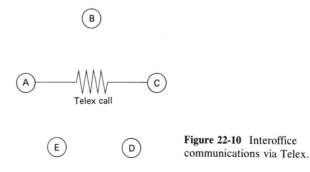

Figure 22-10 Interoffice communications via Telex.

would be to provide each office with a Telex set so that any office could establish a point-to-point connection with any other office through the Telex network. Messages can then be sent along this line, and the connection can be cleared at the end of the message exchange. In such a system, if A calls C, no other stations can call either A or C while they are communicating. Thus, if D wishes to send a message to C, D must keep trying to establish a connection until he can get through. Similarly, if A wishes to send the same message to D and E, he must call each station individually, and, in this case, he will send the message twice.

If a station is out of action, all other stations must hold any traffic that they have for that station. Also, as real circuits are used, all of the terminals must be speed-compatible, code-compatible, and format-compatible.

Provided that there is not too much traffic in the network, such an operation is fine. However, when the traffic builds up, problems arise because the called terminal is likely to be busy when the calling terminal attempts to set up a call.

We can overcome this problem by putting a computer into the system, as shown in Fig. 22-11, with the terminals connected directly into the computer. If A wishes to send a message to E, he sends the message to the computer, which stores the message on its mass-storage system. When E is ready to receive the message, the computer takes it from the mass storage and sends it to B. This is known as a *store-and-forward* message-switching system. If the called terminal is busy, the other terminals can still send messages to it. These messages will be queued on the mass storage and will be output when the called terminal is ready. Priorities can be built in so that urgent messages can take precedence over routine traffic.

If a terminal is out of action, the other terminals can still send messages to it, which will be stored until the terminal is ready. If the same message is to be sent to multiple destinations, the calling terminal sends one copy of the message, and the computer forwards it to the receiving stations.

Because there is a computer in the system, the network allows communication between terminals that would otherwise be incompatible. The computer handles the necessary conversion of code, speed, format, and transmission mode.

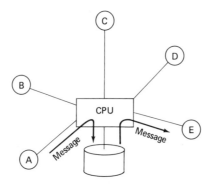

Figure 22-11 Message-switching system.

Many other facilities can be provided such as a retrieval mechanism whereby specific messages can be recovered from the mass-storage system. Also, the computer can keep track of traffic statistics to provide data for the network designer so that he or she can plan for the future.

leased lines

We can lease a line from the communication carrier and use it for purposes other than telephone traffic. When we lease a line, the carrier normally bypasses the switching equipment in the telephone exchanges, which gives us a better-quality connection than if we use the switched network. This is because a lot of the noise that is induced onto telephone lines is caused by switching noises within the telephone exchanges. Leased lines are used for many applications such as monitoring burglar alarms and fire alarms, transmitting facsimile information, and, of course, for data transmission.

The use of the telephone network for data communications is really only in its infancy, and revenues from data communication currently represent a very small proportion of the total revenue of a communication carrier. Data communications is growing extremely fast and would be in the lower left corner of the curve in Fig. 22-2. The growth rate varies from country to country and rates of 30-50% per annum are not uncommon.

data transmission facilities

Because the telephone network exists and is so extensive, we use it for data communications. The network itself was designed for carrying the human voice; as such, it is not ideally suited to carrying data. This was discussed in Chapter 7, where we saw that we required a modem to convert the digital data into a voice-like form that would go smoothly through a telephone network. Most common carriers allow us to use the telephone network in its switched form so that we can establish temporary point-to-point connections between terminals that are connected into the network. In addition, we can lease lines to set up permanent point-to-point or multipoint connections between our computers and terminals.

Switched telephone network

The telephone network is a two-wire network. This means that when we make a telephone call, we set up a logical two-wire connection between the calling and the called telephone. Owing to the nature of the telephone network, we may or may not get a physical two-wire connection between the two telephones.

Most telephone connections are physically two wires from the subscriber's location to the closest telephone exchange or switching office. In a local area, it is quite likely that the connection is made up of physical pairs of wires; over longer distances, we are likely to go through a high-capacity bearer such as a microwave link or a coaxial cable. In those cases we would logically have two-wire connections, but physically that would not be so.

The implication of having a two-wire connection is that as a rule, we can derive only one communication channel from the two wires. Under certain circumstances, however, the modems can electronically manipulate the situation and derive two communication channels from two wires. The speed at which this can be done depends largely on the quality of the telephone network. There are a number of readily available modems which will operate full-duplex on a two-wire line. Commonly available modems are the following:

CCITT V.21	300 bps	Bell 103	300 bps
CCITT V.22	1200 bps	Bell 212A	1200 bps
CCITT V.23	1200 bps/75 bps		
CCITT V.22 bis	2400 bps	Bell 2400	2400 bps
CCITT V.32	9600 bps		

The exact facilities available in a particular country are a function of both the quality of the telephone network and the policy adopted by the common carrier(s) in that country. If we do not have the modems that can electronically derive two channels from the communication facility provided by the two-wire network, we can operate only in half-duplex or one-way modes.

The upper speed limit for transmission over the switched telephone network varies from country to country. Once again this is generally a function of the quality of the telephone network and the policy adopted by the common carrier. Today's more sophisticated modems have adaptive equalization mechanisms built into them which allow the modems to compensate for varying transmission characteristics on the line. When these adaptive equalization modems are used, it is often possible to increase the performance of the switched telephone network to 9600 bps.

A point-to-point connection through the telephone network can be established either by manually dialing numbers on a telephone or by having the computer automatically set up the call. Whether you can use automatic dialing and automatic answering is a function of the policy adopted by your own carrier.

Figure 22-12 illustrates the method of manually setting up a data call. This diagram shows a telephone network with a computer and a terminal interfaced into it. Associated with the modems at each end is a switch and a telephone. When no call is in progress, the telephone line would terminate on the telephone. To initiate a call, the operator picks up the telephone handset and dials the desired number. The network switches the call through to the receiving telephone, which rings. The telephone can be answered by an operator; at this point, the two operators have a point-to-point voice communication line. They can agree to set up a data call, and they can activate their switches, which will cause the telephone

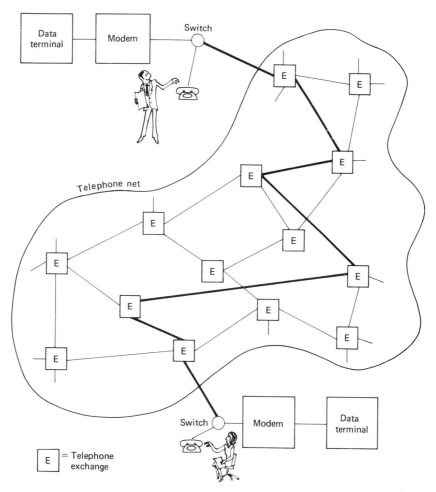

Figure 22-12 Data link established through the switched telephone network.

line to be terminated on the modems. This activates the *connect-data-set-to-line* (or data terminal ready) lead in the V.24/RS-232 interface; when the modem is connected to the line, it will return a signal to the data terminal equipment that says *data-set ready*. This signal indicates that the modem is switched on, connected to the line, and ready for data transmission. At this stage we have a point-to-point connection between the terminal and the computer.

In areas governed by those carriers that permit automatic origination and answering of calls, the computer can originate calls to unattended terminals and extract data from or send data to them.

In many areas, the cost of making telephone calls is cheaper at night than it is by day. By using inexpensive personal computers with local storage (such as floppy disks), it is possible to set up a system whereby remote branch offices can use the PC for local data entry and even for on-line enquiry and update of local files. In the evening, the computer can automatically establish a connection with each PC and cause it to transmit the day's data to the computer. When the data transmission is finished, the call is cleared, and the cost of the call would be the same as the cost of an equivalent telephone call. The computer can process the data and produce a new updated file for transmission to the remote site. This type of facility opens up many interesting possibilities for data communication networks.

Privately leased lines

A privately leased line is one that permanently connects the data terminal equipment so that the data can be transmitted at any time without the need to establish a connection as we did with the switched telephone network. The lines that are used are the same as those used in the telephone network except that they bypass the switching equipment in the telephone exchanges. Leased lines can be used for a wide range of speeds—from less than 50 bps up to 19,200 bps for normal voice-grade telephone channels. Higher speeds, such as 48,000 bps or more, can be achieved over a broadband circuit. The exact speeds that can be used in any given country should be established with the carrier.

A leased line can be a two-wire or four-wire line depending on the speed and mode of operation envisaged. As with the telephone network, a two-wire circuit is usually capable of transferring data in only one direction at a time unless we are using one of the lower-speed modems that enables us to derive two channels from the two wires. At higher speeds, the two wires can be used for half-duplex operation, whereby the data can be transferred in either direction but not simultaneously in both directions. To achieve full-duplex operation at higher speeds, a four-wire circuit is required. This is equivalent to two two-wire circuits, each of which is capable of carrying data in one direction at a time.

Leased lines can be point-to-point or multipoint. By using suitable line-splitting equipment, we can extend the one line to a number of locations to set up a multipoint line. This use of line splitting was described in Chapter 7.

Data-carrying capacity of communications circuits

Because a communications network is made up of different qualities of multipair cables, coaxial cables, and microwave systems, the quality of a given link between two points is only as good as its weakest segment. In a widespread telephone network, the components of lines that are used to put together one temporary point-to-point telephone connection are more or less selected at random from the network, so we can never guarantee from one call to the next whether we would be using the same physical connections between the two points.

Because of this, we cannot condition the lines in the switched telephone network to take care of transmission irregularities that manifest themselves when we are transmitting data. We can, however, use adaptively equalizing modems to compensate for certain transmission characteristics on the line; thus we can stretch the performance of the network as modem technology improves. At present, the general upper limit for transmission speed over the switched network is 9600 bps.

When we lease a line, we can lease a two-wire or a four-wire line, although at high transmission speeds, carriers generally require us to use a four-wire line. Part of the reason for this is that the trunk portion of a telephone network usually consists of four-wire lines, so the long-haul circuits tend to come out of the network as four-wire lines.

A leased line can be conditioned to make it look better than it was to begin with and thus raise its inherent data-carrying capacity. In addition to the line conditioning, we can use adaptive equalization in modems to further improve the performance of the system. At the moment, the general practical upper limit for transmission over the normal type of line that comes from the telephone network is 19,200 bits per second. As indicated earlier, the common carrier can usually provide circuits with higher capacity.

The price of communication lines

The price of communication lines varies dramatically from country to country. If we were to quote any figures, they would rapidly fall out of date, because, along with other areas in the electronics industries, the prices of communication lines continues to fall.

As a general rule, long-haul lines are cheaper per kilometer than short-haul lines, and in the future we can expect the price of short-haul lines to increase somewhat. This is because technological advances allow us to extract more capacity from the type of communication bearers used on long-haul lines, whereas in the local area around a city, the lines generally continue to be physical pairs, the installation and maintenance of these is labor intensive, and the price is likely to continue to rise. The increases in communication capacity that can be provided by the various media are well illustrated by the number of voice channels provided in communication satellites over the 20-year period from 1965 to 1985. In 1965, the Intelsat I satellite was launched with a capacity of 240 voice channels. By 1968, the Intelsat III satellite had a capacity of 1200 voice channels. In 1970, the Intelsat IV satellite had a capacity of 3600 voice channels. And the Intelsat IVa satellite, launched in 1975, had a capacity of 6000 voice channels. Intelsat V, launched in 1980, and Intelsat Va launched in 1984, both have a capacity of 12,000 voice channels. Intelsat VI, has a capacity of 35,000 voice channels. This type of increase in capacity is also being experienced with microwave links and coaxial cables. The tremendous capacity of optical fibers allows for a dramatic decrease in the cost per channel.

new data networks

The telephone network poses a number of problems for data-communications users. The capability of conventional voice transmission techniques limits the transmission speeds we can achieve while maintaining acceptable error rates. In addition, we experience long connect times with the switched telephone network. The connect time, which is the time it takes to set up the call through the network, can be as long as 30 s. This means that if we need a rapid response to an enquiry in an on-line inquiry/update system, we really need to use a leased line.

Most communications lines are grossly underutilized and only carry data for 15% or less of the time. Because most carriers base their charges on the length of the line and the elapsed time for which the line is held, we are usually paying for unused line time.

In some countries, users are allowed to group and share the capacity of a line. Because the cost of a long-haul, 9600-bps line is generally not a great deal more than the cost of a 1200-bps line, the users can reduce their overall costs by subdividing the capacity of a line with multiplexers or concentrators. For example, four users may each use a stream of 2400 bps derived from a 9600-bps data stream, as shown in Fig. 22-13.

Carriers do not generally like users sharing in this manner, because they see it as an infringement on their role as a common carrier and because they may lose revenue. Nor do carriers, in general, like users to resell communication facilities. This means that a user with spare capacity on a particular line is not permitted to sell off some of this spare capacity to another user. Once again, the carriers see this as an infringement upon their role as a common carrier.

An extension of the principle of reselling communications services is the implementation of a *value-added network* (VAN). In this case, the owner of the VAN leases basic communications facilities, such as lines and modems, from the

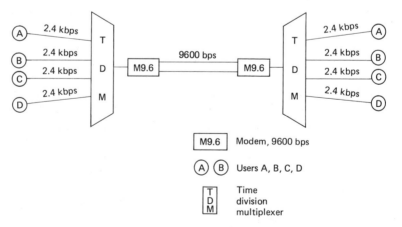

Figure 22-13 Four users sharing a 9600-bps line.

carrier and puts them together into a network. By incorporating suitable equipment, usually based on one or more switching computers, the VAN owner is able to provide a service that would not otherwise have been available from the carrier. Common-user message-switching systems and packet-switching systems are examples of value-added networks. Once again, most carriers do not allow the operation of VANs.

Carriers are being increasingly pressured to provide improved data communications facilities. Users want higher transmission speeds, lower error rates, faster connect times, and lower costs. An ideal situation, from the user's point of view, would be one whereby a terminal could be connected to a computer instantaneously and where the user pays only for the number of bits that are transmitted. If we could achieve virtually instantaneous connect times with a public switched-data network, then even transaction-oriented terminals could establish a fresh connection for each transaction. The call would be held for the duration of that particular transaction and would then be cleared. The happy user would only be charged for the length of time he or she actually held the connection. With suitable transmission equipment, the network would not be devoting any of its expensive long-haul resources to that particular terminal while it is not transmitting or receiving data.

Modern switching systems cannot achieve the ideal, instantaneous connect time, but they can set up calls very quickly. Some systems can establish a connection in 100 ms, although once the connection has been set up, the computers/terminals must exchange signaling information, and the time this takes is largely related to the transmission speed employed. Generally, the overall connect time should be less than 1 s.

23
Digital Data Networks and ISDN

digital transmission networks

Digital transmission systems have been developed that allow us to extract higher bit rates from a given communications line than we could achieve with the conventional analog transmission techniques used in the telephone network. In Chapter 7, we saw that if we send a digital signal down a telephone line, it becomes distorted, as shown in Fig. 23-1(a). This distortion gets worse with distance and with transmission speed. We saw that to send digital signals through the telephone network, we needed to use a modem to convert the digital signals into a smoothly varying analog signal that would travel easily through the telephone network. A modem modulates the data onto a carrier wave, and the maximum data transmission speed we can successfully achieve is directly related to the maximum signal frequency we can send along the line. The maximum sine-wave frequency we can successfully send along the average telephone line is approximately 3000 Hz, and this in turn causes our present practical speed limit over long distances to be approximately 19,200 bps.

Analog signals, like that shown in Fig. 23-1(b), are also subject to distortion, which is related to the frequency of the signal and the distance involved. When an analog signal becomes distorted, there is no way to conveniently remove the distortion and reconstruct the original signal.

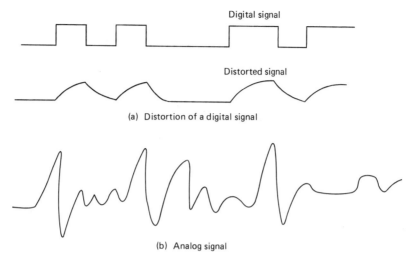

Figure 23-1 (a) Distortion of a digital signal; (b) an analog signal.

With digital transmission systems, the signal quality deteriorates as transmission speed and/or distance increases. Figure 23-2 shows the deterioration of signal quality at fixed speed as the distance increases and, also, for a fixed distance as the speed increases. On the fixed-speed diagram, a line has been drawn to indicate the minimum acceptable signal quality. Below this line, the signal quality is not good enough for us to guarantee that we can always correctly identify the data stream. Above the line, we can correctly identify the data stream, regenerate the signal, and send a fresh clean signal down the communication line. Later we can regenerate that signal as well. If the signal is precisely timed, it is easy to regenerate, because there are only two states that we need to be able to recognize (the 1 state and the 0 state) rather than an infinite range of signal levels that should be recognized in an analog transmission system.

Digital transmission systems give us better error performance than do analog transmission systems. Given that we can precisely regenerate the signal, we can, in effect, remove the distortion from it. We cannot do this with analog signals as they get distorted because, due to the continuously varying nature of the signal, we have no way of telling what the signal looked like in the first place. Therefore, we cannot remove the distortion from analog signals, and the error rate is therefore greater than for digital transmission systems. Generally speaking, the error performance for digital networks is approximately two orders of magnitude better than the error performance in analog networks. The generally accepted error rate for good data transmission over an analog network is 1 in 100,000 (10^{-5}) and therefore the equivalent error rate for a digital network would be 1 in 10 million (10^{-7}). Note that these are bit error rates. We can achieve very high bit rates over a telephone line using digital transmission. As an example, if repeaters are approximately 1 mile apart, we can transmit approximately 2 Mbps over a con-

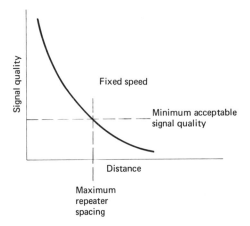

Fixed speed

Minimum acceptable signal quality

Distance

Maximum
repeater
spacing

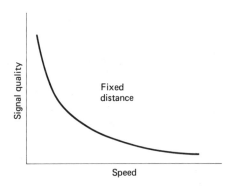

Fixed
distance

Speed

Figure 23-2 Digital-signal deterioration with speed and distance.

ventional telephone circuit. If we are using other communications media, such as microwave radio, satellite, or fiber optics, the speed of transmission that can be achieved is limited only by the characteristics of the communications medium. Speeds of hundreds of millions of bits per second are achievable over satellite and microwave links, and speeds of hundreds or perhaps thousands of millions of bits per second are achievable over fiber-optic links.

Because the data constitute a pure binary bit stream, we can use time division multiplexers to combine the data from many terminals onto a line that otherwise would have supported only one terminal. The common carriers can therefore subdivide the available channel capacity using various stages of multiplexing and therefore share the available channel capacity with a large number of users, thus lowering the communication cost for each user.

Digital transmission networks are expanding rapidly in many countries. As the common carriers continue with the implementation of the integrated services digital network (ISDN) concept, digital transmission will become even more widespread. The ISDN is discussed later in this chapter.

Until we have extensive penetration of digital networks, those users who have terminals and computers close to the digital network will be able to interface with the network using relatively inexpensive interface equipment such as network terminating units, rather than the modems that we use on the telephone network. Users who are a long way from a digital network would use conventional lines and modems to get them to the digital network.

By using a series of time division multiplexers, as shown in Fig. 23-3, it is relatively simple for a carrier to set up a digital transmission system that provides permanent point-to-point or multipoint facilities for its users. This diagram shows a user with a terminal connected through to the computer on a line with an effective speed of 2400 bps. The user's 2400-bps data stream, together with the data stream of other users, goes into a *zero-order digital multiplexer* (ZDME), which produces a composite 64,000-bps data stream. This is fed into a *first-order digital multiplexer* (1DME) together with other 64,000-bps streams from other ZDMEs or direct from users. The output of the 1DME is either 1.544 or 2.048 Mbps. The former speed is used in North America, and CCITT has standards for both speeds.

In Fig. 23-3 the high-speed bit stream is demultiplexed in stages to give the original user data streams. A real-life system may have further levels of multiplexing superimposed on those shown in Fig. 23-3.

Modern switching technology enables circuit switching to be incorporated into a TDM transmission network. These fast connect systems (around 100 ms connect time) provide users with a very flexible, high-performance facility. As indicated earlier, it becomes possible to use a switched service for a transaction-oriented system where a new connection is made for each transaction. This is possible with the switched telephone network, but the long connect times involved limit its usefulness in this kind of application.

Apart from the activities involved in setting up and disconnecting a call, a digital network is transparent to the user. This means that although delayed in time, the information that comes out is the same as the information that goes in. The terminal equipment at each end of a connection must therefore be speed-, code-, and format-compatible in order to be able to use the network. This is the same state of affairs that exists with the telephone network.

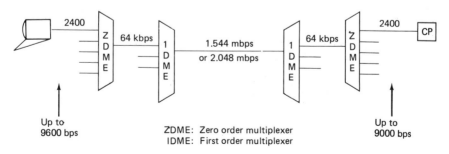

Figure 23-3 Simple digital network.

Being transparent to data, the network is also transparent to network protocols. If we wish to exchange information between different systems, we must ensure that both systems are compatible from the point of view of speed, code, format, error-control method, and overall protocol.

digital network backup and economies of scale

Economies of scale are possible with digital networks by installing the digital multiplexing equipment on the customer's premises rather than in the common carrier's premises. Consider a large organization with hundreds or perhaps thousands of terminals coming back to a centralized computer location. The conventional approach to handling this would be to have hundreds or perhaps thousands of connections from the computer center to the common carrier network. This involves a lot of equipment in the form of communication lines, network terminating units, and so on.

With the digital communication network, the signals from the outstation terminals are multiplexed together within the network, and it is possible to feed a high-speed digital data stream directly into the computer center and install multiplexing equipment on site to demultiplex the incoming high-speed signal to break it down into the individual signals from the terminals. The common carriers can make such a service available to the user at very attractive prices because of the saving in plant and equipment. The equipment saved is, first: A large number of communication lines are replaced with a small number of communication lines, each carrying a high-speed multiplex data stream. Second, on the small number of lines we have only one or two network terminating units, whereas if we had individual lines coming from the network for each terminal, we would have a large number of network terminating units. Common carriers therefore save a lot of money and can pass on some of these savings to the user.

You will note that as it is possible to send a high-speed multiplexed data stream into the user premises, it is now possible to extend this to provide con-

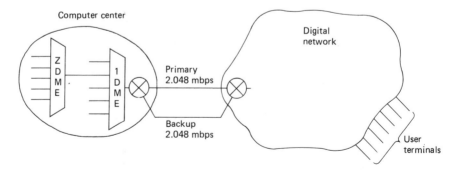

Figure 23-4 Backup link from network to computer center.

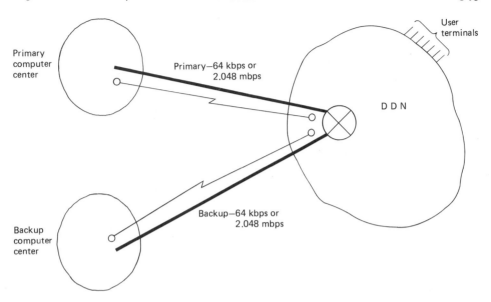

Figure 23-5 Redirection to backup computer center.

venient backup for the user. Consider the situation shown in Fig. 23-4. Here we have a computer center connected with a 2-Mbps multiplexed data stream into the network which is carrying data from several hundred terminals. If we were to lose the 2-Mbps data stream, we would have a disaster on our hands, so it is common practice for the user and the carrier to install a backup 2-Mbps data link which can be switched in automatically if the primary link fails. The backup link may be constructed using microwave radio while the primary link is a conventional wire circuit from a telephone network, so that we have physical diversity in the communication link.

Similarly, many users now have duplicated computer centers. Large organizations such as banks have reached the point where their business depends critically on the computer network, and if the computer itself were to fail, business would stop for the time being. As it is common to have backup computers on-site, what happens if a disaster of one form or another takes out the entire building?

These organizations are now building duplicated computer centers, often in separate cities, and it is possible to have duplicated data feeds coming from the digital network into each of these computer centers, as shown in Fig. 23-5. Normally, the data from the network are funneled to the primary computer center; however, if this computer center fails, the network can switch the data so that they get sent down the path to the backup computer center. It is very easy to arrange this kind of backup for digital networks, and it is very difficult, if not impossible, to arrange convenient backup of this nature using conventional analog lines and modems.

digital data network enhancements

Some Digital Data Networks (DDN) provide a leased line facility while others are circuit switched networks that allow circuits to be set up on demand.

The leased line networks can approximate a circuit switched network if they are equipped with a device known as a "Time Division Cross Connect" (TDCC), as shown in Fig. 23-6. The TDCC allows timeslots within the Time Division Multiplex network to be reassigned so that data paths through the network can be changed from time to time. This reassignment of data paths is not as fast as the call set-up time in a circuit switched network, and it is generally used to allow the common carrier to install customer networks faster than if manual patching had to be used to allocate the routes through the network.

It is possible, however, to give the user some control over the TDCC so that the user networks can be reconfigured as traffic patterns vary. This allows the user to optimize its use of the available transmission capacity.

For example, in Fig. 23-7, a user with two computer centers may wish to have the terminal networks connected to the two computers by day and to have the two computer centers connected together by night. To do this, we would generally need two star-type networks for terminal to host communications and a point-to-point link between the hosts.

Ideally, the user should be able to subscribe to a certain amount of transmission capacity in the DDN. By day, when there is no requirement for computer-computer data flow, the capacity can be dedicated to the terminal networks. By night, while the terminal network is inactive, the capacity can be reassigned to the point-to-point link.

Another scenario involves a user with, let's say, four computer centers. A certain amount of transmission capacity may normally be shared between the four centers but, at times, the whole capacity may be dedicated to two centers for point-to-point high-speed file transfer.

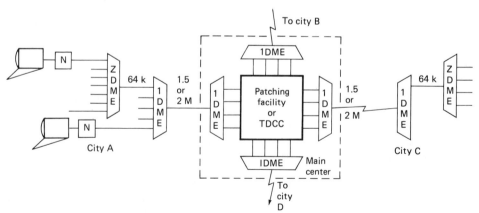

Figure 23-6 Digital network circuit reconfiguration system.

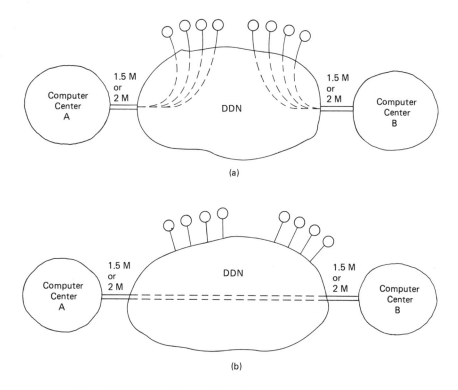

Figure 23-7 (a) Daytime configuration; (b) nighttime configuration.

The TDCCs can be under user control, via a Monitoring and Control System (MACS), which can also provide statistical information to the Network Manager. Indeed, it is a small step to have a computer control the MACS so that the network can be reconfigured dynamically as the traffic pattern changes.

integration of voice, data, and wideband services

Many major business customers now run two or three different types of networks. They have a very large data processing network and they also happen to have very large voice networks as well. Some of the large customers are also operating wideband networks and many more are looking for a more economical approach to wideband services.

There are, therefore, three communications components that users are trying to pull together in order to achieve economies of scale and to centralise some of their operational control. With centralised operational control, the network component would become easier to manage. But, with a decentralised network, how can centralised control be achieved?

Let us first consider voice and data. As we know, voice traffic is very "peaky" with a busy period in the morning, another in the afternoon, and practically no traffic at night. Most voice traffic passes through the telephone switchboard, more appropriately called the Private Branch Exchange (PBX). The old-style Analog PBXs are connected to the telephone network by a number of exchange lines. Limited integration of voice and data was possible for terminals connected to PBX ports by modems.

As illustrated in Fig. 23-8, the new generations of digital PBXs are capable of connecting into a digital network at 1.5 or 2-Mbps, which represents 24 or 30 × 64 Kbps channels. The PBX could allocate this high speed capacity between voice and data depending on the relative traffic patterns for voice and data. Ideally, an Integrated Services Digital Network (ISDN) should be available to handle such PBXs. In practice, however, there are few ISDN facilities in the world; they are expected to be widespread in the early 1990s, however.

In the meantime, a DDN could be made to handle voice as well as data so that users could set up digital tielines between their PBXs in different locations.

An interface unit, often called a "Customer Terminating Facility" (CTF) on customer premises connects into the DDN via a 1.5 or 2 Mbps link. (In the United States, 1.544 Mbps is the standard T1 digital transmission speed. In Europe, the equivalent standard speed is 2.048 Mbps.) Interfaces in the CTF will handle a wide range of data speeds as well as 64 Kbps PCM voice and lower speed digital

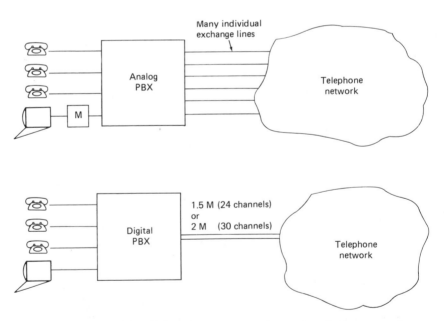

Figure 23-8 (a) Analog PBX needs many connections to the telephone network; (b) digital PBX may connect as in (a) or may use a small number of high speed digital links.

voice. The 1.5 or 2 Mbps output for the CTF can be split up in the TDCC so that the individual data and voice components go to their required destinations. As the demand for capacity between the different locations varies, the voice/data mix can be varied and/or the geographic distribution of the capacity may be changed.

For example, during the voice peak time, the bulk of the capacity may be assigned to provide PBX tieline capability between two main locations. When the voice traffic drops off, the capacity can be reassigned to data, facsimile, Teletex, etc.

Being typically based on CCITT X.50 framing, the network really treats the primary 1.5 or 2 Mbps as being a number of 64 Kbps streams. The network itself is typically based on $N \times 64$ Kbps. Wideband services, such as 1.5 or 2 Mbps video-conferencing, can be handled because the network thinks it is handling 24 or 30×64 Kbps channels, and they will be re-combined at the other end to the original 1.5 or 2 Mbps data stream.

Consider the situation in Fig. 23-9. At the main office, a PBX, a host and a number of terminals connect into the Customer Terminating Facility (CTF). The CTF interfaces to the Digital Data Network via a number of links running at 1.5 Mbps or 2 Mbps depending upon whether it is in America or Europe. The DDN

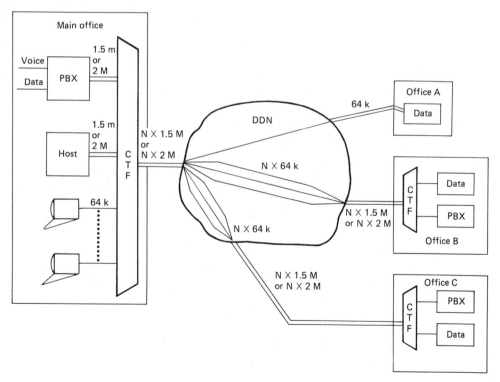

Figure 23-9 Integration of voice and data through a digital network.

breaks the high speeds down into N × 64 Kbps and these streams are routed, via the TDCCs, to the appropriate destinations. One 64 Kbps stream goes to Office A, while the remainder is split between the PBXs and data units in Offices B and C. During the day, the capacity allocated to voice may be changed in accordance with variations in the voice load. The remaining capacity can then be reallocated between the computers and terminals.

These enhanced services provide a valuable bridge between existing dedicated networks for voice, data, and wideband services and the future ISDN. The flexibility provided by the TDCC and customer network management facilities allows users to optimise their own networks from the point of view of cost, reliability, and flexibility. The DDN can, of course, provide gateways into other networks, such as Public Packet Switched Networks and, as it is implemented, the ISDN.

the integrated services digital network

The CCITT defines an Integrated Services Digital Network (ISDN) as a network that provides end-to-end digital connectivity to support a wide range of services, including voice and non-voice services, to which users have access by a limited set of standard multi-purpose user/network interfaces.

The main feature of the ISDN is this end-to-end digital operation and the support of a wide range of voice and non-voice applications in the same network. ISDNs support a variety of applications including both switched and non-switched connections. The switched connections include packet switched and circuit switched and combinations of the two. The ISDN also contains intelligence for the provision of additional service features as well as providing for maintenance and network management functions.

The ISDNs are based on the building blocks of digital switches and digital transmission links. The switches are basically large blocks of Time Division Multiplexers (TDM) in which the time slots can be dynamically reallocated in order to route information through the switch. Figure 23-10 shows an elementary digital switch. The switch consists of two TDMs with a common control element linking them. The control element tells the TDMs which timeslots on the composite link belong to which pair of incoming and outgoing lines. In Fig. 23-10(a) incoming lines A, B, and C are connected to outgoing lines A, B, and C, whereas in Fig. 23-10(b) the demultiplexing has been rearranged so that incoming A, B, and C are connected to outgoing C, A, and B respectively.

A high proportion of the world's telephone networks use digital switching and transmission. The voice signals from a conventional analog telephone are digitized at the telephone exchange, transmitted through the network and converted back to an analog signal at the destination exchange.

The ISDN, however, requires that voice signals are digitised at the custom-

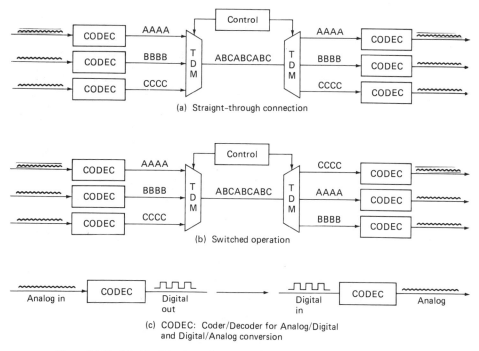

(a) Straight-through connection

(b) Switched operation

(c) CODEC: Coder/Decoder for Analog/Digital
and Digital/Analog conversion

Figure 23-10 (a) Straight-through connection; (b) switched operation; (c) CODEC: coder/decoder for analog/digital and digital/analog conversion.

er's premises either in the telephone instrument or in a PBX. The CCITT recommendations call for digitisation of voice at 64,000 bps. Many systems use lower speeds for digital voice but, for the purpose of this discussion, we will stick with the CCITT recommendation of 64,000 bps.

As shown in Fig. 23-10(c), voice digitisation is performed by a device known as a *codec* (which is a contraction of the words Coder/decoder). The codec takes an analog signal with a bandwidth of 4000 Hz and converts it into a 64,000 bps digital stream. In the other direction, the process is reversed—the 64,000 bps digital stream is converted back into an analog signal.

How does a Codec work?   The codec samples the incoming analog signal as shown in Fig. 23-11. The sample measures the instantaneous amplitude of the signal and this is converted into a 7-bit number, which is transmitted through a digital network. (To simplify the diagram, 3-bit encoding is used in Fig. 23-11.) At the other end, the incoming digital number is fed into a digital-to-analog converter that reproduces the original signal amplitude. If the samples are taken often enough, the original waveform can be faithfully reproduced at the other end as shown. In reality, it turns out that, to get a good reproduction of the signal, the

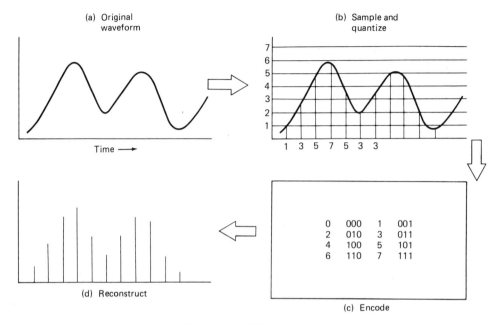

Figure 23-11 PCM encoding.

minimum sampling rate must be twice the maximum signal frequency that is being sampled. With a bandwidth of 4000 Hz for the analog signal, this means that the minimum sampling rate must be 8000 samples/sec. With 7-bit encoding, this requires a digital transmission rate of 56,000 bps and, when some extra bits are added for synchronisation and control purposes, the resulting transmission speed is 64,000 bps.

The technique described is called "Pulse Code Modulation" (PCM) and 64,000 bps is the CCITT standard speed. (There are many other ways of digitising voice at slower bit rates, but the ISDN at present does not recognise the existence of these rates.)

Given that voice can be digitised, it can be transmitted through a common digital network along with data and other digital signals. The network itself may not know whether a particular bitstream is voice or data.

The concept of using digital transmission and digital switching within a telephone network is not new. For years, the common carriers have been using PCM transmission on junction links between telephone exchanges. What sets the ISDN apart is the fact that the analog-to-digital conversions are performed on the customer's premises. The network therefore provides end-to-end digital connectivity.

Because the digitisation takes place on the customer's premises, it is possible for one physical connection to support a wide range of customer applications by multiplexing the various forms of information on to the one circuit.

ISDN customer interfaces

CCITT emphasises that the customer interface will be via a limited set of connection types and multi-purpose user-network interface arrangements. This is because a smaller number of interfaces should make it easier for many suppliers to develop and provide customer equipment.

Two levels of interface have been specified: the Primary Rate Interface operates at either 1.544 Mbps or 2.048 Mbps. The 1.544 Mbps corresponds to the American T1 speed, while 2.048 Mbps is generally regarded as being the European standard speed.

The Primary Rate interfaces carry either 23 (1.54 Mbps) or 30 (2.048 Mbps) separately switched 64 Kbps channels plus a common signalling channel. A digital PBX could interface to an ISDN via a small number of primary rate digital interfaces rather than via a large number of individual exchange lines. Local area networks and communication concentrators are other devices that could interface at the Primary Rate.

The Primary Rate interface is often referred to as 23B + D (American) or 30B + D (European) where the B-channel is a full-duplex 64,000 bps channel and the D-channel is a 64,000 bps channel reserved for signalling. For example, all of the call setup and control messages would be sent along the D-channel while the information transfer related to the call itself would go through the B-channels.

The Basic Interface has been specially developed for ISDN and will be the standard ISDN interface as seen by most users. It will use the existing two-wire metallic circuit that connects the user premises into the network. The interface provides for two 64 Kbps full-duplex channels for each customer, plus a 16 Kbps signalling channel. One of the 64 Kbps channels can be used for voice and the other for data; alternatively, both could be used for non-voice communications.

This configuration is referred to as a 2B + D interface. Once again, the B-channels are separately switchable 64,000 bps full-duplex channels and the D-channel, 16,000 bps in this case, is used for signalling. The B-channels can be regarded as circuit switched paths that are equivalent to Level 1 of the Open System Interconnection model.

The D-channel is a packet switched channel, similar to X.25, which is used mainly for call setup, supervision, and disconnection. The D-channel can also be used for data transmission.

Figure 23-12 shows examples of ISDN interfaces. A wide range of equipment can be connected to an ISDN interface port. A digital telephone and a terminal can connect, via a Network Termination, into the ISDN. The telephone and the terminal can be in use simultaneously communicating over separate paths that have been set up through the ISDN as a result of signalling information carried on the 16,000 bps D-channel.

Alternatively, a number of different types of terminal equipment such as computers, facsimile, Teletex, etc., can be connected in a bus or multidrop con-

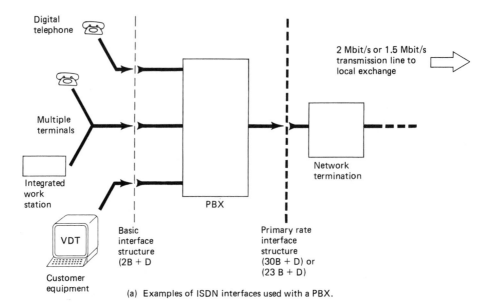

(a) Examples of ISDN interfaces used with a PBX.

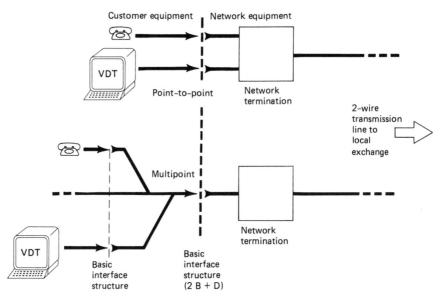

(b) Examples of ISDN interfaces used with a single
pair of wires.

Figure 23-12 (a) Examples of ISDN interfaces used with a PBX; (b) examples of
ISDN interfaces used with a single pair of wires.

figuration into the network termination. These devices can share the capacity of one or both 64,000 bps B–channels.

Unfortunately, the detailed discussion of ISDN is beyond the scope of this book. Ultimately, it is expected that the ISDN will become a "communications utility" rather like the electric supply utilities we have now. We can plug virtually any kind of appliance into an electric power point and, as long as it meets certain requirements in terms of safety and power consumption, it can be expected to work properly without the utility itself having any prior knowledge of the particular appliance.

Likewise, provided that it meets certain basic requirements in terms of transmission speeds, call setup, and disconnection, we can expect to plug virtually any kind of terminal, computer, facsimile, etc., into an ISDN port and have it work properly without the need for the network to have any prior knowledge of the terminal or configuration of terminals.

24
Packet Switching: CCITT Recommendation X.25

packet switching

Another approach to providing a public data network is to use a *packet-switching network* (PSN). A packet-switching network consists of a number of computer-based switching centers interconnected by high-speed communications lines. The communications lines may use analog or digital transmission. A user connects computers and terminals into the network at the nearest switching node. As shown in Fig. 24-1, a number of users have computers and terminals connected into each switching node.

Messages are made into *packets*, each of which is typically about 1024 bits long. Long messages may be segmented into a number of packets that can be individually passed through the network. The packets contain addressing information that enables the switching nodes to send each packet to its proper destination. In addition, each packet has an error-control envelope that enables automatic error detection and correction to be maintained on the links interconnecting the switching nodes. With a large volume of data in the network, the packets belonging to different users are sharing the resources in the switching nodes and the interconnecting trunks. This reduces the cost to each user compared to the cost of establishing a private leased network.

As with the circuit switched network, each user would have a certain amount of equipment dedicated to each of his or her terminals and computers. This would consist of interface equipment, such as modems and the local loops that connect terminals and computers into the packet-switching network. If the user employs the switched network to dial into the packet-switching network, he or she would not have as much equipment dedicated to each terminal.

To exchange packets, we need a standard interface protocol between the network and the computers and terminals that are connected to it. Later in this chapter we examine the standard interface protocol X.25.

Computers and intelligent terminals are capable of implementing such a protocol so they can connect directly into the network. Simpler terminals, however, need to be connected via an intelligent network-access machine. The network-access machine, or *packet assembly/disassembly* (PAD) machine, will accept data from the terminal, "packetize" the data, and forward them into the packet-switching network via the X.25 protocol. The packet-switching network then carries the data through to the receiving terminal or computer.

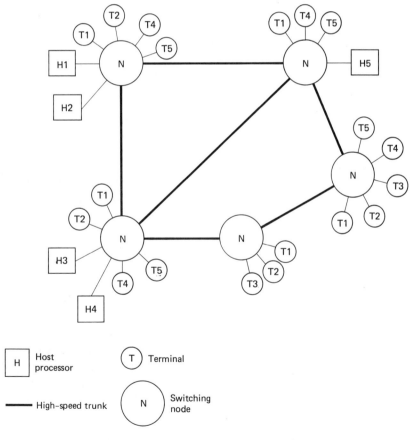

Figure 24-1 Packet-switching network.

packet-switching techniques

There are two main approaches to handling the flow of packets through the network. One approach uses a *datagram* technique; the other uses *virtual circuits*.

Datagrams

A datagram is a packet of data that contains the address of the destination terminal or computer. The packet-switching network treats the datagram as an individual element and passes it on to the destination.

Many packet-switching networks use an adaptive routing technique whereby they continually keep track of the path between any two points that, at the moment, seems to give the best performance. This means that a message consisting of several datagrams could have different packets traveling along different routes so that the packets may arrive at the destination in a sequence different from that in which they entered the network.

Some packet-switching networks rearrange the packets into their original sequence prior to sending them to the receiving terminal; in other systems, this is the responsibility of the receiving terminal. If the packet-switching network reassembles messages, the switching nodes will require more complex protocols to recover lost or damaged packets or to detect duplicate packets; they will also require more buffering capability than they would if they merely passed on the packets in the order in which they were received at that node.

On the other hand, if the receiving terminal is responsible for reassembling packets into sequence, it will require a comprehensive end-to-end protocol operating in conjunction with the sending terminal in order to recover lost packets. When operating in this mode, some packet-switching networks relieve instantaneous congestion by throwing packets away, because the network can rely on the terminal's end-to-end protocols to recover the missing packets.

Virtual circuits

A virtual circuit (or *virtual call* as it is sometimes called) is a logical point-to-point connection between the sending and receiving terminals. The virtual circuit is analogous to the real circuit that would be established through a circuit-switching system except that packet-switching-network resources are not permanently assigned to a particular virtual circuit.

In a virtual circuit system, the packet-switching network delivers packets in the order in which they were received by the network; it also takes responsibility for recovering lost packets and for not delivering duplicate packets. The packets in a multipacket message may or may not go along the same physical route in the network. As described below, CCITT has standardized on a virtual circuit system for public packet switching networks. The networks generally use a diagram technique internally but they maintain packet sequence so as to present a virtual circuit interface to the users.

Virtual-circuit network interface protocol:
CCITT Recommendation X.25

A standard network access protocol has been adopted by CCITT as Recommendation X.25. This protocol defines procedures for setting up a call, transferring data, and clearing down the call after the data exchange is completed. The computers and terminals that interface to the packet-switching network will need to implement the network-access protocol; with the intelligent of terminal equipment, this is a relatively simple exercise. Those terminals that are not capable of handling the network-access protocol will continue to be interfaced via a protocol converter such as a PAD.

Recommendation X.25 contains three levels of protocol as follows:

- *Level 1.* This is the low-level interface protocol that lays down the rules necessary to establish a physical link between a terminal or computer and the PSN. This interface specification is either of the CCITT recommendations X.21 or X.21 bis.
- *Level 2.* This is the link access procedure (line protocol) that lays down the rules for passing information between the terminal or computer and the PSN. This is a version of HDLC asynchronous balanced mode which is sometimes referred to as LAP-B (Link Access Protocol-Balanced).
- *Level 3.* This is the high-level protocol that establishes packet formats and the control procedures necessary to set up a call and exchange information with other terminals or computers.

For the remainder of this discussion, we refer to the Level 3 protocol.

The virtual call must be set up prior to exchanging data, just as a real circuit must be established in a circuit-switching environment. In the case of the telephone network, we establish a call by dialing and waiting for the called party to answer the telephone. Then we "exchange data" while we are having our conversation, and we clear the call by hanging up the telephone.

In the case of virtual circuit, the call is set up as shown in Fig. 24-2. This summarizes the highlights of recommendation X.25 as follows: The calling terminal sends a *call-request packet*, containing the network address of the called terminal, and a *logical channel number*, which will be used to identify the particular virtual circuit during the data transfer operation.

The network converts the call-request packet into an *incoming-call packet*, which is sent to the called terminal. The incoming-call packet will contain the network address of the calling terminal and also a logical channel number, which the called terminal will use during the data transfer operation.

The called terminal can accept or refuse the call. If it refuses the call, it will send a clear-request packet in response to the incoming-call packet. If it accepts the call, it responds with a *call-accepted packet*, which contains the logical channel number and a *call-accepted indicator*. This packet appears at the calling ter-

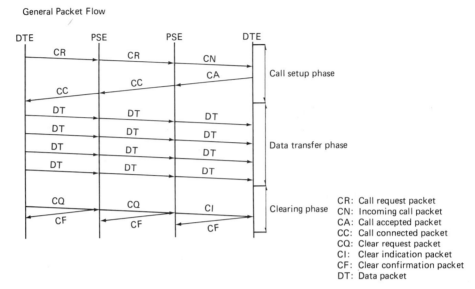

Figure 24-2 Virtual-circuit call establishment and clearing.

minal as a call-accepted packet. At the calling terminal, it will, of course, contain the logical channel number for that terminal. Data packets can then be exchanged, in both directions if desired, between the calling and the called terminals.

At any time, either terminal can terminate the call by issuing a clear-request packet, which contains the logical channel identifier and a ''clear''indication. This packet appears at the other terminal as a clear-indication packet. (All packets have the logical channel number in them.)

As shown in Fig. 24-2, the clear-request packet receives a response of a clear confirmation from the nearest interface. That is, the calling terminal issues the clear request and the clear confirmation comes back from the first packet-switching exchange. Meanwhile, the clear request is propagating through the network and at each packet exchange the clear confirmation is returned to the preceding packet exchange. Finally, at the called terminal, the clear-request packet has been turned into a clear-indication packet, which draws a clear confirmation as a response. The clearing does not require an end-to-end acknowledgement with the clear confirmation going all the way from the calling terminal back to the called terminal because just as on the telephone network if one party hangs up the phone, that clears down the call, there is no need to confirm the fact that the call has been cleared because it has already been done.

Because most terminals implementing the X.25 protocol are intelligent, they have the capability of indulging in simultaneous data exchanges with two or more other terminals. The X.25 protocol handles this by use of logical channel identifiers: A terminal has a different logical channel number for each terminal with which it communicates. This is illustrated in Fig. 24-3, which shows a host with

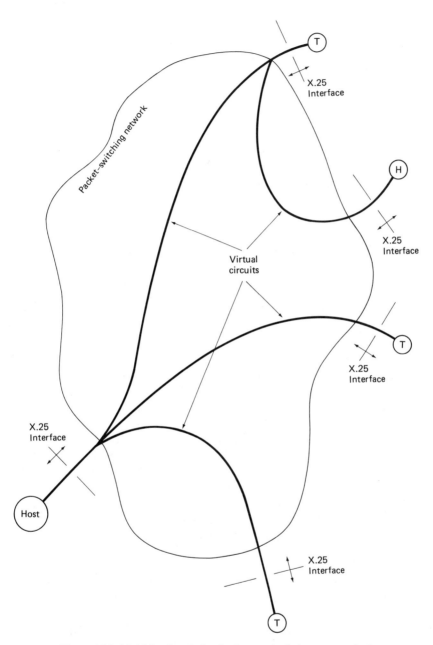

Figure 24-3 Multiple virtual circuits from a single host or terminal.

three simultaneous data exchanges and a terminal with two simultaneous data exchanges.

The logical channel number has local significance. This means that at each X.25 interface there are a total of 4096 logical channel numbers available for use at that particular interface. When a call is set up, the X.25 interface at the calling terminal fishes into the pool of available logical channel numbers and pulls out the first number that it finds. This number is then assigned to that call for the duration of the call. At the other end, the X.25 interface at the called terminal fishes into its pool of available numbers and pulls out the first number that it finds. Thus we will have different logical channel numbers at each end of the same virtual circuit. The network itself carries out the translations between these two logical channel numbers. Clearly, we can have different logical channel numbers for different calls, so that the lifetime of a number is just for the length of a particular call.

Permanent virtual circuits

As you can imagine, the overhead required in establishing and clearing a call could degrade performance for some users. It is possible, therefore, to set up a permanent virtual circuit, which, by definition, is always in the data phase and is never cleared down. The philosophy can be extended to provide a *virtual private network* for a user.

Datagrams versus virtual circuits

There has been a lot of argument as to whether datagram or virtual-circuit systems are better. The datagram system, on the surface, seems better for transaction-oriented systems, which may have only one packet traveling in each direction to constitute a transaction. If we were to use the *switched virtual call* system, we would have a large overhead associated with the transfer of such a pair of packets.

On the other hand, permanent virtual call systems would overcome this problem. Also, X.25 permits the call-request and clear-request packets to contain data, so a transaction that requires only one packet of data in each direction would use the call-request packet for the enquiry and the clear-request packet for the response.

This facility is called *fast select* and is useful for simple message exchanges such as credit card transactions that require one packet in/one packet out. On the other hand, the calling terminal may think that the response to its inquiry is going to be one packet, but in reality the response will require more than one packet. It is possible for a fast select to be converted into a normal virtual call by the called terminal so that it can then respond with a number of packets to the inquiry.

Absolute network addresses can become quite long, especially if a packet is traveling through more than one packet-switching network. Under the datagram method, each packet contains a complete network address, whereas under virtual-circuit operation, each packet contains only the logical channel identifier, which may consist of less than a dozen bits.

The virtual-circuit system will prevail in the future. CCITT's early adoption of the X.25 protocol is evidence of this. Although the network-access protocol is more complex than that required for a datagram interface, the terminals and computers do not require the capability of reordering packets, requesting missing packets, or detecting duplicates, because this is handled by the network. Ironically, it turns out that most virtual-circuit networks in the world today do, in fact, use a datagram switching technique internally in the network, and the network takes responsibility for reordering of the packets before they are delivered to the end users.

X.25: a three-layer interface

CCITT recommendation X.25 describes a three-level interface for packet-switching networks. Let us now have a brief look at how this interface operates.

Consider first the diagram shown in Fig. 24-4, where we have two terminals connected together with a simple two-wire communication line. Each terminal has a buffer which contains the data, which are displayed on the screen of the visual display terminal. The operator on the terminal on the left enters data into the terminal and those data are stored in the buffer and displayed on the screen. What we want to do is have those data transmitted along the line to the buffer in the receiving terminal so that the data can be displayed to the operator at that terminal. In a simple situation such as the one in Fig. 24-4, this is quite easy. All we do is hit the transmit button and the data are transmitted along the line, bit by bit, received at the other end, stored in the buffer, and displayed on the screen. That is the end of the story.

Let us now consider the situation shown in Fig. 24-5, where we have the two terminals connected together via a packet-switching network. The packet-switching network is made up of a number of packet-switching exchanges, in this case, four, interconnected in a mesh arrangement. Each terminal is connected into the nearest packet-switching exchange with a data line consisting of telephone lines and modems, or perhaps digital lines with network terminating units. Sim-

Figure 24-4 Simple point-to-point connection.

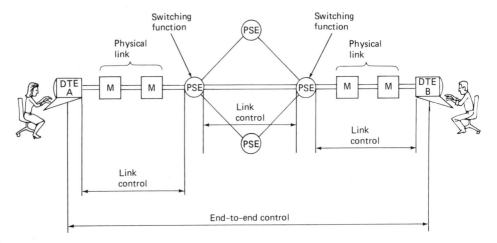

Figure 24-5 Packet-switching network showing different levels of control.

ilarly, the links within the packet-switching exchange can be telephone lines with modems or digital lines with network terminating units.

We can identify several layers of control that are required in order to get a message from one terminal to the other terminal through the packet switch. First, we have the physical interface between each terminal and the packet-switching exchange. This physical interface consists of the combination of lines and modems that are used to connect the two devices. There are three physical interfaces identifiable in the route between the two terminals: from terminal A to the packet-switching exchange; between the two packet-switching exchanges, and between terminal B and the packet-switching exchange.

As we know, the job of the physical interface is to transfer bits of information from one end of the physical link to the other. Errors occur at the physical interface level but they are not detected at this level. If a bit is flipped in transit, the erroneous bit is delivered at the other end of the link.

To detect errors on the lines, we need to have some sort of control exercised over the physical link, and this is the job of the link control procedure. We therefore have link control being exercised across each of the physical data links as shown in Fig. 24-5. The job of the link control procedure is to make sure that if a block of data is presented across the interface at one end of the link, that block of data will be delivered quickly and correctly across the equivalent interface at the other end. This happens on each of the three data links shown in the diagram. A data link control will faithfully deliver a block of data across that link, but once the block exits the link, the link control has no more responsibility for it. We are interested to make sure that the block of data does get from one terminal to another; therefore, there is another level of control built into each of the packet-switching exchanges where a switching function or a routing function is carried out. The purpose of the switching function is to make sure that the block of data transits the packet-switching exchange and exits on the correct data link. There-fore, the combination of the physical layer, the link control layer, and the switch-ing function layer allows us to get a message from one terminal to another. We have shown in this diagram a fourth level of control which operates end to end between the terminals. This is typically called an *end-to-end protocol*, and part of its job is to validate that the block of data does indeed get through the network from one terminal to the other.

Looking at Fig. 24-6(a) we see an x-ray view of the two terminals at the two packet-switching exchanges and the interconnection between them. At the very top we have the dashed-line interface, reflecting the level 4 interface between the data buffer at one end of the link and the data buffer at the other. Below this we have three levels of control, reflecting the switching function level, the link control level, and the physical level.

The dashed line at level 4 is logically equivalent to the physical connection that we had in Fig. 24-4. Really, all we want to do is have the operator enter data into the buffer in terminal A, hit the transmit button, and send the message by magic along the level 4 dashed line to arrive in the data buffer at the other end for display purposes. Unfortunately, such magic does not exist, so what we need to do is take the block of data and feed it down through the layers of control underneath until it can be transmitted across a physical interface level. What happens is described next.

A block of data is split up into segments of a maximum of 1024 bits each. This is because the packet size is usually limited to 1024 bits, so as shown in Fig. 24-6(b), the large data message is split up into two packets. Each packet has a packet header in front of it which contains routing information which will enable the packet to be switched through the network to the correct destination. The packet itself is then delivered to the link control level, where it is wrapped up in an HDLC frame. The frame header and frame trailer is the HDLC framing en-velope, and the HDLC frame is then transmitted across the physical interface bit by bit to the other end of the link. In the packet-switching exchange the link control checks that the block of data was correctly received and it takes the information part of that frame of data and passes it up to the packet-switching control layer, where the routing function is performed based on the information contained in the packet header.

The packet is then fed back down to the link control to the next data link, transported across the physical interface to the next packet-switching exchange, checked out by the receiving HDLC, and the contents of the HDLC frame are fed up to the packet-switching control in the second packet-switching exchange. The packet is routed to the correct link control, to the correct link, and fed down the link control across the physical interface, and finally the data appear in the terminal.

By the time the block of data has arrived at the other end, it has followed the rather torturous path through the network as shown in Fig. 24-7. This is one of the reasons packet-switching networks have relatively long end-to-end transit

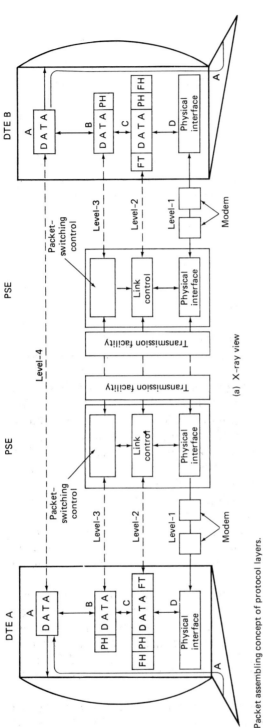

Packet assembling concept of protocol layers.

A Application level e.g. producing transactions to be sent or checking received transactions.
B Transactions from higher level divided into several X.25 packets by adding packet information (e.g. routing information, user facilities etc.). Received packets are assembled into a transaction and forwarded to the higher level.
C Frame level. Packets from higher level are packed in HDLC (LAP–B) frame so that transmission control can be available against transmission error.
D Physical interface level belongs to CCITT V.28, 35, 10, 11. Frames are transformed into electrical signal at this level and forwarded to modem or to other transmission facilities in accordance with suitable physical interface recommended by CCITT.

Note: PH: Packet Header (CCITT X.25)
     FH: Frame Header (ISO HDLC LAP–B)
     FT: Frame Tailer (ISO HDLC LAP–B)
*Packet length is max. 1024 bits. Transactions whose length is over this limit shall be divided into 2 or more packets.

In the node of the packet switching network, the packets are controlled, routed and forwarded according to the information in the packet header at the layer of X.25 level 3.

(a) X-ray view

(b) Packet assembly concept

Figure 24-6 (a) X-ray view of Fig. 24-5; (b) packet assembly concept within X.25.

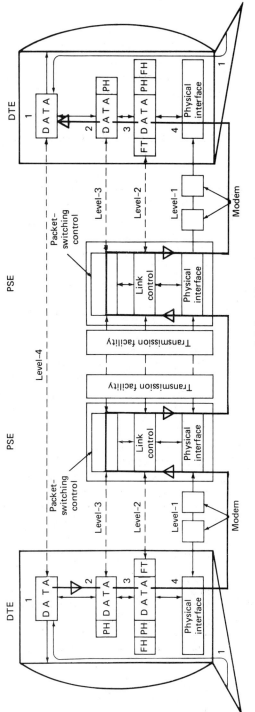

Figure 24-7 The torturous path followed by packets.

371

delays, because the packets have to be processed so much in each packet-switching exchange and also, get retransmitted so many times on the way through the network. The link control exercised across the physical connection in Recommendation X.25 is HDLC asynchronous balanced response mode. This is often called LAP-B, which means Link Access Protocol—Balanced.

character-oriented terminals and packet-switching networks

From the preceding discussions it should be clear that terminals and computers that are capable of communicating in accordance with the X.25 interface rules must be intelligent devices. Most terminals in the world today are not intelligent, and on many occasions we wish to use our existing terminals in conjunction with the packet-switching network. This means that we need to use a protocol conversion device of some kind which will communicate with the terminals in their own native protocol and communicate with the network in accordance with Recommendation X.25.

Consider Fig. 24-8, which shows two classes of terminals. The first is a packet mode terminal, which is a terminal capable of communicating in accordance with Recommendation X.25. The second is a nonpacket mode terminal, which of course is a terminal that is not capable of communicating in accordance with Recommendation X.25. The most common nonpacket mode terminal is a simple teleprinter-style terminal or character-oriented terminal that uses asynchronous transmission, transmitting the data character by character as they are entered into the terminal.

CCITT has specified a particular protocol converter which will handle character-oriented terminals, a device known as a PAD (packet assembly diassembly machine). The character-oriented terminals then communicate with the PAD in accordance with their own character-oriented protocol. The PAD takes the characters as they come in and assembles them into packets and then communicates with the packet network in accordance with the X.25 protocol. In the opposite direction, as packets are received from the network the PAD disassembles the packet and transmits the individual characters out one at a time to a receiving terminal.

There are a number of CCITT standards that define the operation of a PAD and the associated character-oriented terminal. First, CCITT Recommendation X.3 defines the basic characteristics of the PAD. It is necessary for the user of the character-oriented terminal to interact with the PAD, and Recommendation X.28 identifies this interface. Finally, Recommendation X.29 identifies the interface between the packet mode terminal and the PAD.

The interaction between the character-oriented terminal and the PAD arises for a number of reasons. First, these terminals tend to operate in echo mode, whereby a character transmitted from the terminal is not displayed on the screen

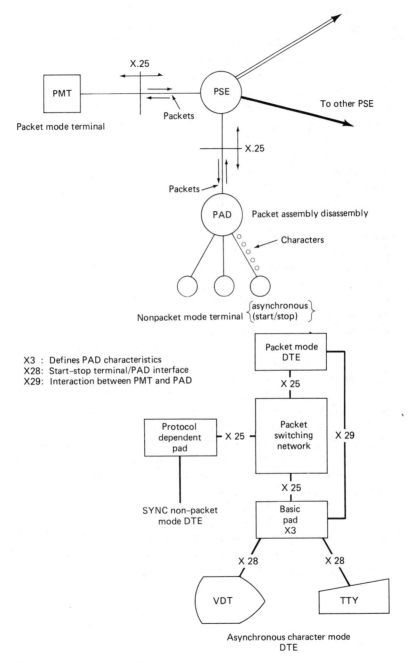

Figure 24-8 (a) Use of PAD in a packet-switching network; (b) network interfaces and protocols.

until it has made the round trip to the host computer. In the case of a packet-switching network, two problems can arise with operating in this mode. First, the round trip can be relatively long, particularly if we go through a number of packet-switching exchanges, and second, it can be expensive. Most packet networks charge based on a volume-oriented tariff, and if the character transits the network twice, we are clearly going to pay more money than if the character transits the network once. It is therefore possible to communicate with the PAD and set up the PAD so that it will echo characters locally rather than requiring the characters be echoed end to end from the host.

Another parameter in the PAD that we may wish to change is the parameter that determines when a packet is dispatched. The tariff for packet-switching networks is normally related not to the number of characters that are sent but to the number of segments that are transmitted. A *segment* is 64 characters, and typically a packet can contain up to two segments. The tariff is based on the number of segments transmitted and the price is the same regardless of the number of characters in a segment. It is possible to transmit one character per segment or 64 characters per segment. If the operator of the character-oriented terminal wants high performance, he or she would wish to send one packet for each character that is entered into the character-oriented terminal. This, of course, could be very expensive. On the other hand, if we want to save money, we would set up the PAD so that it does not dispatch a packet until the segment is full. This means that the operator types away, and every 64 characters a packet goes down the line to the host. This saves money but the performance may drop off. Somewhere between these two extremes is the ideal situation for a particular user. The user can elect to have packets dispatched, for example, when the user enters *carriage return*. This is logical because in a lot of systems the host will not act on the data until it receives a carriage return, so it makes sense to wait until we get the carriage return before transmitting the data down to the host. The number of 64 characters per segment was determined based on studies that were carried out to determine the average number of characters transmitted between carriage returns. It turned out that the average was in the vicinity of 64 characters; therefore, one segment is likely to be able to contain one line of data input.

It is up to the user to determine the best mode of operation. Although it may seem attractive to have local echo rather than end-to-end echo, problems can occur, particularly with handling of passwords. To suppress passwords properly, it is necessary to have end-to-end echoing.

PART FOUR
PLANNING AND MANAGEMENT

25
System Planning Considerations

Planning and design are important preliminary aspects in the development of all projects whether the project is a computer system with a data communication network or whether it is merely the installation of a new lock on a kitchen cupboard.

In the early days of computer-based communications systems, there were many system failures. In this instance, I am using the term "system failure" to mean that the system either did not work or did not achieve its design goals. Generally, the failures occurred because (1) the hardware and software involved were not really suited to communication-based systems, and (2) there was little or no experience available to highlight potential problem areas. We now have a lot of experience behind us, and there are analytical tools available that can help us to predict the performance of a network.

With large systems, the design process and the analysis of system performance can be very complex and costly, involving perhaps the use of simulation packages and other computer-based aids. For smaller systems (this covers the majority of on-line systems and data communication networks in the world), there are a number of simple techniques that can be applied to perform a reasonableness test on a design. A reasonableness test indicates whether the system is likely to work and, if not, where the bottlenecks and problem areas are likely to be. This gives the designer the opportunity to test different system and network alternatives and come up with a workable design, as in Fig. 25-1. A workable system not only satisfies the functional requirements defined in the application specifications but it carries the required load with an adequate response time, provides an efficient interface with the people who will be using the system, is easily expandable, and its cost is not unreasonable.

Let us first look at some of the more obvious factors that need to be considered when planning and implementing an on-line system.

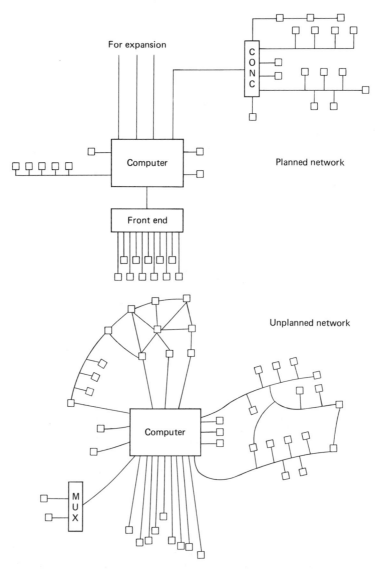

Figure 25-1 Planning in network design.

design considerations

Apart from management problems, there are a number of technical aspects that need to be considered and evaluated for each aspect of the data communication system—factors associated with the computer, the programs, the lines, the terminals, and other equipment required by the system. And there are general considerations that apply to the design of the entire system and that must be kept in mind constantly while the system is planned in detail. These fundamentals provide a foundation from which the overall design may be constructed and from which more detailed questions may emerge about the requirements of the system. These overall considerations are discussed in the following paragraphs.

System performance requirements

This is an obvious factor: The system is being put together for a purpose, and certain functions and services are expected of it. Usually, these requirements, both general and specific, are documented in a *functional specification*, which often forms part of the legal contract between the client and the supplier.

The functional specifications should lay out exactly how each transaction will be processed, what files it requires, what information should be on the files, what screen layouts are required for input and output, and so on. As well as meeting these requirements, the system is generally required to meet certain performance standards; if it does not meet these requirements, the system may be considered a failure (see Fig. 25-2). System performance requirements are generally specified in terms of the load the system can handle—that is, the throughput of the system and also the speed with which the system performs. In an on-line enquiry system, the measurement of speed is usually the response time, which if too long can greatly hamper the operations of the organization.

Consider an airline reservation system that has the following performance specification: The system must provide an average response time of 3 s or less

Figure 25-2 Meeting performance requirements.

at a load of 30,000 transactions per hour. If the system either will not carry the load or provides a long response time, it may be considered unworkable.

At all phases during the specification and design, we need to consider the impact of any design decision on the performance of the system. For example, if we are designing a batch-processing system to run a big payroll, and we underestimate the number of disk accesses required for each transaction by a factor of 2, then we may possibly extend the run time of the program such that we need to continue the operation into the second shift. However, if we make the same kind of mistake in designing an on-line system, it is likely that we could increase the system response time from 3 s to 10 s, which could have a major impact on the operation of the system.

User interface

Most of today's data communication systems are used by people who interact with the system in some way (see Fig. 25-3). Human users may be highly trained programmers and systems personnel, well-trained operators, management, or other staff who only occasionally use a terminal. Users could even be the general public, which is not trained to operate a terminal. The system design must be able to provide an efficient user interface tailored to the particular kind of person that will be interacting with the system.

Until recently, the people who have been interfacing with on-line computer systems have either been programmers and system designers or have been highly trained operators taught exactly how to communicate with the system. In these

Figure 25-3 Efficient interface with human users.

cases the users tend to bend toward the way the computer wants to see the data rather than the other way around. With the continuing reduction in the price of computer systems, they are being integrated into manufacturing and production processes, into distribution processes, and into direct-sales operations.

When we put a computer terminal on the factory floor, the kind of people who interface with the system are not the well-trained people who have been interfacing with computers for years. They are the workers, who may have little or no communication skills one day and be operating a terminal keyboard the next. This problem is compounded by the fact that even in developed countries there is a high level of functional illiteracy.

"Functional illiteracy" refers to the inability to read and understand simple instructions such as how to use a public telephone or how to fill in a form. The level of functional illiteracy among adults varies from country to country, but in many developed countries the level is as high as 14% of the adult population. A high proportion of immigrants also have a problem because, although they may be intelligent, their understanding of the language in their new country may not be sufficient for effective communication.

An example is a factory in Australia where the data processing manager surveyed the factory staff and found that 37 different nationalities were represented and that most of the people in the factory could not read or write English. Interfacing these people to computers can be a big problem. As it has only recently raised its head, not a great deal of work has been done toward finding the best way to handle it. It is a common problem worldwide, and more effort should be concentrated in this area. Like all other areas of data processing, no doubt the wheel will be reinvented many times.

Expansibility

It has been said that a successful on-line system grows until it becomes unworkable. This may or may not be so. In any case, the system should be designed in such a way that it can be expanded without requiring major redesign or degradation in performance (see Fig. 25-4).

Many on-line systems are installed to provide a service where no service existed before. In this case, it is difficult to estimate the loading that will be applied to the system, because we have no yardstick to measure the demand. Perhaps we can solve this problem by implementing a pilot system to observe demand and by using such observations to predict demand for the services of the real system. Should the actual load in real life be greater than that for which the system was designed, then we would want to be able to expand it simply and quickly.

Other types of expansion requirements occur in this changing world. It is difficult for most organizations to predict how much business a company will be doing in two or three years' time, and we must design our computer systems to be capable of handling increases in load that vary dramatically from our original predictions. A change of government or the introduction of new legislation could

Figure 25-4 Expansibility requirements.

modify the environment in such a way as to impose a sudden change in the load on a computer system.

As far as possible, expansion points should be identified at the time of the initial system design, so that added equipment and facilities will fit conveniently into a master plan of the projected system.

Modularity versus specific application design

Both system software and hardware can be designed modularly (i.e., so that small segments or modules of the system can be altered or rearranged without affecting the entire system). This modular design allows flexibility in the system for future developments or changes and for possible interfaces with other systems. However, greater efficiency of operation is almost always obtained if the system is specifically tailored to the particular application (at the expense of flexibility). The relative value of each type of design should be considered for the system in light of the overall requirements and any other limitations placed on the system (see Fig. 25-5). Some systems contain both types of design in different areas of the system.

Cost

Cost is usually the overriding factor in system design, and it must always be considered (see Fig. 25-6). Equipment and lines can be very expensive, so the

Figure 25-5 Modularity versus specific application design.

most economical arrangement should be determined. A certain facility may be desirable for overall system performance, but the cost may be prohibitive. Ingenious thinking may produce an alternative that does the required job at a much lower cost, but sometimes either the budget or the system specifications must be compromised. Each of the first four factors must usually be considered with regard to the cost involved.

Considering all these design factors, there are certain steps involved in the actual design process. Questions are immediately raised: Where do we start? How

Figure 25-6 Cost considerations.

do we examine the various trade-offs that need to be made to come up with a balanced, reasonable system? Some of the variables that need to be resolved are:

- CPU size and speed
- Disk size and speed
- Communications lines
  - —point to-point
  - —multidrop
  - —multiplexers or concentrators
  - —full-duplex, half-duplex, or one-way
  - —transmission speed
- Error-control techniques
- Polling or freewheeling
- Packet switching
- Local area network
- PBX
- Satellite
- Digital network
         etc.

Some of these parameters interact with each other and may be compromised in order to come up with a workable system.

performance criteria

In most on-line/real-time systems, the performance criteria to be met are *response time* and *throughput*. Response time is the measure of the speed of performance of the system, and throughput is a measure of the volume of data that the system will handle.

For an on-line enquiry system, throughput is generally expressed in terms of the number of transactions per hour that the system can handle during the peak hour of operation. In a message-switching system, it may be the number of messages per hour that can be handled by the system in its peak hour; in a data-collection system, it may be the number of characters per hour or per minute that can be handled during the peak.

The speed of performance of a system can be measured in different ways for different systems. In the case of a message-switching system, we talk about a *cross-office delay* or a *transit delay*, which is the time that elapses from when the last character of an input message is received until the message is queued for output on the outgoing line. In an enquiry-and-response system, the measurement of speed of operation is known as the *response time*, which can be defined as the time that elapses from when the operator completes the last action associated with the input of the enquiry until he or she sees the first character of the response at the terminal. This is illustrated in Fig. 25-7, which shows a simple on-line enquiry system. The operator is using a buffered terminal, which means that he can enter the data into the terminal and then initiate its transmission down the communication line by pressing the transmit button. At this point (assuming that the terminal is freewheeling with no polling delay), the input message goes down the line. The time this takes is related to the speed of transmission and the size of the message. When the computer receives the message, it will process the transaction and act upon it. It will most likely look up the file and prepare a response for the operator. The response will then be transmitted back to the terminal and, depending on the type of terminal, will start to appear as the message comes down the line, or perhaps it will wait until the end of the message is received and then display the entire message. Assuming that the terminal is the type that displays the characters as they come off the line, the first character should appear shortly after the beginning of the output transmission. The time from when the computer starts its output until the operator sees the first character will be related to the delays that are encountered in the communication line and also to the number of overhead characters in front of the message block. It could be that there are a number of synchronizing characters and heading characters before the first text character appears.

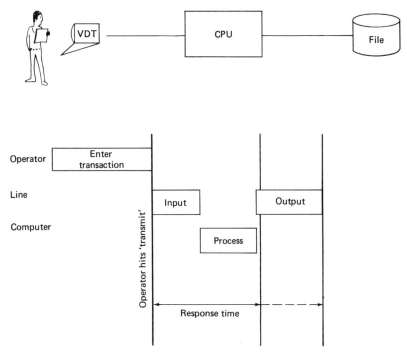

Figure 25-7 Response time for on-line inquiry system.

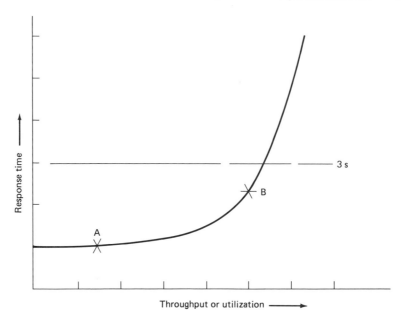

Figure 25-8 Typical relationship between system throughput and response time.

Response time and throughput are usually related, and the relationship is nonlinear. If we were to plot a curve showing the variation in response time with the load on the system, we would generally end up with something that looks like Fig. 25-8. The reason for this shape is that as we apply a load to the system, more and more transactions are competing for service within the system. At various points in the system, bottlenecks can occur that cause congestion. When congestion arises, we have queues of transactions lining up for processing at different parts of the system. Queuing curves have the general shape illustrated in Fig. 25-8. Later we identify some techniques for finding where these bottlenecks are likely to be in a system.

The response-time requirement is usually specified at some particular level of throughput. Let us imagine, for example, that we are required to provide a response time of 3 s or less at a load of 10,000 transactions per hour. It could be that we can meet this requirement by operating at point B on the performance curve in Fig. 25-8. As long as the load on the system does not exceed 10,000 transactions per hour, the system will operate very well, but if the load increases slightly, our response time will deteriorate quite rapidly because we are on the sharp part of the curve. If, however, we had been operating at point A on the curve while providing the required response time, we could apply a large increase in load to the system without a marked deterioration in performance.

The aim therefore is to try to predict in advance where we will be on the performance cure. For most systems in operation today, this kind of prediction has not been made, and a high proportion of data-processing managers would have no idea of where they are on the curve. For most systems, a fairly simple series of calculations can be performed to help us determine the loading on the system and therefore let us work out where we are on the performance curve.

system utilization

To make the mathematics of the situation somewhat simpler, we generally express the load on a system in terms of the proportion of the maximum load that the system can handle. The term we use for this proportion is *system utilization*. Many people use the term *occupancy* instead of *utilization*.

System utilization can be defined in a number of ways. Two common methods are:

$$system\ utilization = \frac{\text{actual load on the system}}{\text{maximum load the system can handle}}$$

or

$$= \frac{\text{time the system is occupied}}{\text{time available}}$$

We usually present system utilization by the Greek lowercase letter *rho*: ρ.

As you can see from the equations, a system that is fully occupied would have a utilization of 1, and the system that is idle would have a utilization of zero. Utilization then lies in the range 0 to 1. Many people use percentages; in this case, the value of the utilization would be multiplied by 100 to give a percentage utilization or percentage occupancy.

Example 25-1: Calculation of the Utilization for a Simple System

Let us work out the utilization of a simple everyday system. Our system is a sandwich shop that sells only peanut butter sandwiches. After a lot of practice, the sandwich-shop owner has organized himself so that when a customer walks in and asks for a peanut butter sandwich, he can make it, wrap it, and give it to the customer in 30 s. Let us suppose that 60 customers arrive every hour. We can compute the sandwich-shop operator utilization as follows:

$$operator\ utilization = \frac{\text{time occupied}}{\text{time available}}$$

The time occupied in making sandwiches is

(30 seconds per sandwich) $\times$ (60 sandwiches per hour) = 1800 s/h

The number of seconds in an hour is 3600, so the operator utilization is

$$\rho = \frac{1800}{3600} = 0.5$$

Alternatively, we could have said that at the rate of 30 s per sandwich, the maximum throughput capability of this one-operator sandwich shop is 120 sandwiches per hour. The actual load on the system is 60 sandwiches per hour; therefore, we could say that

$$operator\ utilization\ = \frac{actual\ load}{maximum\ load}$$

$$= \frac{60}{120} = 0.5$$

Fluctuations in traffic arrival pattern

There is a rule of thumb that states that the performance curve rises very sharply as utilization increases beyond 80%. In fact, we generally aim at designing a system such that the steady-state load on a system will not produce an average utilization of more than 60 to 70%. This leaves room for instantaneous variations in the traffic to take the utilization up around the 80% mark without an undue effect on performance. If we design the system for a steady-state utilization of 80%, instantaneous fluctuations would take us up to 90 to 100% utilization, which could seriously degrade the performance of the system. Let us see how this can happen.

The arrival rate of transactions on a typical system varies with time of day, as shown in Fig. 25-9. We normally try to design the system so that the average utilization during the peak period is at a satisfactory point on the diagram shown in Fig. 25-8.

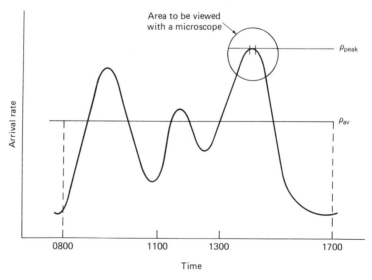

Figure 25-9 Transaction load pattern on a typical system.

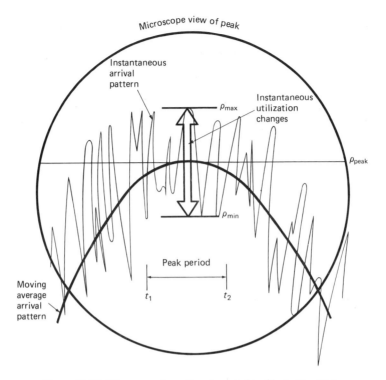

Figure 25-10 Blown-up view of peak-period traffic in Fig. 25-9.

In calculating utilization it is important to pay attention to the period of time over which it is being calculated. For example, in Fig. 25-9 we show two utilization figures. ρ_{av} represents the average utilization over the working day from 8:00 A.M. to 5:00 P.M., whereas ρ_{peak} represents the average utilization over the peak period, which occurs about 2:00 P.M. If we design a system to have satisfactory performance at the utilization level, ρ_{av}, the system performance would be severely degraded during the peaks. Similarly, if we design a system to give adequate performance during the peak period, the system will be relatively lightly loaded at other times of the day.

Let us consider the peak period and examine the peak with a microscope as shown in Fig. 25-10. In this diagram the heavy curved line represents the peak part of the curve from Fig. 25-9, whereas the lighter lines represent the instantaneous arrival pattern, which fluctuates randomly around the heavy lines. If you like, you can regard the heavy curved line as a moving-average representation of the instantaneous arrival pattern. The horizontal line representing ρ_{peak} represents the average utilization over the peak periods, where the period in question ranges, say, from time t_1 to t_2. Although we can work out an average utilization ρ_{peak}, you can see from the diagram that the utilization fluctuates on an instant-by-instant basis in accordance with the instantaneous arrival pattern. This means that the utilization will fluctuate above and below the figure ρ_{peak}.

Refer now to Fig. 25-11, which is a version of the earlier diagram showing the relationship between response time and utilization. Point A on this diagram represents the average utilization, ρ_{peak}. From the diagram we can see that this gives an average response time of approximately 2.25 s. However, the range of utilization change from ρ_{min} to ρ_{max} indicates that we have a corresponding change in response times from approximately 1.25 s through to 6.25 s. In other words, although the average operating point of the system produces a response time of 2.25 s, which appears to be satisfactory, for a considerable amount of the time the response time is going to be beyond 3 s. In other words, from the point of view of the user, the performance of this system would be quite erratic.

If we redesign the system, we may be able to reduce the value of ρ_{peak}. It could be that a communication line is overloaded, and by increasing the speed of the line we reduce the system utilization. Alternatively, some other component in the system may be overloaded and by removing this bottleneck we reduce the system utilization. Consider Fig. 25-12, in which case operating point B represents the new value of ρ_{peak}, which is lower down the utilization curve. Once again we have a range of utilizations from ρ_{min} to ρ_{max}, with corresponding fluctuations in

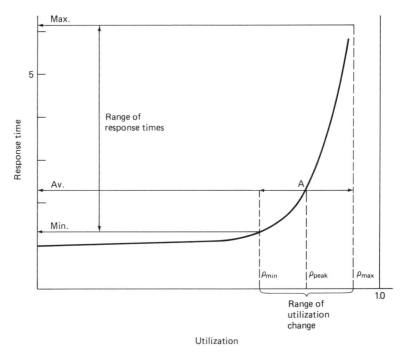

Figure 25-11 Fluctuation in response time caused by instantaneous changes in arrival pattern.

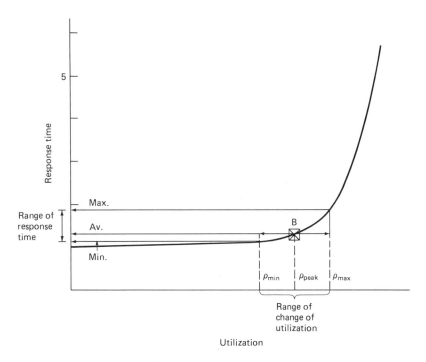

Figure 25-12 Lower utilization gives smaller fluctuations in performance.

response time. Note that the average response time in this case is approximately 1.4 s; the minimum is about 1 s and the maximum is 1.8 s. In this system we have the same range of fluctuation in utilization, but the corresponding fluctuation in response time is smaller because we are operating on a smoother part of the curve.

Queues

Let us now return to the sandwich shop. If the customers arrive regularly—say, every minute on the minute—we could draw a chart as in Fig. 25-13, showing the instantaneous utilization of the operator over the period. Because it only takes 30 s to make a sandwich, when a new customer arrives, the operator will be idle. This means that the new customer will be served immediately, and the operator will then be busy for the following 30 s, at which time he will once again be idle until the next customer arrives. This is an ideal situation—where the time taken to make a sandwich (or, as we often say, the *service time* offered by the facility) is constant, and the transactions also arrive for service at a constant rate.

In reality, transactions generally tend to arrive at random. If the average arrival rate of customers is still 60 customers per hour, but they are arriving at random, then the situation as depicted in Fig. 25-14 could arise. This picture shows one customer arriving when the operator is idle; therefore, he is served imme-

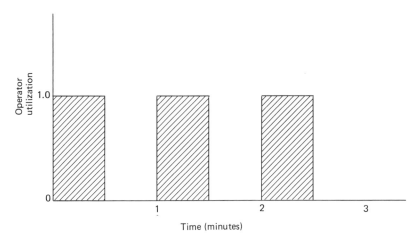

Figure 25-13 Operator utilization with constant arrival rate for customers.

diately. This is followed by an idle period, and then three customers arrive in quick succession. The first one is served immediately, but the second has to wait until the first has finished being served before his service commences. The third customer has to wait for the other two customers to be served before he is served. After that, the operator is idle and two more customers arrive; one of these has to wait while the other is served; and so on.

In Fig. 25-14, we see a queue developing for the facility, and the queue size fluctuates throughout the hour. If we were to examine the queue constantly, we could come up with a figure for the average size of the queue. The average size

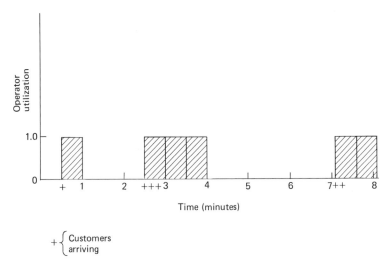

Figure 25-14 Instantaneous operator utilization with random arrival of customers.

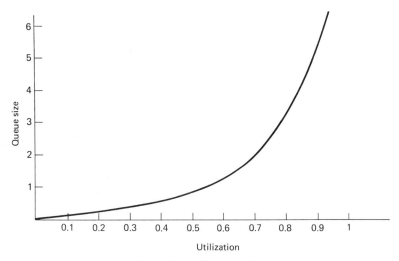

Figure 25-15 Generalized queuing curve.

of the queue is related in a rather complex way to the average utilization of the facility. Generally, if we were to plot a curve of queue size against facility utilization, we would get the shape shown in Fig. 25-15.

Similarly, we could measure the length of time each person spends in the queue. This gives us the *queuing time**** for each person, and we would determine over the period the average length of time that each person spent in the queue. The queuing time is defined as the time from when the transaction joins the queue until it pops out the other end after being serviced. Therefore, the queuing time consists of a component of *waiting time*,* which is the time the transaction spends waiting for service, and then it consists of the *service time*; so we can develop a relationship that says the queuing time is equal to the waiting time plus the service time.

Once again, the queuing time is r^{.l}ited, in a fairly complex way, to the operator utilization. The general shape of the curve showing queuing time versus operator utilization is quite similar to the curve in Fig. 25-15 for the queue size. (The minimum queuing time will be equal to the service time, whereas the minimum queue size will be zero.)

As indicated earlier when we discussed throughput and response times, the curve shoots upward at an increasing rate as the utilization passes beyond about 80%. As a general rule for achieving satisfactory queuing characteristics, we design a system such that the steady-state load does not exceed a utilization of about 60 to 70%.

So far in our example we have offered only one product (the peanut butter sandwich), which was produced with a constant service time. Our sandwich-shop

---

* Some references on queuing theory reverse the definitions of queuing time and waiting time!

proprietor may choose to branch out and offer a wider range of sandwiches, hamburgers, chewing gum, soft drinks, and so on. This will lead to a situation in which different customers require different service times depending on the size of their orders. For example, a person who enters the shop to buy a packet of chewing gum will probably be served in a few seconds, whereas somebody who orders three varieties of sandwiches and a cool drink will be served in much more than the 30 s it takes to provide a peanut butter sandwich.

Based on the example of fluctuating service times, you can probably visualize that for a given customer-arrival rate and for a given average operator utilization, the performance of the queuing situation is going to be worse than that which we encountered when we had constant service times. This is illustrated in Fig. 25-16, where we have superimposed the curves for constant service times and for widely fluctuating service times.

In most of our computer systems, the service time tends to fluctuate somewhat rather than being constant. Once again, the general statements about the sharp part of the curve increasing dramatically beyond the utilization of 80% still apply.

Queues build up at various points in a computer-communications system as the load increases. The queues get larger and the queuing times get longer as the load increases. As with the sandwich shop, the relationship between the queue size and queue time and the utilization of the facility are of the form shown in Fig. 25-16. We call the different parts of the system that are used in handling a transaction the *facilities* within the system. Because each facility can get overloaded we need to be able to work out the utilization of each facility in the system.

The various facilities that are used vary from system to system, but typically they could include the following:

- Processor memory
- Processor time
- Disk storage space
- I/O channel to disk
- Disk access mechanism (seek arm)
- Multiplexer or concentrator
- Communications lines
- Terminal
- Terminal operator

The operator can get overloaded, and then a queue can form for services. The operator uses a terminal connected to the communication line, and there may be a number of terminals connected to that line. This means that each of the operators could be competing for the use of the line. As the load on the system increases, there could be a queue of transactions waiting to get on to the communication line into the computer. Once a transaction gets into the computer, it has to compete with all the other transactions in the computer for the memory space and for the

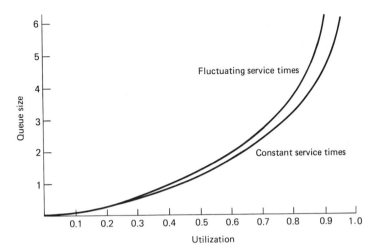

Figure 25-16 Generalized queuing curve for different service times.

processing time in the computer. As the load increases, we could get queues of transactions lining up for these facilities. Most transactions are likely to require the mass-storage system, which may be disk, and the transactions will be competing for the space on the mass storage, for the access mechanisms required to position the read-write heads over the required track, and also for the input/output channel between the computer and the mass-storage subsystem. As the load increases, we can have queues of transactions lining up for these facilities. If we are using concentrators and multiplexers, these can also be potential sources of bottlenecks.

In any system it is important to identify the different facilities that are used to process a transaction so that we can then apply a load to the system and work out the utilization of each facility. We can then identify the facility or facilities that are likely to become overloaded first and therefore cause the bottlenecks. We now examine a simple on-line system to observe what happens when we increase the load on the system.

Example 25-2: Investigation of the Behavior of a Simple On-Line Inquiry System

Let us investigate a simple on-line inquiry system consisting of a computer, one disk, and one communications line with a visual display terminal (VDT) as shown in Fig. 25-17. The system is used by a credit reference bureau; its purpose is to provide an inquirer such as a shopkeeper with the credit rating of a person who wants to buy something with a credit card. (We all know that in modern systems for credit checking we would have a point-of-sale terminal in the shop which is connected directly into the computer. The shopkeeper would wipe the magnetic stripe on the credit card through the credit card terminal and would get a response back directly from the computer. For the purposes of this example, let us assume that we do not have this technology and that it is necessary for the shopkeeper to ring up and speak to the terminal operator.)

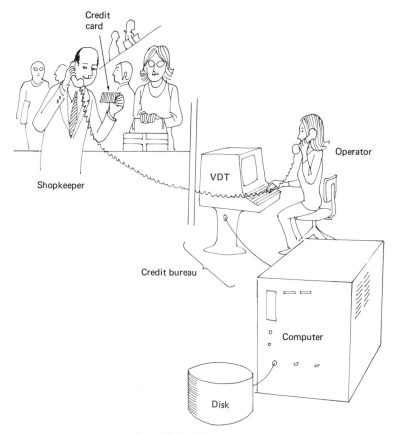

Figure 25-17 Simple system.

The processes involved in a system transaction are as follows:

1. A person walks into a shop and selects an item that she wishes to purchase by using a credit card.
2. The shopkeeper telephones the credit bureau and speaks to the VDT operator, who enters the customer's card number into the VDT. For the purpose of our model, we will say that this operation takes 10 s.
3. The operator then presses the transmit button on the VDT, which causes the message to be sent along the line to the computer. The credit card number is always 15 characters long, and the terminal transmits asynchronously at 150 bps using ASCII code. The VDT is buffered, so the message is transmitted in one block—the total transmission time being 1 s. Only one stop bit is used in this instance, so each character contains 10 bits:

   1 start bit + 7 information bits + 1 parity bit + 1 stop bit

   Therefore,

   $$150 \text{ bits/s} \div 10 \text{ bits/char} = 15 \text{ char/s}$$

4. The computer receives the incoming message and passes it to the application programs for further processing. The application program uses the credit card number to compute a key for accessing the file on the magnetic disk. This computer system is very simplistic and is only required to handle one type of inquiry. So the inquiry-processing program is always resident in the computer's memory and does not need to be read from the disk before processing can begin. Let us say that this initial processing of the message takes 3 ms.

5. Each credit card number has an associated record that contains all the relevant information about that credit account. These records are evenly spread out over the available space on the disk. As the inquiries are entered randomly, the disk arm must be moved across the disk to position the read head above the particular cylinder containing the desired record. The disk arm is said to be *seeking* the desired cylinder, and the mean seek time for this disk is 50 ms.

6. When the arm is correctly positioned, there is a further average delay of 12.5 ms while the disk rotates until the required record comes under the read head. This delay is known as the *latency*, which, on the average, is one-half of the time required for one revolution of the disk. One millisecond is then required to transfer the record from the disk to the computer.

7. The application programs process the data in the record and formulate a response for transmission to the VDT operator. This computer processing takes 5 ms.

8. The computer transmits a response message of 150 characters to the VDT. At 150 bps asynchronous ASCII, it takes 67 ms for the first character to appear on the VDT screen (1000 ms/s $\div$ 15 char/s = 67 ms/char) and 10 s for the entire message to be received (150 char $\div$ 15 char/s = 10 s).

9. When the message has been received, the VDT operator tells the shopkeeper the required credit rating. This conversation lasts 5 s, after which the operator hangs up the telephone and clears the VDT screen in preparation for the next inquiry, taking an additional 3 s.

The overall sequence of events drawn on a time scale is shown in Fig. 25-18. From this diagram we can see that the total time required to handle the transaction is the time between the VDT operator answering the telephone in the credit bureau and the operator hanging up the telephone and clearing the VDT screen. The response time seen by the shopkeeper is the time that elapses between the end of the first conversation with the VDT operator (stating the credit card number) and the first syllable of the operator's response to the inquiry. The response time seen by the operator is the time between initiating transmission of the input message and the display of the first character of the response on the VDT screen. For the time being, we assume that all of the timings for these various processes are fixed and that they are the same for each transaction, although we see later that this a gross oversimplification of what happens in a real system.

Solution   Knowing the times required for each step in the transaction processing allows us to determine the utilization of each facility in our simple system. We can identify the following facilities or servers:

- Operator and terminal
- Communications line

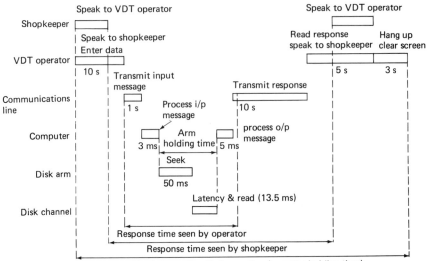

Figure 25-18 Time scale for example transaction processing system.

- Computer
- Disk arm
- Disk channel

The operator utilization can be computed by determining the total time that the operator spends handling transactions in 1 h. This will be equal to the product of the average number of transactions per hour (i.e., the average rate of transactions) and the average time spent on each transaction. We call the time spent by a facility in processing a transaction the *facility holding time*.

Referring to Fig. 25-18, we see that the operator holding time per transaction is the sum of the time taken for each individual process forming the transaction. The operator holding time is thus 29.0715 s (10 + 1 + 0.003 + 0.05 + 0.0125 + 0.001 + 0.005 + 10 + 5 + 3 s). The equation for operator utilization is therefore

$$\rho_{operator} = \frac{\text{time occupied}}{\text{time available}}$$

$$= \frac{(\text{hourly transaction rate}) \times (\text{operator holding time})}{3600 \text{ s/h}}$$

$$= \frac{(\text{transaction rate}) \times (29.0715 \text{ s})}{3600 \text{ s/h}}$$

In our simple system, the operator utilization is also effectively the terminal utilization.

The communications-line utilization can be computed in a manner similar to operator utilization. The total time that the line is in use each hour is the product of the transaction rate and the line holding time. The line holding time has two components: the input transmission time (message traveling from VDT to computer) and the output transmission time (message traveling from computer to VDT; input and output usually refer to directions of transfer regarding the computer as the point of reference). For our simple example, we assume that the line is half-duplex; so the line holding time for a transaction is the sum of the input time and the output time. For full-duplex lines, a channel holding time for each direction would need to be calculated. For example, if our model had a full-duplex line, the input channel would be much less heavily utilized than the output channel, because the transmission time for the output message is 10 s, whereas the input message-transmission time is 1 s.

The equations for the communications-line utilization are:

$$\text{line holding time} = (\text{input time}) + (\text{output time})$$

$$= 1 \text{ s} + 10 \text{ s} = 11 \text{ s}$$

$$\rho_{line} = \frac{\text{time occupied}}{\text{time available}}$$

$$= \frac{(\text{hourly transaction rate}) \times (\text{line holding time})}{3600 \text{ s/h}}$$

$$= \frac{(\text{hourly transaction rate}) \times (11 \text{ s})}{3600 \text{ s/h}}$$

The equations for the computer utilization are similar to the previous facility utilization equations:

$$\begin{array}{l} \textit{computer holding time} \\ \textit{per transaction} \end{array} = 3 \text{ ms} + 5 \text{ ms} = 8 \text{ ms}$$

$$\rho_{CPU} = \frac{(\text{hourly transaction rate}) \times (\text{CPU holding time})}{(3600 \times 1000 \text{ ms/h})}$$

$$= \frac{(\text{hourly transaction rate}) \times (8 \text{ ms})}{(3600 \times 1000 \text{ ms/h})}$$

We can readily see that the computer will be very lightly loaded compared to the other facilities. Even if the transaction rate were 1000 per hour (which is physically impossible with our one-operator system), the CPU would still be utilized less than 1% of the time:

$$\rho_{computer} = \frac{1000 \times 8}{3600 \times 1000} = \frac{8}{3600} = 0.25\%$$

Similarly, the disk-arm utilization is calculated using the following equations:

$$\begin{array}{l} \textit{arm holding time} \\ \textit{per transaction} \end{array} = \textit{seek time} + \textit{latency} + \textit{transfer time}$$

$$= 50 \text{ ms} + 12.5 \text{ ms} + 1 \text{ ms}$$

$$= 63.5 \text{ ms}$$

$$\rho_{arm} = \frac{\text{time occupied}}{\text{time available}}$$

$$= \frac{(\text{hourly transaction rate}) \times (\text{arm holding time})}{(3600 \times 1000 \text{ ms/h})}$$

$$= \frac{(\text{hourly transaction rate}) \times (63.5 \text{ ms})}{(3600 \times 1000 \text{ ms/h})}$$

The disk-channel utilization will depend on the type of disk hardware and also on the type of operating system that is in use. There are three basic approaches to implementing disk hardware. In the simplest systems the disk channel is seized to initiate the disk seek, and the channel is held during the seek, latency, and transfer operations. This means that, on a given disk subsystem, disk accesses must be performed serially.

Newer systems capitalize on the fact that seek times can be relatively long. These systems seize the channel to issue the seek command and then release it until the seek operation has been completed. The system then seizes the channel for the latency and data transfer phase. This means that we could overlap operations on two or more disc drives attached to the one control unit. Several seeks could be initiated in quick succession on different drives, and the one that terminated first would seize the channel. In this situation, there is, of course, a possibility that one of the other drives may find the channel busy when it wants it, and it may have to go around again.

TABLE 25-1 FACILITY UTILIZATION[a]

Hourly transaction rate	Operator	Line	Computer	Arm	Channel
10	0.08	0.03	—	—	—
20	0.16	0.06	—	—	—
30	0.24	0.09	—	—	—
40	0.32	0.12	—	—	—
50	0.40	0.15	—	—	—
60	0.48	0.18	—	—	—
70	0.56	0.21	—	—	—
80	0.65	0.24	—	—	—
90	0.73	0.27	—	—	—
100	0.80	0.30	0.0002	0.0017	0.00037
110	0.89	—	—	—	—
120	0.96	—	—	—	—
200	1.61	0.61	—	—	—
300	2.42	0.91	—	—	—
400	3.24	1.22	—	—	—
600	4.75	1.83	—	—	—
1000	8.00	3.05	0.002	0.017	0.0037

[a] A facility cannot be utilized more than 100% of the time ($\rho = 1.00$), but the figures are included here to show the overload occurring on the operator and line when the CPU and disk facilities are still barely utilized.

The newest systems incorporate rotational position sensing so that once the seek has been initiated the channel is not needed until the data come under the read head. This allows greater overlapping of operations on different drives and gives us better system performance.

In our model, we are using the second type of disk, so the channel will effectively be tied up only during the latency and data transfer period. Hence the equations for disk-channel utilization are

$$\frac{channel\ holding\ time}{per\ transaction} = latency + transfer\ time$$

$$= 12.5\ ms + 1\ ms = 13.5\ ms$$

$$\rho_{channel} = \frac{time\ occupied}{time\ available}$$

$$= \frac{(hourly\ transaction\ rate) \times (channel\ holding\ time)}{(3600 \times 1000\ ms/h)}$$

$$= \frac{(hourly\ transaction\ rate) \times (13.5\ ms)}{(3600 \times 1000\ ms/h)}$$

In all the facility-utilization equations we have developed, the hourly transaction rate is the unknown variable. We can investigate how the transaction rate effects the load on the different facilities by constructing a table showing utilization of each facility at different transaction-arrival rates. Obviously, as the transaction rate increases, the loading on the facilities will increase. Table 25-1 shows that in our simple system the facilities become fully occupied in the following order:

- Operator
- Communications line
- Disk arm
- Disk channel
- Computer

The theoretical maximum number of transactions per hour that could be handled by each facility is

Operator: $\frac{3600\ s/h}{29.07\ s/trans} = 123.83\ trans/h$

Line: $\frac{3600}{11} = 327.27$

Disk arm: $\frac{3600}{0.0635} = 56,693$

Disk channel: $\frac{3600}{0.0135} = 266,666$

CPU: $\frac{3600}{0.008} = 450,000$

The inquiry rate that the credit bureau can handle is limited in this case by the operator.

Table 25-1 shows us that the maximum load the system can handle is approximately 120 transactions per hour; the 80% utilization mark arises at about 100 transactions per hour, and the maximum safe limit for loading is in the vicinity of 80 transactions per hour, because this is the point at which the system utilization is 65%.

Based on that information, we could draw a curve illustrating the relationship between transaction volumes and shopkeeper queuing time. We assume that the credit bureau has a queuing telephone system. This means that if when a shopkeeper rings up, the operator is speaking to someone else, the shopkeeper gets a ring tone rather than a busy signal. When the operator finishes dealing with one shopkeeper, she will find that the next one is there waiting to be served. This means that we will have a queue of shopkeepers on the telephone waiting for service as the load on the system increases. Figure 25-19 broadly illustrates the relationship between queuing time for the shopkeepers and the hourly transaction rate that is being applied to the system.

If we wish to improve the system throughput to increase the number of transactions per hour that can be handled, we must remove the bottleneck that caused the system to have the limitation of 120 transactions per hour. In our case the bottleneck was the operator, because the operator utilization increased beyond the safe upper limit at a transaction rate of about 80 transactions per hour.

In any system there are two main approaches to improving throughput. The first is to reduce the total amount of time it takes to process each transaction, so that we can fit more transactions into the available time. The second approach is to increase the number of transactions that can be handled in parallel, thereby increasing the total number of transactions that we can feed through the system.

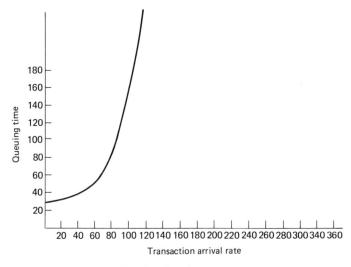

Figure 25-19 Queuing time for one-operator system.

Looking at the system utilization table, we can see that the computer, the disk arm, and the disk channel are very lightly loaded even at very high transaction rates. For the purposes of this analysis, we can therefore assume that the computer is capable of handling any transaction load that we can reasonably expect to apply to it. This leaves the operator and the communication line as the main potential bottlenecks in the system. Let us examine the approach to increasing system throughput by decreasing the total amount of time it takes to handle a transaction.

We can see from Fig. 25-18 that there is very little scope for reducing the amount of time that the operator spends speaking to the shopkeeper either at the beginning or at the end of the transaction, because these times are already minimal. Similarly, there is little to be gained by decreasing the time it takes to process the message in the computer or to look up the disk, because these times are measured in milliseconds, whereas the other times in the time chart are measured in seconds.

The communication line, however, is operating at only 150 bps, and it is used for a total of 11 s for every transaction. It would be feasible to increase the speed of the line to 1200 bps; this would in turn reduce the line holding time to 1.37 s. This would in turn reduce the total time required to handle each transaction to 19.44 s, thus boosting our theoretical maximum transaction rate to 3600/19.44 = 185.18 per hour, which is a significant increase over the previous figure of 123.83 transactions per hour.

If we were to analyze the loading, we can work out the facility utilization for the different facilities as we apply a load to the system and come up with the critical points, as illustrated in the following table:

Arrival rate (transactions/h)	Facility utilization	
	Operator	Line
37	0.2	0.113
74	0.4	0.226
111	0.6	0.339
148	0.8	0.452
185	1.0	0.565

This shows that the 60% utilization mark is at an arrival rate of 111 transactions per hour, and the 80% utilization mark is at an arrival rate of 148 transactions per hour, and the 100% utilization mark is at a transaction-arrival rate of 185 transactions per hour. We could plot a rough curve showing shopkeeper queuing time as the transaction rate increases. Figure 25-20 shows such a curve superimposed on the curve that we had in Fig. 25-19 for the system with a line speed of 150 bps. We can see from Fig. 25-20 that the new system gives better performance in that it not only carries more load but it has reduced queuing time because the service time has been reduced.

Another point to note is that, in this particular system, we would not achieve a great deal at this point by increasing the line speed beyond 1200 bps. The improvement in shopkeeper queuing time that would be achieved by increasing the line speed would be quite small because of the small impact this would have on the total time it takes to process each transaction.

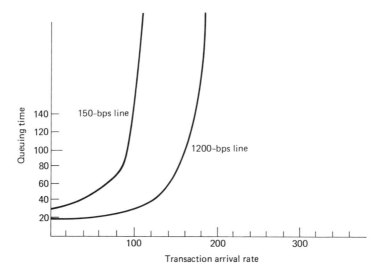

Figure 25-20 Queuing time with different line speeds.

Let us now return the line speed to 150 bps and examine other approaches to improving system throughput. An obvious way of increasing the load-handling capability of the system is to add a second operator, as illustrated in Fig. 25-21. If we retain our queuing telephone system, either operator can take the next transaction from the head of the queue. The time scale illustrated in Fig. 25-18 would still hold, because even though we have added another operator, we have not changed the length of time it takes to handle the transaction through the various facilities. Because the operators are sharing the load between them, the operator utilization at a given load would be one-half the operator utilization in the earlier example. The line utilization would also be one-half the line utilization in the earlier example. On the other hand, the computer and the mass storage are processing all the transactions, so the utilization of the computer, the seek arm, and the disk channel would be the same at a given transaction rate as they were in the first example.

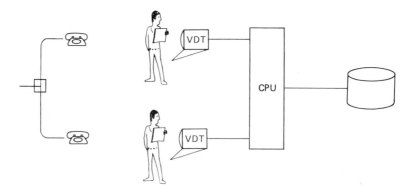

Figure 25-21 Two-operator system.

Once again, we can evaluate the load on the various facilities as we apply an increasing transaction rate to the system, and we can draw up the following table:

Arrival rate (transactions/h)	Facility utilization	
	Operator	Line
160	0.65	0.24
200	0.80	0.30
240	0.96	0.36

In this case the maximum load that the system can handle has doubled, and the critical points of 65% utilization and 80% utilization occur at roughly double the load at which they occurred in the previous examples.

If we plot a curve showing the shopkeeper queuing time against the number of transactions per hour that are applied to the system, we get a graph roughly like the one shown in Fig. 25-22. This shows the two-operator system performance curve superimposed on the performance curve of the single-operator system.

Similarly, we could add a third operator to the configuration shown in Fig. 25-21, and we could evaluate the utilization of the various facilities as we apply a load to the system. We could then determine the critical points for a curve as illustrated in the following table:

Arrival rate (transactions/h)	Facility utilization	
	Operator	Line
240	0.65	0.24
300	0.80	0.30
360	0.96	0.36

We could plot a curve as shown in Fig. 25-23, which superimposes the three-operator system curve on the two-operator and one-operator system performance curves.

An alternative approach to the system expansion is to add the additional terminals on the same communication line and incorporate some kind of cluster controller to prevent contention from arising on the line. This is illustrated in Fig. 25-24. In this case the single communication line is carrying the traffic from all the terminals, which means that the line utilization will increase as the traffic increases. This in turn will ultimately result in a queue arising at the cluster controller as the operators contend for the capacity of the line. This is illustrated in the simplified time-scale chart shown in Fig. 25-25. The box labeled "computer" on this chart contains the sequence of events including computer processing, disk seek arm, and disk channel operations from Fig. 25-18.

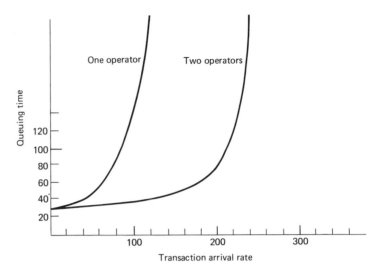

Figure 25-22 Queuing time for two-operator system.

The time taken to process each transaction includes a component of waiting time in a queue for the communication line on the input side and also another component of waiting time for the same communication line on the output side. There is actually only one queue for the line, although it is physically distributed with the input transactions at one end and the output transactions at the other. These waiting times will increase exponentially with the load on the communication line; this in turn will cause the operator holding time to increase quite dramatically as the load on the system gets to the point where the communication line is being heavily utilized.

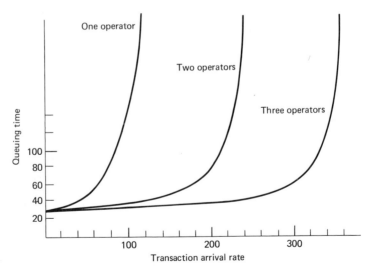

Figure 25-23 Queuing time for three-operator system.

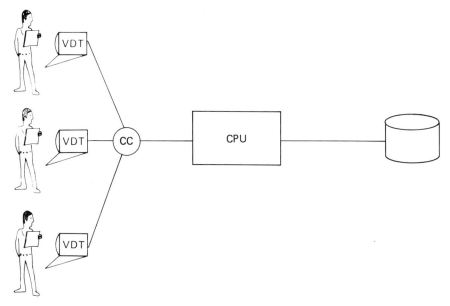

Figure 25-24 Three-operator system with single communications line.

This in turn will cause the operator utilization to increase faster than it otherwise would have, and that will cause the shopkeeper's queuing time to increase quite dramatically. This is, if you like, an illustration of the fact that the shopkeeper queuing time is an exponential function of an exponential function, which will produce a rapid decline in system performance as the load on the system increases.

With three terminals on the line, there is a limit to the length of time a transaction would spend in the line queue because there could never be more than three transactions in the queue. With a large number of terminals, the queuing time for the line could be quite significant. This situation could be alleviated by going back to the original premise of increasing the line speed to 1200 bps. This would reduce

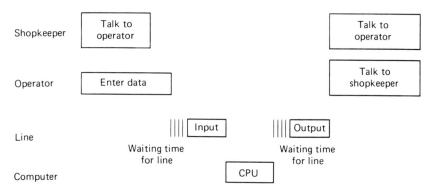

Figure 25-25 Time chart for three terminals on one line.

the line utilization, even at fairly heavy transaction rates, so that we would not get a severe queuing problem for the lines. This would also reduce the operator utilization, so that the system performance would be much more stable.

The type of analysis we have been performing can be extended to the internal processing in the computer. You can imagine queues of transactions lining up for the different processing segments and also for the disk arm or disk channel. As the load on the system increases, these queues could become excessively long. If the utilization of any facility gets above about 80%, this could be the item that would cause the system performance to degrade.

For ease of understanding the situation, we grossly oversimplified this system. Real systems may have 10, 20, or even hundreds of transaction types, each with their own processing requirements, different input message lengths, and different output message lengths. Also, the operator will not spend a constant amount of time speaking to each person who calls. Some will be processed quickly, and others will take a long time, depending on the interaction between the operator and the inquirer. Internally, different transactions will require varying amounts of computer time and disk operation time. Some transactions will require no disk accesses, whereas others may require 20, 30, or perhaps a hundred.

For real systems, therefore, we need to apply some statistical methods to work out average message lengths, average transmission time, average processing time, disk operation timings, and so on. We can then build models based on the techniques covered in this book and incorporate queuing theory, as described in Chapter 28, into the analysis of the system performance.

26
Network Management

network management considerations

Once you have a network, it is a good idea for you to see to it that it is run properly. This means that you must have the right combination of people, equipment, software, and procedures.

The hardest thing to find, of course, is the people. There are not that many trained network management personnel on the market at the moment, and most organizations adopt the approach of training their own network managers. They take people from within the company who seem to have an aptitude for the technicalities of the job and feed them through training courses, both public courses and those run by their computer suppliers. They also provide on-the-job training and expose the people selected to network management centers in other organizations.

The equipment required in a network management center includes testing equipment that is used for diagnosing faults, and reconfiguration equipment such as patching facilities and switching facilities so that the network can be reconfigured in the event of a fault. In this way it can continue to give some kind of service while a fault is being diagnosed and rectified.

The software facilities include, among other things, the generation of performance statistics which allow us to keep track of how the system is performing. These performance statistics are outlined in the following pages.

The ISO model for Open System Interconnection is to include network management. At the time of writing, the ISO has started to study those aspects of network management that should be incorporated into the model. In the meantime, there are several proprietary software packages that perform network management functions for particular network architectures.

performance statistics

A good system keeps track of its own operation, gathers statistics on its own performance, and makes these statistics available every day or perhaps even on demand to the network management systems personnel. It can also provide regular performance figures to data processing management. The following statistics may be collected in the host itself or perhaps in the front-end processor. Alternatively, intelligent terminal control units may collect statistics on response times, and it may also be necessary to use external test equipment to gather some specific information.

Statistic	Network total	Line and/or terminal total	Applic. and terminal total
Characters in/out	✓	✓	✓
Messages in/out	✓	✓	✓
Timeouts	✓	✓	
Retries in/out	✓	✓	
Response times Average Range	✓ ✓	✓ ✓	✓ ✓
Line loading		✓	

Figure 26-1 Useful statistics for an on-line system.

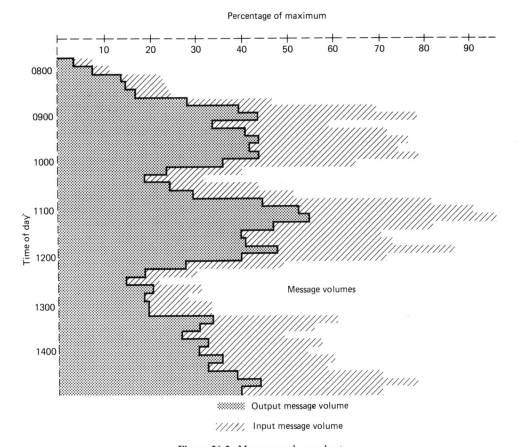

Percentage of maximum

Figure 26-2 Message volume chart.

Figure 26-1 provides a list of general statistics that it is nice to be able to collect in a network. Not all networks may be able to provide all this information, but it is nice if they can be provided. Also, in some systems there may be specific statistics available from the operating system which are not included in the list in Fig. 26-1.

For some statistics we are interested in figures for the network as a whole, whereas for others we are interested in details for a single communication line or perhaps even for a single terminal on that line. On the other hand, other statistics are useful on a per application basis so that we can see who is doing what. We may even break these statistics down further, so that we can see which applications are being accessed by which terminals.

The statistics are summarized at frequent intervals. The interval depends on the loading pattern in the system. In the examples provided in Figs. 26-2 and 26-3 the figures are summarized at 10-minute intervals. In other systems they may be summarized at 30-minute or even 1-hour intervals. The statistics can be dumped

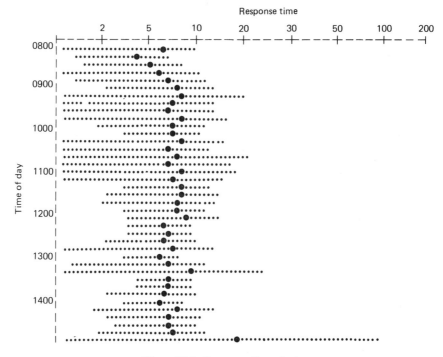

Figure 26-3 Response-time chart.

in either graphical or tabulated form for analysis by the network management personnel.

The purpose of each of the various statistics is summarized below.

- *Characters in/out; messages in/out.* These tell you the loading on the system and allow you to see how the traffic fluctuates during the day and also helps you to keep track of traffic growth so that you can plan future expansion. Ideally, figures should be collected for the system as a whole, for each terminal, *and* for each application that is accessed from the terminals. This allows you to see where the traffic originates and who makes how much use of each application.
- *Polls sent.* The number of polls issued on each line can be a useful statistic, particularly on networks using statistical multiplexers, because polls contribute to the loading on the main link between the statistical multiplexers.
- *Retries.* Indicates the number of messages that are retransmitted. Collected for the network as a whole, for each line, *and* for each terminal, this statistic can be a useful diagnostic tool and can foreshadow a potential network component failure.
- *Timeouts.* Indicates how many polls or messages sent to terminals did not get a response. As with retries, this statistic can indicate a faulty network

component or can foreshadow a potential fault. (On the other hand, a large number of retries may just indicate that a terminal operator has switched off the terminal and gone home.)

- *Response times.* Both the average response time and the range of response times experienced over the time interval can be recorded. This is both a planning tool and a diagnostic aid. It is not always possible to measure response times, but if you can do it, you will find it a very valuable exercise.
- *Line utilization.* Gives an indication of the loading on a line. This is a useful planning tool.

Some system software provides you with some of these statistics in one form or another, whereas others do not. In the latter case, you would have to get into the software yourself, and that may or may not be an easy task.

Figure 26-2 shows a message volume plot which gives an indication of the volume of input and output messages for each 10-minute interval during the day for a particular organization. Note that the display is normalized with respect to the maximum amount of traffic experienced during any 10-minute interval during the day. It therefore shows relative traffic. This particular printout, while useful in its graphical form, is backed up by a table showing the absolute traffic volume.

In Fig. 26-3, we have plotted response time for this organization. The horizontal axis is response time on a logarithmic scale going from 2 s through to 200 s, and the vertical axis is time of day in 10-minute intervals. The range of dots for any 10-minute interval indicates the range of response times experienced, and the heavy dot in the middle represents the average response time during that 10-minute interval.

Response times can also be produced in the form of a table which gives a more detailed breakdown and allows percentiles to be established. Referring to Fig. 26-4, we see that we have three columns, the first column giving the range of time, the second column giving the percentage of transactions that occurred during the time range, and the third column giving the cumulative percentage of transactions that have response times less than the upper limit of the time range given. For example, looking at the second time range 3 to 5 s, we can see that 43% of all transactions had response times in the range 3 to 5 s, and cumulatively 51% of transactions had response times of 5 s or less.

Time	Transactions	
(s)	(%)	(cumulative %)
0–3	8	8
3–5	43	51
5–7	25	77
7–10	14	91
10–15	5	96
15–20	2	98
20–30	1	99
30–50	0	100
50–100	0	100

Figure 26-4 Response-time percentiles.

TABLE 26-1 *STATION STATISTICS*: FIGURES FOR EACH TERMINAL ON A MULTIDROP LINE

Terminal number	Messages		Characters		Errors		Average response time
	In	*Out*	*In*	*Out*	*Timeout*	*Parity*	
1	69	115	1,032	54,067	4	11	10.000
2	426	493	49,911	94,457	10	8	5.702
3	339	380	30,860	53,983	21	5	5.932
4	3	9	105	430	0	0	0
5	34	68	294	3,213	32	0	0
6	14	19	234	7,532	5	494	13.340
7	1	4	0	158	0	61	0
8	174	184	18,512	25,286	11	9	5.893
9	1	75	0	20,174	0	0	0
10	0	1	0	70	0	0	0
Total	1,061	1,348	100,948	259,370	83	588	

Figure 26-4 also backs up the general rule of thumb about average response times, 90th and 95th percentiles. Referring to the diagram, the 91st percentile response time is 10 s and the 96th percentile response time is 15 s. The 51st percentile response time is 5 s; therefore, we could say that, roughly speaking, the average response time is 5s. The 90th percentile is 10 s, which is twice the average, and the 95th percentile is 15 s, which is three times the average.

Table 26-1 shows station statistics, which are figures for each terminal on a multidrop line. The complete block of data represents statistics for one communication line, and each horizontal line on this table shows statistics for one terminal on that line. We have details of messages in and out and characters in and out, which are the volume-related statistics. We also have error-related statistics such as buffer overflow errors in the front end, timeout errors, carrier loss errors, parity errors, and also the average response time for each terminal on the line. Looking at the response times, we can see that the average response times are different, and this implies that the terminals are accessing different applications. In fact, some response times are zero, which implies that that particular terminal is indulging in a one-way data transfer. Also looking at the parity error column, we can see that during this particular day there was a total of 588 errors on the communication line and, of those, 494 came from one terminal. This ought to tell the network management people something about that terminal. Maybe it has a fault in the interface, or maybe there is a fault in the modem or the tail of the line going out to that terminal.

Table 26-2 shows application statistics for each application being run on the host. There are about 20 to 30 applications on this particular machine. Table 26-2 shows the message and character volume statistics for each application and the average response time.

TABLE 26-2 *APPLICATION STATISTICS:* FIGURES FOR EACH APPLICATION BEING RUN IN THE HOST

Application number	Messages		Characters		Average response time
	In	*Out*	*In*	*Out*	
1	7	4	337	539	11.586
2	14	8	1,104	2,188	3.193
3	14	11	681	2,640	14.986
4	43	35	1,406	6,836	7.344
5	135	126	11,087	21,332	3.819
6	29	22	1,355	4,837	7.210
7	5	2	111	292	14.800
8	29	7	135	2,634	8.779
9	31	25	379	6,825	2.374
10	25	19	391	10,980	7.284
11	28	7	155	1,433	2.625
12	4,227	5,629	768,531	1,095,082	7.310

The person who has the information outlined in the preceding tables and figures is in charge of his or her systems. This person knows how the system is performing and can spot trends; that is, as the load increases, she can observe the traffic growing on a weekly/monthly basis. She can thus predict when there are likely to be problems due to going up the steep part of the queuing curve and can anticipate expansion requirements or complaints from users if the response times are starting to get too long.

network reconfiguration equipment

As you can imagine, from time to time faults will occur in the network and we may need to troubleshoot the network or reconfigure the network to minimize the effect of the fault. Figure 26-5 shows a generalized network which has two hosts, each with a front-end processor and a number of communication lines. The communication lines are all connected to front-end processor A, which has a spare port; we also have a spare modem. Front-end processor B is completely spare. If a fault occurs we may wish to connect modem M1 to a spare port on front-end processor A. We can do this by disconnecting the cables and reconnecting the cables to the appropriate ports, as illustrated in Fig. 26-6.

Alternatively, we may wish to test the line with a serial data analyzer. This could involve unplugging the V.24 interface on the modem, connecting up the serial data analyzer, and reconnecting the modems. Although this allows us to test the network, it does interrupt service to the users on that line.

Alternatively, it may be necessary to reconfigure the network so that all the lines are connected to front-end processor B. This would be the action we would take in the event of a failure in host A or front end A, and we can disconnect all the cables and plug them into B, as shown in Fig. 26-7.

Although reconfiguring cables does work, it has a number of problems. First, it is relatively slow; second, it can cause interruptions to the service, particularly in the case where we are connecting test equipment into the line; and third, it can cause future problems. Future problems arise because the pins in the plugs

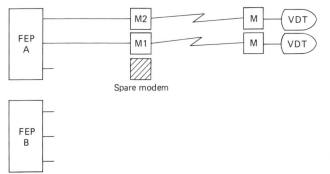

Figure 26-5 Generalized network.

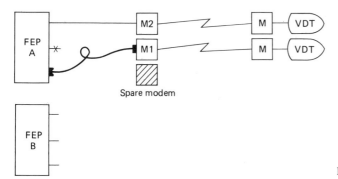

Figure 26-6 Cable reconfiguration.

and sockets used in the connectors can become loose as they are plugged and unplugged a number of times, and this can cause intermittent problems in the future. Many connectors, particularly those used for V.24/RS-232 interfaces, are designed to be fixed into place with screws, so that once they are installed they are meant to be left there and not disturbed very often.

Generally speaking, we need methods of reconfiguring the network and being able to insert test equipment that is faster and more reliable than physically disconnecting the modems and reconnecting them. The available reconfiguration equipment falls into three major categories:

1. Patch panels
2. Unintelligent switches
3. Smart switches

Let us look briefly at these in sequence.

Patch Panels

These fit into the system as shown in Fig. 26-8. A patch panel looks and behaves rather like an old-fashioned telephone switchboard, where we have a large number of sockets on the switchboard and we connect any telephone into

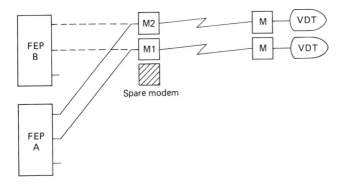

Figure 26-7 AB changeover using cables.

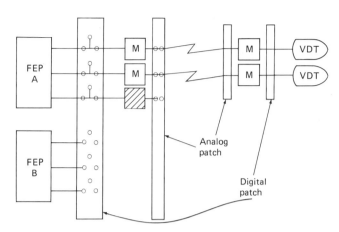

Figure 26-8 Patch panels.

any other telephone by connecting a cord into the appropriate sockets on the switchboard. On a patch panel we have the capability of connecting anything to anything, and as shown in Fig. 26-8, we have two types of patch panel: a digital patch, which sits between the modems and the front-end processor, and the analog patch, which sits between the modem and the communication line. The digital patch panel allows any modem to be connected to any computer port. It also has a monitor socket attached to each interface, which enables us to plug a piece of test equipment into the monitor socket so that we can observe the data going along the line without interrupting service. Similarly, the analog patch panel allows us to connect any communication line to any modem.

It is therefore possible to bypass a modem and patch in a spare modem in the event of a failure in a modem by putting patches on both the digital and analog side of that modem. Similarly, we could patch any modem to any spare computer port or we could connect all the modems from front end A across to all the ports on front end B by using the appropriate patch cords. Patch panels are relatively inexpensive and their operation is relatively fast and easy, although problems can occur if there are lots of lines to be reconfigured.

Unintelligent switches

The next reconfiguration equipment to consider are the unintelligent switches. These are often known as AB switches or perhaps XY switches. The general characteristics are that they are more expensive than patching; however, they are much faster but not as flexible. Examples of these are the AB switches or changeover switches, which can be used to gang switch a group of lines from one front-end processor to another. This is illustrated in Fig. 26-9. In this case, the AB switch allows the network lines to be connected to ports on either front end A or front end B. Generally, all the lines are connected through front end A,

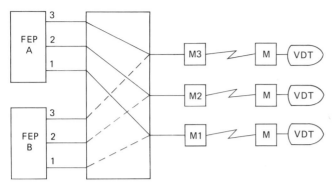

Figure 26-9 AB changeover switch.

but in the event of a failure in front end A we can press a button on the switch panel and that will automatically switch all the lines to front end B.

Although the changeover is extremely fast, it is inflexible in that once a switch is wired up, the modems can be connected to the designated ports only. For example, it is not possible to connect modem 3 to port 2 on front end B without rewiring the switch. A variation on the theme includes both patching and switching capability in one unit and many organizations go for this kind of arrangement so that they can have the flexibility of patching and the rapid backup changeover of the AB switch.

Smart switches

A more expensive switching device, often called the matrix switch, provides the flexibility of patching with the speed of switching. The matrix switch sits in the interface between the modems and the front-end processors as shown in Fig. 26-10. Here we have a number of front ends and a number of modems and the matrix switch allows any modem to be connected to any computer port. It can be reconfigured instantly under command from the network control center operator via a control visual display terminal.

Individual lines can be switched, or a group of lines can be preprogrammed to be switched from one machine to another. For example, we could set up a command so that all the lines normally connected to front end 1 or front end 2 could be switched across to front end 3 in the event of a failure in either front end 1 or 2.

Also, the matrix switch has a number of test access ports available and the network operator can have test equipment connected into the test access ports. He or she can command the switch to connect the test equipment to any interface in the network, so that without leaving the control position, the network control operator can observe data going across any interface in the network, can perform loopback tests on any line, and so on.

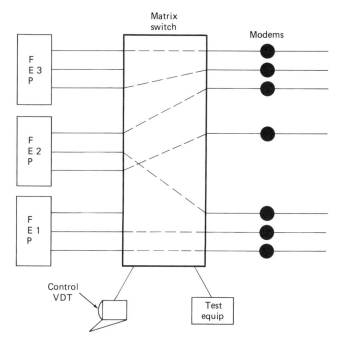

Figure 26-10 Matrix switching.

Port selection units (Data PBX)

A variation on this theme is the port selection unit or Data PBX. It is similar in many ways to the matrix switch, but generally speaking these are under the control of the individual visual display terminal operator. With character-oriented terminals, these terminals are normally connected on point-to-point lines to the host and they are dedicated to particular ports on the host computer. The port selection unit provides a switching capability so that character-oriented terminals can indulge in switched operation so that they can be connected to any one of a number of computer ports.

A typical configuration is shown in Fig. 26-11. Here we have two front ends: front end A has two classes of port, and front end B has a third class of port. The terminals are connected into the port selection unit on the right-hand side, and any terminal operator can request the port selection unit to connect the terminal through to any one of the classes of port. If a port is available, the terminal is connected; if the port is not available at the time, the terminal is informed that the port is busy and that the operator should try again later.

This allows us to share a number of ports between a large number of users. In many applications the character-oriented terminals are very lightly loaded. For example, one client of ours had 100 terminals, each utilized less than 1% on average during the day. Rather than dedicating 100 ports on the computer to the terminals (which was difficult because the computer had a maximum of 64 ports),

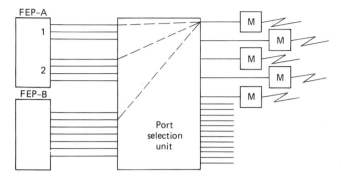

Figure 26-11 Port selection unit.

we used a port selection unit which allowed us to share about 15 to 20 ports between the 100 terminals. Due to the light loading on the terminals, it was highly unlikely that all 20 ports would be used in any given instant so that, generally, when an operator does want a port, he or she gets connected straight through to the appropriate port.

Like the switching multiplexers mentioned below, data PBXs can be interconnected in quite complex networks to provide switching capability to simple, character-oriented terminals.

Switching multiplexers

There are many other components on the marketplace including switching multiplexers. A switching multiplexer combines the characteristics of both the port selection unit and the statistical multiplexer. As shown in Fig. 26-12, terminal

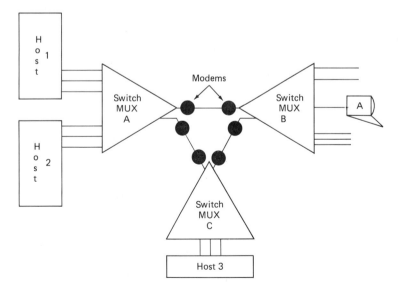

Figure 26-12 Switching multiplexers.

A, connected into switching multiplexer B, can indulge in a dialogue with the switching multiplexer and have itself connected through to host 1, 2 or 3. In the process of transmitting, the data from A will be statistically multiplexed with data from other terminals along the link. Quite complicated networks can be set up using combinations of switching multiplexers and statistical multiplexers which allow terminals to get access to a large range of host computers at various places throughout a network.

test equipment

We also need to be able to troubleshoot the network, that is, to identify a faulty item when failure occurs, and this means that we need test equipment. There is a whole host of test equipment on the market; new pieces appear on the market every day, so what we will do is sample the possibilities.

Indicator lamps

Probably the simplest test equipment in existence are the test aids that come with your standard data communications equipment. This includes the indicator lamps on modems, patch panels, and so on. Most modems have indicator lamps attached to some or all of the V.24 signals, such as request-to-send, clear-to-send, transmit data, receive data, and carrier detect, and operators become accustomed to the general status of these lamps and to the rhythm of the lamps flashing on and off. The operators get to the point where they can glance at the modem or patch panel and tell that all seems to be well. When a fault does occur, these indicator lamps provide useful indications of the status of the V.24 interface as a first level of troubleshooting.

Breakout boxes

The next level of test equipment is the breakout box, which is a portable hand-held unit that gives access to V.24 interfaces and is useful for troubleshooting at remote sites. The breakout box is connected into the V.24 interface between a modem and a terminal, and it gives access to all the V.24 signals. Indicator lamps show the status of most of the V.24 signals, and usually there are switching or patching facilities. These enable the operator to get access to the V.24 interface for manipulating the leads and for simulating the operation of the interface.

Serial data analyzers

An essential piece of data communications test equipment is the serial data analyzer. This analyzer fits into the network as shown in Fig. 26-13. They are microcomputer-based devices which typically would plug into the monitor socket

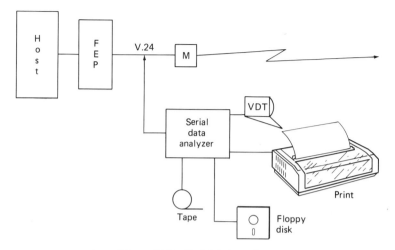

Figure 26-13 Serial data analyzer.

of the V.24 interface patch panel. The microcomputer will capture the status of each V.24 interface line for each bit time on the interface. It will make the information available either on a screen or a printer, and it may save it on a tape or disk for future analysis.

The serial data analyzer shows all traffic on the line in both directions and generally shows relative timing or measures time delays in relation to the network. This analyzer is your window into the network. Without it you are blind and do not know what is happening.

A typical display shows transmit data in normal video and received data in inverse video. They come in all shapes and sizes, ranging from small, inexpensive portable units through to very expensive, intelligent units which can be programmed so that they can behave as an active network simulator.

Figure 26-14 shows a printout from one model which shows polling messages and no traffic responses and also data messages being returned in the network. This network uses half-duplex protocols and the printout also shows timing relationships.

The top line of the printout shows the transmit data from the computer, the bottom line shows the received data from the network, and the middle line is encoded to show the status of some of the V.24 interface signals. The letter T in the middle line means that the figure under this letter is a time indication which shows the number of milliseconds that elapsed from the end of the last message to the beginning of the next message. From this we can work out reaction times and loop delays.

For example, we see a poll being transmitted from the computer; 26 ms later a no-traffic response comes back. The 26 ms is loop delay. After the no-traffic response, 8 ms later the next poll goes out. The 8 ms is reaction time.

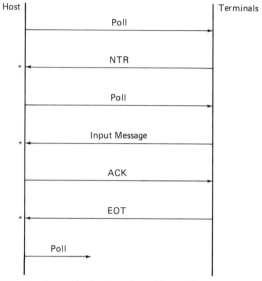

*Reaction time at host = 8 ms; loop delay = 26 ms

(a)

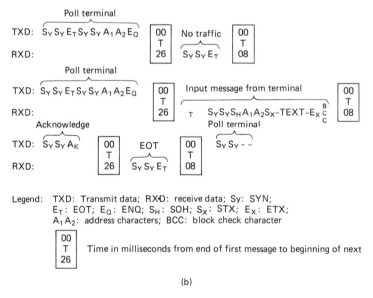

Legend: TXD: Transmit data; RXD: receive data; Sy: SYN;
E_T: EOT; E_Q: ENQ; S_H: SOH; S_X: STX; E_X: ETX;
$A_1 A_2$: address characters; BCC: block check character

00
T
26

Time in milliseconds from end of first message to beginning of next

(b)

Figure 26-14 (a) Protocol sequence; (b) printout from a serial data analyzer for protocol sequence in part (a).

Equipment such as this can be used for evaluating all the components of loop delay in a network, and this is in fact the best way to determine the components of loop delay for your own particular network.

Loopback testing

Smarter serial data analyzers can be used for network testing; that is, they can be plugged into the modem side of the patch panel, which breaks the V.24 interface between the modem and the computer port, and the test equipment can now exercise the line. A common method of line testing is loopback testing, as indicated in Fig. 26-15. The terminal operator may have discovered a fault in his or her terminal and called the network manager for assistance. The network manager initiates a loopback on the digital side of the remote modem and then transmits a test pattern from the network diagnostic system through the network out to the remote modem, then back again through the network to the network diagnostic system. The NDS compares what it receives with what it sent, and if they match, there is a reasonably fair indication that the fault lies in the remote terminal cluster.

If the test did not work, the manager will then perform a loopback on the analog side of the instation modem and transmit data through that modem. If this test works but the other test did not, there is a reasonable indication that the fault lies somewhere in the network or in the remote modem. By using loopback tests

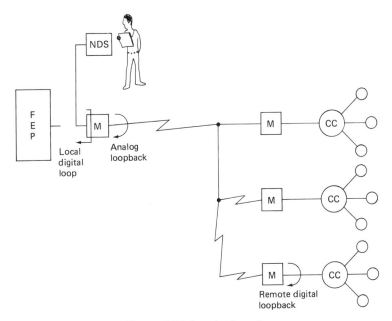

Figure 26-15 Loopback testing.

and progressively looping back at different locations in the network, it is possible to identify reasonably accurately where the fault lies in the network.

Centralized network management systems

The ultimate in network management is a centralized network management system, which allows all or most of the components in the network to be monitored and controlled from a central point. Many of these systems are based on the use of intelligent modems. Many modems now have microcomputers built in to assist in the general operation of the modem and in the performing of equalization. The microprocessor is capable of monitoring the status of the modem, measuring parameters on both the analog side and the digital side, and making this information available to the central site. To perform these tasks, modems need to derive two communication channels from each pair of wires in the communication link. The primary channel is the high-speed data channel used for the data transfer from the host to the terminals. The secondary channel, typically running at 75 to 150 bps, is generally used as the control channel for communication between the modems, as shown in Fig. 26-16. This channel is connected to the network management system computer, which allows commands to be sent out by the network operator, and then the status of the network can be reported back. For example, the network operator may issue a command to the remote modem to report its own status. That modem will then respond over the secondary channel and report its identification by perhaps giving its serial number, details of the power supply voltages, and the configuration of the modem (i.e., how its ports are configured, whether it runs as a 9600 bps single stream or is split into two streams of 4800 bps.) It will also report the incoming analog parameters on the primary channel, such as signal-to-noise ratio, receive signal level, and so on. It can also report the status of the V.24 interface connections on the digital side. With all this information available at the central site, you can imagine that the network control operator has quite a powerful tool at his or her disposal.

For those of you who are interested, Fig. 26-17 shows how the primary and

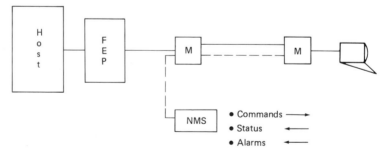

Figure 26-16 Centralized network management system.

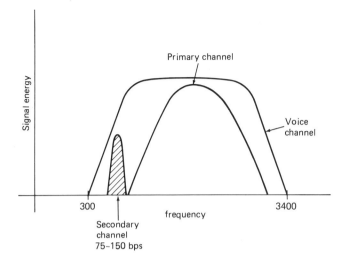

Figure 26-17 Derivation of primary and secondary channels from a voice channel.

secondary channels are derived. The typical telephone voice channel has a bandwidth of around 3000 Hz, typically going from 300 to 3400 Hz. The primary channel uses most of the bandwidth for information transfer, but it leaves a small slice which can be used for the secondary channel.

The functions of the network management system include monitoring analog parameters on the incoming primary data channel and monitoring modem characteristics such as power supply, voltages, V.24 interface status, the configuration of multistream modem ports, and so on. It can also record faults and threshold violations. For example, rather than expecting detailed reports on the status of the modem, the operator can tell the modem to report threshold violations. In other words, if the received signal-to-noise ratio drops below a certain level, tell us all about it; otherwise, don't bother. Also, in some systems we can switch modems on and off or switch in backup modems. On a multipoint line we can detect which modem is streaming, if we have a streaming modem, and send out a command on the secondary channel to tell that modem to switch itself off.

Modem independent management systems

The system we described uses intelligent modems. Most modems in the world today are not intelligent and there are network management systems which can be used with unintelligent modems. This equipment consists of an electronic wraparound box which, as shown in Fig. 26-18, wraps around the modem on both the digital interface side and the analog interface side. The wraparound box electronically derives the two communication channels from the line so that we can have the secondary channel connected back to the network management system computer. The wraparound box will measure the incoming analog parameters and

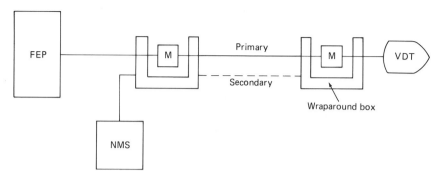

Figure 26-18 Modem-independent network management system.

the status of the V.24 signals on the digital side of the modems. Therefore, this type of equipment can provide functionally very similar performance to that obtained through intelligent modems.

One thing to be careful about when using electronic wraparound boxes is to make sure that the existing modems do not use the entire bandwidth of the communication line. In other words, we need to make sure that there is sufficient bandwidth left over so that we can derive the secondary channel.

Other test equipment

There are many other kinds of test equipment on the market, such as bit error rate testers, block error rate testers, and pseudo random code generators. These are the types of equipment we often use when conducting loopback tests. Nowadays, however, these functions are often integrated into the serial data analyzer.

Analog testing

Of course, analog testing is something else again. Quite often the network management system can do it for you because it is capable of measuring the incoming analog parameters on the communication line. Otherwise, you need a range of equipment and procedures to suit the analog side of the modem. In this book we do not go into analog testing in detail, as it is rather complex and to have a proper understanding of what goes on the analog side of a communication line, you generally need to have some form of engineering training. Those of you with engineering training probably have access to suitable documentation which will explain that in the correct level of detail. More often than not, of course, analog testing is the domain of the common carrier because most common carriers in the world do not really like users to play around with the communication lines themselves.

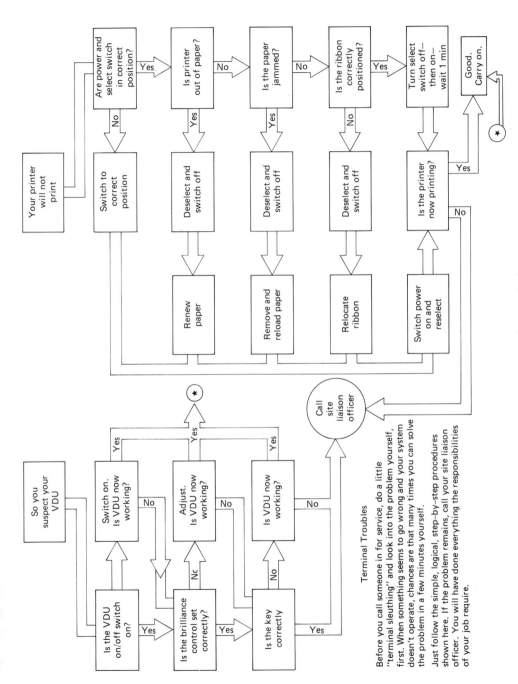

Are power and select switch in correct position? — Yes → Is printer out of paper? — No → Is the paper jammed? — No → Is the ribbon correctly positioned? — Yes → Turn select switch off—then on—wait 1 min → Good. Carry on.

Your printer will not print

Are power and select switch in correct position? — No → Switch to correct position

Is printer out of paper? — Yes → Deselect and switch off → Renew paper

Is the paper jammed? — Yes → Deselect and switch off → Remove and reload paper

Is the ribbon correctly positioned? — No → Deselect and switch off → Relocate ribbon

Is the printer now printing? — Yes → ⊛
Is the printer now printing? — No → Call site liaison officer

Switch power on and reselect

So you suspect your VDU

Is the VDU on/off switch on? — Yes → Is the brilliance control set correctly? — Yes → Is the key correctly — Yes

Switch on. Is VDU now working? — Yes → ⊛
Switch on. Is VDU now working? — No

Adjust. Is VDU now working? — Yes → ⊛
Adjust. Is VDU now working? — No

Is VDU now working? — Yes → ⊛
Is VDU now working? — No → Call site liaison officer

Terminal Troubles

Before you call someone in for service, do a little "terminal sleuthing" and look into the problem yourself, first. When something seems to go wrong and your system doesn't operate, chances are that many times you can solve the problem in a few minutes yourself.

Just follow the simple, logical, step-by-step procedures shown here. If the problem remains, call your site liaison officer. You will have done everything the responsibilities of your job require.

Figure 26-19 Terminal check chart.

Operator self-help test procedures

It is usually a good idea to give the terminal operators some form of troubleshooting guide so that they can minimize the number of times they need to call for help from network managers. This is because many of the faults that occur out of terminals are the result of finger trouble caused by the operator.

Figure 26-19 is a flowchart that is given to terminal operators by one of our client organizations. This simple flowchart allows operators to do some basic testing on their terminals and printers before they call for help.

PART FIVE
QUEUING AND STATISTICAL CALCULATIONS

27
Basic Statistics

The study of statistics came about because not everything in life is fixed. If you look around, you will notice that not everybody is the same height, messages flowing through a message switching system are not necessarily all of the same length, and not all trees are the same shade of green. Where all the items in a population are the same—for example, if all the messages in a system are exactly the same length—it is fairly easy to describe the system mathematically. However, when the individual values in a population can be different, it becomes more difficult to handle. The mathematics of statistics have been developed to enable us to handle these populations more simply.

A common piece of statistical terminology is *probability*. Probability is the measure of the likelihood of occurrence of an event. We say that something that will *never happen* has a probablilty of 0, and something that is an *absolute certainty* to happen has a probability of 1, and everything else lies in between. Consider Fig. 27-1. At the bottom we have never-happen probability 0 events, and at the top we have the absolute-certainty probability 1 events.

Two events which are generally regarded as having a probability of 1 are death and taxes; at the other end of the scale something that has a probability of 0 at the moment, given our current understanding of technology, is that it would be impossible for me to go back in time and "unwrite" this book. In between these two figures, if we toss a coin, the chance of the coin landing as a head on

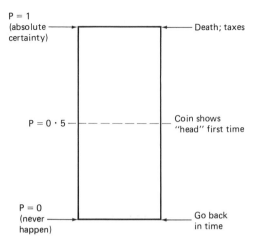

P = 1
(absolute →
certainty)

← Death; taxes

P = 0·5 — — — — — — —

Coin shows
"head" first time

P = 0
(never →
happen)

Go back
in time

Figure 27-1 Probability scale.

the first toss is one-half; if we throw a die (singular of "dice") the probability of getting a 6 is going to be one-sixth (i.e., 0.166), and so on.

The probability of most events can be calculated one way or another. Sometimes it is easy, sometimes it is hard, but most events can be calculated. For further details, refer to one of the numerous texts on statistics and probability theory.

describing a population of variables

The most common descriptor of a population is the *average* value of the items in the population. In statistical terminology we call the average the *mean* value of the population.

The mean of a set of numbers is the sum of all the numbers divided by the total number of numbers. Mathematically, we may write

$$E(x) = \frac{X_1 + X_2 + X_3 + \cdots + X_n}{N} = \frac{\Sigma X}{N}$$

where $X_1, X_2, \ldots, X_n$ are the values and $E(x)$ is the mean of these numbers (E is for "expected value"; that is, if we take an item at random from the population, we would expect it to be the average value). N is the total number of samples and Σ indicates the sum of all the values (a useful shorthand notation).

The mean of a set of values tells us something about the data, but not enough in most cases. We generally need to know how the data are distributed about the mean value. For example, Table 27-1 lists message lengths and the frequency of occurrence of these message lengths in a hypothetical system.

We can express these data graphically as shown in Fig. 27-2. This diagram, known as a *histogram*, plots the distribution of message lengths in the system and

TABLE 27-1 MESSAGE LENGTHS

Message length, X_i	Number of messages/hour, N_i
40	2
50	4
60	8
70	12
80	10
90	7
100	3
110	0
120	1

gives us an indication of the frequency of occurrence of each value. By looking at this diagram we can see that the mean message length is around about 70 to 80 characters. To make the curve easier to handle visually, we draw a smooth curve through the histogram as shown in Fig. 27-3. We could determine the mean value of the messages in this particular distribution. This would be a useful figure, but it is not enough to describe the data accurately. We also need to know how the data are distributed about this mean, and for this purpose we determine a value known as the *standard deviation* of the distribution. The standard deviation

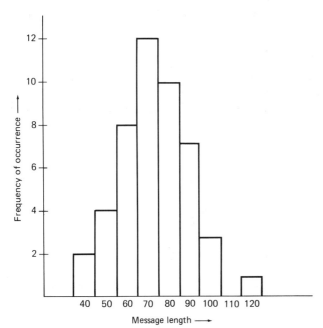

Figure 27-2 Histogram of data of Table 27-1.

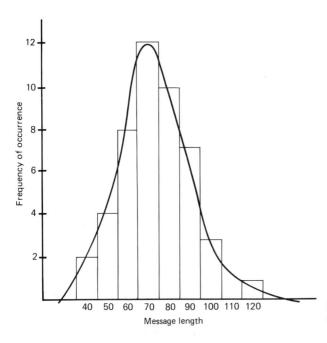

Figure 27-3 Frequency distribution curve for data of Table 27-1.

is defined as the *root-mean-square deviation* of all the values from the mean. The standard deviation is represented in this book by the Greek lowercase letter σ.

In a distribution where the standard deviation is small compared to the mean, the individual values are distributed fairly closely about the mean value; in other words, it is a tight distribution. In a distribution where the standard deviation is large relative to the mean, the values are scattered widely about the mean; in other words, the distribution is fairly loose. This can be illustrated diagramatically as shown in Fig. 27-4, which illustrates three curves that have the same mean value but different standard deviations.

If these curves represent message lengths going into the on-line systems,

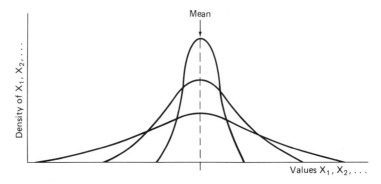

Figure 27-4 Curves with the same mean but different standard deviation.

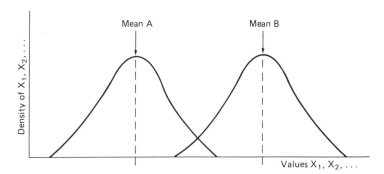

Figure 27-5 Curves with different means and same standard deviation.

we would expect the system with the tight distribution of message lengths to give us much more stable operation than the system with the broad distribution of message lengths. To put this into perspective, the tight distribution could be the distribution of message lengths for credit card numbers going into a credit-checking system, whereas the broad distribution could be the distribution of message lengths going into a commercial time-sharing bureau. The distribution in the middle could be an average message length distribution for a typical commercial data processing operation.

Similarly, it is possible to have curves that have the same standard deviation but different means. This is illustrated in Fig. 27-5. This situation arises quite often. For example, if we were to measure the message lengths in a system in terms of the number of characters entered into a visual display unit, we may plot a curve such as the one on the left of Fig. 27-5. When these messages are transmitted down the line, a constant overhead may be added to each message, which would cause the distribution curve for the length of the messages on the line to be shown as the curve on the right of Fig. 27-5. Adding a constant overhead does not alter the *relative* size of the messages; therefore, the standard deviation would be the same in each case.

28
Introduction to Queuing Theory

queuing theory*

A queue can be defined as a line of transactions waiting for some kind of service. As shown in Fig. 28-1, we have a line of people waiting for a bank teller and the queue is defined as consisting of all the people in the system, *including* the one who is being served.

If a careful record were kept of the time we spent in various queues, we might be surprised at the amount of time we spend just waiting for some kind of service. Indeed, it sometimes seems as if we move from one queue to another during the course of a typical day—lining up for the morning bus, lining up at the bank teller's window to get enough cash to queue in a lunch counter to buy sandwiches, waiting to be served at a hardware store, waiting on the telephone for the attention of an airline reservation clerk, standing in line in a taxi rank, and so on.

Queues may also develop for the services provided by a computer communications system. In fact, queues can develop internally within the system. Any facility within the system may have a queue of users waiting for that particular service.

---

* The terminology, equations, and graphs in this chapter follow the conventions used in *Systems Analysis for Data Transmission* by James Martin (Englewood Cliffs, N.J.: Prentice Hall, Inc., 1972).

Figure 28-1 Queue of customers waiting for a bank teller.

A *facility* is any part of a system that is used in processing a transaction. As the traffic through the system increases, transactions compete for the available facilities and where this competition occurs, queues arise. Following is a list of typical facilities in an on-line real-time computer system that may constitute points of queue buildup:

- Computer memory
- Computer processing time
- Peripheral file storage: disks, floppy disks
- Computer input/output channels
- Access mechanisms, such as read/write heads of disks
- Communication lines
- Transmission devices, such as concentrators and statistical multiplexers
- Terminals
- Operators

It is obviously desirable to design a system that is capable of providing a certain standard of service under varying load conditions. To design such a system, the behavior of the queues for all the facilities in the system must be known. Average queue sizes and queuing times and their associated standard deviations must be determined for each facility under different loading conditions and utilization factors, so that adequate facilities can be provided to handle the predicted demand. The probability that a certain facility will be busy under certain conditions may need to be determined. The effects on system response time and throughput caused by changing particular aspects of a system may need to be considered.

These types of calculations can be made by the use of a mathematical tool called queuing theory. The equations of queuing theory allow queues to be described mathematically so that realistic numerical values for queue lengths and times can be obtained. In the following discussion of queuing theory, we will not present the detailed mathematics involved, as this is beyond the scope of the book and it is not really necessary for understanding how to use queuing theory in system design. We outline the basic parameters used in queuing-theory equations, explain how to use standard curves to obtain the desired numerical answers, and define the limitations and relevance of queuing theory to the types of calculations that need to be made in a computer communications system analysis.

The equations and curves of queuing theory assume that the users for a facility arrive at *random*. Intuitively, we know that events which occur randomly just happen "at will," with no particular pattern or order guiding the occurrence of the events.

A random arrival pattern occurs in many on-line systems such as airline reservations and banking systems. People ring up the airline to make bookings at random, people walk into banks at random, and this applies in many other on-line systems as well. Generally speaking, a random arrival pattern is regarded as being a worst-case arrival pattern; any other arrival pattern usually provides better performance than we would get if the arrivals were random. In this book we assume that the random arrival pattern is the one used in any models that we develop.

Assuming a random arrival process, we can now investigate what happens when users arrive at a facility and queues for service begin to form. The simplest queuing situation is one in which there is a single server. Single-server systems can be represented diagrammatically as shown in Fig. 28-2.

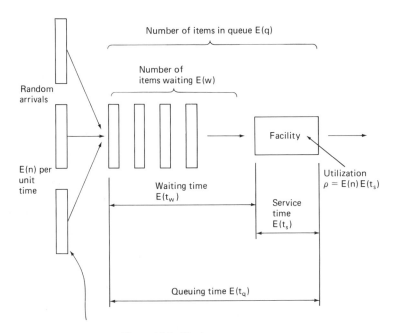

Figure 28-2 Single-server queue.

It is necessary to define the relevant variables in the single-server queuing situation, so that we may build up the formulas for dealing with the queue behavior. The following symbols will be used:

t_s = service time for one item in a queue; $E(t_s)$ = mean service time

σ_{ts} = standard deviation of the service time

q = the total number of items in the system both being served and waiting; $E(q)$ = mean number of items in the queue including the item being served

t_w = waiting time for one item, the time an item spends waiting for service; $E(t_w)$ = mean waiting time

t_q = queuing time, which is the sum of the waiting time and the service time for an item, the total time an item spends in the system; $E(t_q)$ = mean queuing time

The mean of any value, x, will be represented as $E(x)$; that is, the mean of the service time, t_s, is $E(t_s)$. When we were investigating our simple example system in Chapter 25, we defined the facility utilization, ρ, as

$$\rho = \frac{\text{load on a facility}}{\text{maximum load the facility can handle}}$$

or

$$\rho = \frac{\text{time the facility is occupied}}{\text{time available}}$$

A precise way of determining the facility utilization is given by the equation

$$\rho = E(n)E(t_s)$$

where $E(n)$ = mean arrival rate of transactions

$E(t_s)$ = mean service time for one item

The basic formulae for single-server queuing theory were developed by Khintchine and Polloczek; we will present the relevant equations which are the basis of the various curves and tables describing queue behavior, but it is not necessary to understand the method of derivation of these equations to use queuing theory successfully in system design. All the equations contain the variable ρ (facility utilization), which is a very important factor. We will see that to use queuing-theory curves correctly to obtain information, we must always compute the facility utilization first. The information we are most often interested in are queue sizes and queuing times under different facility utilization and service-time conditions, and the four relevant equations follow.

The average number of items waiting for service is given by

$$E(w) = \frac{\rho^2}{2(1 - \rho)}\left\{1 + \left[\frac{\sigma_{ts}}{E(t_s)}\right]^2\right\}$$

The average number of items in the queue is given by

$$E(q) = \rho + \frac{\rho^2}{2(1 - \rho)}\left\{1 + \left[\frac{\sigma_{ts}}{E(t_s)}\right]^2\right\}$$

The average time an item spends waiting for service is given by

$$E(t_w) = \frac{\rho E(t_s)}{2(1 - \rho)}\left\{1 + \left[\frac{\sigma_{ts}}{E(t_s)}\right]^2\right\}$$

The average time an item spends in a queue is given by

$$E(t_q) = E(t_s) + \frac{\rho E(t_s)}{2(1 - \rho)}\left\{1 + \left[\frac{\sigma_{ts}}{E(t_s)}\right]^2\right\}$$

Note: The queuing time is the sum of waiting time and service time. Also, at any instant the average number of items being served is ρ, so the average size of a queue will be ρ plus the average number of items awaiting service.

When we are designing a system, we often make calculations which will cope with the worst situation; this way, we know that our estimates are not totally accurate, but at least we have erred on the side of safety! In considering our simple system in Chapter 25 we assumed initially that all the service times for each particular facility were constant, and later we said that constant service times are rarely the case in real systems because the service times will vary. This variation can be described by computing the mean and the standard deviation of a

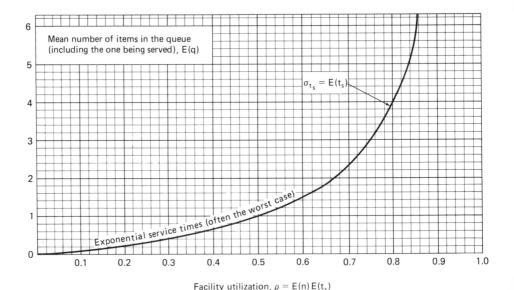

Figure 28-3 Mean queue sizes for single-server queues with Poisson arrival pattern.

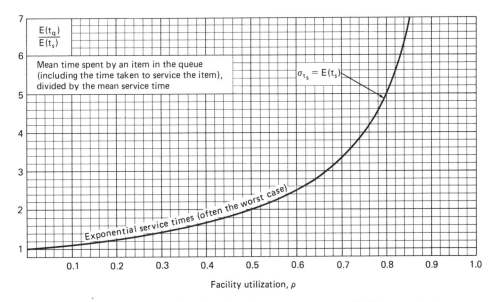

Figure 28-4 Mean queuing times for single-server queues with Poisson arrival pattern.

particular facility's service times. The best case occurs when the service time is constant, that is, the standard deviation = 0 (there is no deviation, so to speak, from the mean value). The worst case occurs when the service time follows an exponential distribution, that is, when the standard deviation = the mean value (this is a very large value for a standard deviation, showing that there are a wide range of service time values). However, most service times in a system fall somewhere between these two extremes, with the standard deviation usually being less than the mean value. A warning should be noted: An exponential distribution (i.e., a standard deviation equal to the mean) is not always, in reality, the worst case; for example, the mean of the values 5, 10, 20, and 200 is 58.75, but the standard deviation is approximately 81.

Because our treatment of queuing theory is simplified, we are going to consider only the worst-case situation. Figure 28-3 shows a curve which gives the average queue sizes for a single-server queue with a random (Poisson) arrival pattern for transactions. The horizontal axis of this curve is the facility utilization, which runs from 0 to 1. The vertical axis gives us the mean or average number of items in the queue, including the one being served. To use the curve, we go along the horizontal axis to the desired utilization, look up vertically until we intercept the curve, and then travel horizontally from the point of intersection to where we meet the vertical axis and read the number of items in the queue from the vertical axis.

Figure 28-4 allows us to work out the average or mean queuing times for a single-server queue with a random arrival pattern. Once again, the horizontal axis is utilization. In this case, however, the vertical axis does not give us the queuing time directly; it gives us the queuing time divided by the service time $[E(t_q)/E(t_s)]$. Therefore, whatever we read off the vertical axis must be multiplied by the service time to find the queuing time. The queuing time curve is put together in this manner so that we can use the same curve regardless of the service time.

As an example of how to use these curves, consider the case of the sandwich shop, in Example 25.1 with an average service time $E(t_s) = 30$ s. Let us work out the average queue size, queuing time, and waiting time at various customer arrival rates.

Example 28-1: Queuing Example No. 1

Take a sandwich shop with an average service time $E(t_s) = 30$ s (assume the worst-case distribution). What is the average queue size $E(q)$, the average queuing time $E(t_q)$, and the average waiting time $E(t_w)$ at customer arrival rates of 60, 80, 100, and 110 transactions/h?

Solution   First, build a model of the queue. Consider the arrival rate of 60 transactions/h. The sequence for calculating the answers is as follows:

1. Find the facility utilization:

$$\rho = E(n)E(t_s)$$

$$= \text{arrival rate} \times \text{service time}$$

$$= \frac{60 \text{ transactions/h} \times 30 \text{ s/transaction}}{3600 \text{ s/h}}$$

$$= 0.5$$

Note that we divide by 3600 s/h because the units for arrival rate and service time are not compatible.

2. Look at the single-server queue size graph (Fig. 28-3) at a utilization of 0.5. This gives an average queue size $E(q) = 1.0$.

3. Look at Fig. 28-4 to find the average queuing time. Note that the vertical axis is average queuing time divided by average service time, so we must multiply by the service time to get the correct answer. The chart gives

$$\frac{E(t_q)}{E(t_s)} = 2.0$$

So

$$E(t_q) = 2E(t_s)$$

or

$$\text{queuing time} = 2 \text{ (service time)}$$

$$= 2 \times 30$$

$$= 60 \text{ s}$$

4. The waiting time is (queuing time) − (service time):

$$E(t_w) = E(t_q) - E(t_s)$$

$$= 60 - 30$$

$$= 30 \text{ s}$$

The other solutions are obtained using the approach shown above. The results are best expressed in the form of a table as follows:

Arrival rate (transactions/hr)	Utilization	Average queue size	Average queuing time (s)	Average waiting time (s)
60	0.5	1	60	30
80	0.67	2	90	60
100	0.83	4.8	180	150
110	0.92	?	?	?

At 92% utilization, the curves disappear off the top of the page, which is why we show a question mark as the answer. In this case you could use the equations if you wish. (For the worst-case service-time distribution, they become quite simple.)

multiserver queues

A multiserver queue is a system where we have a number of identical servers processing a single line of transactions. The transaction at the head of the queue goes to the first available server to be processed. A multiserver queue is illustrated in Fig. 28-5(a), and it is to be contrasted with the arrangement in Fig. 28-5(b), which is actually a number of single-server queues in parallel. If we had identical servers in each case and identical arrival patterns, but in the case of single-server queues the transactions jumped at random into a particular queue and once in that queue remained there (in other words, queue jumping is illegal), we would find that the performance of the multiserver queue would be far superior to that of single-server queues in parallel. This is because in the case of the single-server queue it is possible to have one or more idle facilities while other facilities have queues behind them; this would never happen in the multiserver situation because as soon as the facility becomes idle, the transaction at the head of the queue will move to that facility for processing.

The mathematics of multiserver queueing are a little too difficult for a book of this level, so once again we will be using graphs. A number of assumptions need to be made to use these graphs, which give us an approximatation to the queue sizes and queue times in multiserver queues. For a more detailed examination of multiserver queues, I refer you to the books by James Martin or other authors in the field of queuing theory.

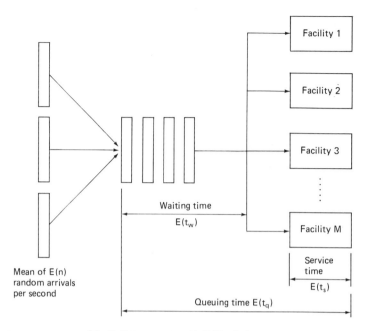

(a) Multiserver queue with M identical servers

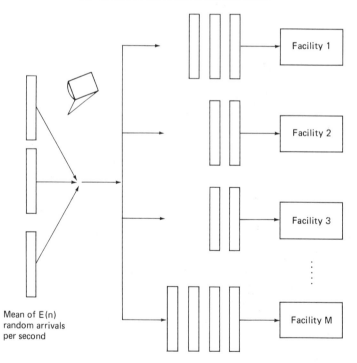

(b) M single-server queues in parallel

Figure 28-5 Multiserver queuing versus many single-server queues in parallel.

The equations for multiserver queuing theory assume that the arrival times of the items to be served follow a Poisson (random) distribution and that items are served on a first-in, first-out basis. These assumptions were applied to the single-server queue equation which we have just investigated. Two further assumptions are made about multiserver queuing behavior which limits the use of these equations to fewer situations. It is assumed that the service times follow an exponential distribution (a worst-case situation) and that all the facilities have identical service-time distributions. There are no simple equations that describe multiserver queues which have a better-than-exponential service-time distribution, but a useful mathematical approximation factor for estimates in these situations does exist. [See *Systems Analysis for Data Transmission* by James Martin (Englewood Cliffs, N.J.: Prentice-Hall, Inc., 1972).]

Once again, we must know the facility utilization of each server to use the multiserver queuing curves correctly. In the single-server queue situation the utilization for the one facility was described by the equation

$$\rho = E(n)E(t_s)$$

where $E(n)$ = mean number of items being served
$E(t_s)$ = mean service time for one item

But in a multiserver queue situation we have M identical servers, each getting the same share of the work. So the correct equation for the facility utilization of each facility in a multiserver situation containing M servers is

$$\rho = \frac{E(n)E(t_s)}{M}$$

Curves similar to those for single-server queues exist which describe multiserver queue behavior. These curves allow us to estimate average queue sizes and average queue times for multiserver queues. Figure 28-6 allows us to work out the queue size in a multiserver queuing system. Notice that the horizontal axis is still utilization, in this case taking into account the number of servers, M. The vertical axis gives us the average number of items in the queue, including the one being served, *divided by the number of servers*. This means that when we read a number from the vertical axis, we must multiply that number by the number of servers to work out how many people are in the queue. Notice that there are a family of curves and the parameter describing the curve is M, the number of servers, in our case going from $M = 1$ for a single-server queue to $M = 10$.

To use the curve we would identify the number of servers in the system, calculate the utilization for the facilities, and then move along the horizontal axis to that particular utilization figure. Moving vertically until we intersect the appropriate curve for the number of servers that we have, we would read the number off the vertical axis and multiply that number by the number of servers.

Figure 28-7 allows us to work out the average queue time for a multiserver queuing situation. Again, the horizontal axis is utilization and the vertical axis,

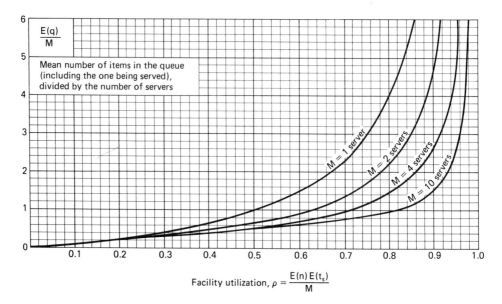

Figure 28-6 Sizes of queues in a multiserver queuing system.

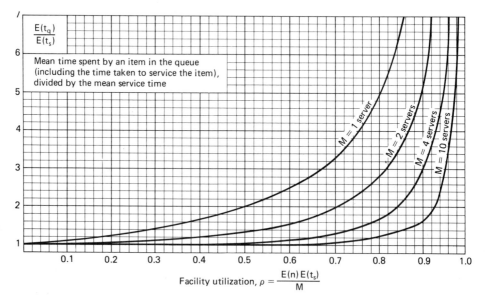

Figure 28-7 Queuing times for multiserver queues.

as with the single-server queue time curve, is the queuing time divided by the service time. Also, we have a number of curves—the parameter, once again, being the number of servers going from $M = 1$ for the single-server situation to $M = 10$ for a 10-server queue. To use the curve we would identify the number of servers, work out the utilization, move along the horizontal axis to the utilization, travel vertically until we intersect the appropriate curve for the number of servers that we have, and then read the number off the vertical axis. This number would then be multiplied by the average service time to give us the average queuing time for that particular case.

Example 28-2: Queuing Example No. 2

As an example of the use of the multiserver queuing graphs, let us work out the average queue size and queue time for a sandwich-shop system where we have an average service time of 30 s, two servers, and an arrival rate of transactions of 200 transactions/h.

Solution   First we must calculate the utilization, which we do using the following equation:

$$\rho = \frac{E(n)E(t_s)}{M}$$

$$= \frac{200 \text{ transactions/hour} \times 30 \text{ s/transaction}}{3600 \text{ s/hour} \times 2}$$

$$= 0.83$$

Using Fig. 28-6, we go on the horizontal axis to a utilization of 0.83, move up vertically until we intersect the $M = 2$ servers curve, and read the number 2.7 on the vertical axis. Remembering that the vertical axis gives us the mean queue size divided by the number of servers, we take this number, 2.7, and multiply it by the number of servers, which is 2, to give us an average queue size of 5.2.

Similarly, to work out the queuing time, we go to Fig. 28-7, 0.83 utilization, and we see that we intersect the $M = 2$ curve at a value of 3.25. This tells us that the queuing time is going to be 3.25 times the service time, which gives us a figure of 97.5 s.

These figures could be compared with the equivalent results for Example 28-1, where we had an arrival rate of 100 transactions/h, giving a utilization of 0.83 for an average queue size of 4.8, with an average queuing time of 180 s—a dramatic improvement in queuing time.

Example 28-3: Queuing Example No. 3

We are not always given problems in such a straightforward way. Often the problem we are faced with is one that cannot be solved directly from the graphs. We first need to take a guess at what the solution might be, solve the problem based on that guess, and then see whether the solution needs improving. If so, we modify the guess, solve the problem based on the new guess, and so on, until we finally iterate in on a solution.

For example, you wish to open a sandwich shop. You believe that the average service time $E(t_s)$ will be 30 s. The peak hour arrival rate will be 300 transactions/

h. You wish to keep the average waiting time for customers below 15 s. How many servers do you need?

Solution   To solve this problem, you need to do a little guesswork. There is not enough information to calculate the exact answer, so you guess a number of servers and see how that system performs. Based on the results of that analysis, you modify the number of servers, analyze the new system, and keep doing this until you find the solution. First, let us see what we can find out from the information we have been given.

If average waiting time $E(t_w)$ must be less than 15 s, average queuing time must be less than 45 s (because queuing time = waiting time + service time). Also,

$$\text{utilization} = \frac{\text{arrival rate} \times \text{service time}}{\text{number of servers}}$$

$$= \frac{E(n)E(t_s)}{M}$$

$$= \frac{300 \text{ transaction/h} \times 30 \text{ s/transaction}}{3600 \text{ s/h} \times M}$$

$$= \frac{2.5}{M}$$

So let us take a guess at M.

Clearly, $M = 1$ will not work because the server would be 250% busy. Similarly, $M = 2$ will not work, so we will try $M = 3$. If $M = 3$,

$$\text{utilization} = \frac{2.5}{3} = 0.83$$

Look up the multiserver queuing chart, Fig. 28-7; for $M = 3$ the chart gives

$$\frac{E(t_q)}{E(t_s)} = 2.35$$

which gives the average queuing time

$$E(t_q) = 2.35E(t_s)$$

$$= 2.35 \times 30$$

$$= 70.5 \text{ s}$$

Clearly, $M = 3$ is not enough servers. Try $M = 4$:

$$\text{utilization} = \frac{2.5}{4} = 0.63$$

Using Fig. 28-7 with $M = 4$ gives

$$\frac{E(t_q)}{E(t_s)} = 1.2$$

So average queuing time

$$E(t_q) = 1.2E(t_s)$$
$$= 1.2 \times 30$$
$$= 36 \text{ s}$$

This gives an average waiting time of 6 s, which is within our specification. Therefore, we need four servers.

Example 28-4: Queuing Example No. 4—Simple System

In this example a credit reference bureau is being used to answer credit inquiries from shopkeepers. (We recognize that with modern technology, we would not need the operators because the shopkeepers would have credit card terminals. Nevertheless, this makes a convenient model.) The credit bureau facility consists of an operator with an unbuffered terminal connected to a computer by a half-duplex 150-bps line. Input messages are of 15 characters and the responses are 150 characters. Asynchronous transmission is used with one stop bit on each ASCII character. We will assume that the computer can process transactions in an average time of 3 s/transaction regardless of the traffic volume and that it can process a number of transactions at the same time.

The terminal operator has a queuing telephone system so that shopkeepers are placed in a queue rather than receiving a busy tone. We will apply a load to the system and calculate the performance of the system. As the load increases and it becomes necessary to add operators, we will assume that all operators behave in an identical way and that they share the load evenly between them. As the operators are added, each will have a terminal on a dedicated line. The equipment configuration is shown in Fig. 28-8.

Problem   Calculate the average queue size, average queuing time, and average waiting time for shopkeepers at the following transaction arrival rates:

(a)   80 transactions/h
(b)   160 transactions/h
(c)   320 transactions/h
(d)   800 transactions/h

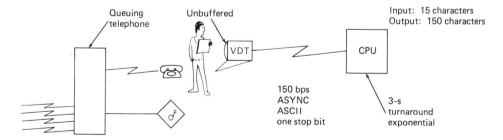

Figure 28-8 Network for Example 28-4.

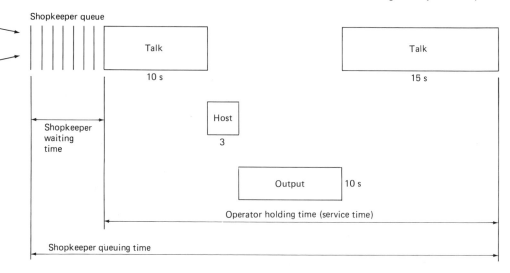

Figure 28-9 Model for analysis of Example 28-4.

Assume that the shopkeeper and the operator talk to each other for 10 s at the beginning of the transaction and for 15 s at the end.

Solution   The first step in a problem like this is to build a model of the system to see what happens to a transaction. The model will look like that in Fig. 28-9. During the first "talk" period, the 15-character credit card number is being entered into the terminal. As it is an unbuffered terminal, the characters go straight down the line and the next block is therefore the host processing. The output transmission takes 10 s which is calculated as follows:

$$\text{time} = \frac{\text{message length}}{\text{line speed}}$$

$$\text{message length} = 150 \text{ characters at } 10 \text{ bits/character}$$

$$1 \text{ character} = 7 \text{ information bits} + 1 \text{ parity bit}$$

$$+ 1 \text{ start bit} + 1 \text{ stop bit}$$

$$= 10 \text{ bits}$$

Therefore,

$$\text{transmission time} = \frac{\text{message length}}{\text{line speed}}$$

$$= \frac{150 \text{ char} \times 10 \text{ bits/char}}{150 \text{ bps}}$$

$$= 10 \text{ s}$$

The operator holding time is 38 s, calculated as follows:

	Elapsed time (s)
First "talk"	10
Host time	3
Output transmission	10
Second "talk"	15
Total	38

The operator holding time is also the service time for the queue of shopkeepers.

Operator Utilization   To analyze the queue, we need to know the operator utilization. This is calculated using the equation

$$\text{utilization} = \text{arrival rate} \times \text{service time}$$

$$= E(n)E(t_s)$$

$$= \frac{80 \text{ transactions/h} \times 38 \text{ s/transaction}}{3600 \text{ s/h}}$$

$$= 0.84$$

To find the queuing time, look up the single-server queuing curve in Fig. 28-4. Alternatively, use the $M = 1$ curve (single server) on Fig. 28-7. You will read 6 on the vertical axis for utilization = 0.84. The vertical axis is

$$\frac{E(t_q)}{E(t_s)} = \frac{\text{queuing time}}{\text{service time}}$$

So if

$$\frac{E(t_q)}{E(t_s)} = 6$$

Then

$$E(t_q) = 6E(t_s)$$

$$= 6 \times 38 = 228 \text{ s}$$

$$\text{waiting time} = \text{queuing time} - \text{service time}$$

$$= E(t_q) - E(t_s)$$

$$= 228 - 38$$

$$= 190 \text{ s}$$

Average queue size is calculated in a similar way. Using Fig. 28-6 ($M = 1$, single server), we read the average queue size from the vertical axis of 5.3. So $E(q) = 5.3$.

These results are best expressed in the form of a table.

Arrival rate (transactions/ h)	Number of servers	Utilization	Average queue size	Average queuing time (s)	Average waiting time (s)
80	1	0.84	5.3	228	190
160	2	0.84	5.7	129	91
320	4	0.84	7.0	76	38
800	10	0.84	11.0	53	15

As the load is increased and extra servers are added, remember to use the $M = 2$, 4, or 10 curve, as appropriate. Also, remember that the number read off the vertical axis of Fig. 28-6 must be multiplied by M (the number of servers) to find the average queue size.

Note: The waiting-time figure can be somewhat misleading because not all shopkeepers are delayed. See the solution to Example 28-5 for further details.

Example 28-5: Queuing Example No. 5—Single-Thread System

The credit bureau from Example 28-4 has been modified. There are now 10 operators, each with a buffered, freewheeling terminal, connected to the host via a cluster controller and a 1200-bps half-duplex asynchronous line. We ignore protocols in this example to simplify the calculations. (See the solution to Examples 16-2 and 16-3 to see how protocol analysis is incorporated.) The configuration of equipment is as shown in Fig. 28-10. Assume that the dialogue between the shopkeeper and the operator is 10 s at the beginning and 15 s at the end. Work out the following:

(a) Average waiting time for shopkeepers.
(b) Average response time for the terminal operators.

Do these calculations for two transaction arrival rates: 320 transactions/h and 620 transactions/h.

Solution   The first thing to do is to draw a bar chart showing the time sequence of events involved in processing a single transaction. This enables the queues in the system to be identified and we can then figure out how to go about solving the problem. The bar chart is shown in Fig. 28-11. Things to observe about this model:

- The line holding time includes the host processing time because it is a single-thread system.
- The line queue is a single-server queue with service time = line holding time.
- The operator holding time will increase as the load increases because it contains the line queue.
- The shopkeeper queue is a multiserver queue with 10 servers.

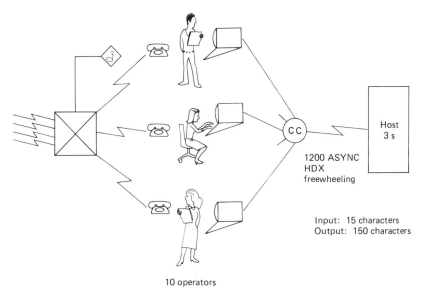

Figure **28-10** Network for Example 28-5.

How to Solve It
You start from the middle and work outward in the following sequence:

1. Work out the line holding time:

$$\text{input} + \text{host} + \text{output} = 0.125 + 3.0 + 1.25$$

$$= 4.375 \text{ s}$$

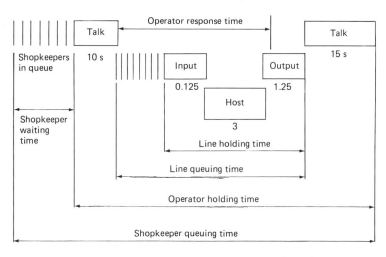

Figure **28-11** Model for analysis of Example 28-5.

2. Work out the line utilization:

$$\text{arrival rate} \times \text{service time} = \frac{320 \text{ transactions/h} \times 4.375 \text{ s/transaction}}{3600 \text{ s/h}}$$

$$= 0.389$$

$$= 0.39 \text{ (round the number off to 0.39;}$$
$$\text{do not truncate it to 0.38)}$$

3. Look up the single-server, worst-case, queuing chart, Fig. 28-4, to find $E(t_q)/E(t_s)$ for the line queue. This gives

$$\frac{E(t_q)}{E(t_s)} = 1.6$$

So

$$\text{queuing time} = 1.6 \text{ (service time)}$$

$$E(t_q) = 1.6 E(t_s)$$

The service time for the line queue is the line holding time, so

$$E(t_q) = 1.6 \times 4.375$$

$$= 7 \text{ s}$$

This is the line queuing time.

4. Subtract the output transmission time (1.25 s) from the line queuing time to get an approximate answer for operator response time.

$$\text{Operator response time} = 7 - 1.25$$

$$= 5.75 \text{ s}$$

5. Add the two "talks" to the line queuing time to get the operator holding time.

$$\text{Operator holding time} = \text{talk} + \text{line queuing time} + \text{talk}$$

$$= 10 + 7 + 15$$

$$= 32 \text{ s}$$

This is the service time $E(t_s)$ for the shopkeeper queue.

6. Find the operator utilization. Remember that it is a multiserver queue with $M = 10$.

$$\text{Operator utilization} = \frac{E(n)E(t_s)}{M}$$

$$= \frac{320 \text{ transactions/h} \times 32 \text{ s/transaction}}{3600 \text{ s/h} \times 10}$$

$$= 0.284$$

7. Look up the multiserver queuing curve for $M = 10$ on Fig. 28-7 to find the queuing time. The chart shows for utilization = 0.28 and $M = 10$ that

$$\frac{E(t_q)}{E(t_s)} = 1$$

This means that the queuing time, in this particular case, is equal to the service time. The queuing time is, therefore, 32 s.

8. Calculate the average waiting time by subtracting service time from queuing time.

$$E(t_w) = E(t_q) - E(t_s)$$
$$= 32 - 32$$
$$= 0$$

Comment: At first glance this result looks strange but, upon consideration, it is reasonable. With 10 operators and 28% utilization we can say that, on average, seven operators are idle and that most shopkeepers therefore get straight to an operator and so have zero waiting time.

Increased Load

The following summarizes the results for the increased load of 640 transactions/ h:

1. Line holding time = 4.375 s.

2. Line utilization $= \dfrac{640 \times 4.375}{3600} = 0.78$

3. Line queuing time $= \dfrac{E(t_q)}{E(t_s)} = 4.6$

$$= E(t_q) = 4.6 \times 4.375 = 20 \text{ s}$$

4. Operator response time = line queuing time − output transmission time

$$= 20 - 1.25$$
$$= 18.75 \text{ s}$$

5. Operator holding time = talk + line queuing time + talk

$$= 10 + 20 + 15$$
$$= 45 \text{ s}$$

6. Operator utilization $= \dfrac{E(n)E(t_s)}{M}$

$$= \frac{640 \times 45}{3600 \times 10} = 0.8$$

7. Shopkeeper queuing time (from Fig. 28-7, $M = 10$)

$$\frac{E(t_q)}{E(t_s)} = 1.25$$

$$E(t_q) = 1.25E(t_s)$$

that is,

$$\text{queuing time} = 1.25 \text{ (service time)}$$

$$= 1.25 \times 45$$

$$= 56 \text{ s}$$

8. Waiting time = queuing time − service time

$$= 56 - 45$$

$$= 11 \text{ s}$$

The results for the two arrival rates are summarized below.

Arrival rate (trans-actions/h)	Line util.	Line queue time (s)	Op. resp time (s)	Op. hold time (s)	Op. util.	S'kpr queue time (s)	S'kpr waiting time (s)
320	0.39	7	5.75	32	0.28	32	0
640	0.78	20	18.75	45	0.80	56	11

Comment

- The first solution is okay because the system is relatively lightly loaded.
- The second looks okay at first, but it is not very good because both the line utilization and the operator utilization are up around 80%, which means that we would have quite erratic behavior.
- The waiting time, 11 s, is the *average* of *all* shopkeeper waiting times.

In a situation like this not all shopkeepers are delayed. The only time a shopkeeper has to wait for service is if all the operators are busy when he or she rings up.

Figure 28-12 is a series of graphs which give us the probability that all the servers are going to be busy in a multiserver queue at different facility utilizations. There are a family of curves, each curve relating to a particular number of servers. As you can see, the curve for $M = 1$, that is, a single-server queue, is a straight line. This means that the probability that the server is going to be busy at a given instant is equal to the average utilization of the server. If a server is 50% busy, the probability of that server being busy when a shopkeeper rings up is 50%. On the other hand, in a two-server queue, although each server may be busy 50% of the time, the chances of them both being busy at a given instant is going to be less than 50% because one may be busy while the other one is idle. As the number of servers

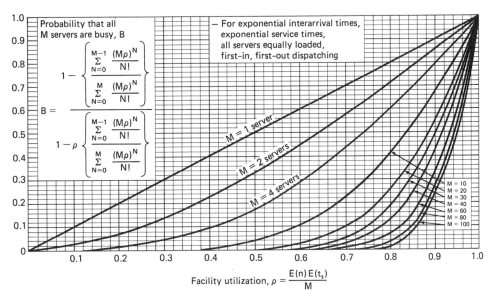

Figure 28-12 Probability that all servers are busy in a multiserver queuing system.

increases, the chances of all operators being busy at the same time for a given utilization decreases. In our case, if you look at Fig. 28-12, you will see that at 80% utilization, with 10 operators, the probability of all operators being busy is 42%. This means that 58% of shopkeepers get straight on to an operator and so experience no delay.

The average delay experienced by those that are delayed will therefore be longer than 11 s. $(E(t_d) = E(t_w)/B$, where $E(t_d)$ is the average delay time and B is the probability that all operators will be busy. Refer to *Systems Analysis for Data Transmission* by James Martin (Englewood Cliffs, N.J.: Prentice-Hall, Inc., 1972) for further details of delay times in multiserver queues.

Example 28-6: Queuing Example No. 6—Multithread System

In Example 28-5 the reason the performance was so bad as the arrival rate increased was the fact that we were running single thread. In a single-thread system, when a transaction gets the communication line for input the line is dedicated to that transaction until the output response has been transmitted. This means that while the computer is processing that transaction the line cannot be used for anything else. In the examples we are using, we have a host processing time of 3 s, so the communication line is tied up for 3 s while the host does its work. Although increasing the line speed can improve the performance, even an infinite increase in line speed would be of limited use because of the fact that in the limit the 3 s of the host processing time is going to be the minimum line holding time.

One approach to improving the throughput of the system is to run it multithread. In a multithread system, once a transaction has finished using the line for input, it releases the line so that while the transaction is being processed in the host, the line can be used to handle other inputs or other outputs. In this way it is possible to overlap operations on the line and in the host.

In a multithread system the model needs to be changed as illustrated in Fig. 28-13. Here we see the shopkeeper talking to the operator and the operator enters a credit card number into the terminal. The operator then hits the transmit button and the transaction jumps into a queue for the line so that the input message can go down the line. The message is then processed in the host for 3 s, and when the host is ready to send the transaction, the transaction jumps in a queue for the line before it can be output. In this system, therefore, we have two queues for the communication line.

An interesting question is to consider the relationship, if any, between the two queues shown in Fig. 28-13. Careful consideration of the model shows that they are in fact the same queue. There is exactly one facility providing a service—the communication line—and this facility is used by both input and output transactions. So we have one queue, even though it is physically distributed with input transactions lining up at the cluster controller and the output transactions lining up at the host.

In reality, we would need a protocol to manage the line to enable the inputs and the outputs to be handled in an orderly fashion along the line. For the time being, however, we will assume that somehow (by magic perhaps), the line is being managed without a protocol. Later we examine how we can include protocol analysis with the queuing analysis.

By reflecting on the dynamics of the queues we can come to the conclusion that the average length of time a transaction waits to get on the line is going to be the same for both an input transaction and an output transaction. This can be visualized if you imagine an input transaction jumping in the queue. In front of the input transaction will be a random collection of inputs and outputs. This random collection of inputs and outputs will take a certain time to be processed, and this time is, in effect, the waiting time for the input transaction. Similarly, when an output transaction jumps into the queue, in front of it is also a random collection of input and output transactions. On average, the length of time to process this random collection of inputs and outputs will be the same as the length of time it takes to process

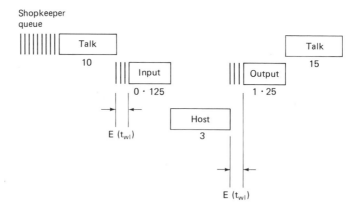

Figure 28-13 Model for multithread Example 28-6.

457

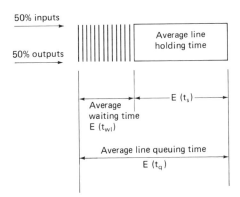

Figure 28-14 Model for analysis of line queue.

the previously mentioned random collection of input and output transactions, which were in front of the input message. Therefore, on average the length of time a transaction waits to get on the line will be the same regardless of whether it is an input or an output transaction. This, of course, assumes that we have equal priorities for inputs and outputs in the system. In our case, as we are using a magic nonexistent protocol, we can assume that we have equal priority for inputs and outputs. In reality, when we are using a protocol it is possible to manipulate the relative priorities of inputs and outputs so that one of them can wait a longer or a shorter time than the other.

To calculate the average waiting time for a transaction, we need to build a model of the line queue. This is generally a simple model because of all the transactions going along the line, typically, we have exactly 50% of the transactions as inputs and the other 50% as outputs. We can then build a model as shown in Fig. 28-14. The average line holding time is the average length of time the line is in use when it is in use. When the line is in use for an input it is used for 0.125 s, and when it is in use for an output it is used for 1.25 s. The average length of time the line is in use will therefore be the average of the input and output, that is,

$$\frac{\text{input} + \text{output}}{2} = \frac{0.125 + 1.25}{2} = 0.6875 \text{ s}$$

The transaction arrival rate at the line queue is, in fact, double the transaction arrival rate at the operators, because for each operator-level transaction, the line sees both an input and an output message.

The line utilization can be calculated by taking the arrival rate of transactions at the line and multiplying this by the average line holding time. In our case if we had an arrival rate of, say, 2000 transactions an hour, the line utilization would end up being

$$\rho = \frac{2000 \text{ transactions/h} \times 0.6875 \text{ s/transaction}}{3600 \text{ s/h}} = 0.38$$

Looking up the single-server queuing chart in Fig. 28-4, we can see that for a 38% utilization the ratio of queue time to service time is 1.6.

$$\frac{E(t_q)}{E(t_s)} = 1.6$$

This means that the queuing time is

$$E(t_q) = 1.6E(t_s)$$

$$= 1.6 \times 0.6875$$

$$= 1.10 \text{ s}$$

The waiting time is therefore going to be equal to the queuing time minus the service time, which is

$$E(t_w) = E(t_q) - E(t_s)$$

$$= 1.1 - 0.6875 = 0.41 \text{ s}$$

This is therefore the average length of time that either an input transaction or an output transaction waits for a communication line.

As indicated earlier, it is possible through the use of protocols to manipulate the relative priorities of inputs and outputs so that the relative size of the waiting times of inputs and outputs can be adjusted.

Example 28-7: Queuing Example No. 7—Full-Duplex System

Another way to improve the performance of the system in Example 28-5 is to change the line into a full-duplex communication line. In this case the model would look similar to that which we had in Example 28-6, except that we now have two physically separate queues, as shown in Fig. 28-15. We have one queue for the input channel and one queue for the output channel. These, as indicated earlier, are completely independent queues and would be analyzed independently.

Each queue is a single-server queue, and in our particular example, the input queue could never be of significant size because when we reach the point where the output channel is 100% busy, the input channel would be no more than 10% busy.

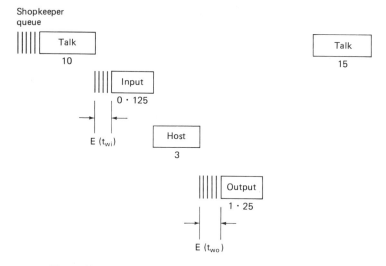

Figure 28-15 Model for analysis of full-duplex Example 28-7.

incorporating protocol analysis in queuing models

So far we have been analyzing queuing models by assuming that we have magically been able to control the flow of data along the line without a protocol. In reality, we need a protocol; let us now examine how we can combine protocol analysis with queuing.

In the queuing models we have been analyzing block diagrams of the form shown in Fig. 28-16. This diagram is for a half-duplex multithread on-line inquiry

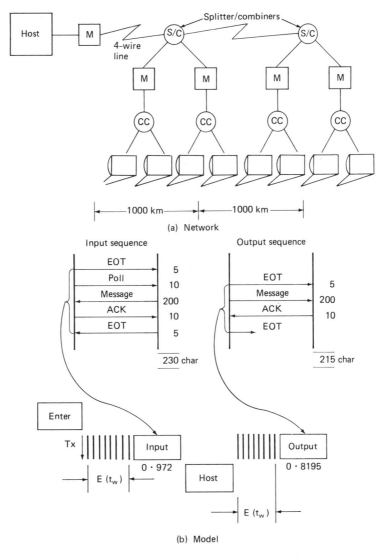

Figure 28-16 Incorporating protocol analysis in a queuing model.

system, similar to the one that we developed in Example 16-2. For queuing analysis we take the box labeled "input" and the box labeled "output" and work out an average line queue based on the average line holding time, which is the average of the input and output times. From that we can work out the line utilization based on the transaction arrival rate at the line, and from that we can look up the single-server queuing system to work out the queuing time and thence work out the waiting time for the line.

When we were analyzing protocols in Chapter 16 we also developed block diagrams very similar to that shown in Fig. 28-16. In this case the box labeled "input" contained all the protocol messages illustrated, and the box labeled "output" contained all the output protocol messages shown in the diagram. When doing the protocol analysis we worked out the protocol sequences, the loop delays, and so on, and from that we were able to calculate how long the line was going to be occupied for an input message sequence and how long the line was going to be occupied for an output message sequence. This time can be shown on the block diagram in Fig. 28-16.

Figure 28-16 looks remarkably similar to Fig. 28-13, which is the one that we have been using for queuing analysis. It follows, therefore, that we should be able to use the same approach to the analysis of the queuing behavior for Fig. 28-16, and in fact we can. We say that the average length of time the line is in use when it is in use is going to be the average of the inputs and the outputs, and in our case this will be the average of 0.972 and 0.8195, which is 0.9. We can then build an average model of the line, as shown in Fig. 28-17, where we have transactions arriving and the transactions consist of exactly 50% inputs and 50% outputs. Using the techniques outlined earlier, we can determine the line utilization at the transaction arrival rate, look up the single-server queuing curve to find the line queuing time and from that determine the average line waiting time by subtracting the average service time from the average queuing time. This gives us the average waiting time or, as we have called it in previous sections, the interference time delay.

By reducing the models to block diagram levels for both queuing analysis

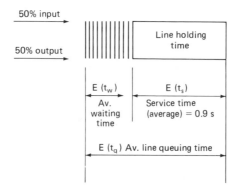

Figure 28-17 Model of the line queue in Fig. 28-16.

and protocol analysis, it is usually relatively easy to incorporate the two by building a single model that handles both queuing and protocol analysis, as outlined above.

final comment

That completes the network design aspect of this book. We have dealt largely with single lines in the examples because any network is nothing more than a collection of single lines. In a complex network, the output of several lines may be combined in a concentrator to become the input to a single line. That line can be analyzed using the techniques in this book.

This would be a good time to go back and re-read the "good advice" in Chapter 21, *Network Design Summary*. You will find that it is unlikely that any of the examples in this book will correspond directly with your own situation. You will also find differences in detail between what I cover in this book and what you come across in your own environment. Nevertheless, the general principles that I have covered will apply to your network. You will still have to supply the most important ingredients yourself—thorough analysis and clear thinking. You must analyze the equipment and software that you are working with so that you can uncover any idiosyncracies that may be present. You must think clearly about what is happening in the network so that you can build a model for analysis.

Clear thinking, clear thinking, and more clear thinking is, I believe, the key to it all. Re-read Chapter 21 and practice these techniques first on your existing network and then on new networks and I am sure that you too will experience the satisfaction of designing a data communications network that has predictable performance.

Index